Sovereignty and Authenticity

Sovereignty and Authenticity

Manchukuo and the East Asian Modern

Prasenjit Duara

ROWMAN & LITTLEFIELD PUBLISHERS, INC.
Lanham • Boulder • New York • Oxford

ROWMAN & LITTLEFIELD PUBLISHERS, INC.

Published in the United States of America
by Rowman & Littlefield Publishers, Inc.
A Member of the Rowman & Littlefield Publishing Group
4501 Forbes Boulevard, Suite 200, Lanham, Maryland 20706
www.romanlittlefield.com

P.O. Box 317, Oxford OX2 9RU, United Kingdom

Copyright © 2003 by Rowman & Littlefield Publishers, Inc.

British Library Cataloguing in Publication Information Available

Library of Congress Cataloging-in-Publication Data
Duara, Prasenjit.
    Sovereignty and authenticity : Manchukuo and the East Asian Modern /
Prasenjit Duara.
        p.   cm.
    ISBN 0-7425-2577-5
    1. Nationalism—East Asia.   2. Imperialism—East Asia.   3. Manchuria
(China)—Politics and government.   4. Manchuria
(China)—History—1931–1945.   I. Title.
JC311 .D83   2003
320.54'095—dc21   2002151157

Printed in the United States of America

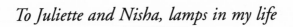
To Juliette and Nisha, lamps in my life

Contents

~

Acknowledgments

Given the unjustified obscurity of Manchukuo, I ought properly to begin by expressing gratitude to the celebrated Italian filmmaker Bernardo Bertolucci for having made *The Last Emperor*. I learned to rapidly dispel the vacant looks that greeted my introduction of Manchukuo as the subject of my research by mentioning the film, and such factoids as fascist Italy and the Vatican having been among the thirteen states to recognize the Japanese puppet state. The experts on Manchukuo—or of the area that is universally recognized today as China's northeast—have of course been much more directly and substantially helpful for my project. I apologize in advance for the inescapably formal alphabetical listing of names that seems to be in the nature of acknowledgments. The work of Mark Elliot, Suk-jung Han, Rana Mitter, and Yasutomi Ayumu has shaped the project in significant ways, and their detailed comments on the manuscript have been invaluable. Others who read and commented on the final manuscript are Dipesh Chakrabarty, John Fitzgerald, Takashi Fujitani, Sheldon Garon, Haiyan Lee, David Strand, Jung-min Seo, and Wen-hsin Yeh. My warmest thanks go to them for taking time out of their busy schedules to read about a subject distant from their own research interests. Elizabeth Perry, the editor of the series in which this book appears, and Susan McEachern, editor at Rowman & Littlefield, shepherded the book in its final stages. I am grateful to Liz for her enthusiasm, critical eye, and judicious direction, and to Susan for going beyond the duty of any editor, much less a busy executive editor.

More than ten years have passed between the conception and production of the book, and many institutions and people have helped it along the way. Among libraries and archives, I wish to thank the directors and staff of the Library of Congress in Washington, D.C., and the East Asian Library at the University of Chicago. I acknowledge my gratitude to the staff of the municipal libraries in Changchun, Dalian, and Shanghai; the library of Northeast Normal University in Changchun; the archives of Jilin and Liaoning provinces; and the Number Two National Archives in Nanjing for giving me such free access to their abundant resources. I am also grateful to the staff of the Tōyō Bunko and the Tōyō Bunka Kenkyūjo in Tokyo, and to the faculty and library of the Modern History Institute of Academia Sinica in Taiwan. The leaders of the Wanguo Daodehui in Taiwan generously made their resources available to me, and I am most thankful to them. I wish to personally thank Mr. Okuizumi Eizaburo of the University of Chicago's East Asian Library and Dr. Liu Huijuan, director of the Changchun Library, for their special efforts.

The list of other individuals who have helped and facilitated my research is very long, and I apologize to those whose names I may have missed. I recall well the assistance of professors Chang Cheng, Kong Jingwei, Lü Qinwen, Mao Jiaqi, Sun Zhongtian, Wang Kuixi, and Zhu Huan in China. In Japan, Professors Linda Grove, Hamashita Takeshi, Hirano Kenichiro, Igarashii Akio, Ishikawa Yoshihiro, Nakami Tatsuo, Nakao Katsumi, Nishimura Shigeo, Ozaki Fumiaki, Yamamoto Eishi, Yamamuro Shinichi, and Sasaki Tōru were all most helpful. Professor Howard Goldblatt at the University of Colorado, Boulder, kindly gave me unlimited access to his personal collection of library materials from Manchukuo and made our stay in Boulder very pleasant. I would like to express my deep appreciation of all they have done for me.

Many good friends and colleagues have read and discussed different parts and early versions of the book's chapters. I acknowledge here my gratitude to Ann Anagnost, Leora Auslander, Bryna Goodman, Bruce Cumings, Joshua Fogel, Joan Judge, Linda Kerber, John Kelly, James Ketelaar, Philip Kuhn, Thomas Lahusen, Claudio Lomnitz, Bruce Lincoln, Tessa Morris-Suzuki, Tetsuo Najita, Marshall Sahlins, James C. Scott, William Sewell, Shu-mei Shih, Ronald Suny, Mariko Tamanoi, Stig Thogersen, David Der-wei Wang, Mayfair Yang, and Dingxin Zhao. Whether as research assistants, discussants, or cautious critics, the help of students, as always, has been indispensable. Without the assistance of Richard Burden, Juliette Chung, Todd Hall, Taka Nishi, Viren Murthy, Shi-chi Lan, Scott Relyea, and Yi Wang, the book would have been very much longer in the making. My thanks to Phil Schwartzberg for the customized production of the maps, to Scott Relyea for his help with the maps and other technical matters, and to the University of Chicago Digital Media Laboratories. Over these many years, I have also presented lectures based on this work to well over a hundred institutions in several countries. Since it would be quite impractical to name them all, I wish to express my thanks to those who listened, questioned, criticized, and helped, and I hope they will read the book to see how it turned out.

Parts of several chapters have appeared in various publications. Some of chapter 1 was published in *History and Theory* 37 (October 1998): 287–308, as "The Regime of Authenticity: Timelessness, Gender, and National History in Modern China." Parts of chapter 3 appeared in "The Discourse of Civilization and Pan-Asianism," *Journal of World History* 12 (March 2001): 99–130. A part of chapter 4 appeared as "Of Authenticity and Woman: Personal Narratives of Middle Class Women in Modern China," in *Becoming Chinese: Passages to Modernity and Beyond*, ed. Wen-hsin Yeh (Berkeley: University of California Press, 2000), 342–64, and a significant part of chapter 6 appeared as "Local Worlds: The Politics and Poetics of Native Place," in *South Atlantic Quarterly* 99 (Winter 2000): 13–50.

I have also been fortunate to receive several fellowships and research grants to complete the project. In 1993–1994, the Committee on Scholarly Communications with the People's Republic of China gave me a fellowship to spend a year in northeast China and facilitated the beginnings of my research. A short-term grant from the Modern History Institute of Academia Sinica and the Chinese University of Hong Kong allowed me and my family to get away from the bitter cold of the northeast for a couple of winter months. In 1996–1997, I received a Guggenheim Fellowship to write up some of the chapters, and I was also granted a short-term Social Science Research Council grant, permitting me to travel to Taiwan and Japan for further research. In 2000–2001, I received fellowships from the National Endowment of the Humanities and the American Council of Learned Societies, which permitted me to extend my leave and complete the book. I am most grateful to these foundations and to my home institution, the University of Chicago, for their support and flexibility.

Finally, I wish to express my thanks to my beloved family (and Kola) for cheerfully tolerating everything and giving balance to my life. This book is dedicated to them.

A Note to the Reader

Because sources in Manchukuo are in either Chinese or Japanese (and sometimes both), I identify sources in the language as I have found them. The *pinyin* system of transliteration is used for Chinese words and macrons are included on long Japanese vowels. In both languages exceptions are made for words and place names that are familiarly used in English (e.g., Tokyo, KMT).

Location of Manchukuo

Introduction

Until recently, the subject of Manchukuo, the Japanese puppet state established in the Chinese northeast (Manchuria) between 1932 and 1945, has not seemed worthy of new exploration, since more details appeared only to confirm the well-known story of the cruelty and duplicity of the Japanese rulers and the victimization of its subjects. This story continues to be absolutely necessary to grasp the history of Manchukuo, but it is no longer sufficient. As new work has reopened the subject in the last several years,[1] Manchukuo appears as a place of paradoxes, where it becomes difficult to disentangle imperialism from nationalism, modernity from tradition, frontier from heartland, and ideals of transcendence from ideologies of boundedness. While these paradoxes are a product of the political project of Manchukuo, they are also symptomatic of the problematic conditions of modernity in the early twentieth century. This nexus between the particular and wider processes represents the point of departure of this book.

It is significant that no matter how imperialistic the intentions of its builders, Manchukuo was not developed as a colony, but as a nation-state. The Manchukuo state urgently sought international and domestic recognition of its sovereignty even after the League of Nations, following its first, most extensive investigation, determined against Manchukuo's claim. This book is centrally concerned with how its claim to sovereignty derived in large part from its claim to represent the authentic culture of the land and peoples. Manchukuo was a product of the post–World War I era, when imperialism became increasingly illegitimate and political and economic competition among states was expressed through the forms of nationalism. As such, Manchukuo reflects the persistent and complex relationship that existed between nationalism, imperialism, and modernity at least through the end of World War II.

During the inter-war period, older colonial relationships in many parts of the world came to be shaped by experiments in limited political or electoral representation, nationalist forms, and developmental agendas. But if imperialism had to adjust to the new ideological conditions, nationalism too had to adapt to the territorial imperative that historically drove the competitive and expansionist modern state by

1

devising new political forms. Among these were forms embodying the promise of emancipation and development, of identity representation and supranational brotherhood. Each was opposed to traditional imperialist forms, but each also held the potential of developing into new modes of domination. Pan-Asianism, *kominka* (imperial citizenship), and the multinationalism of Manchukuo were some Japanese expressions of these political forms. New nation-states, such as the Soviet Union, India, or China, which sought to expand their sovereignty claims upon regions and groups with fragile links to the core, also developed parallel political forms to accommodate these claims.

Because it was such a transparently constructed entity in a contested region, Manchukuo provides a window into the modern processes of nation making, state building, and identity formation. As a national *idea*, Manchukuo was predictably weak, because the commitment of its makers to independence from Japan was weak and variable. The national idea was, however, contained within the framework of Asian civilization, a framework of identity for a multinational state that was continuous with nationalism and generated strategies for representing sovereignty similar to those of nation-states.[2] The blueprints, materials, technologies, techniques, and problems encountered in the construction of Manchukuo reveal the ways nation-makers sought to found the sovereignty of the nation-state in a discourse of cultural authenticity.

Given that these resources and techniques were mostly drawn from the historical experiences of China and Japan, nation making in Manchukuo discloses a great deal about what it took to become a modern nation in East Asia. As the site of Sino-Japanese interactions and discursive convergence, the cultural representations and identity-building projects in Manchukuo illuminate certain obscured ways in which they were constructed and naturalized in the successful nation-states of China and Japan. The distinctive ways of demarcating and representing the spheres of modernity and tradition, state and society, nation and self in Manchukuo not only reflected processes in the two societies, but drew from cultural resources circulating between them.

Nation-makers deployed Confucian civilizing processes (*jiaohua, kyōka*), redemptive religion (*jiushi, kyūsei*), the model of the self-sacrificing woman (*xianqi liangmu, ryōsai kenbo*), and the vernacular tradition of the knight-errant (*lülin haohan*), among other strategies. Japanese ideas of authentic Eastern civilization were shaped considerably in response to the widespread presence of Chinese redemptive societies, whereas Japanese efforts to incorporate "primitive" peoples within narratives of belonging in Manchuria influenced Chinese reformulations of these peoples as part of the nation-space. Manchukuo reveals the lineaments of a *regional* understanding of how older formations are culturally constructed as sovereign nations in East Asia.

What I call the East Asian modern is a regional mediation of the global circulation of the practices and discourses of the modern.[3] I am particularly concerned with how the impetus, assumptions, categories, norms, schemata, and methods from an emergent world culture are "translated" to constitute and legitimate nations and states as morally authentic sovereigns. The process of dissemination hardly develops on a level or open field, but through historically specific expressions of power, namely imperialism and a system of unequal states.[4] This inequality in the flow of global culture from West to East was also expressed within East Asia in the early twentieth century in the hegemonic dominance of Japanese neologisms and re-significations of classical Chinese terms in the modern Chinese and Korean vocabulary. Recent studies exploring cultural translation reveal a justified anxiety about losing sight of the ways in which the translating society adapts the imported meanings according to its own understandings and needs. Lydia Liu outlines an approach to grasping the changed meaning in her idea of "translingual practice."[5] At the same time, we cannot afford to lose sight of how globally circulating categories *function* to make nations homologous, if not equal.

I will consider how historical, local, and regional practices and conceptions, vocabulary and symbols, translate and mediate global ideas to constitute nations. Of course, these mediations also do much more, including constituting the region itself anew. For instance, in order to understand certain modern cultural and economic practices that constitute the urban experience, a map joining major East Asian cities such as Shanghai, Tokyo, Hong Kong, and Harbin may be more relevant than the national one. Another regional network is formed by the lexicon of modernity. When re-signified words from the classical Chinese returned to China, by way of Japan, they appeared to establish a transparent relationship of the present to the Chinese past. Terms such as nationality (*minzu, minzoku*), culture (*wenhua, bunka*), religion (*zongjiao, shyūkyō*), or native place (*xiangtu, kyōdō*), widely considered to represent ancient continuities, were either invented or returned to China with new significations requisite for a modern nation. In practice, this "lexical effect," made possible by historical regional relationships, actually inserted Chinese intellectuals into a new regional discourse of the modern, causing a closer discursive resemblance to their Korean and Japanese counterparts than, for instance, to their peasants. In such ways we may see how the global was remade *regionally* into the national.[6]

The concept of the *modern* that I explore in this book (see chapter 1 in particular) is a temporal structure centered upon a historical self-consciousness. The ineluctable novelty of historical progression in this consciousness—I am not speaking only of East Asia—is premised not on a simple rejection of the past, but upon a complex encompassing or supercession of it. The "East Asian modern" occupies this labile interface between novelty and the past in the region. As such, it addresses problems of identity, change, and authenticity that politically powerful forces seek to appropriate for their particular projects. The term East Asian modern represents both an analytical category, where the past is repeatedly re-signified and mobilized to serve future projects, and a substantive category, referring to the circulation of practices and signifiers evoking historical authenticity in the region. People in the period—notably Japanese state-builders in Manchukuo—may have been quite aware of what they were circulating and appropriating. My task is to explore the ways in which the region's past was being re-signified, often in the name of the eternal or authentic, to speak to a range of different needs and goals.

Thus, the East Asia I am proposing here is not an essential category, but a historical and changing one. For instance, in the Chinese imperium, the old tribute area including Burma and Nepal was the relevant sphere, whereas the Japanese in the inter-war era increasingly saw Siberia and Central Asia as part of this region. Further, the integrity of the space diminished considerably during the early Cold War, when China became more meaningfully part of the socialist bloc and Japan more integrated with the United States; and today it has once again emerged with different contours. In the period from 1900 to 1945, the conditions of Sino-Japanese interaction in this region included Japanese strategic, military, economic, and cultural projects in China; Chinese students, businessmen, professionals, and political exiles in Japan, and their return; and the circulation of the regional lexicon of modernity. Many works in English, Chinese, and Japanese have studied these interactions, including those by Tam Yue-him, Sanetō Keishū, Akira Iriye, Ramon Myers, Joshua Fogel, Douglas Reynolds, Douglas Howland, and Lincoln Li. This work is an indispensable foundation for my understanding of the history of the Sino-Japanese encounter. At the same time, I want to show how this very history and the idea of the regional modern was itself utilized as a resource in the construction of nations.

It should be clear by now that I am not arguing that China and Japan came to look the same. Rather, the modernity of each was forged in a complex regional matrix. Models and practices frequently emerging from powerful nation-states were mediated by this regional matrix, and perceived as authentically national or civilizational. Perhaps one of the most politically significant paradoxes of nationalism, elaborated in chapter 1, is the transnational origins of its claim to historical and contemporary distinctiveness. The modern state produces both the reality and the reification of the territorial nation. However, the local, regional, and global sources of its construction have always produced, and continue to generate, the most fundamental tensions in the national form.

The book is organized methodologically to reflect its major substantive concern: the manner in which the history of a place—Manchukuo—presents a space of conversion and transformation of global discourses into discourses of national or civilizational authenticity. My effort is to track the interactions of certain practices across three spatial levels: within Manchukuo, in the East Asian regional context, and in the global system of nation-states. It is a spatial (or perhaps hyperlinked) mode of historical writing that presents a challenge to linear histories based mainly upon a causal and evolutionary method. Nonetheless, it is also clear that we cannot sustain any concept, whether of system, institution, or space—such as capitalism, nationalism, the state, or region—without engaging some kind of causal or linear analysis. My goal is to avoid the teleology and determinism that arise with the generalization of this method.

I have divided the book into three parts. The first part consists of two chapters introducing the basic concepts of the study and providing a historical overview of

Manchuria. These chapters call for a more causal and linear approach. The remaining four chapters (parts II and III) are more synchronic, reflecting upon the interactions of global, regional, and local forces in the making and unmaking of Manchukuo.

Chapter 1 seeks to grasp nationalism in a comparative and systemic framework, as the new global ideology of the late nineteenth and early twentieth centuries, and examines its relationship with imperialism, expansionism, and militarism. I argue that in the epoch-defining nexus between nationalism and global capitalism, the problem of authenticity and identity becomes central to the definition and struggles over sovereignty. Incidentally, readers eager to get to the story of Manchukuo may skip the last two theoretical sections on authenticity and return to them later. Chapter 2 narrates the history of Manchuria since the late nineteenth century in the light of its contested historiography, and with a view to grasping the problem of sovereignty in the region. This problem is examined from the different perspectives of the League of Nations, the Japanese military, expansionists and settlers, Chinese nationalists, local warlords, landowners, and popular society. I hope to provide a complex but coherent historical background for readers to contextualize and judge the behavior of different actors.

Part II explores the advent of a new discourse of civilization in the post–World War I period. How did the Manchukuo regime draw upon this new global discourse in the conceptualization of the nation-state? What were the old social and cultural formations in East Asia that it was able—or unable—to mobilize in order to realize these conceptions? In chapter 3, I focus on popular Chinese redemptive societies that during this period also developed links with other—Japanese and global—societies, and on the efforts of Manchukuo pan-Asianist ideologists to co-opt them into their political projects. In chapter 4, I examine the ways in which this civilizational authenticity came to be embodied in women, who were, in the process, brought out of the home and into the projects of governmentality. Through a set of personal narratives, I am able to probe the tensions and ambivalences of this kind of modern subject formation.

Finally, part III considers the ways in which the new *spatial* formations and representations of the nation were expressed in Manchukuo. How were regions, localities, and frontiers historically perceived in the old empires, and how were they transformed by modern states? As a contested borderland in East Asia, Manchukuo was a unique space, simultaneously represented as frontier and nation, and as periphery and heartland. Chapter 5 examines how different forms of modern knowledge, particularly ethnography, produced the frontier and the indigenous inhabitants— focusing initially on Japanese studies of the Oroqen (*Elunchun* in Chinese, and *Oronjon* or *Orochon* in Japanese)—as the authentic repository of the frontier nation. This ethnographic activity in the Chinese peripheries triggered a new ethnographic and historical understanding in China itself, which sought to assimilate the indigenous peoples and the lands of the periphery anew into the national *imaginary*. Chapter 6 studies the nostalgic reflection and formal knowledge of the native place in the modern representation of the local or the homeland. Perceived globally as the locus of timeless traditions or of "the pastoral" threatened by the market, urbanization, and reform, it is a deeply sentimentalized space of authenticity. I analyze the Chinese native-place novel, written in Manchukuo by Liang Shanding, called *Green Valley* (*Lüsede gu*). The only Chinese novel written in and about the region after 1934, it became involved in a complicated political battle that remains meaningful to this day. By examining historically the reception and appropriation of the novel among different political forces, I track the role of affect and identity in the production of the space that has now come to be known as the northeast, or *dongbei*.

Notes

1. See Han Suk-jung, "Puppet Sovereignty: The State Effect of Manchukuo, from 1932 to 1936" (Ph.D. diss., University of Chicago, 1995); Rana Mitter, *The Manchurian Myth: Nationalism, Resistance, and Collaboration in Modern China* (Berkeley: University of California Press, 2000); and Louise Young, *Japan's Total Empire: Manchuria and the Culture of Wartime Imperialism* (Berkeley: University of California Press, 1998).

2. As we shall see later, the line between the multinational state and the multicultural nation is difficult to distinguish.

3. For global circulation in this period see John Boli and George M. Thomas, eds., *Constructing World Culture: International Nongovernmental Organizations since 1875* (Stanford: Stanford University Press, 1999).

4. Lydia Liu, ed., *Tokens of Exchange: The Problem of Translation in Global Circulations* (Durham, N.C.: Duke University Press, 1999).

5. Lydia Liu, *Translingual Practice: Literature, National Culture, and Translated Modernity, China 1900–1937* (Stanford: Stanford University Press, 1995).

6. The "East Asian modern" is not something that I study exhaustively or precisely. Trained principally as a scholar of China, I have a more limited knowledge of Japan, and still more so of Korea—to which there are only occasional references. Nonetheless, as a recognizable collection of circulating ideas and practices, the concept of the East Asian modern enables me to situate a historical perspective that is not hopelessly limited by nationalist ideology; see my *Rescuing History from the Nation: Questioning Narratives of Modern China* (Chicago: University of Chicago Press, 1995). My goal is to engage some of the more important features of "the modern" embedded in Sino-Japanese interactions and provoke other strategies of transnational historical understanding. By using the term modern in the title as a noun rather than an adjective I seek to highlight the idea of the modern as a set of temporal practices and discourses that is imposed or instituted by modernizers. As such it is a hegemonic project among other temporal practices, rather than a preconstituted period or a given condition.

PART ONE

COMPARATIVE AND HISTORICAL PERSPECTIVES

~

CHAPTER ONE

Imperialism and Nationalism
in the Twentieth Century

Throughout the nineteenth century, imperialist conquest, annexation, assimilation, and colonialism were closely associated with nation-states. Perhaps the most distinctive feature of nationalist *ideology* in the twentieth century is the peeling away of imperialism from nationalism—an ideological divergence obviously prominent in anti-imperialist nationalism. It has shaped our view of nationalism and imperialism as two very different phenomena. Nationalism is characterized by citizenship, equality, and development, whereas imperialism has historically produced domination, exploitation, and the reproduction of difference between ruler and ruled in the colonies. A goal of this chapter is to show that nationalism was not able to easily overcome the long practical *history* of the nation-state's association with imperialism in the competition for dominance of the capitalist world. Moreover, the evolving relationship between the two in the inter-war years meant that imperialism too came to be penetrated by nationalist rhetoric, forms, and practices.[1]

The difficult relationship between twentieth-century nationalism's ideology and history necessitates a methodology capable of joining the history of modern nationalism with the understanding of nationalism as the producer of history—both in its material effects and, especially, in its enormous ideological capacity to code history as national. I examine the relationship between nationalism and imperialism in the historical context of the expanding system of competitive nation-states and a global culture.

In this period, nationalism becomes the driving force of expansionism. It draws its authority, or moral sovereignty, from an immanent conception of history and what I call "the symbolic regime of authenticity." Ironically, these morally drenched conceptions emerge even as nations are being practically shaped by circulating discourses of the global system. This chapter explores the comparative historical and theoretical context in order to grasp the relevance of the imperialism–nationalism problem for Manchukuo. Later chapters, especially in parts II and III, exemplify how the symbolic regime of authenticity is formed and operates in Manchukuo and more widely in East Asia.

Nationalism and Imperialism

The ideological divergence between nationalism and imperialism became most visible at the end of World War I, when a major constellation of forces produced the political and discursive conditions for anti-imperialist nationalism. Wartime mobilization of both European nations and the colonies, the loosening of imperialist control of the economy in large countries like China and India, and the concomitant strengthening of urban nationalism in these places were part of these conditions. Moreover, the balance of global power was beginning to move away from Europe and toward the Soviet Union and the United States. Under Lenin and Woodrow Wilson, "prophets of a new international order," these powers were not only committed to national self-determination, but competed with each other to champion the cause of national independence, and, we might add in hindsight, nationality formation itself.[2] This environment facilitated an unprecedented global outpouring of criticism against centuries of imperialism and the horrors of imperialist wars—in particular the most recent war, the scale of which portended the end of the world. We will turn to the new moral authority generated by the critique of Western civilization in chapter 3; let us note here that this novel understanding of nationalism was accompanied by the simultaneous emergence of the idea of the nation-state as a universal political form and of nationalism as a natural condition of humanity.

It is sometimes easy to forget how recently the idea emerged that the globe was divided into nations—awakened or unawakened—even among the colonized and semicolonized. According to Eric Hobsbawm, although the nation-state was the dominant political entity in Europe through much of the nineteenth century, *nationalism,* as we understand it from the last twenty years of that century, did not exist. Only "advanced" or "civilized" societies, in the evolutionary discourse of the period, qualified as nation-states; the rest would either disappear through extinction or assimilation, or, we may add, become colonized. We can infer from Hobsbawm's observation that conquest, assimilation, and colonization—in a word, imperialism—was the privilege of the nation-state in the period. The corollary to this was that nationality was not a birthright or an ascriptive status. Patriotism in the eighteenth-century revolutions of America and France was seen to be a largely voluntary affair. To be sure, the territorial nation-state did produce the cultural homogenization that was a condition for nationalism. But ethnicity, language, and other markers of collectivity were not to become the natural basis of claims to sovereignty until the last decades of the century. Hobsbawm may be criticized for ignoring earlier, individual manifestations of these phenomena, but we can hardly deny that the idea of nationalism as a universal condition emerged only in the later period and became gradually realized in the aftermath of World War I.

I accept Ernest Gellner's definition of modern nationalism as the congruence of the political and the cultural, but find it of limited value. Such a definition requires distinguishing between a homogenized, politicized Self and Other, an identification based upon a historicist conception of community. To anticipate a later discussion in this chapter, it is precisely because the self-conception of a community is over-whelmingly a temporal or historical one that the problem of change and identity is central to it. The problem of identity is not simply a question of how we can be what we *were*, but is fatefully entangled with the politics of who we *are* in relation to contemporary interests, needs, and visions of the future. Thus, who we are not, and how to define and treat those who are not us, are constitutive questions of nationalist ideology.

Reflecting to some degree the needs or the political entanglement of the time, the Other can be constructed flexibly, through either a sharp or a graded demarcation, including the production of "the internal frontiers of the nation" or the "truest" core of the national community.[3] Nonetheless, the possibility of sharp demarcation or the hardened boundary is intrinsic to the nationalist form. When this hardened community is simultaneously moralized and valorized, it is not difficult to see how it might develop into imperialism, authorizing the annexation or colonization of the Other. Although the nation's imperative for territorial control contributes signifi-cantly to the tendency toward exclusiveness, if we foreground the problem of time and identity in the ideology of the national form, the territorial state is theoretically not essential. Indeed, if cyber-technology enables decision making and resources to flow through the power nodes of a de-territorialized "nation" (linking homelands and diasporas, for instance), we may still be left with the nationalist form and its intrinsic capacity for closure.

However, from its earliest appearances in Europe, the territorial state has been historically necessary to the realization and existence of nationalism. In the under-standing of world systems analysts such as Immanuel Wallerstein and Giovanni Arrighi, nationalism is to some extent a by-product of the relationship between state building, modern capitalism, and global domination. According to Arrighi, the cre-ation and maintenance of global capitalism was made possible by the fusion of "two logics," territorial and capitalist: the capture of mobile capital for territorial and pop-ulation control, and the control of territories and people for the purposes of mobile capital. From the seventeenth century, the territorial state—possessing absolute jurisdiction within its boundaries and growing military and organizational capabili-ties—became necessary to control the social and political environment of capital accumulation on a world scale. In Arrighi's scheme, the hegemonic power in the competitive system of European states, such as the Dutch in the seventeenth and eighteenth centuries and the British in the nineteenth century, was successively chal-lenged by latecomer territorial states. These latecomers, in their drive to become globally competitive, sought to mobilize the economic and human resources first within their jurisdictions, thus producing some aspects of nationalism.[4] Wallerstein is more explicit, declaring that nationalism became the very means whereby a state or social formation sought to leverage itself out of the periphery of the world system into the core.[5]

Although Arrighi's pattern suggests that nationalism was part of the state strategy in the British and French challenges to Dutch hegemony in the eighteenth century, in general it is agreed that full blown nationalism as we understand it emerged in the late nineteenth century, when Germany, the United States, and Japan sought to challenge British economic domination of the world. They took the lead in developing nationalism and forging a closer relationship between this nationalism and the state.[6] Political and capitalist elites in these newly industrialized societies, which later also included Italy and Russia, gradually undermined the classical liberal principles of free trade—enabling and enabled by British hegemony—by adopting neomercantilist policies toward securing a state-protected national economy.[7] Leaders deliberately fashioned nationalist, neomercantilist, developmental, and regulatory regimes, and states came to play an important role both for national development and to enhance global economic competitiveness. Economic nationalism also appeared in societies such as China and India, where early-twentieth-century nationalist movements were built around campaigns to boycott imperialist products and promote nationally made goods.

To be sure, competition for global economic domination was not the only condition for the rapid spread of nationalism in Europe and the world from the late nineteenth century. Nationalism, as we shall see, was linked to the politics of mass mobilization that emerged with the increasing democratization of European polities after 1880. Gellner associates nationalism with industrial society's need for mass literacy and interchangeable skills, which in turn necessitated the state–culture congruence. Karl Deutsch first saw the importance of the mass media for nation-building projects, and Benedict Anderson emphasized the connection between media and capitalism in "print capitalism" capable of producing the imagined community of the nation.[8] Certainly, some of these conditions—such as the mobilization of certain identities or a form of "print capitalism"—could be found in imperial China and elsewhere. Nonetheless, it was the simultaneous development of all or most of these conditions within an evolving system of inter-state competition that produced the national form by the end of the nineteenth century. That form embedded many different aspirations, but it was also seen to be the most effective means to achieve global dominance or imperialism.

War provides the perfect optic to view the relationship between competitive imperialism and nationalism. World War I and World War II were Germany's response, not simply to the structure of power in Europe, but to the British empire and the developing world empires of the United States and Russia.[9] Nationalism was functionally important in mobilizing the population and resources for war preparation and the war itself. The call for national autarky, which preceded World War I but was especially developed during the war and inter-war crises, presupposed the nationalism that it was producing, and mandated state mobilization of human and material resources in the name of the nation. The German planned war economy of 1914–1917 was an important model for much autarkic national development, including that of the Soviet socialist economy and China and Manchukuo.[10] World War I, the first long, mass war for global dominance, marked the height of nationalist mobilization. In what was for many societies the first episode of mass production, appeals to maximize production and rein in consumption were pitched to national loyalty.[11] Indeed, as Gregory Kasza has shown, administered mass organizations, allegedly representing the will of the people, began with the experience of insufficient civilian support for World War I. They first emerged in countries like Japan, which were not directly involved in the war but saw the need to mobilize for its future eventuality. Later these mass organizations became everyday fixtures of the nation-state.[12]

Imperialist nationalism turned out to be a significant means of integrating and subordinating the different classes and groups in these nation-states. Although, as noted by Lenin and Marxist scholars, the imperialist payoff was clearly an important part of the subordination of these classes, this payoff was not only economic, and perhaps even more symbolic (witness defeated inter-war Germany). In a move that appears somewhat dated today, Hannah Arendt sometimes attributed the great appeal of imperialism to the "mob" or the lumpenproletariat. But she also commented that imperialists appeared as the best nationalists, because they claimed to stand above the reality of national divisiveness and represent the glory and authenticity of the nation.[13] As we will see, the discourse of civilization also played a role in creating not only nationalist identification but a transnational identity of world-conquering nations with high moral purpose.

Note, however, in Arendt's observation, how imperialism actually comes to be authorized by nationalism, which has become the primary force. If in an earlier period nationalism was a response to imperialist competition, it had now become the ground reality. The symbolic power of nationalism to subordinate and discipline all manner of difference to a greater cause is, of course, important not only for imperialism but for domestic projects as well. From the 1880s until the end of World War I, nationalism revealed a strong communal and conservative character, violently opposed to ideas of class struggle and the labor movement.[14] Nonetheless, there may be little better to focus the national mind than dominance and glory at another's expense.

So far we have seen how imperialism, while necessary to nationalism, is still something external to it—applied to people outside its imagined community. However, nationalist principles were also extended or deployed for imperialist ends or with imperialist consequences. Ideals of assimilation or brotherhood often ended up in a brutal imperialism. During the French revolutionary imperialism, several French thinkers saw colonialism as a way to integrate the colonies into the universal project of the Enlightenment; yet the civilizing mission entailed and reinforced "the right to intervene."[15] In what she called "continental imperialism," Arendt described latecomer nationalists who sought to develop their empires through the pan-German and pan-Slav racist movements.[16] They pursued a nationalism that saw itself as authorized to imperialistically annex territories belonging to other states. The fate of those who were identified as not belonging to the community is well known. Japanese pan-Asianism, based on the purported solidarity of a common civilization (and sometimes common race), was deployed to build an empire. Twentieth-century nation-states have exercised imperialism in the name of common civilization, socialist brotherhood, and democracy.

The world system perspective has enabled us to see the function of modern political forms in relation to the imperative of global competition in the dual logic of territory and capital. Nationalist and imperialist practices were combined and often fused to gain competitive advantage. If nationalism had imperialist consequences in the pursuit of interests or the national "will," some imperialist states also recognized the importance of autonomy or formal independence in mobilizing or motivating the colonized or semicolonized population in pursuit of its competitive interests. As Manchukuo shows, zones of imperialist domination could be re-territorialized as part of "regional economic blocs" where patterns of investment and economic modernization resembled those of nation-states.[17] This pattern would become clearer in the post–World War II era, when hegemonic powers controlled many formally independent nations. But the rapid spread of the legitimacy of nationalist discourse underlying these formations cannot be understood only through world-systems theory. Nationalist ideology came to have an autonomous power capable of generating nationalist rights as well as the symbolic power to exclude.

Citizenship, National Rights, and Imperialism

> The greatest adversary of the rights of nationality is the modern theory of nationality.
>
> —Lord Acton, *Essays in the Liberal Interpretation of History*

Since the French revolution, the nation-state, nationalism, and national mobilization have been accompanied by the doctrine of "rights," which has been an important component of their appeal and promise. While the historical relationship between rights and nations continues to be a subject of considerable disagreement,[18] we can, without going into this history, make a few observations that are relevant to twentieth-century nationalism. It has been pointed out that the French Revolution combined the declaration of the Rights of Man with the demand for national sovereignty. Thus human rights were only protected and enforced as national rights.[19] Moreover, as quickly became evident with the emergence of French revolutionary imperialism, these rights applied only to some nations; and, whether in France, Britain, or the United States, they applied only to some groups within the nation.[20] Nonetheless, in these nations, citizenship rights evolved before the period of high nationalism of the late nineteenth century, and the tension between these rights and national rights were yet to be fully articulated.

By the end of the nineteenth century, the liberal ideal of the individual citizen's rights was frequently ignored or subordinated to the rights of the collective nation in many nationalisms of the period.[21] Whereas it is certainly true that those societies with developed democratic institutions were better able to protect the rights of individual citizens, the tension between national rights and citizenship rights cannot be reduced to another version of the duality between Western, civic nationalism and Eastern, ethnic nationalism. Classical liberal philosophers such as John Locke presupposed the common cultural framework of an identifiable people for the operation of citizenship rights,[22] and J. S. Mill was convinced that "free institutions are next to impossible in a country made up of different nationalities."[23] Alexis de Tocqueville understood national pride as one of the prerequisites of democracy, since it inculcated the republican spirit that would promote civic virtue. Tocqueville even declared that colonialism was necessary for reinforcing the nationalist sentiment that was the sole way to transcend individual interests.[24] The "freedoms" of many minorities or underprivileged groups in democratic societies were premised upon assimilation, often forced, into the dominant culture of the civic nation until at least the middle of the twentieth century.[25]

The tension between individual and national rights continues into the post–World War II era. The charters of the United Nations—founded by democratic sponsors—reveal the tension between these two sets of rights. Article 1 of the Universal Declaration of Human Rights states that "everyone has the right to take part in the government of his country, directly or through freely chosen representatives." But the International Covenant on Economic, Social and Cultural Rights and the International Covenant on Civil and Political Rights declare that all "peoples have the right to self-determination. By virtue of that right they freely determine their political status and freely pursue their economic, social and cultural development."[26] Thus, as Clarke and Jones point out, liberalism holds that political authority derives from the consent of the governed; but this is in tension with the "givenness" of national affiliation, to which the question of consent does not arise.[27] While nationalism has no necessary need for liberalism, liberalism cannot do without the authority of the nation, if only because it cannot have people opt out of the nation-state.[28]

On the other hand, nondemocratic nations were and are still bound to a conception of rights as the informal contractual basis of the legitimacy of the national regime. These rights are not associated with ideas of liberal individualism or political freedoms but typically with rights to livelihood and economic betterment, or what T. H. Marshall called "social rights."[29] How and why such rights should have developed and disseminated around the world by the first half of the twentieth century is far too vast a problem to enter here. At the very least, we can say that they are associated with the participation of states in the widening system of nation-states (discussed below), which disseminated ideas of governmentality, sovereignty, and nationality. Although in the early twentieth century competition was a very important threat to the system, nonconformance to the discursive conditions of nationality—and even worse, nonrecognition by the superior powers—entailed significant risks and losses that could weaken a state at home and abroad. However these ideas were disseminated, they were usually justified through the discourse of the rights of nations, as for instance in China, where Republican regimes in the twentieth century deferred democratic rights in the name of the collective national interest, economic security, and tutelage necessary to produce proper citizens. In Manchukuo, rights were conceived as the rights of nationalities within a purported Asian civilization.

Thus we can see that rights are indeed closely related with nationalism, but the relationship is not simply an emancipatory one. On the one hand, nation-states are expected to guarantee certain rights to their citizens, whether these be individual rights or rights to economic and material improvement. We shall see later how this expectation must be related to the phenomenon Foucault has called "governmentality."[30] On the other hand, the bearer of rights is not only, nor even primarily, the individual, but the nation. As the bearer of rights, the nation has sovereign power over its individual citizens and in dealings with the outside world. Until the end of World War I, and in a problematic and confusing way beyond that date, the logic of rights facilitated the transformation of the nation into the imperialist nation. The racialist ideas of social Darwinism further enabled this transformation and the quest for global domination.

Several authors have observed how a virtual blurring between races and nations occurred in the last third of the nineteenth century.[31] Nations were perceived as unique and homogenized products of biological and cultural factors. However these "civilized" nations functioned domestically, externally they functioned in a naturalized world "red in tooth and claw," where one was equipped, biologically, environmentally, and culturally, to dominate—or else be dominated. Nations as self-conscious civilized bodies had the right to dominate and colonize those who were not: the primitive and the heathen. For many of the dominated, social Darwinism was also the discursive path to survival. The writings of Chinese and Japanese thinkers of the late nineteenth and early twentieth centuries closely reflected these assumptions, if only to transform themselves into civilized nations. There was, however, no line separating survival from domination. At the same time, the logic of rights continued to unfold, as nationalism was also subject to claims of national rights made by others, particularly if they succeeded in claiming systemic recognition.

Imperialism and Anti-imperialist Nationalism

Anti-imperialist nationalism of the post–World War I period shared most of the characteristics of its late-nineteenth-century predecessor, including the mode of producing national identity and rights. These ideas were sustained in the international system of states, which sought to shape these new forces, though not without enormous tensions and conflicts. Participation in the international system entailed varying degrees of commitment to a regime of rights, whether national or individual, socioeconomic or political. On the other hand, what distinguished this expression of nationalism was the renunciation of imperialism and the social Darwinist characterization of nations, including to some degree the underlying theories of race. In its place—or sometimes as a supplement—nationalists in many countries, including ones in East Asia, developed or gave a new salience to ideas of "culture" or cultural unity in the narrative of national integration.

We shall explore this notion of culture at various places in the book; suffice it to say here that it played an important role in the new nationalism in several ways. First, it was a means of dis-embedding the project of national homogenization from race and its association with imperialism. Ideas of culture underlay the new discourse of civilization, which authorized nationalism and forged narratives of brotherhood, often contradicted in practice. Second, culture introduced a paradigm of voluntarism (at least in theory) for the process of assimilation and homogenization, particularly in the face of growing awareness of nationality rights among various people within the claimed territory of the new nation-state. This factor made the "national question" considerably more problematic for the new nations than for the older nation-states, where assimilation had largely—although, as we know, not wholly or irreversibly—taken place before the generalization of such nationalist-rights consciousness. In some ways, this cultural nation was exemplified by the American mechanism of the "melting pot," but unlike the exceptional case of America, most of the relevant groups did not volunteer to come into the new nation. Culture, as produced in the new nationalism, represented an important and novel form of knowledge to address problems generated by the divergence of imperialism and nationalism.[32]

How should we grasp the relationship between this novel system, with its anti-imperialist liberatory rhetoric, and the powerful historical imperatives that had made the imperialist nation-state such a compelling model of power in the world? Since the dynamic of national strengthening was inseparable from the expansion of capitalism, these nations were subject to a set of imperatives that also obtained for all nation-states in the twentieth century seeking to survive and compete in the capitalist world—or, as in the case of socialist states, to be economically competitive with capitalism. These include the maximization of the territorial control of the state in order to command resources and markets; the building of military and security systems that had difficulty maintaining a stable line differentiating defense from aggression; and nationalist claims upon territories and people that amounted to imperialism.

The nineteenth-century nation-state, which wore its imperialism with pride, was imperialist in more than the usual sense of possessing colonies abroad. The process of nation formation, it will be remembered, was simultaneously a process of state formation that entailed conquest, pulverization, and homogenization of relatively autonomous communities, whether in the heartlands, peripheries, or neighboring regions of these states. The extraordinarily violent and imperialistic means by which the national territory of the United States of America was created in the nineteenth century is a case in point. It was also an uneven process and regions annexed to the nation-state at a later date frequently retained their peripheral, semicolonial status well into the twentieth century. The homogeneous nation was more frequently an ideal than a reality.

In East Asia, the case of Okinawa (like Hokkaido) in the Japanese nation reflects the problematic ways in which nations were imperialistically constructed. With the incorporation of Okinawa—an autonomous kingdom with multiple political affiliations—in 1879, the Japanese nation-state determined the national territorial limit of Japan and sought to differentiate it from the "outer territories" that were later to become its colonies. Yet, as Tomiyama Ichiro says, Okinawa problematizes the idea of a colony as having to be outside the nation, since Okinawa was historically closer to the "outer territories" and economically, too, it was incorporated much like a colony. However, since it was geographically and administratively part of the nation, it could not be dealt with rhetorically and politically as a colony. As neither colony nor quite of the nation, Okinawa became a place in need of welfare and relief administered by the benevolent national center in Tokyo.

Perhaps one of the most problematic and enduring manifestations of the imperialism–nationalism continuum for the anti-imperialist nation may be found in the transition from empire to nation. Nationalists of the dominant ethnicity or group made claims upon regions or territories of the old empire through the doctrine of *uti possidetis* (the principle of inheriting imperial boundaries). But it was practically difficult for Indian, Russian, or Chinese nationalists, for instance, to extend or sustain the principle of nationality among several groups within the empires of the British, the Romanovs, or the Manchus. The peripheral regions of these empires had multiple and flexible political affiliations (such as Okinawa or the Liu Qiu islands, which sent tribute both to China and the Satsuma domain in Japan). Moreover, incorporation into an empire may have been based on patronage of common religious or other cultural symbols, rather than the modern conception of absolute belonging to a territorial nation.

In other words, the principle of belonging to a national territory was incommensurate with the historical principle of multiple affiliations and flexible incorporation into empire. This was the basis, for instance, of the rejection by Muslims of the British Indian empire to join with the Republic of India, the Tibetan and Mongol refusal to participate in a Chinese nation, and so on. The Japanese claims to Manchukuo were made with an opportunistic grasp of this incommensurability. Moreover, dominant nationalists were often making their claims precisely at a time when elites of these regions or communities, such as the Mongols or British Indian Muslims, were also developing a national consciousness. Dominant nationalist claims on these regions—made with the belief in anti-imperialist brotherhood, common culture, or history, but often resulting in "internal colonialism"—produced acute tensions and political innovations that are important to this study.[33]

Finally, an aspect of nationalism not typically regarded as imperialistic is the mode whereby nationalists seek to transform identities. If, however, we accept the broad definition of imperialism as "the extension of rule or influence by one government, nation, or *society* over another,"[34] then the process of remaking people according to alien (modern) values—often violently—is a form of cultural imperialism. By ignoring this mode of domination, we may be slipping into the normalizing categories of the nation-state. Nationalist efforts to cultivate national loyalty or identification among peasants and other classes in the new nations of the twentieth century were often instituted in the absence of effective nationalist educational systems and with the expectation of quick results. In these societies, nation building not only meant the imposition of an abstract sense of the nation over and instead of other religious or local loyalties, it also meant the imposition of a modern, Westernized figure of a rational, hygienic, and scientific subject in place of much that was meaningful to the people. Judging by the reaction of peasants in China, who violently resisted the efforts by modernizers to appropriate their temples and festivals, this process must have been experienced as the imperialistic imposition of an alien culture. Once again, the Japanese architects of Manchukuo moved in to mobilize the rejected identities for their own purposes. The rural population in China was often caught between the alienating forces of nation- and state-building by Chinese elites and the appeals of the alien Japanese forces who claimed to champion their values.

To sum up: In principle, the nation-state system, which can perhaps be most appropriately dated to its explicit articulation by Emmerich de Vattel in the late eighteenth century, assumed that states respected the territorial integrity of other similarly constituted states.[35] The practice of competition between these states, however, entailed not only military conquest and colonization, but also annexation or domination of each other's territories. In other words, imperialism was intrinsic to the logic of the system. Before the late nineteenth century, nationalism tended to emerge as a functional support for imperialism. By the twentieth century, there is reason to believe that the stimulus for functional reciprocity between the two may have moved to nationalism as an ideology. Imperialism came to be justified by nationalism and the power of the nation-state came to be authorized by the symbolic regime of nationalism.

The period after World War I witnessed two contradictory forces: a strengthening nationalism justified aggression and domination, whereas an expanding system of nation-states introduced, if not reprisals or constraints upon aggressiveness, then the extension of some of the principles of citizenship to the dominated. Both old and new nations reflected to a greater or lesser degree this contradiction in their policies and practices. Older imperialist nations were faced with the moral and systemic pressure of the growing idea that nationalism was the legitimate mode of political belonging in the world. Colonial nations had to find means other than formal colonialism in order to control resources and remain globally competitive. Sometimes this meant developing client states and other subordinate political forms instead of colonies. It also involved pursuing developmental policies characteristic of nations, such as we will find in Manchukuo.

At the same time, anti-imperialist nationalism was also shaped by the contradiction between its imperialist practices and its commitment to anti-imperialism. In its ideology, imperialism became fully identified with colonialism, and thereafter the two were expunged from nationalism. Nationalism was identified with the principle of rights, equality, and brotherhood (if not sameness), whereas imperialism was identified with inequality and difference between ruler and ruled, characteristic of nineteenth-century colonialism. It is just as fruitless, I believe, to see this ideology simply as false consciousness as it is to accept its own pious declarations. Rather, the contradictory effects that issued from its constitutive form and its ideology were packaged in new institutions and policies that sought to redress but did not resolve these tensions. It is similarly fruitless to focus either on the covert imperialist intentions or the avowed developmental goals of an imperialism shaped by nationalism. Both old and new nations were being increasingly shaped by and into a single competitive world.[36]

Sovereignty and World Culture

Nationalism as a global ideology only tacitly accepts that sovereignty may derive from recognition by the system of nation-states. Rather, it declares that its sovereignty is immanent in the preconstituted communal body of the nation that is usually represented by the nation-state. This immanence can be deciphered in the history and culture of the national geo-body.[37] We will return to this extremely powerful doxa of nationalism and the symbolic regime of power that sustains it. But in order to grasp it as doxic, we need to understand that other obscured source of sovereignty.

Recent analyses of sovereignty have challenged certain of the assumptions that have long dominated its understanding. Thus, mainstream international relations theory treated the nation-state precisely as the preconstituted actor or subject that represented the sovereign, indivisible power of a people in a territory. Sovereignty was assumed to have evolved historically as political society matured and the state came to be based on the idea of a general will and common interest. Indeed, sovereignty was considered indivisible because it expressed this general will and vice versa. The historical work of F. H. Hinsley, long considered classic on the subject, plotted the evolution of this political society. Sovereignty first emerged internally, as citizen and community came to exercise political and ethical restraints upon the modern state; subsequently, internal sovereignty became the basis for external sovereignty, conferring upon the state a right to play a role in the inter-state system.

Aside from reflecting the views of nation-states themselves, there was a strong moral component in this thinking linking sovereignty closely to arguments of culture and civilization. According to Jens Bartelson, the argument made in international relations theory starts from an anterior origin of sovereignty in human nature or in the social bond. It then ventures to explain the transition from this origin as a gradual overcoming of otherness or estrangement. As such, the transition is mediated by culture and each move marks a step on the ladder of civilization, culminating in the triumph of man over the dark forces of nature (anarchy) in the fully sovereign state. Of course, this dark force is never completely overcome and is transferred to the conflict among nations for global dominance. But in theory, the inter-state system itself serves as the monitor regulating this conflict. Certainly, nineteenth-century imperialism justified its sovereignty over its colonial lands by the argument that these lands were uncivilized and could thus scarcely claim sovereign status. Ironically, this civilizational discourse underpinning sovereignty retained enormous significance for the new nationalism of the twentieth century.[38]

Early critics such as Harold Laski argued that the doctrine of the sovereign state representing all citizens was significantly undermined by the reality of class stratification within national society. Indeed, this theory of sovereignty was manipulated to allow the state to expand its prerogative within domestic politics.[39] More recently, Anthony Giddens has shown that it is simplistic to assume the sovereign state pre-existed the inter-state system. He says, "The European state system was not simply the 'political environment' in which the absolutist state and the nation-state developed. It was the condition and in substantial degree *the very source* of that development."[40] The sovereignty of a modern state depends upon a reflexively regulated and monitored set of relations between states. The system orders both what is internal and external to states, "presuming a system of rule that is universal and obligatory in relation to the citizenry of a specified territory but from which all those who are not citizens are excluded."[41] Not only was sovereignty an essential condition of belonging to the system, the latter would shape the very form of the sovereign nation.

By the time of the emergence of the new anti-imperialist nationalism in the aftermath of World War I, this self-regulating state system had begun to expand in principle to participation of all nation-states beyond the select club of "civilized" powers. The expanded system found institutional expression and was reinforced by new global institutions and fora such as the League of Nations, the Court of International Justice, the Multilateral Treaty of Paris, the World Disarmament Conferences, and the like.[42] Despite the catastrophic competitiveness among states, the inter-war years saw a deepening and shaping of the system's role with respect to these nations, old and new.[43] Although institutions such as the League were not successful in achieving their primary goal of peace, by integrating and reinforcing the dependency of nations upon the system, discursively and practically, they enhanced the primacy or even naturalness of the nation as the only basis of the sovereign polity. New nations were dependent upon the standards and procedures of these international bodies for recognition, and the League also became a means of channeling the processes of global information control and monitoring upon which modern states depended.[44] The question of Manchukuo's sovereignty was not only determined by the League, but the Lytton Commission report upon which the judgment was based represented an enormous enterprise in information gathering.

Whatever its long-term effect on internationalism, the League of Nations could not overcome the problematic relationship between imperialism and nationalism discussed earlier. This was frequently expressed as a tension between the rights of states and the rights of nations, which becomes noticeable particularly with the rise of anti-imperialist nationalism. Woodrow Wilson, champion of the right to national self-determination and the new internationalism, was the leading advocate for the League of Nations in the Paris Peace Conference in 1919. When the United States Senate refused to ratify the Treaty of Versailles, which contained the Covenant of the League, America was not able to participate in the League and its leadership of the new internationalism came to an end.[45] Subsequently, the philosophical principles of the League came to be formulated and guided by a group of British diplomats, professionals, and thinkers belonging to the "liberal idealist" tradition.[46] Most prominent among these thinkers was Alfred Zimmern—a League diplomat, Foreign Office advisor, first professor of international relations at Oxford University, and teacher of Arnold Toynbee.[47] Zimmern, like Woodrow Wilson, was committed to an internationalism based upon cooperation among nations—the individual families of mankind.

Despite the reality of nationalist aggression, fascism, and imperialism, these thinkers thought of nations as organic communities; like families, they were necessary for humanity. They were committed to the Wilsonian idea of making state boundaries coincide with those of nationality and language. This principle frequently unleashed bloody nationalist violence and has prompted Hobsbawm to remark that Hitler was a "logical Wilsonian nationalist."[48] To be sure, Wilson was also committed to human rights and hoped that the League as the organization of "democratic world opinion" would counter narrow nationalism.[49] Similarly, according to Morefield, the liberal idealists were "firm believers in the unifying power of a higher 'international mind'" based on the idea of a common civilization underlying nationalism. This same nationalism, however, also mandated that the sovereignty of existing states not be compromised in the least. The insistence on the inviolability of external sovereignty of states was consistent with, and perhaps reflected, the League's highly ambivalent attitude to imperialistically acquired state rights (and colonialism), which we shall see in relation to Manchukuo. It was manifested not only in the relative powerlessness to enforce compliance upon Japan, but also in its rhetoric respecting the special state rights acquired by treaties. Dominated as it was by imperialist nations, the League was forced to reconcile the reality of imperialism with the new rationale of national self-determination.

Thus we cannot afford to lose sight of the extent to which the domination of the system—the shaping standards and rules, the continued pursuit of imperialism by the major powers, old and new—continued to reflect the power of the older Western states. Indeed, with the exception of resource extraction, global processes tended to flow from the powerful or advanced nation-states to the poorer and weaker ones throughout the twentieth century. But the regulation and shaping of nations by these systemic forces and the principle of the juridical equivalence of nation-states was an equally influential, and perhaps more long-term, result. Let us turn to these shaping forces.

Nations have been constituted by norms and practices deriving not only from the system of nation-states, but from a "world culture" that accompanied this system since the late nineteenth century. World culture may be thought of as a wider system that circulates and disseminates authoritative standards, norms, and practices—and the cognitive principles underlying them—among nations. A group of scholars, mainly sociologists, under the leadership of John Meyer has tracked the dissemination of "world culture" over a range of different institutions, practices, and movements. For instance, the notion of the child has become increasingly standardized as the institutional rules governing childhood were diffused to all types of nation-states over the last hundred years.[50] The conduits for this circulation also include nongovernmental organizations, such as trade, labor, professional, and knowledge-producing groups. For example, the International Electrotechnical Commission established standards in fields of power generation, radio communication technology, and basic electrical devices, and disseminated international units such as the hertz. Formed in 1906, by 1939 it included representatives from China, Argentina, the USSR, and even colonies such as India and Egypt.[51]

The concept of world culture, while not incompatible with current theories of globalization, was distinctive and usable for an earlier period precisely because it was not transgressive of the nation-state but rather constitutive of it, at least through much of the twentieth century.[52] Recognition of a nation was—and is—not merely a political act; it has a cognitive and ontological dimension. A nation has to be constituted as a type of being with political practices capable of being read as signs of sovereignty in order to be re-cognized as such. Entire societies, as we shall see with regard to China and Japan, have not only to be remade into modern economic, political, and military structures, but the very basic perceptions of time, space, and the self need to be overhauled. The ability of societies to learn to see themselves as progressing (or stagnating) in a linear universal time—history—is an essential condition for sovereign nationhood, as is the ability to recognize a diverse population as an authentic "people" or "culture." The doctrine of rights and ideas of governmentality become rooted in a society because they are part of what is systemically acceptable as national—and sometimes, as in the case of Manchukuo, despite its rejection by the nation-state system. Such assumptions, conceptions, and cultural technologies, as well as the tensions and contradictions inherent in them, are absorbed from the circulatory system of world culture.

Although governmentality comes with as many faces as there are nations in the world, it is constituted by certain shared principles and goals of modern state power and governance in general. Governmentality is a more complex way to understand what we have called "modernization," which tends to be normative, one-sided, and teleological. According to Foucault, the birth of the modern state, the "reason of state," refers neither to God nor to the prince's patrimony, but to itself, to its own rationality and its own finality. The thesis that the aim of government is to strengthen the state itself led to techniques and practices—rationalities—that sought to define, regulate, control, mobilize, and expand the capacities of its most basic source of power: bio-power, or what came to be called "population."[53] The welfare of the population, the improvement of its condition, the increase of its wealth, longevity, and health becomes a goal of government.[54] At the same time, governmentality is not benign. It is a "power knowledge" that produces its own forms of domination and is capable of monstrous violence, as we shall see below. But its most novel and dangerous aspect is the form of power it represents: disciplinary power.

Foucault considers disciplinary power in the formation of subjects to be characteristic of modern society. Power operates through and on the subject, constituting the subject as subject through the sciences and the techniques of self-knowledge, as well as through the extension of disciplinary models emerging from the prison and the military. Within this framework, governmentality is concerned with policing, surveillance, control, and intervention in the population to both extend and control bio-power. In Foucault's view, while governmentality reflects the rationale of the modern state, it is not solely the purview of the state. The growing administration of society takes place at a number of different levels, often outside the state in the realm of what we call civil society. He argues that modernity is characterized less by the "'étatisation' of society," than by "the 'governmentalization' of the state."[55] What has been called the East Asian model of development—which in my view is significantly rooted in the East Asian modern, incorporating a Confucian statecraft tradition, state penetration of society and economy, total surveillance, and high levels of mass education, among other features—exemplifies a historical, regional, and cultural mediation of governmentality.[56]

We will consider later the problems with Foucault's deliberate effort to diminish the distinction between civil society and state as two realms and mechanisms of governmentality. For the moment, I want to underscore here the phenomenally significant role of disciplinary power in nationalism and the nation-state, political forms that Foucault never specifically considered. Anthony Giddens emphasizes this characteristic of the modern nation-state: "there is no type of nation-state in the contemporary world which is completely immune from the potentiality of being subject to totalitarian rule."[57] The specific mechanisms that produce this potentiality, according to Giddens, are the high level of surveillance of society by the nation-state, based on the multiple modes of documenting and coding information about the population and on expanded supervision of the conduct of significant segments of it.[58] We may add, following Foucault, that these functions are performed not only by the state but increasingly by a variety of social organizations. Even more significantly, the disciplinary production of national subjects or individuals, when joined with these mechanisms of social power, has the *capacity* to mobilize the social or national body, for purposes of closure, with the authority of personal, moral, and scientific truth—or the regime of authenticity.

Thus, on the one hand, the inter-state system has been a crucial source of national sovereignty, and world culture has been the source of many circulatory practices transforming societies into nations. The advent of nationalism as a world ideology, on the other hand, tended to identify sovereignty solely within the people and culture of the nation. Sustaining such an immanent conception of sovereignty necessitates a misrecognition of the systemic or wider source and impetus of many national developments and of the ideas, techniques, and practices of nation formation. Symbols like the national flag or national anthem are good, if obvious, examples. In their history, form, design, and usage, they are truly emblematic of the circulatory process, yet they can evoke powerful emotions as symbols of the primordial nation. There are also more subtle mechanisms of misrecognition.

Consider China. Apart from the many thousands of new words coined to express the language of world culture, an entire class of paleonyms—deriving from the classical Chinese but re-signifed (usually in Japan) with meaning and function drawn from Western conceptions of history—such as the words for feudalism (*fengjian*) or revolution (*geming*), emerged in the Chinese vocabulary. Frank Dikötter has discussed the signifier *zu*, which historically referred to the lineage or descent line, but came to be translated into the late-nineteenth-century concept of race or a community of blood ties (*zhongzu, shuzoku* in Japanese). Revolutionary nationalists like Chen Tianhua were able to able to draw upon the historical values embedded in lineage ideology to produce and disseminate the idea of the nation as kin group: "The Han race is one big family. The Yellow Emperor is the great ancestor, all those who are not of the Han race are not the descendants of the Yellow Emperor, they are exterior families. One should definitely not assist them."[59] A new conception of political community encased in old symbols became naturalized as the historically deep nation. Misrecognition is particularly enabled by the East Asian modern.

If nations have been formed by external impulses, does this mean that the people and historical cultures of these new nations are mere automatons or puppets of an impersonal world culture? Misrecognition is an important ideological device serving a political function, but it is also a new cultural resource. The paleonym *fengjian*, which had possessed a positive value in the late imperial critique of autocracy, acquired a negative value in the East Asian modern, but simultaneously signaled an agenda for change.[60] Regional and local, popular and elite groups engage, select, reject, and contest world culture, thus remaking it into local and national culture. The complex relationships and gaps between historical reality and these goals or ideals form the stuff of this book. Nonetheless, we would fall headlong into the traps of nationalist ideology if we were to ignore the global stimulus of nation formation.

Time, History, and Authenticity

In the remainder of this chapter I probe the ideological mechanism by which the nation-state or its ideologues adapt the external sources of sovereignty and nation formation into the immanent conception and its consequences. This process generates and is sustained by a regime of authenticity that grants those who can speak for it sovereign authority both within the nation and without. The mechanism was deployed in Manchukuo with particular transparency, but I hope to show here that the process applies, in varying degrees, to all nation-states. The regime of authenticity is a regime of symbolic power capable of preempting challenges to the nation-state or nationalists by proleptically positing or symbolizing the sacred nation. This regime does not simply possess a negative or repressive power. It also allows its custodians to shape identities and regulate access to resources.

The problem of identity, so characteristic of modern societies, is most fundamentally a problem of time. It is a quest to retain a sense of self when everything around is perceived to be in flux. Politically, the identity problem arises in the ability to claim sovereignty in the foundational ideals of a regime when the ideals may no longer be viable, or when the conditions underlying them are no longer sustainable. In other words, the search for identity is an effort to grasp, retain, and extend presence. Identity and authenticity become particularly salient in politics when accelerating linearity becomes the dominant mode of representing time and history.

To be sure, the representation of time as linear is historically hardly new, and one may find evidence of it in certain thinkers or practices all over the world.[61] Nonetheless, I believe that a constitutive difference between historical and modern societies lies in the *dominant* representation of historical time. Linear history is enabled by the increasing pervasiveness of a representation of time associated with the rise of capitalism. This time is linear, abstract, or, as Walter Benjamin put it, "empty and homogeneous."[62] At the same time, I want to emphasize that even in mature capitalist societies, abstractness and linearity are dominant *representations* of time that coexist with and sometimes obscure other conceptions—religious, apocalyptic, or cyclical (such as the business cycle).

Modern linear history is distinguished from traditional histories principally in that the meaning that the latter almost always seeks in history refers to an earlier presumed existent ideal, or to a transcendent time of god. Traditional historiography usually has a cyclical structure whereby time will reproduce, return to, or approximate a "known certainty." Linear history frequently dispenses with god and replaces it with the model of a unified actor—the subject, the nation—moving forward in time, conquering uncharted territories. Just as linear time in capitalism is the dominant one, so too linear history is often a hegemonic conception; it is imposed upon, and sometimes resisted by, various groups in society whose lives respond to different rhythms or conceptions of time, whether seasonal or ritual.

Recently Michael Puett has argued that in early Chinese history, during the period of the Warring States and the early Han, strong claims were made for discontinuity, change, and the creation of new institutions that were transgressive of the past and the divine; in other words, some Chinese statesmen advocated a conception of time as secular and innovative. Nonetheless, even while scholars like Sima Qian affirmed—however ambivalently—historical creation, the claim that came to dominate the empire was one of continuity with the patterns of the ancient sages and the normative order of Heaven. Puett's argument is consonant with my own about the *hegemonic representation* of time and history, which obscures other perceptions, like the one Puett has excavated. The task remains to explore how, and with what effects, conceptions of time become tied to structures of power.[63]

There are several views regarding the emergence of the modern conception of history in Europe. Reinhart Koselleck's is perhaps the most concise. By the end of the eighteenth century, the impact of capitalism and the industrial revolution, together with the developing notions of linear time, produced what Koselleck describes as the increasing gap in perception between "experience" and "expectation." Where, up to this time, the bulk of the population in Western Europe had expected to live their lives as did their fathers and forefathers, the accelerating pace of change in their lives now caused their expectations to diverge from experience. From this tension emerged the concept of historical time as we know it. Linear history was experienced and formulated as unique in that the past became distinct from the future, not simply in one case, but as a whole.[64]

From the late nineteenth century, linear history, disseminated through world culture and the nation-state system, became a most important means of constituting nationhood and the rights of nations. Nationalists seem to have tried to institutionalize it both in societies where the process of making a "people" was well underway and in those where this relationship would call or "awaken" the people into being. By the twentieth century, individuals were increasingly educated to identify with nation-states that had supposedly evolved over a long history. Individual and state were to attain a self-conscious unity and the collective subject would be poised to acquire mastery over the future. History became the history of a people or nationality and a territory.[65]

Historically, all kinds of communities, and not only religious ones, were capable of developing a strong sense of Self versus Other and hard boundaries in relation to outsiders. What these movements lacked was not self-consciousness or identity per se, but the historical claim arising from the idea of a sovereign people evolving within a delimited territory. The three-way relationship between a people, a territory, and a history produces the rights of nations and distinguishes nationalism from other types of identity movements that preceded it.[66]

However, national history is not only about linear evolution; it is also about timelessness. While writers like Koselleck provide us with persuasive accounts, their objective is to grasp the creative, open dimension of this history: a "totality opened toward a progressive future."[67] I will argue not only that linear time conditions the possibility of a progressive or linear movement of history, but that the aporia and the anxiety embedded in that time also generates a representation of timelessness that serves as an anchor for identity in modern histories and a foundation of the symbolic regime of nation-states. It is perhaps because it contradicts or complicates the idea of history as progress or change that timelessness is obscured in historical accounts. Linear histories have certainly become dominant in the era of capitalism and nation-states, and the unchanging does not have the primacy it once had in traditional histories. But it has not disappeared.

The writings of poststructuralist thinkers like Jacques Derrida and Paul Ricoeur have been centrally concerned with the issue of time at a philosophical level, but its implications go to the heart of identity politics such as nationalism. The anxiety of identity becomes particularly pronounced in the perception of linear time, in which it is impossible to grasp the "present" or the "now." Phenomenologically, the "now" or "instant" (*nun*) can only be approached as "being-past" or "being-future." Derrida describes the paradox of the linguistic "now" as the "intemporal kernel of time, the nonmodifiable nucleus of temporal modification, the inalterable form of temporalization."[68] He shows that beings, substance, essence—and, we may add, the authentic—are all linked in meaning to the form of this present participle. According to Ricoeur, the conception of linear time that is bound to posit time as a series of "nows"—of unrelated instants—necessarily generates an aporia manifested as a disjuncture between the past and the present. Expressed in Saint Augustine as a sorrow for the fleeting and dread of the future, the anxiety associated with this linear representation of time can neither be fully overcome by the philosophy of time nor by narrative itself. This representation of time requires an artifice, equivalent to the linguistic now, which allows it to negotiate or conceal the aporia—but the aporia itself will persist.[69]

Koselleck's identification of the tension between experience and expectation in the emergence of history, corresponds, I believe, to Ricoeur's aporia of linear time, and the conceptions of progress and utopia, which Koselleck observes came to overlay the horizon of expectation, may be seen as the artifices necessary to negotiate this tension. But perhaps the most exemplary device developed to redress the aporia of time is the very subject of history—the ahistorical kernel of historical time. Ernest Renan, who confronted the problem of the nation's history as early as 1882, put the matter directly: "Man, Gentlemen, does not improvise. The nation, like the individual, is the culmination of a long past of endeavours, sacrifice and devotion. . . . The Spartan song—'We are what you were, we will be what you are'—is, in its simplicity, the abridged hymn of every *patrie*."[70] In order to be recognizable as the *subject* of history, the core of the nation has to be perceived as unaffected by the passage of time.

This core often refers to none other than the unity of a people and its territory. In the nation's evolution there are historical vicissitudes during which a people may be driven out of its territory or enslaved, or become separated and lose consciousness of their original unity. But the historical destiny of the nation lies in the fulfillment or restoration of this unity and sovereignty of a people. National history is fully teleological in that its ends are to be found in its beginnings.

Yet even the evidentiary pyrotechnics of nationalist history is inadequate to sustain the irony of "unity within change." This should come as no surprise, given that historically people did not think in terms of their unity for future nationalisms, nor in terms of territorial sovereignty. Thus the timeless unity of the nation—the stillness of the true—has to be deciphered in the signs of authenticity. The truth of this originary unity is simulated and sublimated by symbols of the pure, the honorable, the good, and the spiritual. It is their immateriality, after all, that renders them insusceptible to historical corrosion.

The Regime of Authenticity

The unchanging essence of the past, endowed with a special aura of sanctity, purity, and authenticity, is located at the heart of a modern discourse of progressive change that is otherwise entirely synchronous with the quickening pace of change—the transformative drive—of global capitalism. It is possible to think of the aporia of linear history as demarcating two regimes: of capitalism and of (national or transnational) authenticity, which institute two poles of authority. Certainly linear, measurable time is necessary for capitalism (where time is money), but the corrosive effects of capitalism (where all that is solid melts into air) are also made visible by this very conception of time. It is not simply the disruption caused by rapid material change that necessitates the production of an abiding truth. It is ultimately the dominant temporal conception that exposes this change as having no goal or meaning that necessitates a continuous subject of history to shore up certitudes, particularly for the claim to national sovereignty embedded in this subject.

The opposition between authenticity and capitalism is an old one and I need to outline the specificity of my argument. The tradition of modern writing on "authenticity" tends to locate it as the ethically and ontologically positive, if fleeting, term in the opposition between the self and the market or modernity. Alessandro Ferrara argues that it derives from Rousseau's notion of authenticity as "man in the state of nature." The tradition develops through the thought of Hegel, Kierkegaard, Nietzsche, and Heidegger, and in such contemporary thinkers as Daniel Bell and Christopher Lasch, who deplore the corrosion of authenticity and the reduction of self to pure exteriority.[71] Notably this tradition focuses on authenticity of the self, or personhood. Ferrara also identifies an assumption of authenticity in the thought of social thinkers like Marx or Durkheim, whether located in the concept of the worker or the "species being," or in ideas of community or *gemeinschaft*. Here the role of such concepts as Marx's alienation, Weber's rationalization, or Durkheim's anomie seem to indicate that authenticity is under constant threat of erasure. Most of all, for all of these thinkers, the loss of authenticity spells the destruction of social identity.

The authentic that I want to explore here refers primarily neither to selfhood nor to any ontological category. Authenticity in my formulation refers primarily to an order or regime simulated by representations of authoritative inviolability. It derives this authority from "being good for all times," which is tantamount to being beyond the reach of time. My understanding of the regime differs fundamentally from the modern conception of authenticity as an attribute of some *being* that is endangered, although the perception of danger remains central. Rather, the regime is a power that repeatedly constitutes itself as the locus of authenticity. The hegemony of linear time accompanying the transforming drive of capitalism necessitates the repeated constitution of the unchanging subject of history precisely because it is this very combination of capital and linear time that erodes it and simultaneously exposes the spectacle of erosion.

Herein lies the distinctive irony of authenticity among nations. Global competitiveness, industrialization, urbanization, and other accelerating forces of transformation erode identity in an unprecedented manner. The nation-state and modernizers frame many of these transformations in the new historical optic of progress or development upon which they stake their legitimacy. But as representatives of identity polities, they are equally forced to simulate symbols of timeless authenticity that are, nonetheless, destined to erode. In this way, while authenticity was unquestionably important in prenational polities, its distinctiveness in the twentieth century emerges from its generation within an accelerating, linear temporality that requires the constant renewal of timelessness.[72]

While the authentic is not primarily about the self, my argument also seeks to clarify a method of linking selfhood to wider political ideas and institutions. I hope to show that authenticity is the anvil upon which the truth of the self is forged in relation to political identities. As such, the self may be formed with reference to an authenticity that is not necessarily controlled by the nation-state—although the nation-state has the distinct advantage of controlling much institutionalized knowledge production. Ideals of the authentic self may derive from religious faith or civilizational, regional, or local fashionings of the true. These ideals, I shall show in the discussion of redemptive societies in part II, frequently gain sanction by becoming intertwined with circulating world cultural ideas. A person's quest for identity may in such a way elude the boundaries of the nation-state and attach to these alternative, even transnational conceptions of community sometimes capable of challenging the nation-state system. But while the regime of authenticity may link individual subjectivity to various conceptions of political community, this regime develops and derives its greatest power by symbolizing the identity of an entire body politic. Thus, in neither premodern polities nor, until recently, in transnational communities has the regime of authenticity had effects as powerful as in the nation-state.[73]

In China, some of the more familiar representational practices that sustain the order of authenticity include the movement in politics and culture to identify essences and search for roots. Among these are the early-twentieth-century search for "national essence" associated with Zhang Taiyan, the National Culture of Hu Shi, the New Life essentialism in the KMT (Kuomintang Party), the folkloric or people's culture movement among communists and noncommunists, the "native place" or "search for roots" literature in more recent times, and what Rey Chow has called "primitive passions" in contemporary Chinese cinema. In Japan we have the state cult of authenticity or purity (*junsuisei*) centered on the divine emperor and the myth of a two-thousand-year continuous history of the imperial institution.[74] Beyond the state cult, several scholars have traced the various efforts to recuperate the authentic in the landscape and folk traditions of the Japanese countryside.[75] In postwar Japan, perhaps most revealing is the culture industry known as *Nihonjinron* (theories of Japaneseness), described by Yamamoto Shichihei as the "cultural theology of Japan," which constantly seeks out the bases of Japanese authenticity.[76]

What kinds of beings or objects are selected to represent the authentic? To be sure, the authentic tends to be differently represented by different powers, whether the nation-state or nationalist intellectuals or militarists, and at different moments in time, depending, say, on whether the women's movement has flowered or whether the aboriginal has been domesticated by state making. But at the outset, there appear to be two desiderata for the role: that the representation, or perhaps representative, be productive of deep affect, and that it be denied agency in the public realm. The sentiments that underpin authenticity derive from a range of attitudes about the possible erosion of the true. They include fear, vigilance, devotion, dutifulness, discipline, self-abnegation, sacrifice, and militancy. Moreover, loss is not only existential but may be experienced as dishonor, desecration, and defilement (by commodification or sexualization).

Authenticity is frequently embodied in living persons such as the child, the woman, the rustic, the aboriginal, and royalty. Each invokes symbolic affects in various historical cultures, including the association of timelessness with the royalty, innocence with children, naturalness with the primitive, rootedness with peasants, and motherhood or chastity with women—the last three of which I will explore in later chapters. Each has also had a dependent status. The problem arises, of course, not only from their agency, which might challenge the image of timelessness, but simply from the fact that their lives will change in time.

Similar problems also arise with representative objects such as a constitution or a monument. Here it is their changing meaning or interpretation that must be discounted, as can be seen in the effort to restore the original intent of the United States constitution. With certain social practices or traditions, like annual festivals, historicity is concealed by the pace of change, which is not synchronous with change in other spheres. But the human embodiments are most powerful because, having (ideally) internalized the authentic in their sense of the self, they are capable of producing empathy. However, they are also the most ephemeral, since the risk of their not living up to the unchanging ideal in time is considerable. These symbolic figures must be contained within representational and often physical or spatial apparatuses that conceal their lived reality: the home, the reservation, or the castle. When this is not possible—when, for instance, the women's movement seeks to blur the line between the domestic and the public—the embodiment of authenticity must be found elsewhere.

Who are the agents involved in the process of selection and construction? Given the split time of the nation, the agents most interested in reconciling the demand for an unchanging unity of nationhood with a changing modern future are representatives of the national community (such as nationalist intellectuals) or the state. They seek to do so by constituting and policing the regime of authenticity. Globally circulating discourses of nation formation are usually processed by state organizations, quasi-state agencies such as universities or mass organizations, self-strengthening societies, or the modernizing press. These agents are critically positioned: on the one hand, they are discursively affiliated with modernizing forces in the nation-state system; on the other, they have linguistic and social links with wider segments of the society.

This positioning enables the agents to engage in two kinds of mediations: to translate global categories and techniques—say, of feudalism or public speech making—into historical or vernacular expressions, thus indigenizing them; and to recast existing cultural objects, practices, and "traditions" as embodiments of the authenticity of nations. This dual process, as we shall see, is at the heart of the East Asian modern. The two translations are not necessarily performed by the same people or groups, but the one often implies the other. Moreover, the project of transforming culture can implicate modernizers in a complex and frequently hostile relationship with vast segments of popular society. Since this opposition undermines their claims to national representativeness, the consolidation of a symbolic regime becomes still more urgent.

Functionally, in an ideal nation, the representation of identity generated by the regime of authenticity grants its custodians the authority to regulate the relationship with other nations and global capitalism, as well as to regulate and shape the identity of national citizens. These agents typically need to balance and police the boundaries between the regimes of authenticity and capitalism, both global and domestic. Even though the authentic imagines a fixity, these boundaries can hardly be fixed. Attention to the constitution and reconstitution of this boundary allows us to see a complex relationship between the two orders.

On the one hand, the authentic can be mobilized to produce opposition to capitalism and modernity, as fundamentalist and nativist movements the world over (whether the Taliban or Showa Restorationists) have shown. Through most of the twentieth century, even when the symbolic regime was being significantly shaped by world culture and the nation-state system, anti-imperialist nationalism was able to mobilize considerable opposition to global capitalism by drawing precisely from the authority of this regime. At the same time, the symbolic regime should not be seen to be in contradiction with global capitalism; after all, modern regimes are equally legitimated by global success. The symbolic regime is rather an autonomous authority deployed by nationalists to contain capitalism's effects and regulate its role. On an everyday level, the regime of authenticity authorizes a range of representational practices that are in constant traffic with the practices of the capitalist order, a traffic that produces an elaborate economy of authorization and delegitimation, and that the nation-state would like to control.

The question of the nation's historical unity is, of course, inseparable from the problem of its contemporary diversity. The idea of a collective actor or subject—the self-conscious, sovereign nation-people—that a national history ultimately presupposes is practically often challenged through counter-histories, different modes of life, or the assertion of rights by classes, ethnicities, races, or minorities. The demand of the nation-state that we exist first and foremost as national subjects turns out to be mostly hortatory. In so urging us, the nation-state strives every day to *produce* the idea that the nation is prior to us. The regime of authenticity contributes significantly to this production through representations that simulate the priority of the nation. Because of their inviolability, these representations are able to preempt challenges to the nation and limit political and human rights.

But this authority is not simply a repressive one. The symbols of timeless identity are deployed as ideals to produce disciplined bodies for purposes of governmentality, and can be mobilized to legitimate state building. In much of the rest of the book I will explore the representation and politics of authenticity in the discourse of civilization, the model of the self-sacrificing woman, the "natural primitive," and the peasant of the heartland in Manchukuo.

The purpose of this chapter has been to demonstrate two theses: first, that nationalism and imperialism have been historically and functionally interconnected in the pursuit of dominance and survival in a competitive capitalist world; second, the systemic attributes underlying this relationship and transnational conditions—the circulatory conceptions, practices, and techniques—of nationality and sovereignty formation were misrecognized as immanent phenomena. The immanent conception, based upon a deep history of a people, could only be sustained by a symbolic regime of authenticity that in turn created the possibility of a morally absolute, unilateralist, and imperialist nationalism.

I believe that the anti-imperialist movement was necessary and morally right. At the same time, we can scarcely retain a clear historical picture by pitting a world-emancipating anti-imperialist nationalism against imperialist forces. The nationalisms of the twentieth century were too intimately shaped by—and shaped to respond to—the ideals, tensions, and practices of the nation-state system, world culture, and global capitalism to generate long-term systemic opposition. By the inter-war years, the discourse of developmentalism and practices of governmentality had so penetrated the system that even imperialist powers undertook nationalistic development and governmentality in the colonies, whatever their true goals may have been. On the other hand, even the most stoutly anti-imperialist nationalisms did not refrain from imperialistic practices to garner territory and resources in a competitive world. Most importantly, despite socialistic or civilizational ideals of human emancipation accompanying the new nationalism, this nationalism continued to be built upon an identity politics of closure sanctioned by the regime of authenticity.

The symbolic regime authorized a new type of relationship between nationalism and imperialism. As Hannah Arendt pointed out, compared to the earlier imperialism of nation-states, which was more sensitive to the balance of power in the interstate system, nationalism possessed few constraints in its pursuit of imperialist projects. Nationalism is able to consider itself morally autonomous and absolute precisely because it misrecognizes the systemic basis of national power. Considerations of inter-state relations become epiphenomenal and may be ignored, particularly where nationalism no longer sees the state as representative of sovereign authenticity. The inter-war political history of Japan is a case in point.

From early in the Meiji period, Japanese imperialism was justified by nationalism.

Mainland northeast Asia was characterized as the outer zone of national defense. The security of the Japanese nation was depicted in popular representations of the Korean peninsula as a dagger poised at the heart of the nation. Japanese expansionism in northeast Asia during the first three decades of the twentieth century was accompanied by the rhetoric that Korea, Manchuria, and Mongolia (successively, *Man-sen* and *Man-mo*), represented the "lifeline" of the Japanese nation.

In the 1920s, Japanese nationalism grew out of several different social sites. There was, of course, the continuation of the Meiji orthodox nationalism built around the emperor system by the state and the *minkan* publicists—the journalists and intellectuals of popular society.[77] Other sources included the radicals of an "authentic" agrarianism (*nōhonshugi*) responding to widespread rural immiseration of the time, a military generally disaffected by disarmament programs, and, especially, young disgruntled military officers, the Showa Restorationists, who felt that the capitalists, politicians, and bureaucrats had abandoned the true *bushido* spirit of the Japanese nation.[78] The radical nationalism that began to coalesce around these forces was centered on powerful symbols of authenticity and on continuing expansion in deliberate defiance of an inter-state balance of power perceived as unjust to a sovereign Japan. It was facilitated by the ideology of pan-Asianism, which claimed to protect an authentic Asia and thus justified the expansion as a holy war against the West. Note here that Japanese militaristic expansion into Manchuria in the early 1930s was enthusiastically welcomed by the entire social body of the Japanese nation, which was efficiently mobilized to support it.[79] Let us also note that if the nation was behind imperialism, the imperialism of Japan in Manchuria was also shaped by nationalist ideas and practices.

Imperialist in intent, the global circumstances we have outlined pushed the rulers of Manchukuo to fashion it much like a nation. While it would be folly to ignore the intent, it would nonetheless represent an intentional fallacy to ignore the effects and products of this strangely contradictory enterprise. I will examine why and how Manchukuo's makers sought to produce it as a nation. Each of the four representations of authenticity discussed in parts II and III reflects the double translation: to convert circulatory ideas and forms into immanent conceptions, and to re-signify social and cultural entities to represent the authenticity of this state. Since these translations frequently processed cultural materials, practices, and techniques circulating in China and Japan, we gain an opportunity to view these societies through the lens of Manchukuo.

Notes

1. I follow the definition of imperialism as "the extension of rule or influence by one government, nation, or society over another," *Columbia Encyclopedia*, 6th ed. Note that imperialism does not specify a mode of rule; it might involve the assimilation of conquered or dominated peoples (as in French imperialism), or, as was more usual in the nineteenth-century colonialism, the maintenance of difference between ruler and ruled. While working

definitions are indispensable, defining such historical formations as imperialism, colonialism, or culture and civilization has become epistemologically problematic. The realities to which these signifiers refer are fluid and change according to time and place. By the time we access them as analytical categories they have already been deployed in language games by different powers and ideologies. Thus, while recognizing that any encompassing definition of imperialism can only have limited value, I employ the widest definition in order to grasp how and to what ends particular groups or ideologies—such as nationalism, discussed above—have delimited its usage.

2. Geoffrey Barraclough, *An Introduction to Contemporary History* (Hammondsworth, England: Penguin, 1964), 119, 120–25.

3. Etienne Balibar, "The Nation Form: History and Ideology," in *Race, Nation, Class: Ambiguous Identities*, ed. Etienne Balibar and Immanuel Wallerstein (London: Verso, 1991), 94–95.

4. Giovanni Arrighi, *The Long Twentieth Century: Money, Power, and the Origins of Our Times* (New York: Verso, 1994), 34–58.

5. Immanuel Wallerstein, "The Construction of Peoplehood: Racism, Nationalism, Ethnicity," in *Race, Nation, Class: Ambiguous Identities*, ed. Etienne Balibar and Immanuel Wallerstein (London: Verso, 1991), 81–82.

6. The appearance of the idea of the "people's economy" (*Volkswirthschaft*) or "national economy" (*Nationaloekonomie*)—as opposed to the contemporary British understanding of the economy as political economy—can be traced to German thinkers like Friedrich List, whose ideas were much influenced by the nineteenth-century American debates on the national economy. See Eric Hobsbawm, *Nations and Nationalism since 1780* (Cambridge: Cambridge University Press, 1990), 29–30.

7. Arrighi, *Long Twentieth Century*, 59.

8. Ernest Gellner, *Nations and Nationalism* (Ithaca: Cornell University Press, 1983); Karl W. Deutsch, "Social Mobilization and Political Development," *American Political Science Review* 55 (1961): 493–514; Benedict Anderson, *Imagined Communities: Reflections on the Origins and Spread of Nationalism*, rev. ed. (London: Verso, 1991).

9. Barraclough, *Introduction to Contemporary History*, 115–16.

10. Hobsbawm, *Nations and Nationalism*, 132; William C. Kirby, *Germany and Republican China* (Stanford: Stanford University Press, 1984), 162.

11. Anthony Giddens, *The Nation-State and Violence*, vol. 2 of *A Contemporary Critique of Historical Materialism* (Berkeley: University of California Press, 1987), 234–39.

12. Gregory J. Kasza, *The Conscription Society: Administered Mass Organization* (New Haven: Yale University Press, 1995), 18–19.

13. Hannah Arendt, *The Origins of Totalitarianism* (1948; reprint, New York: Harcourt Brace, 1973), 152–53.

14. Hobsbawm, *Nations and Nationalism*, 102.

15. Tzvetan Todorov, *On Human Diversity: Nationalism, Racism, and Exoticism in French Thought*, trans. Catherine Porter (Cambridge: Harvard University Press, 1993), 254, 261.

16. Arendt, *Origins of Totalitarianism*, 222–23.

17. Ramon H. Myers, "Creating a Modern Enclave Economy: The Economic Integration of Japan, Manchuria, and North China, 1932–1945," in *The Japanese Wartime Empire, 1931–1945*, ed. Peter Duus, Ramon Myers, and Mark R. Peattie (Princeton: Princeton University Press, 1996), 136–70.

18. Giddens, *Nation-State and Violence*, 198–200.

19. Arendt, *Origins of Totalitarianism*, 230; Giorgio Agamben, *Homo Sacer: Sovereign Power and Bare Life*, trans. Daniel Heller-Roazen (Stanford: Stanford University Press, 1998), 126.

20. Philip Spencer and Howard Wollman, "Good and Bad Nationalisms: A Critique of Dualism," *Journal of Political Ideologies* 3 (1998), 263–65.

21. Michael Freeman, "The Right to National Self-Determination," in *The Right of Nations: Nations and Nationalism in a Changing World*, ed. M. Desmond Clarke and Charles Jones (New York: St. Martin's, 1999), 49–50; Hobsbawm, *Nations and Nationalism*, 121.

22. See M. Desmond Clarke and Charles Jones, eds., *The Right of Nations: Nations and Nationalism in a Changing World* (New York: St. Martin's, 1999), 1–5.

23. John Stuart Mill, *Considerations on Representative Government* (1861; reprint, Buffalo: Prometheus, 1991), 310.

24. See Todorov, *On Human Diversity*, 197.

25. Anthony Smith, "Theories of Nationalism: Alternative Models of Nation Formation," in *Asian Nationalism: China, Taiwan, Japan, India, Pakistan, Indonesia, The Philippines*, ed. Michael Leifer (London: Routledge, 2000), 16–17.

26. United Nations, "International Covenant on Economic, Social and Cultural Rights," and "The Covenant on Civil and Political Rights," at www.hrweb.org/legal/undocs.html#CPR (accessed June 19, 2002).

27. Clarke and Jones, *Right of Nations*, 14–15.

28. Of course, we can still make the argument that democratic institutions are the only guarantee against the absolutism of the nation's symbolic regime. The verdict on this question is still out and the debate will have to weigh the evident value of democratic institutions not only against the symbolic regime's power of closure, but also its perception of the nation's Other and the outside-of-the-nation more generally.

29. T. H. Marshall, *Class, Citizenship and Social Development* (Westport, Conn.: Greenwood, 1973).

30. Note how all of these guarantees of political and/or economic rights by nation-states necessitate tasks that require an unprecedented maximization of information, surveillance, and intrusion in the lives of the population; thinkers like Michel Foucault and Anthony Giddens have considered this the hallmark of the modern state and modernity itself.

31. Richard Hofstadter, *Social Darwinism in American Thought* (Boston: Beacon, 1955); Hobsbawm, *Nations and Nationalism*; and George W. Stocking, Jr., *Victorian Anthropology* (New York: Free Press, 1987).

32. Of course, the voluntarist paradigm hardly applies to many groups in the United States. It excludes not only African Americans and native peoples, but also the population that was incorporated in the westward expansion of the United States. That it does not accord with the view of many segments of the American population is perhaps clear from the new importance of the multiculturalist model of the nation in recent times.

33. For "internal colonialism," see Michael Hechter, *Internal Colonialism: The Celtic Fringe in British National Development, 1536–1966* (Berkeley: University of California Press, 1975).

34. See note 1 above.

35. Stephen D. Krasner, "Organized Hypocrisy in Nineteenth Century East Asia," *International Relations of the Asia-Pacific* 1 (2001): 177.

36. In our own times the re-territorialization of nation and state may be generating new fault lines, leaving behind these old contradictions.

37. For "geo-body," see Thongchai Winnichakul, *Siam Mapped: A History of the Geo-Body of a Nation* (Honolulu: Hawaii University Press, 1994).

38. Bartelson's work demonstrates that sovereignty meant and functioned very differently in the political discourse of different periods. The modern notion of sovereignty, an eighteenth-century development, was quite different from the earlier classical, absolutist, Renaissance, or late-medieval ideas of sovereignty. Indeed, before the classical period of the absolutist state, the discourse of sovereignty did not incorporate an autonomous idea of states in their sovereign particularity and individuality; nor was there a firm line of demarcation between the inside and outside of a state. See Jens Bartelson, *A Genealogy of Sovereignty* (Cambridge: Cambridge University Press, 1995), 134.

39. Harold J. Laski, *The Foundations of Sovereignty and Other Essays* (1921; reprint, Freeport, N.Y.: Books for Libraries, 1968), 27–28.

40. Giddens, *Nation-State and Violence*, 112, emphasis mine.

41. Giddens, *Nation-State and Violence*, 281.

42. Arnold J. Toynbee, "World Sovereignty and World Culture," *Pacific Affairs* 4 (September 1931): 753–78.

43. Giddens, *Nation-State and Violence*, 234–38.

44. Giddens, *Nation-State and Violence*, 258–59.

45. Frank A. Ninkovich, *The Wilsonian Century: U.S. Foreign Policy since 1900* (Chicago: University of Chicago Press, 1999), 75. Note that American scholars continued to be informally engaged in the League's efforts to codify international law; see Hatsue Shinohara, "Forgotten Crusade: The Quest for a New International Law" (Ph.D. diss., University of Chicago, 1996), 82.

46. Jeannie Marie Morefield, "'Families of Mankind': Liberal Idealism and the Construction of Twentieth-Century Internationalism" (Ph.D. diss., Cornell University, 1999).

47. Morefield, "'Families of Mankind,'" 198.

48. Hobsbawm, *Nations and Nationalism*, 133. Rana Mitter has pointed out to me that this is rather an unfair judgment, in part because Wilson often only advocated the autonomous development of "peoples," rather than a perfect match between state and nationality.

49. Ninkovich, *Wilsonian Century*, 67–68.

50. John Boli-Bennet and John W. Meyer, "The Ideology of Childhood and the State: Rules Distinguishing Children in National Constitutions, 1870–1970," *American Sociological Review* 43 (1978): 797–812.

51. Thomas A. Loya and John Boli, "Standardization in the World Polity: Technical Rationality over Power," in *Constructing World Culture: International Nongovernmental Organizations since 1875*, ed. John Boli and George M. Thomas (Stanford: Stanford University Press, 1999), 172–73. A great deal more work could be done in this area, such as to study the dissemination into nations of international conceptions of norms and deviance deriving from the procedures of international statistical or psychiatric associations.

52. Indeed, nationality and national citizenship are preconditions for a fuller participation in "world culture." Citizens of countries such as Taiwan, which have all the characteristics of a nation-state but without recognition in this system, find themselves greatly handicapped both in their economic projects and individual sense of self; see Wang Horng-luen, "In Want of a Nation: State, Institutions, and Globalization in Taiwan" (Ph.D. diss., University of Chicago, 1999).

53. Michel Foucault, "The Political Technology of Individuals," in *Technologies of the Self: A Seminar with Michel Foucault*, ed. Luther H. Martin, Huck Gutman, and Patrick H. Hutton (Amherst: University of Massachusetts Press, 1988), 160.

54. Michel Foucault, "Governmentality," in *The Foucault Effect: Studies in Governmentality*, ed. Graham Burchell, Colin Gordon, and Peter Miller (Chicago: University of Chicago Press, 1991), 100.

55. See Mark Neocleus, *Administering Civil Society: Towards a Theory of State Power* (New York: St. Martin's, 1996), 71.

56. For the East Asian model, see Bruce Cumings, "Colonial Formations and Deformations: Korea, Taiwan, and Vietnam," in *Parallax Visions: Making Sense of American–East Asian Relations at the End of the Century* (Durham, N.C.: Duke University Press, 1999), 69–94.

57. Giddens, *Nation-State and Violence*, 302.

58. Giddens, *Nation-State and Violence*, 303.

59. Chen Tianhua, quoted in Frank Dikötter, *The Discourse of Race in Modern China* (Stanford: Stanford University Press, 1992), 117.

60. See Duara, *Rescuing History from the Nation*, chaps. 5 and 6.

61. Eviatar Zerubavel, *Hidden Rhythms: Schedules and Calendars in Social Life* (Berkeley: University of California Press, 1981), 38–39, 111–13.

62. Moishe Postone has described the differences between capitalist and precapitalist conceptions of time as one between an independent variable and a dependent variable. As an independent variable, capitalist time is conceived as a preexisting (empty) and abstract (homogeneous) measure of events and processes (such as labor), whereas the "concrete" time of precapitalist societies is dependent upon and shaped by events. The former is linear, while the latter is characterized less by direction than by its dependent status. See Moishe Postone, *Time, Labor, and Social Domination: A Reinterpretation of Marx's Critical Theory* (Cambridge: Cambridge University Press, 1993), 200–201, and Zerubavel, *Hidden Rhythms*, 56–57.

63. Michael Puett, *The Ambivalence of Creation: Debates Concerning Innovation and Artifice in Early China* (Stanford: Stanford University Press, 2001).

64. Reinhart Koselleck, *Futures Past: On the Semantics of Historical Time*, trans. Keith Tribe (Cambridge: MIT Press, 1985), 276–81. The historical transition from the transcendent time of god to the secular, linear history of modern society is also the subject of J. G. A. Pocock's *The Machiavellian Moment: Florentine Thought and the Atlantic Republican Tradition* (Princeton: Princeton University Press, 1975). Pocock explores Christian and Renaissance conceptions of time: true meaning lay in divine or rational virtue that existed outside time. For Machiavelli, natural law was true, and history was irrational and corrupting. The "moment" consists of the deferral of the inevitable collapse of virtue in mundane time. It was ultimately the Puritan extension of timeless grace into the temporal world that had the effect of developing a secular history through the search for the kingdom of god on earth—the city on the hill. Pocock's insight into the Machiavellian moment has resonances for the conception of time in imperial China. The idea of the dynastic cycle embeds something very like the Machiavellian moment in the cycle of virtue and corruption, and the Tongzhi Restoration (1861) has been interpreted precisely as an effort to extend the regime of virtue in the face of impending collapse.

65. Prasenjit Duara, "Transnationalism and the Challenge to National Histories," in *Rethinking American History in a Global Age*, ed. Thomas Bender (Berkeley: University of California Press, 2002), 25–46. For the trope of "awakening" in nationalism, see John Fitz-

gerald, *Awakening China: Politics, Culture, and Class in the Nationalist Revolution* (Stanford: Stanford University Press, 1996).

66. Duara, *Rescuing History,* chap. 2.

67. Koselleck, *Futures Past,* 281. Pocock refers, in a rather panglossian moment, to the acceptance of the "incessant qualitative transformations of human life"; see *Machiavellian Moment,* 551.

68. Jacques Derrida, "Ousia and Gramme: Note on a Note from *Being and Time,*" in *Margins of Philosophy,* trans. Alan Bass (Chicago: University of Chicago Press, 1982), 40.

69. Paul Ricoeur, *Time and Narrative,* 3 vols. (Chicago: University of Chicago Press, 1984–88), 1:1–30, 3:138–41. Ricoeur has been identified as a hermeneutic poststructuralist in contrast to Derrida's deconstructive poststructuralism. In the former, a metaphor posits a connection rather than a congruence. Ricoeur seeks to stress the commonality in the reading experience and the "similarity that rises out of the ruins of semantic impertinence"; see *Reflection and Imagination: A Paul Ricoeur Reader,* ed. Mario J. Valdes (Toronto: University of Toronto Press, 1991), 25.

70. Ernest Renan, "What Is a Nation?" in *Nation and Narration,* ed. Homi Bhabha (New York: Routledge, 1990), 19.

71. Alessandro Ferrara, *Modernity and Authenticity: A Study of the Social and Ethical Thought of Jean-Jacques Rousseau* (Albany: State University of New York Press, 1993), 30, 148–50.

72. The symbolic regime of authenticity also permits us to revisit the tradition–modernity binary, which has had a peculiarly suspended existence in the literature following the devastating critiques of modernization theory in the 1970s and 1980s. Although few subscribe to the general theory of modernization, we still refer to certain continuing processes as "traditional" and new ones as "modern," often as a convenience. Yet if continuing processes are also being signified anew in the present, that distinction is not so simple to sustain. Tradition and modernity, as a binary structure, are categories generated by the aporia of linear time. Although any pastness that survives into the present is equally determined by the present, the need to posit and delimit a realm of pure continuity is first and foremost a constitutive element in the ideology of nationalism.

73. The subjective dimension of authenticity also makes this a more powerful idea than the notion of "legitimacy."

74. Carol Gluck, *Japan's Modern Myths: Ideology in the Late Meiji Period* (Princeton: Princeton University Press, 1985); Takashi Fujitani, "Inventing, Forgetting, Remembering: Toward a Historical Ethnography of the Nation-State," in *Cultural Nationalism in East Asia: Representation and Identity,* ed. Harumi Befu (Berkeley: University of California Press, 1993), 77–106; and Stefan Tanaka, *Japan's Orient: Rendering Pasts into History* (Berkeley: University of California Press, 1993), 57, 65–66. For the importance of Japanese "purity" during the Pacific War, see John W. Dower, *War without Mercy: Race and Power in the Pacific War* (New York: Pantheon, 1986), 203–33.

75. Marilyn Ivy, *Discourses of the Vanishing: Modernity, Phantasm, Japan* (Chicago: University of Chicago Press, 1995), and Alan S. Christy, "Representing the Rural: Place as Method in the Formation of Japanese Native Ethnology, 1910–1945" (Ph.D. diss., University of Chicago, 1997).

76. Yamamoto Shichihei, quoted in Harumi Befu, "Nationalism and *Nihonjinron,*" in *Cultural Nationalism in East Asia: Representation and Identity,* ed. Harumi Befu (Berkeley: University of California Press, 1993), 127.

77. Gluck, *Japan's Modern Myths*.

78. Ian Nish, "Nationalism in Japan," in *Asian Nationalism: China, Taiwan, Japan, India, Pakistan, Indonesia, The Philippines*, ed. Michael Leifer (London: Routledge, 2000), 182–89.

79. Louise Young, *Japan's Total Empire: Manchuria and the Culture of Wartime Imperialism* (Berkeley: University of California Press, 1998).

all secondary sources

CHAPTER TWO

~

Manchukuo: A Historical Overview

The region known in Chinese as northeastern China, or simply the Northeast, was, from at least the eighteenth century, referred to as Manchuria by Europeans and the Japanese. The rapid settlement of the region by Han Chinese from north China in the latter half of the nineteenth century began to integrate the region with China more closely, making it a distinct part of the Chinese nation. However, I continue to use the term Manchuria for this period so as not to foreclose what was still an open-ended historical situation by imposing the perspective of subsequent historical developments and nationalist historiography.[1]

Today Manchuria is "unalterably Chinese," in the words of the Lytton Commission, largely as a consequence of the demographic and cultural integration that took place in the first half of the twentieth century and not because of some primordial or age-old claim to it.[2] This period was thus one characterized by a contest over whether Manchuria would remain autonomous or be fully incorporated into the Chinese nation. Such an incorporative process was not only challenged by the Japanese, Russians, and other historical groups of the region, there were also considerable differences within Chinese groups as to how, and under what conditions, the integration might take place.

An Interpretive History of a Contested Borderland

The representation of Manchuria as a distinctive space is perhaps traceable most of all to the Manchu emperors themselves, who ruled China from 1644 until 1911. After the Manchu conquest of China, the emperors determined to turn their own homeland into a preserve of Manchu heritage unspoiled by Chinese or other foreign immigration. The Manchu policy of "seal and prohibit" (*fengjin*) sought to restrict Han Chinese to lands within the Willow Palisade. The palisade represented a symbolic division of the Manchurian territory into a northern Manchu preserve, a Mongol domain in the west, and the region of southern Fengtian (roughly today's Liaoning) long occupied by Han Chinese. The Manchu desire to restrict Han immigration beyond the palisade was not only connected to a sense of identity, but was also political and economic. Perhaps most significant of all was their keen awareness that an alliance between the Han and indigenous peoples, both Manchu and non-Manchu, could pose the same threat to the rulers of the Chinese empire from the strategic launching pad of Manchuria that they had themselves done. There were also lucrative trades in ginseng and sables that the Manchus sought to monopolize. A threefold strategy was designed to secure the cultural isolation of the region: the ban on Chinese migration, an alliance with the non-Manchu Tungus and Mongol peoples based on the tribute system, and the establishment of the system of banner garrisons throughout as the principal means of political control of the region. The hereditary bannermen, originally drawn from different ethnic groups, had been the principal instrument of the Manchu victory, and were transformed in Manchuria as elsewhere in the empire into a kind of a loyal military caste designed to keep alive the separate identity of the Manchus.[3]

Through the eighteenth century, as the policy of cultural isolation was being challenged both by the Sinicization of the banners and the increasing penetration of the region by Chinese, the emperors tended increasingly to romanticize and reify Manchu identity and the region in various ways. Sacrificial rituals to ancestors, which were part of Manchu shamanic tradition, were performed at Manchurian locations such as Mukden and especially Changbai mountain. The latter—which Korean nationalists also regarded as the ancestral birthplace of the Korean nation (see part III)—was declared the ancestral birthplace of the Manchus and sacrifices there were institutionalized early by the Kangxi emperor. Because all members of the tribe were considered to be descendants of a single ancestor, this practice was intended to memorialize the homeland for every Manchu.[4]

The Qing court also sought to ritualize shamanism, a historically fluid and multi-form practice in the region. Shamanism can be generally described as the belief in the effective determination of the living, visible world by invisible spirits that the shaman seeks to control. The court imposed a form of petrified, patriarchal shamanism upon Manchus and other Tungus groups to symbolize ethnic exclusivism and frontier manliness.[5] In the hands of the Qianlong emperor, shamanism came to represent the pure culture from the frontier, which would revive the center corrupted by Chinese society.

By examining historical maps of the region, Mark Elliott has recently shown that the toponym Manchuria was by no means absent in the Manchu and Chinese imagination. Although Chinese maps of the early twentieth century mostly refer to the region by the name of the three northeastern provinces, there are a good number of them that refer to *Manzhou* (Chinese for Manchuria) as well, including the largest publisher of the time, Commercial Press. Elliott suggests that it was the atlas of China commissioned by Kangxi and produced through the mapping techniques of the Jesuits around 1720 that did the most to generate the notion of Manchuria as a separate territorial entity. The atlas was designed to define the imperial territory (particularly in response to Russian advances), but it also had the effect of enhancing

Manchu identity. The first map in the atlas was that of greater Mukden, showing the full range of the Manchu ancestral territories. Visualizing the extent of their homeland apparently filled the Manchus with pride, and their special identification with it was indicated by writing all place names on the map north of the Great Wall in Manchu, in contrast to those south of the wall, which were written in Chinese.[6] In this way, we may see how the toponym Manchuria may be traced to the Manchu cultural construction of the region in the eighteenth century.

No matter how much the Manchu emperors sought to boost Manchu identity and preserve the region as the land of the Manchus and their allies, in practice, of course, the policy of cultural isolation was a failure, particularly after the flood of immigration beginning in the second half of the nineteenth century. Even before the Manchu invasion of China and the subsequent policy of isolation, political forces in Manchuria tended to become involved in China. Whereas Mongolia was a radically different, nonagricultural society, there was historically greater mutual interaction between China and Manchuria. Nor was Manchuria merely a frontier region of imperial China. Indeed, the region defies the usual spatial classifications of historical regions. According to Owen Lattimore, a significant part of the region—particularly the south, which had contact with imperial China—functioned as a "reservoir."[7] The physical characteristics and resources of the reservoir were such as to enable successive historical groups, or more strictly speaking, alliances, to gain and maintain control over China itself. Before the Manchus, the Tungus in the region had produced the Jurchen or Jin dynasty (1125–1234) and the Khitan (907–947) and Liao (947–1125) dynasties emerged from the Mongols.

The peculiar capacity of the region to generate the resources to dominate the Chinese empire derived from several factors. First, it was able to avoid control by a foreign group from within China proper. The region was too vast and varied for premodern imperial Chinese armies to supply and sustain an extended campaign. This diversity extended to different modes of livelihood—the Mongol nomads of the west, the hunters and gatherers of the mountains and forests, the agricultural communities of Chinese to the south, and rice-farming Koreans to the east. More so than was true of other frontier civilizations, Manchuria sustained a hybrid culture and permitted more contact with China. The successful, dominant groups in the region were able to access and absorb Chinese goods, techniques, and culture. They were thus able to strengthen themselves and, while eluding Chinese control, could at least partially use these resources to create alliances with different communities within Manchuria. In these ways, the region would provide the dominant groups with the necessary resources, whether they sought to control China or already did so. For this reason as well, the importance of the Chinese frontier for Manchuria far surpassed that of the Korean, Siberian, or Mongolian frontiers.

But if Manchuria was historically destined to be entangled with China, it retained its sense of independence right until the end of the nineteenth century. Lattimore has suggested that the regional importance of the reservoir transcended racial and cultural differences. A Chinese population moving into the reservoir became conscious of how it could exercise control over the China it left behind rather than push into the undeveloped lands and primeval forests. In the seventeenth century, the Chinese population in southern Manchuria that had settled there during the Ming joined the rising Manchu power and turned back to bring down the Ming.[8] The absorption of the Han into the banner system and the amalgamation of Manchus and Han in southern Manchuria contrasted markedly, as Lattimore reminds us, with the way Mongol and Han tended to remain separate because of the differences between the agricultural and nomadic modes of livelihood.[9]

All of these factors—the reservoir function, the sense of autonomy, the "turning back" to China—were to be dramatically affected by the migration flood of the late nineteenth century. The imperial court's decision to relax the ban on Chinese immigration, gradually extended to the entire region by 1902, was made in response to the Russian and, later, Japanese expansionist designs in the region. The land hunger of an overpopulated north Chinese countryside, the capacity of the railroad to transport immigrants to remote places (and also ensure military control of the region), and the lure of high-value crops like opium led to one of the largest population transfers and the most rapid colonization movements in the twentieth century. Between 1890 and 1942, an average of half a million migrants and sojourners flowed into the region every year, and over eight million people were added to the population from outside during this period.[10] This rivaled the heaviest flow of European immigration to the United States over a comparable period in the nineteenth century. Already by the end of the Qing, the demographic profile of the two newly created northern provinces, Jilin and Heilongjiang, which had historically had a far smaller Han population than the southernmost province of Liaoning, was completely transformed. In 1787 the total Jilin population was 150,000, and in 1850 about 327,000. By 1907 the Chinese population alone in Jilin was 3.8 million, and the banner population was about 400,000. In 1808 the Heilongjiang banner population was 136,000. In 1887 it was 252,000. By 1907 the total population was 1.5 million, of which only 81,000 were in areas where non-Chinese were in the majority.[11]

In many ways, the Chinese immigrants transformed the landscape in the image of their natal villages in north China. The wood and mud-walled banner garrisons surrounded by settlements of soldiers and farms of the early Manchurian frontier towns gave way to the architecture and material culture of northern China in villages, temples, schools, and residences where Chinese became the common spoken language.[12] But even as the Manchu clan villages and the landscape were becoming Sinicized, there were also significant spatial differences between these new settlements and those in north China. Yasutomi Ayumu has recently shown that Manchurian villages were unlike those south of the pass, where economic relationships were largely embedded in the periodic market communities that G. W. Skinner has called the standard marketing town.[13] Villages had little direct ties with the most important extremity of administrative power, the county seat, even during the Republic. However, such periodic market towns were largely absent in central and northern Manchuria and appeared only in the south, the area of traditional Chinese settlements

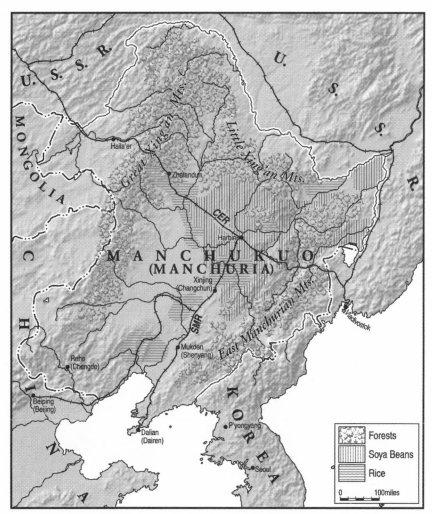

Principal Railroads and Agricultural and Natural Features of Manchukuo
CER = Chinese Eastern Railroad; SMR = South Manchurian Railroad

west of the Liao River. Even here, Yasutomi finds these markets to be more thinly distributed than in north China and declining in number during the Republic. Consequently, marketing activities in Manchurian villages came to be concentrated in the county seat, which corresponded to a midsized market town.[14] The coextensiveness of the economic and political realms enabled the county administrative power to exercise much greater control over the villages than elsewhere in China.

In Yasutomi's analysis, railroads were not the only factor behind this spatial pattern, since there is evidence that it preceded the building of certain lines. Soya, which was the overwhelmingly dominant agricultural product, could be transported on horse carts (plentifully available because of Mongolian ponies and lumber) on frozen rivers, roads, and fields from village to county seat and railroad station, obviating the need for periodic markets. The small retail needs of the villagers were met by itinerant traders traveling from village to village. Merchant associations, together with local landlords, were able to control the soya bean trade from the county seat. At the same time, they were susceptible to domination by—or compelled to share power with—the political power based there.[15] Thus, climate together with commerce and transportation technology contributed to this novel space of power.

The soya export boom was closely entwined with the distinctive political economy of the Manchurian locality. The emergence of the county as the basic marketing sphere and transportation hub encouraged peasants to specialize in soya production, resulting frequently in the increased dependence of peasants on county soya merchants for their capital and consumption needs. The financial base of the warlord Zhang Zuolin clique (see below), built upon foreign exchange acquired from its control of banks and soya trading houses, derived ultimately from the ability to control the merchants who in turn controlled the soya producers throughout the county. Yasutomi also attributes the rapidity with which the Guandong Army (*Kantōgun*) acquired control of the entire region after the Manchurian Incident—in contrast to the rural quagmire that sank this very army in north China—to the unprecedented concentration of state power at the local level.

Meanwhile, by the end of the nineteenth century, the agrarianization of the landscape increasingly transformed the older spaces of forested mountains inhabited by hunters, ginseng diggers, woodsmen, and miners, and of the grasslands to the west, dramatically affecting the livelihood of the Mongol, Manchu, and other Tungus communities. Manchu relations with the largely Tungusic tribespeople of the region had been one of patronage. Although large numbers of the Tungus, along with their tribal culture, were decimated or absorbed during the Manchu ascendancy over Manchuria between the fifteenth and sixteenth centuries, once they controlled the Chinese empire, the Tungusic groups, like the Mongols to the west and northwest, became firm allies of the Manchus in the latter's effort to keep the region as the pristine land of the Manchus. The tribal command of the region was part of a strategy of maintaining it as a buffer zone, not only against a potential Han–tribal alliance, but against the emerging power of Russia to the north. The Manchus sought to secure tribal fealty by honoring the elites and establishing a tribute system in which the tribes received a fair exchange for their valuables, such as sable furs and ginseng. To be sure, tribals were also exploited by local officials in the later part of the nineteenth century, but observers of the tribute system such as Mamiya Rinzo, the Japanese explorer who observed the tribute scene on the banks of the Amur in 1809, described it as official but warm.[16] Thus the Manchus succeeded in maintaining equilibrium in their relations with the tribal groups until the end of the nineteenth century, when the massive migration of Han Chinese into the area inevitably upset this arrangement.

The conversion of vast primeval forests into agricultural lands led to the shrinkage of hunting and fishing grounds. Added to this was the competition of Chinese hunters and fishers, and undermining of the tribals' traditional lifestyle.[17] V. K. Arseniev wrote in 1907,

> These aborigines having adopted Chinese culture could not absorb it, and succumbed to the influence of the Chinese themselves. As farmers and tillers of the soil they could not live, and they forgot the arts of the hunter and trapper. The Chinese have taken advantage of their spiritual poverty and made themselves indispensable to them. From that moment the natives lost all independence and became converted into slaves.[18]

With the establishment of the Frontier Agricultural Settlement Bureau in 1908, lands were increasingly appropriated from the tribals as well as the Mongol herdsmen. Conflicts between Mongol herdsmen and Chinese cultivators became especially acute after the Republic, when expropriation and agricultural colonization became a matter of national policy.[19]

Thus, toward the end of the Qing dynasty, the distinctive characteristics of Manchuria, guarded by the banner garrisons and the tributary system, gave way to the demand to integrate the region more closely with China proper. The turnabout in Qing policy toward the isolation of Manchuria and Manchu identity can be understood in terms of Benedict Anderson's notion of "Russifying nationalism," whereby the dynasts' effort to distinguish their lineage from those whom they ruled was reversed because of the pressure from nationalism below and from imperialism without. Indeed, Manchuria became the laboratory to experiment with administrative, judicial, and legislative reforms conducted by the Qing in the last decade of their rule. At the same time, these reforms spelled the end of the banner governance of the frontier and the ascendancy of Han administrators, politicians, and militarists over the region.[20] The reservoir function also fell away, as immigrants sought not to "turn back" to China proper but to push ahead and colonize the vast interior.

The irony of the Chinese demographic and administrative domination of the region by the early twentieth century was that it was taking place at the same time that, and to some extent because, outside claims on the region were being made by the imperialist powers of Russia and Japan, who financed and ran the first railroads. The victory of Japan over China in the Sino-Japanese War of 1895 and the Japanese demand to cede the Liaodong peninsula was reversed by the Russian-led intervention. In turn, Russia acquired the right from the Qing imperial government to build, and maintain military and territorial control over, the Chinese Eastern Railroad. The Boxer crisis of 1900 gave the Russians military control over the entire region. The Treaty of Portsmouth, which concluded the Russo-Japanese War of 1904–1905, while acknowledging in theory China's sovereignty in Manchuria, granted Japan the Russian lease on the Guandong peninsula and the South Manchurian Railroad.

From this time onward, Japan replaced Russia as the dominant foreign power in the region, with its interests and influence growing particularly after the annexation of Korea in 1910 and during the imperialist power vacuum in East Asia during World War I. Through Group II of the Twenty-one Demands that it imposed on China in 1915, Japan acquired privileged economic rights in southern Manchuria and eastern Inner Mongolia, secured by several railway, industrial, and loan contracts and agreements. The Republican government, however, succeeded in resisting the demand that Japanese be permitted to own (as opposed to lease) land in the region, a resistance that thwarted Japanese efforts to colonize the land with settlers and agricultural corporations.[21]

The economic and political affairs of these leased territories were managed by the Guandong government and the South Manchurian Railroad Company, a quasi-governmental corporation with many subsidiary enterprises beyond railroads and one of the largest research organizations in the world until 1945. The establishment of the railroads linking the southern port of Newchwang to regions as far north as Harbin, and the opening of several ports in the first decade of the twentieth century, including Dairen (Dalian), which would come to rival the Shanghai port facilities, led to rapid economic growth, particularly in agriculture. Agriculture was stimulated both by demand from the increasing population, which appears to have more than doubled between 1898 and 1908,[22] and by the continuous rise in export demand for soya.[23] The soya bean and its derivatives, which probably constituted as much as 80 percent of the export of Manchuria in the early years of the twentieth century, continued to be the most important export of the region until the late 1920s, with the region producing 59 percent of total world soya production.[24] Destined largely for Japan, it later found a market as European cattle feed. Lacking growth rate figures for the economy as a whole during this period, economists look at the high rate of export growth—11 percent per year from 1907 to 1929—as indicative of the dynamism of the economy.[25] Cities like Harbin and Dairen, enriched by agricultural growth, trade, and foreign investments, began to rival Shanghai and, according to Lattimore, were more modern than mainland cities like Nanjing and Beijing.[26]

As the Manchurian economy grew, both mainland Chinese and Japanese interests in the region developed correspondingly. Between 1903 and 1928, the Manchurian share of the foreign trade of China went from 3.5 percent to 32.5 percent, and the bulk of it was with Japan.[27] In 1931, Manchuria was still principally an agrarian economy, but one with a growing factory industry, chiefly devoted to production of consumer goods. It was an important source of agricultural goods for China, Japan, and Korea, and, of course, a most important outlet for the surplus population of rural north China. Perhaps almost as important were the financial remittances to the rural economy of north China.[28] As for the Japanese, they controlled the major coal and iron mines, the foreign trading and shipping companies, the electric supply, and the trunk railway lines, and also provided the financial backing for many Chinese railroads. By 1927, 85 percent of Japanese foreign investment was in China, and 80 percent of this was in Manchuria. The investment of the South Manchurian

Railroad Company in 1920 alone was 440 million yen. By 1932, Japan's share of the total industrial capital in Manchuria was 64 percent, while China's share was 28 percent.[29]

The incorporation of Manchuria into the Chinese nation during a period of high imperialism presented considerable problems. While its demographic Sinicization should have made the political claim of Chinese nationhood easy, it was precisely the historical image of Manchuria as a frontier, a virgin land of "primitive" and martial peoples unrelated to the Chinese, that was to undergird imperialist—especially, but not only, Japanese—claims to the area. Thus Manchuria became a contested borderland where China, Russia, and Japan were the main competitors, though at another historical moment the Koreans and the Mongols could have been included as well. The notion of a borderland has been introduced by American historians Jeremy Adelman and Stephen Aaron to distinguish this political condition from both the premodern imperial frontier and the boundaries of the modern territorial nation-state.[30] The borderland is a kind of a liminal and indeterminate historical space often characterized by warfare, but also by opportunities for local elites who are able to play off one outside power against another.

To be sure, Manchuria does not fit with this scheme in all respects, but it allows us to comprehend the rise of the illiterate soldier-bandit Zhang Zuolin—as well as almost every other warlord leader in Manchuria—to governor of Fengtian province (now Liaoning) and supreme warlord in all Manchuria. Zhang assisted the Qing government against the Russians in the aftermath of the Boxer uprising. But whereas other bandit leaders supported the Japanese in the Russo-Japanese War, he supported the Russians. Nonetheless, he was able to convince the Japanese of his usefulness to them. It is possible that he played a double game; but despite many frustrations on both sides, the Japanese backed him all the way until 1928, when they finally murdered him.[31]

There are two paradoxically contrary ways in which the Manchurian case does not fit the borderland model. First, the original model of Adelman and Aaron presupposed the borderlands to be inhabited by ethnically and culturally different indigenous peoples, whereas by our time Manchuria was overwhelming populated by Han Chinese. Second, despite this ethnic domination by Chinese, the political ambitions of elites like Zhang Zuolin were not restricted to carving out a temporary political space by eluding the domination of a single power; rather, their ambitions could attain imperial heights: Zhang was bent on bringing China itself under his sole command. In this way, the relevance of Lattimore's insight into Manchuria as a reservoir—a resource base for the domination of China—had not quite faded despite many fundamental reversals. At the same time, given these reversals, such ambition could only be sustained because the borderland situation allowed him to maximize his political resources.

In his splendid study of Zhang Zuolin, Gavan McCormack has outlined the fundamental political tensions in the region during the period of Zhang's ascendancy, 1911 to 1928.[32] Zhang and the Japanese needed each other to satisfy their ambitions. The Japanese were caught in a contradiction: they had economic and considerable political power in the region, but no sovereignty. They were interested in cultivating Zhang as a strongman who could protect their interests. Zhang, on the other hand, needed Japanese financial and military support not only against his warlord rivals within Manchuria, but even more, against the other warlords vying for control of Beijing itself. For the sake of this latter goal, which occupied a good deal of his energies till the end of his life, Zhang had already fought several exorbitant and unsuccessful wars bankrupting the Fengtian provincial treasury and causing much hardship on the people. Despite his continental goals, however, Zhang had developed a good relationship with many in the Fengtian provincial assembly and implemented several state-building and modernizing reforms. He had built up a significant core of civilian support in the Mukden clique which by the mid-1920s was moving him in the direction of increasing independence from Japan.

But Zhang's ambition to control Beijing took primacy over all and so weakened his support even among the loyal supporters in his administration, such as Wang Yongjiang. The administrators and assemblymen launched a campaign to contain his ambitions called the *baojing anmin* movement (to protect the borders and secure the people of the region), which has been interpreted widely, and especially by the Japanese, as a movement of regional autonomy. Indeed, Zhang himself had set the precedent in 1922 when he declared the independence of the three Eastern provinces, Rehe, Chahar, and Inner and Outer Mongolia. Zhang was responding to President Xu Shichang's dismissal of him as governor of Fengtian because of his role in the1922 Zhili Fengtian war. He even entered into independent treaties with nations like the Soviet Union.[33]

For somewhat different reasons, a similar declaration of regional autonomy was made by the Association of the Three Provincial Assemblies, the chambers of commerce, education associations, and many other groups.[34] This popular upsurge was part of south China's spreading federalist movement, which sought the autonomy of the region to implement democratic reform at a time when the center was chaotic and oppressive. The *baojing anmin* movement of the later 1920s appears to have been triggered by a similar impetus, although, dominated as it was by conservative administrators and assemblymen, it was rather cautious about mass nationalism and democratic change.

While their interests were different, the disillusionment of the assemblymen and administrators with Zhang coincided with the frustration of the Japanese, who began to fear that Zhang's increasing military involvement south of the Great Wall would devastate the economy, and even more, that his defeat would bring in a government hostile to the Japanese.[35] When both sides decided to abandon him, Zhang's end was clear. But nothing was solved for the Japanese. While some members of the Mukden clique were anti-Japanese and succeeded in moving Zhang towards their position, Zhang was no modern nationalist. As McCormack has said, he was a traditional dynast waiting in the wings for the dragon throne.[36] However, the times had changed and Zhang had been caught up in a growing nationalist movement he did not fully comprehend. His son, Zhang Xueliang, who succeeded him in power, while subject to charges of corruption and drug use, was distinctly more nationalistic. Besides, he was surrounded by a dynamic group of intellectuals and bureaucrats who would go on to form the nucleus of the Northeast National Salvation Society (*dongbei jiuguohui*); they were fervently devoted to the nationalist cause.[37]

At the end of 1928, Zhang Xueliang hoisted the national flag and declared his allegiance to the KMT government of a unified China. But it was not only the political allegiance that caused the Japanese to strike down the regime. Two other major issues, equally representative of the growing Chinese nationalist feelings, caused the Japanese military to believe that it would need to become the dominant political power in Manchuria. One was the younger Zhang's continued building of railway lines competitive with the South Manchurian Railroad Company (SMR); the other was the denial of landownership to Japanese nationals. Many Chinese were discouraged and disallowed from leasing land to the Japanese, who used Koreans with Chinese citizenship in Manchuria for this purpose. Koreans working on large-scale Japanese farms (leased originally from the Koreans) competed with Chinese farmers—a displaced expression of the Sino-Japanese competition that sometimes erupted in violence. One such flare-up helped to instigate a reaction against Chinese in Korea and provided the provocation for the Japanese to strike down the Zhang Xueliang regime.[38] On September 18, 1931, the Guandong Army set a bomb on an SMR line near Mukden and used the explosion as an excuse to occupy all of Manchuria by the end of 1932. In March of 1932 it proclaimed the independent Republic of Manchukuo.

The League of Nations and Sovereignty Claims

Manchukuo had a global significance as the first important test put to the new international institution for settling disputes peaceably and nonimperialistically within the nation-state system, the League of Nations. Certainly, the verdict delivered by the League condemning Japanese expansionism lived up to the new rhetoric of the age of anti-imperialism. But the details and practical actions taken revealed the severe limits of the new system. The failure to back its verdict with suitable action suggests a number of questions: Was the system truly representative of the interests of nationalism, or was it a disguised tool of imperialist nations? Did it point to the limits of nationalism itself, shaped by the expansionary impulse of the modern territorial state? Manchukuo presents us with a similar set of problems.

The verdict of the League, delivered in the fall of 1932, was based on the voluminous report of the Lytton Commission, which was submitted to the League in September 1932 after six months of intensive investigation. However, from the start, the League was impotent to impose sanctions or take action against Japan because of the contrary opinions of Great Britain and the nonparticipation of the United States in the League. It could do little more than declare nonrecognition of the new state and call for the evacuation of Japanese troops in Manchuria from outside the railway zone. It also recommended beginning negotiations for the reorganization of Manchuria under Chinese sovereignty, but with considerable autonomy.

The Lytton Commission report deemed the crisis to have arisen from a situation where both parties claimed to have rights and interests that were not clearly defined by international law. Moreover, although the Commission recognized the disputed territory to be legally an integral part of China, this territory had a local administration of sufficiently autonomous character to carry on direct negotiations with Japan on the matters that lay at the root of the conflict.[39] Thus, on the one hand, the Lytton report was unambiguous in its view that Manchuria had been formally a part of China at least since the Manchu conquest of 1644, and was influenced by Chinese culture long before that. It was also unambiguous in condemning Japan's actions in the Manchurian Incident as unlawful, a violation of China's sovereignty and international law. As we shall see, Japan sought relentlessly to demonstrate that China was not an organized state and therefore not a nation. It seized upon the "Law of Nations" invoked by the Lytton report—"a State must possess and continue to possess one supreme Government"[40]—arguing that China lacked precisely this condition. The Lytton Commission, however, was satisfied that China, as "a nation in evolution," was in the process of gradual but distinct modernization.[41] The report did express concerns about antiforeignism in China, which tended "to kindle patriotism with the flame of hatred, and to build up manliness on the sense of injury," but attributed this more to the communists than to the established government.[42]

On the other hand, as the dispute was complex and characterized by a lack of clarity regarding rights on both sides, the report did not come out completely on the side of Chinese nationalism. Indeed, it often tended to take a middle position between the Chinese and Japanese. For this reason, although KMT officials endorsed the Lytton report, the communists denounced it.[43] The first principle the Commission report proposed was that the League's decision should be compatible with both Chinese and Japanese interests. The fourth principle stated that the "rights and interests of Japan are facts that cannot be ignored,"[44] and the report even went on to argue that seeing Manchuria as part of China would better promote Japan's interests as well. It recommended that the government of Manchuria should be modified so as to secure, in a way consistent with the sovereignty and administrative integrity of China, a large measure of autonomy designed to meet the local conditions and special characteristics of the three provinces.[45]

The verdict of the assembly of the League of Nations based upon the Lytton Commission report also reflected its framework of understanding. While the League clearly acknowledged Chinese sovereignty, it also sought to recognize the historical autonomy of Manchuria and acknowledge the treaty rights of other powers such as the Japanese and the Russians in the region. In other words, while the League acknowledged that sovereignty was based upon historical claims of belonging and culture, it also was wary of denying the rights of states—states that had imperialistically acquired rights in an earlier period. Other realpolitik concerns also weighed heavily in the verdict, as in the report: the need to strengthen the KMT against the communists in China and the fear that Japanese rule in Manchuria would affect the Open Door policy and principles of free trade, and thus harm foreign interests (in addition to the people of Manchuria).[46] As the Chinese communists never tired of pointing out, the great powers that dominated the League of Nations were hardly free and neutral agents themselves. In a way, the practical if not always rhetorical ambivalence of the League, given the preponderant role within it of imperialist powers, matched the practical role of Japanese expansionism in contrast to its rhetoric. However, the rhetoric did not merely seek to hide an old and ugly reality. In both cases, the rhetoric and some of the innovations reflected the power of new forces that would have significant effects.

In their response, the Japanese side rejected the fundamental assumptions of the Lytton Commission report and finally withdrew from the League of Nations in 1933. Where the report of the League emphasized Manchurian autonomy but not independence from China, the Japanese emphasized the de facto independence of Manchuria. The Japanese representative to the League, Matsuoka Yosuke, rejected the Commission's claim that Manchuria had historically been an integral part of China. He asserted that the union of Manchuria with China had only been "temporary and accidental." Matsuoka cited the authority of M. Escarra, an advisor to the Nanjing government, who had argued that Manchuria was never a vassal of China, since, on the contrary, it was the Manchu family that conquered the Chinese empire.[47] The empire had been the product of a personal union and could not be considered a question of China's rights over Manchuria. M. Escarra was of the view that imperial and national claims to sovereignty were simply incommensurable. He urged that since the Manchu family had disappeared, another juridical formula had to be developed to explain the reconnection of China and Manchuria.

Not only did Matsuoka deny the claim that Manchuria was an integral part of China in the deep historical perspective, he rejected the claim that the recent history of the settlement of Manchuria by Han Chinese made Manchuria a part of the Chinese nation—a denial that few non-Japanese would find acceptable. He invoked the idea of common political consciousness as the basis of nationhood. Manchuria's numerical domination by Chinese did not mean that it was part of the nation, because "the Chinese have *not* a keen sense of nationality."[48] However, Matsuoka had to walk a thin line here. He had to show that while the Chinese inhabitants of Manchuria may not have had a Chinese national consciousness, they had a sense of Manchurian identity. He pointed to the presence of the *baojing anmin* movement, "a movement based on Manchurian independence,"[49] not only during the rule of Zhang Zuolin but also under Zhang Xueliang, who had declared allegiance to the KMT. He suggested that these aspirations came together spontaneously after the Manchurian Incident.

> When the authorities who, under General Chang Hsueh-liang, were responsible for the maintenance of order in Manchuria disappeared, as they mainly did after the

events of September 18th, some organization was evidently necessary in order to carry on the normal machinery of daily life; local vigilance committees were formed by the local leaders, and the Japanese Army welcomed their co-operation and assisted them. . . . [T]that these nuclei of government eventually coalesced and developed into a genuine State is no matter for astonishment. . . .[50]

While we need not accept Matsuoka's interpretation of these committees (whom we will encounter again), they were quite critical to the reestablishment of order in the region.

At the same time, Matsuoka asserted that China had neither a strong state nor an acceptable nationalism.

[S]ince the Revolution of 1911, [China has] fallen into a condition of confusion bordering upon anarchy, and remains in the same condition at the present moment. . . . [U]nder present circumstances, it is entirely impossible to tell when China may come to have a strong and permanent central government, even if we grant the ultimate possibility of that event.[51]

Thus, not only was it incapable of governing Manchuria (or restraining the warlords there), it could not ensure the security of foreigners' life and property, guaranteed by treaty rights. Matsuoka seized on a statement in the Lytton report that held antiforeignism in China—particularly the economic boycott and antiforeign education—to have also contributed to the present conflict. While the report found this antiforeignism to be an expression of a negative rather than a positive nationalism, Matsuoka sought to draw the lesson that China was anarchic and possessed of neither nation nor state.[52]

The position of the government of the Republic of China as publicized to the outside world was perhaps best summarized by Chih Meng, associate director of the China Institute in America, in its 1932 publication *China Speaks*. Meng's view was supported in most respects by the most authoritative account of the conflict at the time, that of W. W. Willoughby. Willoughby, an American professor who had served as a legal advisor to the Chinese government between 1916 and 1919, and W. W. Yen, China's chief delegate to the League of Nations, both endorsed Meng's account in their respective prefatory comments to the book, in which Chih Meng claimed that "Manchuria is part of China because of priority in political affiliation and by explicit international recognition."[53] By the former he meant that since China and Manchuria were ruled jointly by the Manchus, Manchuria had been part of China for nearly three hundred years. Although, according to Meng, there was a period of time in the Qing when the government attempted to stop Chinese migration into Manchuria "to reserve the land for the Manchus," that law was never effectively nor strictly enforced. He added the argument that China needed Manchuria more than did Japan. It is noteworthy that Meng's argument for establishing Chinese sovereignty included a mix of recent historical developments and practical factors. It was by no means the deep historical view that later emerged.

More important than the historical claim was Meng's effort to establish China's sovereignty over Manchuria by means of its recognition in legal statements, international law, and international precedents. Meng cites the constitution of China and, more importantly, Article 10 of the Covenant of the League of Nations and Article 1 of the Nine Power Treaty of 1922, which recognized China's sovereignty over the region.[54] Even the recent historical process of Han Chinese colonization that he had cited gains its significance by international comparison: "The Manchus in Manchuria today are somewhat in the position of Indians in the United States, except that the Manchus have been entirely assimilated into Chinese culture."[55] The appeal to international precedent in order to establish sovereignty claims appears again in the bid to demonstrate that China was a genuine nation-state. Meng says that although China is an ancient and the world's most continuous civilization, it had also begun recently to awaken to a modern nationalism:

> The seemingly unchanging China has been changing, and rapidly, during recent years. China has awakened. She instinctively thinks first of self-preservation. She discovers Nationalism, the secret power of the modern nation, and the modern definition of sovereign rights. . . . Call it anti-foreignism, if you wish; it is anti-foreign injustices [sic]. In this sense, the Thirteen Colonies of America were also "anti-foreign."[56]

Thus Meng acknowledges, through his complex argument integrating antiforeignism with nationalism by way of international precedent, the systemic principle that only nation-states have the right to reject foreign occupation.

Manchukuo as event allows us to observe how history becomes central to the claims of nationhood. One is hard pressed to find Chinese historical scholarship laying deep historical claims on Manchuria, whether based on racial, cultural, or political ties, at the time of the Manchurian Incident. As Feng Jiasheng, who was to subsequently publish his historical researches on the Northeast, pointed out in an early issue of *Yugong* in 1934, the history and geography of the Northeast had been utterly neglected by the Chinese and was far behind the scholarship of the Russians and the Japanese.[57] The very few extant works on Manchuria in Chinese published before 1931 seem to have been written precisely to alert Chinese to the impending Japanese threat. They bemoan the ignorance and indifference towards the region among the Chinese, who had tended to regard it as an insignificant wasteland. They too do not delve into long-term historical questions. Even a historian like Fu Sinian, who was close to the political establishment, writing on the first anniversary of the Manchurian Incident in 1932, emphasized how it was the recent colonization of Manchuria in the last century by thirty million immigrants from the provinces of Shandong and Hebei that had changed it into Chinese territory.[58]

Moreover, historians at the time were also conscious of the problems of making deep historical claims. Among the century's finest and most provocative historians, Gu Jiegang, wrote a brilliant essay in which we may see how the spatial representation of China as the eternal geo-body had been historically constructed during momentous political transformations such as the Qin–Han unification of 221 B.C. In his 1926 essay on the image of the world during the Warring States (fifth–third century B.C.) and its transformation after the Qin unification, Gu showed that spatial conceptions of the world as the "four seas" or the "nine *zhou*" from earlier eras such as the Xia and the Zhou were mistakenly regarded as literal and unchanging representations. Thus people from times following the Qin believed the territorial extent of China to have been continuous with these earlier representations. Gu showed that in fact these abstract spatial representations not only hid changing territorial realities, but were hypothetical. They represented a scheme for unification that only took place under the Qin. Gu was interested in exploring the functions of this "laughable ignorance" of history.[59]

A few years after the Manchurian Incident, historical writing on Manchuria developed a momentum and tended to make deep claims. Although there developed more complex strategies by professional historians to claim the region historically as a part of China, the more crudely nationalist writing relied on flimsy evidence. Thus Wu Shangquan wrote, twenty years after Gu's piece, that the Northeast was a distinct part of the nine *zhou*. He even sought to naturalize the relationship between the Northeast and China proper by showing how the mountain chains are linked to the mainland, and how the northeastern rivers belong to the same system as those in the mainland.[60] Such deep historical claims continue to this day. For instance, considerable historical energy has been spent on demonstrating that 1998 was not the hundredth anniversary of the founding of Harbin (by the Russians, who built the China Eastern Railroad). Instead, unconnected historical traces have been utilized to construct a historical claim to the region for many hundreds of years before 1898. Soren Clausen and Stig Thogersen have grasped the means whereby this history was created: "Since Manchu and Mongols and others are today incorporated in 'Chinese people' (*Zhonghua minzu*), the area can be said to have been inhabited by Chinese for a very long time."[61]

Doubtless, the appropriation of Manchuria into the Chinese geo-body within Chinese historical writing has to be understood in the context of the inefficacy of the League and the Japanese denial of Chinese sovereignty, whether in the long or short history. Matsuoka's claim discussed above was consistent with Japanese historical scholarship before 1931, which held that it was not until the second half of the nineteenth century that efforts were made to integrate Manchuria with China. As Nishimura Shigeo has pointed out, scholarship after the Russo-Japanese War and the annexation of Korea was conducted increasingly under the dominant ideology that Japan had special rights in Manchuria and Mongolia because these regions represented Japan's lifeline.[62]

Thus, long before 1931, Japanese historians tended to celebrate the autonomy of the region. Consider the detailed introduction to Inaba Kunzan's 1918 history of the region written by the great Sinologist Naitō Kōnan. In Naitō's view, both the Chinese and Japanese developed their political interests in Manchuria during the Koguryo rule of the region, which lasted for seven hundred years, from the late Han until the Tang. During the succeeding three hundred years of rule by the Bohai, the ancestors of the present Manchus, the state's political and economic ties with Japan were actually closer than those with China. Indeed, if it had not been for the Khitan, who occupied the region between them and the Chinese proper in western Liaoning, the Bohai could have established their power over China. Later it was the Jin or Jurchen, also ancestors of the Manchus, who defeated the Song dynasty in China. While the Jurchen suffered a setback during the Yuan-Ming period, their Manchu descendants went on to found the Qing empire in China. It was not until the middle of the nineteenth century that the Qing began to encourage Han settlement in Manchuria. Naitō evokes the image of a region with an autonomous history disrupted only recently by accidental developments. For three thousand years, he writes, the land has had its own natural history, its own monuments, routes, and relics. Only in the last two to three hundred years has this pattern changed with the intrusion of agriculture and other developments. It is also in recent centuries that we have become aware of this ancient history and its importance for understanding the present. At the same time, Naitō urges against a historical determinism. The future, he says, can always unfold a different history.[63]

The main text by Inaba Kunzan fills out this natural history with thick descriptions of primeval peoples hunting in the green woods, fishing, pearl diving, digging for ginseng, and trapping for fur. Of course they had periodic contact with Chinese culture, but they always returned to their primeval forests and mountains. The policy of the Qing to ban agricultural settlement by outsiders reinforced the nonagricultural character of the region. The Han had always dreamed of this virgin land as a vast agricultural garden, and Inaba fears that they had made it so in recent years, and not only in Manchuria proper but in Mongolia and Siberia as well. He warns his compatriots to fear the Chinese. Poor and weak as they seem, they have strong national ties and will make a formidable foe!

The historical narrative sketched by Naitō and Inaba seemed to structure many of the official publications that poured out of Manchukuo. The introduction to the official 1940 text known as *Kōmin* (citizen or civic person), produced by the Police Department for the instruction of police officers, constructs its own deep history of Manchuria, celebrating in particular the Koguryo period of rule over much of this land and Korea over 1,600 years ago. It follows through with the Bohai and their close links to Nara and Heian courts, and then settles down to the Khitan/Liao and Jin ancestry of the Manchu clans. Subsequently, the Russians are blamed for encroaching into the region and releasing the modern period of ethnic struggles. The historical segment closes with a discussion of how notions of ethnic harmony and the "kingly way" have finally brought peace to the region. Note, however, that the Chinese are not even mentioned.[64]

In a way, Japanese historical scholarship was not too distant from the view of Western historians like Lattimore with regard to the history of Manchuria as frontier. Yet the contemporary population of Manchuria overwhelmingly by Chinese did not lead the majority of these Japanese scholars to acknowledge Chinese sovereignty either, although, as the League report pointed out, neither did they deny this sover-eignty before September 1931. After the Manchurian Incident, Matsuoka and oth-ers sought to hammer home the point that the autonomy of Manchuria had also meant that the region had no sense of Chinese nationhood. The historical narrative of an autonomous Manchuria suddenly became the history of an independent Man-chukuo.

Note also the transformation of Chinese sovereignty claims. Chih Meng and oth-ers did not initially make deep historical claims, emphasizing instead the practical needs of an existing population. This was in accord with the Lytton report: "China, at first, showed little activity in the field of development in Manchuria. She almost allowed Manchuria to pass from her control to that of Russia. . . . Meanwhile the immigration of millions of Chinese farmers settled the future possession of the soil, and Manchuria is now unalterably Chinese."[65] Yet the basis of the claim to sover-eignty transmuted into a deep historical one. Given the Japanese use of history, there were presumably few alternatives. However unsuitable or inapplicable it may have been in sorting out territorial claims, history, in the sense of a long and continuous presence, had become implicated in the claim to national sovereignty. In the same essay cited above, Gu Jiegang captures the painful moral dilemma presented to the historian—who is both professional and national—by the use of historical mala-propisms.

It is laughable that people identify the territory of the Warring States period with that of the earlier Xia, Shang, and Zhou periods without historical knowledge. But we really should not laugh at them. We need to know if the capacity of China for unity has to depend on such a preposterous historical view. We can only eliminate racial prejudices and create the territory of China as an organized federation if we have such a notion of "past unity." In the past, when Chinese saw the tattoos on the people of Wu and Yue and heard the butcherbird-like sounds of the Chu people, they thought of them as disgraced convict-soldiers of the Zhou. Once, however, they developed the concept of the "nine *zhou*," everyone felt that we and they were of the same family. No matter that they lived at some distance from each other, we all developed a famil-iarity. Since then, the various Chinese states (*zhuxia*) and the barbarians began to feel a sense of natural intimacy. Moreover, when the ancestors of each state were strung together in a single lineage, it caused the people to feel as if they were all the descen-dants of the Yellow Emperor, and this generated a still greater intimacy among them.

Nowadays we hear of the "Republic of Five Races," but we cannot generate any feelings of friendship of the Han people towards the Manchus, the Mongols, the Mus-lims, and the Tibetans. This is because the Han have known them to have been "bar-barian states" (*fanbang*); they harbor arrogance towards them in their minds and cannot feel an intimacy. If the Han today were ignorant in the same way as the ancients and followed those who constructed a false history, believing that the territor-ies of the Manchus and the Mongols were in the realm of the Yellow Emperor, Yao, and Shun, and that the people of those regions were descendants of these sage kings, then they would see the Manchus and the Mongols as the same as one from the eighteen central provinces, and the five races could *truly* become a republic (*wuzu jiu zhen keyi gonghele*).[66]

This is an extraordinarily revealing passage that suggests that the fabrication of a deep history is necessary for the production of true national loyalty. Once the Japanese invasion had occurred, Gu's work became increasingly torn between relatively objective historical research and propagandistic historical writing.[67] As we shall see later, Gu and other concerned historians would try to conceive of the relationship between national unity and historiography at a different epistemological level—one that would perhaps transcend what Benedict Anderson has characterized as the "necessary forgetting," or, as Gu himself put it, a "laughable ignorance." For the moment, however, we may wonder if a legitimate nationalism called up to defend people who have been attacked may not have transmuted into an essentialist doctrine demanding unconditional loyalty—one that, in being purposefully forgetful of other histories, is also homogenizing, exclusive, hierarchical, and unable to distinguish between defense and aggression.

Manchukuo

Historical cases like Manchukuo present the historian with a facile clarity. A great deal is written about them, but what is written tends not to stray from the accepted narrative shaped by the judgment of the case, here Manchukuo, as an unspeakable abomi-*nation*. When writing of the experiences of people, whether ordinary or elite, the expectation is that they cannot but be reduced to symbols of victimization, collaboration, or resistance. My objection to this position is not that we should not denounce a brutal regime, but that this narrative itself is shaped by a nationalist politics that channels history into very narrow passages. This is true not only of contemporary Chinese writings, but also of much Western and postwar Japanese historiography.

Manchukuo was established in March 1932 as the Republic of Manchukuo and was subsequently renamed an empire. Despite the claims to independence, there is no question that the real power behind it was the Japanese Army—hence the Western historiographical designation of it as a "puppet state." Chinese scholarship refers to it as the "false Manchukuo" (*wei Manzhouguo*), its falsity referring to its illegitimacy. While both designations capture important aspect of the polity, these characterizations tend to shape the kind of scholarship that is produced and obscure a wide range of historical issues. Until recently, much scholarship tended to concentrate on the negative effects of state policies on people's lives. The wider effects of Manchukuo's massive industrialization, urbanization, and modernization—perhaps more massive than elsewhere in Asia during the period—have barely been probed.[68] Socially, the vast range of activities and complex responses to political power that do not conform to victimization, collaboration, or resistance are deemed to have little consequence. Finally, the puppet designation suggests a scarcely veiled colonialism and cannot capture the novel institutional arrangements that produced results very different from the old colonial states.

I have found it useful to think of a fourfold distinction in discussing the polity of Manchukuo: its power structure, regime form, state form, and sovereignty claims. The puppet state designation clarifies the *power structure* of the polity, which was a form of disguised imperialism. Real power resided with those whose principal loyalty was often to Japan or to Japanese groups. However, while the power structure did influence policy and institutions, it was not as central or overwhelming as we have believed. Many of the institutions, policies, and experiences were shaped by the other three factors.

I will define *state form* here as the rationale, goals, and "rationalities" that enable the legal exercise of power in society. The state form is capable of encompassing several different regimes and I believe Manchukuo belongs to the modern state form that we have identified as "governmentality." To be sure, governmentality cannot be applied mechanically to Manchukuo or East Asia generally. We will consider later how Foucault's slighting of the distinction between state and civil society does not aid our understanding of governmentality in this region. Moreover, specific expressions of governmentality articulate with historical representations from the East Asian modern, regarding, for instance, gender and morality (*jiaohua*), which equally shape lived experience. But as a modern state form, Manchukuo is to be distinguished not only from premodern states, but also from most nineteenth-century colonial states. These states usually sought to reproduce the difference between rulers and ruled, and were not preoccupied with the rationalities of the modern state except insofar as they needed to implement them to extract resources or maintain the colonial order.

The *regime form* specifies the decision-making institutions and methods of implementing policies. We may characterize the regime form of Manchukuo as "military fascist" to emphasize the central role of the Guandong Army in place of the supreme leader.[69] To be sure, fascism here is to be construed loosely, and there are aspects of the central European model that do not apply, most conspicuously and ironically Manchukuo's commitment to a multicultural polity in opposition to fascism's homogenizing imperative. But similarities include the nondemocratic and narrow circle of decision-makers, policies of state-led industrialization and modernization, implementation through a state-sponsored mass organization (the Concordia Association, *Xiehehui*, *Kyōwakai*), and a corporatist system in which each group has its place and function within the state. Finally, the Manchukuo state severely restricted individual rights and often exhibited a dictatorial and brutal conduct. Interestingly, both the Japanese and the Chinese KMT state also shared important features of this fascist model and thus bear a closer resemblance to the Manchukuo regime than might appear at first sight.

Finally, in its *sovereignty claims,* Manchukuo devised, deployed, and sometimes pioneered the rhetoric of the emerging anti-imperialist nationalism. It made the rather outrageous claim that it was not merely a nation, but one that embodied utopian ideals. While it soon became clear that these ideals were often appropriated for militaristic purposes, they nonetheless shaped several policies and the lives of many people. One of these was the multiculturalism embodied in the Concordia Association; another was the redemptive universalism of the many religious and "Eastern" civilizational organizations that flourished in Manchukuo; and a third was the effort to realize a modern utopia blending the best of East and West—which could only be attained in this last frontier of the East. Although the bulk of this book is devoted to exploring the historical process whereby cultural formations and practices were transformed into sovereignty claims, this process cannot be grasped apart from each of the other dimensions. Most of all, any understanding of Manchukuo will have to grapple with the contradiction between a disguised imperialist power structure and the three other dimensions, without reducing the latter to the former.

Visions: Utopian and Colonial

Why was Manchukuo established as an independent, civilian nation-state, however formal, rather than as a colonial and military state? To be sure, key elements of the Guandong Army that drove out the Zhang Xueliang government were not necessarily committed to its independence from the start. Senior officer Ishiwara Kanji, perhaps the single most forceful figure behind the creation of Manchukuo, initially saw the Japanese possession of Manchuria as necessary for the survival of Japan and its continued control over Korea. The "strategic autarky" or "Japan's lifeline" argument, which had gained currency in the army from the end of World War I, always figured Manchuria at the center of a sphere of self-sufficiency that would be critical to the outcome of any battle in the future. According to Tak Matsusaka, Japanese military analysts came to this conclusion after observing the close relationship between state and resource mobilization during World War I. Manchuria and China would be necessary for the sphere of Japanese self-sufficiency, whether through voluntary cooperation or, if necessary, occupation and coercion. In other words, an imperialist intent distinctly pervaded the enterprise.[70]

The general view regarding the proclamation of independence is that it was a fig leaf designed to mollify the League of Nations and fend off Chinese nationalist charges. But it is noteworthy that Manchukuo remained a formally independent nation even after the withdrawal of Japan from the League and at a time when Japan and other powers continued to possess colonies. Two other factors merit consideration. First, in order to effectively attain its goals, the Japanese military had to develop an alliance with key groups in Manchukuo, both Chinese and Japanese. In order to do so meaningfully, it was compelled to champion the rhetoric of these allies, which included the framework of a sovereign state. Ishiwara and his associates in the Guandong Army, Itagaki Seishiro and Doihara Kenji, recognized that they could ignore the new discourse of rights and autonomy only at their own peril.[71]

Second, ideas of strategic autarky and an "economic bloc" came to be interpenetrated by pan-Asianist discourse. While figures like Ishiwara were motivated by Japanese nationalism, this nationalism was itself framed by a vision of the inevitable confrontation between East and West. The cooperation of China and Manchuria under Japanese leadership was necessary for success in this holy war or righteous duty (*zhengyi, seigi*).[72] Ishiwara became a convert to the pan-Asianist idea of the formal equality of Asian nations; there was no contradiction between viewing the alliance as representing the supposed difference between Asian ideals and Western imperialism and treating it as a tool in the final war for global dominance.[73]

Thus, while the idea of an autarkic Japan–Manchuria bloc was influenced by models of autarky in Europe, it was grasped within the civilizational discourse of pan-Asianism. The bloc idea grew by the mid-1930s into the East Asian League *(Tōa renmei)* and the East Asian Community (*Tōa kyōdōtai*), and still later into the idea of the Greater East Asian Co-prosperity Sphere (*Dai-Tōa Kyōeiken*). Indeed, figures associated with the propagation of these ideas, such as Ozaki Hotsumi, Kada Tetsuji, and Shinmei Masamichi (whose lecture tours in Manchukuo were sponsored by the SMR), were critical of Nazi ideas of racial superiority and emphasized cooperation with the Chinese in a regional alliance under Japanese leadership.[74] Commitment to the idea of an alliance—and even that Japanese should renounce extraterritoriality in Asian countries—hardly meant that the Japanese were not thought to be intrinsically superior or that Asian nations need not accept the leadership of Japan. Yet it is impossible to fully understand why the military encouraged the rapid modernization and industrial buildup in Manchuria without grasping its framing within pan-Asianism.[75]

The discourse of Manchuria as an autonomous place fostering a new type of polity had been advocated by a variety of Japanese groups within Manchuria. Some were idealistic and some even utopian, finding in Manchuria a frontier where they could realize a vision that many considered impossible to achieve in the established society of Japan. Yamamuro Shinichi has said that in the entire history of Japanese expansionism, Manchuria is arguably the only place that held a romance for Japanese. Idealists and visionaries of every hue saw there a frontier of boundless possibilities. And yet, as he further notes, the reality of the Japanese imperial system stood in their way; indeed, convinced as they were of the superiority of Japanese personality and institutions, it stood *inside* their way as well.[76]

Groups like the *Mantetsu Shainkai* and the *Daiyūhōkai* were formed by employees of the SMR. The former advocated the ideals of racial harmony and a new state, while the latter was inspired by Buddhist universalist ideas of divine compassion.[77] Another important group whose ideas informed the new Manchukuo state was the Manchurian Youth League (*Manshū Seinen Renmei*), formed by the Japanese settler society in Manchuria. This group was particularly sensitive to the rise of Chinese nationalism and, although a paramilitary outfit, it was painfully aware that Japanese interests in Manchuria were doomed without some kind of compact with the Chinese communities or a framework of Sino-Japanese coexistence. Under its idealistic leader Yamaguchi Jūji, the League developed the idea of *kyōwa*, or cooperation between races or nationalities and the rejection of colonialist attitudes. This idea would ultimately incarnate in a fascistic mass organization in Manchukuo known as the Concordia Association. Though fascist, the association was built upon a rhetoric of eternal peace embedded in East Asian ideals and a framework of mutual cooperation among the different peoples. It advocated anti-imperialism and even conceived of a new type of anticolonial state that would replace all imperialist powers—including the Japanese.[78] Although the history of Manchukuo since the mid-1930s is one of subordination to Japanese expansionism, the effects of these early ideas and policies should not be underestimated.

In all these groups—although with different emphases or in different combinations—we see the modern progressive, even radical, ideals of the equality of gender and peoples combined with notions of the distinctiveness of Eastern civilizational traditions. Thus Buddhist thinkers such as Kasagi Ryōmei of the *Daiyūhōkai* and Ishiwara emphasized Easternness, while the Youth League and Tachibana Shiraki sought more progressive ideals. But it was really Tachibana Shiraki who synthesized this duality in a way that was suitable for the new state. A well-respected Sinologist and a journalist in Manchuria, Tachibana began to work for the influential SMR Research Department in 1925.[79] He was perhaps more sympathetic to Chinese nationalism than most other Japanese, and his goal was to create a new East that was modern, progressive, and socialistically egalitarian.[80] At the same time, he was convinced that the East was organized around different ethical and spiritual principles than the West. He was much struck with Sun Yat-sen's appeal to *wangdao*, or the way of the ethical monarch of Chinese antiquity, as a means of countering the "way of the hegemon" represented by both Western powers and the local warlords.

Ironically, the Manchukuo state would seek to deploy precisely such Chinese ideals as *wangdao* and their own supposedly more genuine version, the Republic of Five Nationalities of 1912, in the *minzu xiehe* (Concordia of Nationalities). Not only did both these ideas refer to Sun's rhetoric, they also alluded (as had Sun) to Chinese civilizational categories, including the Qing notion of the federated empire. As creative as he was in his efforts to synthesize the modern West and ancient East, and to channel Japanese expansionist energies toward the construction or restoration of China and other Asian societies, Tachibana's desire to see Asia unified under Japan led him to work with the military.[81] Tachibana's implication in the core reality of the military power, like that of all the other idealists who dreamed of building a new world on the frontier, would lead him to compromises and even the reversal of his ideals.

In 1931, Tachibana became associated with the Manchurian Youth League by accepting the editorship of their journal *Manshū Hyōron*.[82] At the same time, because of his connections to the economic research group of the SMR, which in turn was actively allied with the radicals in the Guandong Army, he was well positioned to represent the different Japanese interests in Manchuria and serve as the architect of the new state.[83] In the immediate aftermath of the Manchurian Incident on September 18, his principal political task was to direct the Self-Government Guidance

Department (*zizhi zhidaobu*), which sought to build the apparatuses of local administration from among local elites who had been associated with the earlier autonomy movement and who probably saw de facto Japanese rule as their best available option. In March 1932, when the guidance department was disbanded, Tachibana threw himself into building the Concordia Association, which replaced the Machurian Youth League. He sought to build upon the ideas of Yamaguchi, who had articulated the vision of a new society in which all the different groups in "Man-Mo" (Manchuria and Mongolia) would "participate in politics equally and without discrimination."[84]

Despite Japanese military control, there was no shortage of Chinese—autonomists, opportunists, "Eastern" religious salvationists, revolution-fearing elites, and war weary masses—who could be persuaded or coerced to join the "peace maintenance committees" that served as the effective administration under the Self-Government Guidance Department. At the top level, most of the important military generals, such as the Manchu Xi Xia in Jilin, Zang Shiyi in Fengtian, and Zhang Jinghui in Heilongjiang, swiftly switched sides and became the new provincial governors. Thus, by January 1932 pro-Japanese regimes had been established in all three provinces. At the local level, a group of Chinese politicians, merchants, and local notables formed the Peace Maintenance Committee of Liaoning Province, with Yuan Jinkai as its chairman. There is considerable scholarly consensus that the most significant basis of Chinese support for the Manchukuo regime came from the landed classes who tacitly promised support in return for stability and anticommunism.[85] In large measure because of the ways in which corrupt officials and land companies distributed the land for settlement and cultivation in the late nineteenth century, Manchuria had an extremely unequal profile of land distribution. The investigation of the Land Records Bureau, set up in 1936, revealed that 3 percent of the rural households in northern Manchuria owned 50 percent of the land, and 4 percent of the rural households in southern Manchuria owned 40 percent of the land, while 84 percent of rural households in the north and 65 percent in the south owned very little or no land.[86] It is for this reason that the first reform item on Tachibana's agenda—radical agrarian reform, which grew out of his socialist agrarian philosophy (*nōhonshugi*)—was shelved, and the rural sector remained stagnant during the entire period. In general, the refusal of the Guandong Army to interfere with the interests of the landed classes made several of the projects of the radicals impossible.

The leader of the Guidance Department, Yu Chonghan, was a representative of landed interests and also had financial interests in an SMR company.[87] Yu had been an advocate of the autonomist *baojing anmin* movement and was also a leader of a group of top civilian administrators in the Zhang administration known as the *wenzhipai* (civilian rule group). When he came out of retirement to accept the offer to lead the department, Yu declared the necessity of constructing a new, independent state based upon the principles of *wangdao,* which involved, among other things, reform of the taxation, official compensation, and police systems. He also advocated an industrialization policy and, most curiously (although consistent with the spirit of *wangdao*), the abolition of the national defense forces, a policy that Tachibana also advocated in the early stages.[88]

Rana Mitter has shown how various forms of local alliances, in particular, the county-level peace maintenance committees, were crucial to ensuring a relatively smooth takeover by the Guandong Army of much of Manchuria.[89] The economic integrity of the county and the effective control of county elites was perhaps most in evidence in the financial panic following the Manchurian Incident, when the Guandong Army seized the banks of the old government. Many counties were able to forestall the slide into economic and political chaos by issuing their own currencies. That these currencies circulated countywide—unlike other parts of Republican China, where one could find multiple currencies in a single county—not only reflects the integration of county power, but Yasutomi Ayumu and Fukui Chie argue, it also permitted the relative ease of political control in Manchukuo.[90]

Once regular administration was reestablished, particularly after the formation of the Republic of Manchukuo in March 1932, these county-level committees were formally dissolved, but the spirit of (doubtless forced) cooperation that lay behind them was to be sustained through two institutions: the Concordia Association and the principally Chinese associations that I have called the modern redemptive societies, such as the *Daodehui* (Morality Society) and the *Hongwanzihui* (Red Swastika Society). The tacit alliance that the Manchukuo state formed with Chinese landed groups, local elites, autonomists, and redemptive societies, as well as modernizing bureaucrats and modernizing elements in the Concordia Association, shaped the rhetoric of its sovereignty claims.

Political Economy: Violence and Development

The political structure of Manchukuo exemplified the contradictions between its sovereignty claims and strategies (based on social alliances) and the structure of power. At the same time, its broader macrosocietal agenda indexed its difference from the older colonial model and revealed many of its contradictions to be characteristic of modern governmentality, particularly as expressed in the Manchukuo regime form. This governmentality was expressed in its slogan of *jianguo* or *kenkoku* (founding the nation-state).

Despite the rhetoric of self-rule or local self-government, the political structure was carefully controlled by the Guandong Army. Puyi, who had reigned as child emperor until the fall of the Manchu dynasty in the Republican revolution of 1911, was designated head of state in 1932 on the model of the KMT presidency, and became emperor again in 1934.[91] Much has been written and at least two movies made about this somewhat tragic, if colorless and powerless, emperor. In his role as the titular ruler of an independent state, Puyi was initially considered equal to the Japanese emperor. After the Japanese invasion of China in 1937, he was increasingly subordinated to the Japanese emperor. He was induced to worship at holy shrines

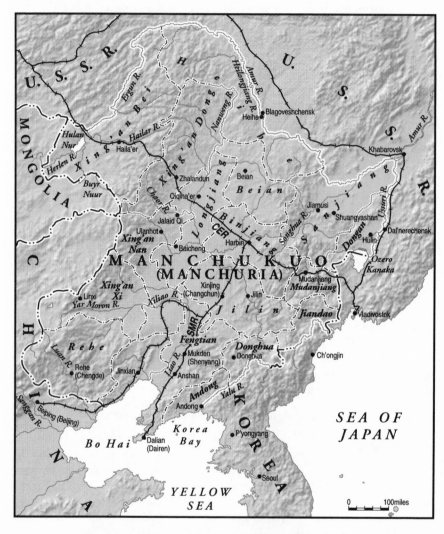

Provinces, Cities, and Principal Railroads of Manchukuo

of Ise, and in 1939 a shrine for Amaterasu was installed in his palace in Xinjing, the new capital built in the old city of Changchun. In 1940, Puyi underwent a ritual rebirth from the womb of Amaterasu, thus becoming the younger half brother of the Japanese emperor. In the view of the authoritative Chinese history of Manchukuo, such an act made "the Chinese people into Japanese imperial subjects."[92] By 1937, and especially after the outbreak of the Pacific War, the symbolic independence of Manchukuo was seriously compromised, as it increasingly became an important supply base for the Japanese war machine in inland China.

Initially, the army sought to control the administrative structure directly, and Muto Nobuyoshi, commander in chief of the Guandong Army, was also appointed governor of the Guandong-leased territory (as well as Japanese ambassador to Manchukuo). The civilian governorship was separated from the other posts soon after,[93] and by the mid-1930s army officers had to share power with a host of "reform bureaucrats" from Japan who envisioned Manchukuo as a "modern national defense state" that would serve as a model for Japan. Totalitarian in conception, the vision of these bureaucrats involved the rational and efficient mobilization of material, political, scientific, and cultural resources under state control. Although more closely identified with Japan than were the Guandong Army officers, their conception also involved winning the "hearts and minds of the people" through propaganda and the Concordia Association, which developed into an administered mass organization.[94]

The reform bureaucrats and the army controlled the wider administration through the General Affairs Board (*zongwuting*) of the State Council, the most powerful administrative body. It consisted of the six bureaus of planning, legislation, personnel, accounts, statistics, and information. The board made the budget and supervised all important hiring and firings. Most of the top political and administrative positions in the government as a whole were occupied by Chinese, although they were closely supervised by a high-level Japanese who was said to report to the board. The director general of the General Affairs Board was always Japanese.[95] The first prime minister was Zheng Xiaoxu, a Qing loyalist and Confucian scholar who apparently hoped for a genuine return to the principles of Confucian governance. He was gradually ousted from power and replaced by the former warlord Zhang Jinghui in 1935.[96] Many of the Chinese administrators were locals, frequently educated in Japanese institutions in the SMR-leased regions or in Japan itself.[97]

Manchukuo did not have a formal constitution, but bureaucrats and scholars referred to the Proclamation of the Establishment of the State (*Jianguo xuangao*) of 1932 and the Government Organization Law (*Zhengfu zuzhifa*) as containing the fundamental laws of the state. According to these laws the political system was a modern one, containing an executive, a legislature, and a judiciary. However, there was no true separation of powers and Yamamuro has aptly called the system "apparent constitutionalism." The language of the laws frequently referred to the rights and duties of citizens (although there was no explicit citizenship law), but couched as it was in the familiar imperial Japanese metaphor of the family-state, the obligations of the citizen overwhelmed her rights: "National citizenship is the expanded version of family membership. Just as the family member has an obligation to obey the family unconditionally, so does the citizen have to obey the state."[98]

Groups and nationalities, rather than individual citizens, were more frequently seen as rights-bearing units: "No matter what race or religion, all the people are guaranteed to enjoy equality in the nation. . . . We are a country of different nationalities/races (*minzoku*) and religions, and the nation-state guarantees equality among them."[99] Such legal statutes underpinned the corporatist organization of society, which was managed at an everyday level by the Concordia Association and the various redemptive societies. The political constitution of Manchukuo was a sham as far as democratic rights and checks were concerned. But the regime was by no means an old-style colonial power moved to intervene in society simply in order to secure its power and profits. It was a fascistic regime whose laws were designed to produce its vision of a disciplined and mobilized society. As the war beyond its boundaries expanded, it became ever more committed to mobilizing the population, regardless of ethnicity, for its political, economic, and ideological projects.

The most modern part of the state was the economic system, particularly the urban, industrial sector.[100] The modern sector of the economy grew more rapidly and developed a more advanced industrial base than any part of Asia outside Japan. Kung-tu Sun calculates that industrial production tripled between 1933 and 1942, and producer goods output grew the fastest.[101] The establishment of a unified currency equivalent to the Japanese yen was very important to the economic recovery of the region after years of fiscal irresponsibility. It also enabled Manchukuo to integrate with the Japanese economy, forming a "yen bloc." The banking system was reorganized and unified. There was a dramatic rise in Japanese investments—according to Louise Young, to almost 6 billion yen between 1932 and 1941 (in 1941 exchange rates), a figure far greater than that for any other transfer from a metropole to colony. By 1945, Japanese investment in Manchukuo exceeded the combined total of investment in Korea, Taiwan, and the rest of China.[102] This economic growth meant that immigration from China continued to rise as a whole, although the Japanese made efforts to control and reverse it during the early period, when they hoped to settle the land with Japanese and Koreans.[103] As a result of these efforts, migration into Manchuria from north China in 1931–1938 fell to below half the levels of the preceding years, but with the industrialization drive of the war years immigration picked up again, to an average of 1.2 million per annum between 1939 and 1942. Most of this labor force went into the industrial sector.[104]

Ramon Myers has argued that the establishment of Manchukuo marked a break from the older colonial pattern of economic domination, which involved the emergence of a small Westernized industrial sector alongside a much larger, traditional agricultural sector. There was also little transfer of capital or technology or significant economic integration between colony and metropolis. Myers argues that between 1931 and 1945 the Japanese military and government began to create a "modern enclave" economy in Manchukuo and, later, north China, comprising the full panoply of modern economic enterprises and services such as hospitals, schools, and research centers. Capital assets in this sector far exceeded the size and value of Chinese-owned mining and manufacturing south of Manchukuo. As Louise Young says, "The truly radical and novel facet of Manchurian development lay in the plans for heavy industrialization and the hope to make Manchukuo the advance guard of Japanese industrial capitalism. By turning Manchukuo into a testing ground for industrial management and planning techniques, Japan departed from existing colonial practices."[105] The modern enclave economy idea fits our efforts to characterize the complexity of Manchukuo. On the one hand, the massive modernization of economic and social life is continuous with the modern state's imperative of governmentality. On the other hand, this buildup was itself designed to create a war machine dominated by an imperialistic power structure.

Scholars have tended to divide economic development during the fourteen-year period from 1931 to 1945 into three stages. In 1931–1936, the Guandong Army was relatively responsive to the various Manchuria based Japanese utopian and visionary groups, such as the *Daiyūhōkai*, the *Mantetsu Shainkai*, the Manchurian Youth League, and others.[106] This early influence by no means precluded the establishment of Japanese dominance, but rather emphasized the independence of Manchukuo from both the Japanese government and from *Zaibatsu* capitalists.[107] From the mid-1930s, the bureaucrats arriving from Japan increased their influence, and by 1936 the government announced the first of a series of five-year plans based on extensive state control of the industry and commerce that had been built up over the preceding years. Special companies in charge of a particular industry were set up, usually as state corporations in which the government was a principal or important shareholder. However, since the available capital was still insufficient, the army began to abandon its vestigial anticapitalism and invited the *Zaibatsu* to establish joint ventures with the state corporations.[108] Most important among the houses was the new and supposedly less plutocratic *Nippon Sangyō Kaisha*, or Nissan, headed by Ayukawa Yoshisuke.[109]

The dependence on Nissan grew after the invasion of China proper in 1937, as it became increasingly clear that Manchukuo would serve as a principal supply base. Nissan became a holding company controlling most of the state enterprises—increasingly at the cost of the South Manchurian Railroad Company, which was reduced to a transportation company and research organization.[110] Thus, while the period before 1936 saw considerable industrial development, it was far surpassed by industrial growth in 1937–1941.[111] There are no reliable statistics for the second five-year plan, which began in 1942, because of the wartime statistical blackout, but most economists believe that production increased still faster, judging from available data. In 1945, total thermal and hydroelectric production was around 3 million kilowatts, compared to the unmet annual target of 1.4 million from 1937 to 1941.[112] The maniacal increase in industrial production and the diversion of resources to feed the war machine came at a terrible price. Inflation and increased taxes began to burden the people as early as 1937. But it is after the outbreak of the Pacific War in 1941 that we get a palpable sense of the reduction in living standards, especially among the urban Chinese population.[113] The increasing costs of maintaining the Japanese armies led to shortages and still more stringent state control of the distribution system, which in turn led to popular dissatisfaction and black-marketing. This period was increasingly shaped by the fascistic regime structure and tensions generated by a Japanese imperialist racism, which blatantly contradicted the sovereignty claims of the multicultural ideology of Concordia.[114]

In addition to these wartime problems, Chinese authors have pointed to many injustices produced by the inequality between Japanese and Chinese. They note the monopolistic nature of the industrialization drive; the Manchukuo government and Japanese houses controlled 72 percent of the total invested capital, making it hard for Chinese capital to compete.[115] Moreover, the wage differential between Chinese and Japanese workers in the factories was staggering; in 1939, for every one hundred yuan made by a Japanese, a Chinese worker made 29 yuan.[116] Conditions of work in the mines were especially appalling. In the agricultural sector not only was there no reform, but the means used by the government to settle Japanese and Korean farmers produced much tension and conflict. The Land Records Bureau set up in March 1936 turned out to be a means to grab the best land for Japanese settlers.[117] Chinese farmers were evicted with a token compensation of 5 yuan, or else their land was bought in August, when the price was lowest. By the end of 1939, over one million hectares of land—representing about one-sixth of all the cultivable land in Japan—was under Japanese cultivation. Nineteen percent of this land had already been under cultivation.[118]

The brutality of the regime cannot be doubted. Some of this was, not unexpectedly, directed at resistance forces. Given Chiang Kai-shek's policy of nonresistance, followed, however reluctantly, by Zhang Xueliang, most of the existing military forces in the Northeast either fled Manchuria or capitulated to the Japanese. A few warlord armies, most famously that that of Ma Zhanshan in Harbin (studied by Rana Mitter) and such disparate entities as student groups, "patriotic landlords," and secret societies, particularly in the old Chinese regions of southern Liaoning, offered resistance, but they were routed by 1933.[119] After 1933, as the Soviet Union felt more emboldened to encourage the Chinese Communist Party to attack the Japanese, the CCP brought together many of the resistance forces into the *Yiyongjun* (or Righteous/Volunteer Army) and put up considerable resistance. Communist-led uprisings continued, particularly in the Korean-dominated Jiandao region, but the Manchukuo and Japanese armies were able to decimate them by the late 1930s. Whole villages were wiped out, including the killing of 2,500 villagers in the Pingtingshan massacre. Altogether almost 66,000 people were slaughtered between 1932 and 1940.[120] According to Lee Chong-sik, the principal reason for Japanese success lay in their draconic counterinsurgency measures. In response to suspected peasant support for anti-Japanese guerillas in the Jiandao border region with Korea, 5.5 million rural residents were forcibly relocated, by the end of 1937, to 10,629 hamlets. These concentration camplike hamlets came with three-meter-high walls, barbed wire, and squads of forced labor.[121] As Japanese forces cut off supplies to the guerillas, the latter were forced to raid the hamlets themselves, which gradually led to the deterioration of villager–guerilla relations.

In contravention of the 1925 Hague Convention ban on bacteriological warfare and experimentation, the Japanese government sanctioned germ warfare experimentation in Manchuria and elsewhere in China. Unit 731 in Harbin, where over 3,000 deaths took place between 1937 and 1945 alone,[122] has become the most notorious symbol of this cruel experimentation with humans, but there is evidence of experimentation in Xinjing and other places as well. Colonel Ishii Shiro ran his own bacteriological factory in Pingfang (Unit 731), equipped with a private airstrip, railway line, and other facilities. Here they experimented with the transmission of deadly infections such as the plague and typhoid; they also conducted vivisection, freezing, and dehydration experiments on people.[123] Recently the Japanese government has undertaken to clean up the site.

Manchukuo presents us with two faces. On the one hand, we have a record of cruel violence; on the other, one of a developmental state. Nishimura Shigeo has plotted these recurring phenomena as the plunder and development phases.[124] However, it is worth noting that it was the same state that underwent both phases. Although the contrast between development and violence seemed particularly sharp in Manchukuo, Foucault has pointed out that this antinomy is typical of the modern state.

> In all history, it would be hard to find such butchery as in World War II, and it is precisely this period, this moment, when the great welfare, public health, and medical assistance programs were instigated. . . . One could symbolize such a coincidence by a slogan: Go get slaughtered and we promise you a long and pleasant life.[125]

If the modern state is increasingly driven by the autonomous logic of governmentality to intervene to take care of men as population, it does so for its own sake. And since population is nothing more than what the state takes care of for its own sake, says Foucault, the state is also entitled to slaughter it, if necessary.[126] The case of Manchukuo suggests that we also need to invoke the "regime of authenticity" to grasp how the distinctions between authentic and inauthentic groups of people—based on ethnicity, class, or gender, even within the nation—could generate such contradictory forces within governmentality.

Even while it killed people mercilessly, the Manchukuo state sought to ensure high levels of investment, enjoyed considerable success in state building, eliminated banditry, and disciplined the warlord armies, turning them into the Manchukuo army. A very important propaganda item of this regime was that it had brought security from warlord disorder. With regard to infrastructural development—the construction of world-class dams, ports, railroads, planes, automobiles, and spectacularly modern cities—its achievements were greater than those of most other states in Asia. Japanese city planners who failed to realize their dreams in Japan sought to do so in Manchukuo. Xinjing, for instance, was designed as a futuristic world-class city to showcase the progressive Japanese leadership of Asia. Indeed, the state was the precursor of the postwar Japanese "construction state" (*doken kokka*), endlessly building Manchukuo.[127]

Other aspects of governmentality include the punctiliously detailed censuses and surveys; the extensive and complex plans for settlements; the close attention to hygiene and welfare, making available education, drinkable water, and shelters; and the mobilization of the population for forced inoculations—sometimes at gunpoint.[128] No state in the region had ever been so busy classifying, surveilling, managing, and directing the lives of the people. Suk-jung Han's important work has shown how the Ministry of Civil Affairs (*Minzhengbu*) under one-time warlord Zang Shiyi

> pok[ed] its nose into all realms of daily life, even examining bathroom designs of new buildings, dogs, carts, and checking the health conditions of prostitutes monthly. . . . Each provincial office was a small scale replication of the ministry with similar sections (such as personnel, finance, statistics, police, welfare, land, construction). The ministry sent a hundred directives annually to local officials for them to report on endless items (from the condition of roads to that of Confucian shrines). . . . It also devised an extreme measure for directing local offices. It finally graded them for their achievement in various fields.[129]

There is perhaps no better symbol of the antinomian structure of the modern state in Manchukuo than the police. According to Han, who is fascinated by the multifarious and moralized role they were assigned, Manchukuo had a huge police force that was relatively well paid and regularly trained, and that engaged in every kind of supervisory, surveillance, regulatory, mobilizational, and educational activity.[130] Indeed, they appear to have occupied the much broader role of the *polizeistaat,* which according to Foucault heralded governmentality in eighteenth-century Europe.

The rationality at work in hygiene and welfare was also at work in the elaborately planned isolation of peasants in their hamlets, the cold-blooded science of human experimentation with lethal bacteria, and the mobilization of the population for a deadly war. But many modern states exhibited this duality. The governmentality that characterized Manchukuo was typical of the modern nondemocratic regimes of the inter-war years, such as fascist Italy, Nazi Germany, the Stalinist Soviet Union, and Japan. Even KMT China sought to emulate these examples. In contrast to the democratic regimes of the period, in which the functions of governmentality were distributed between state and nonstate organizations of civil society, in this other type of regime the administration itself and its extensions—what Gregory Kasza has called "administered mass organizations"—reached into every sector of the population to control and manage. The particular combination of the state form and the fascistic regime form characterized the governmentality of Manchukuo. What made it different from other modern states was that it did not have the legitimacy of a nation. Governmentality does not eliminate the need for sovereignty, and sovereignty in the post–World War I era was increasingly embedded in the discourse of nationhood. The failure to secure recognition from the League on the basis of state rights pitted the Manchukuo government all the more against the deep claims made by Chinese nationalism. The story of Manchukuo—at least during the early phase—is the story of a state in search of a nation. Let me turn to one of its principal claims to be a sovereign nation: what it regarded as its prized innovation, the Concordia Association.

Sovereignty, Mobilization, and the Concordia Association

In conception, the Concord of Nationalities, the doctrine of the Association, was supposed to be two stages ahead of the old colonial ideas of the nineteenth-century West. Not only was it supposed to reject exploitation and the reproduction of difference between ruler and ruled, it was also designed to counter the homogenization of differences produced by nationalism itself, which had led to such insoluble conflicts in the early twentieth century. By allegedly granting different peoples or nationalities their rights and self-respect under a state structure, it saw itself as a nation in the mode of the Soviet union of nationalities or today's multicultural nations.[131] But where in the eyes of a Yamaguchi or Tachibana or even an increasingly sympathetic Ishiwara, the Concordia Association was to represent the will of the people and was ultimately destined to replace the Guandong Army, by mid-decade it was purged of its original leadership and made into an instrument of the army and government.[132] It became less the means of ethnic, cultural, and occupational representation than of their surveillance and mobilization. Nonetheless, in the process, it could not avoid confronting the problem of identity politics of modern nationalism.

As a mediator between local structures and the center, the Concordia Association enrolled all officials, teachers, and important figures in society. Several scholars have referred to it as a totalitarian party, and indeed the Guandong Army decided against calling it a party precisely because parties were too closely associated with partisan interests and hence insufficiently "total." According to the commander in chief of the Guandong Army, it was in theory "the ideological mother of government."[133] Members often wore uniforms and served as propaganda agents, whether through making films, training youth, or organizing meetings, while also undertaking lower-level administrative functions, such as surveillance and even labor mobilization during the Pacific War. As an organ for mass mobilization, all youth aged sixteen to nineteen were compulsorily enrolled in the Concordia Youth League from April 1937. McCormack notes that the Association's numbers grew from 1 million in early 1938 to 4.28 million by June 1943 (of a total population of approximately 40 million).[134] While the CCP enrolled 5 percent of the population, it enrolled over 10 percent.[135] Gradually, as in "administered mass organizations" of this kind of regime, most of the population was organically woven into one part or another of the Concordia Association structure.

The Concordia Association was also the nucleus of a fascistic *corporatism*. Analysts of fascism have used the notion of corporatism to describe the actualization of twentieth-century fascist theories of "organic society" into social organizations that emphasized solidarity of the national community rather than competition between individuals or classes. The Concordia Association claimed to be both anticapitalist and anticommunist, and sought to overcome class and other divisions by organizing people through their communities. These communities were occupational or professional, cultural (generational, gendered), and ethnic. Developed originally as a framework to represent the different ethnic communities, such as Mongols, Manchus, or Hui Muslims, the association was particularly important for mobilizing the support of the elites of these ethnicities who allegedly represented the masses in their communities. These elites were themselves often divided into an older, traditional group and a younger, modernizing one, reflecting a split within Concordia ideology.

Many Japanese ideologists, such as Tachibana, did not see any contradiction between the modern ideals of republicanism, equality, and modernization and "Eastern" values of community solidarity and the moral state (*wangdao*). After all, had not Japan exemplified the synthesis and represented the best of both worlds? As Tachibana declared,

> Since the Manchurian Incident, the warlord regime in the Northeast has collapsed. With this collapse, the 30 million people of Manchuria and Mongolia (Man-Mo) and the 300 million Chinese people have been liberated from the shackles of semifeudalism. Moreover, this liberation has directly awakened the Asian essence (*honshitsu*) of Manchurian society. By turning to these traditions (*dentōteki seikatsu shisō*; literally, traditional life ideas) and self-governing capacities, a new *ōdō* (*wangdao*) nation has been created. Hence, the establishment of the *ōdō* nation-state possesses a historical and social inevitability.[136]

Yet when these ideas were the bases not merely for talking points but for different interests and programs, the tensions were very real.

On the one hand, having declared its sovereignty to be founded upon the distinctive and superior essence of Asia, the corporatism of the Concordia Association necessitated a notion of Asiatic traditionalism. This form of corporatism often strengthened the regime's control of local society because it preserved the existing power structure intact. It was similar to the *baojia* system of community self-surveillance, an imperial Chinese method of local control that the Association also implemented among the Han Chinese communities in Manchukuo. By the 1940s, the Concordia Association was organizing Hui mosque communities, Mongol lama monasteries, and Manchu villages, among others. To promote the goal of solidarity, the Association sought to emphasize the so-called values of communalism or *kyōdō-tai* within religion; to celebrate pan-Asianism, which they allegedly found even among Muslims and Central Asian peoples; and to support the religious leadership among these peoples, such as Mongol lamas, Manchu and Daur shamans, Muslim ahongs, Buddhist monks, and Confucian moralists. Thus traditional pan-Asianism was an important aspect of maintaining the specific nature of corporatist control in this fascist regime. At the same time, we can see how the regime form in Manchukuo served to bolster or even produce its sovereignty claims based on the implicit compact with conservative forces in the society.

However, the sovereignty claims of the regime also incorporated modernity; indeed the modernity of Asian tradition was implicit in the idea of the "kingly way." It was expressed most clearly in the forms of governmentality that characterized state power. We have already attended to the large-scale state projects of modernity such as cities, dams, ports, hygiene programs, five-year plans, and the like, whereby the modern state performs—or perhaps, calls up—the modernity through which it will legitimate its rule. James Holston writes,

> Like prophets gathering flocks, modern states invent nations where they do not yet exist and create polities to which they later belong. And like prophets, they often do this inventing by means of public works that are supposed to demonstrate their capacity to create an imagined, usually alternative future and to fashion new subjects and subjectivities for it. . . . [S]uch projects aim to cultivate the belief that states can produce the future-modern by accelerating history ("Fifty Years of Progress in Five") [and] dematerializing distance ("National Unification through Highway Construction").[137]

Technocrats, bureaucrats, and other modernizing elites tied in one way or another to state projects were the advocates of this vision.

It should not be forgotten that the Concordia Association was originally designed to realize a visionary modern polity. Many of its early recruits, especially among the younger elite of the minorities, turned out to be quite fiercely iconoclastic. Thus Mongol tribal youth who served in border armies were decidedly against the lama priests and demanded modern education. A Daur intellectual and member of the Association wrote a savage critique of shamanism. Even Japanese reformers were appalled at the massive state expenditures in building temples to Chinese gods such as Guandi and others. At the highest level, Chinese supporters of the regime were fiercely divided between those who wanted to keep Manchukuo a modern republic and those, such as Zheng Xiaoxu, who sought to make Puyi, the last Manchu emperor, an emperor once again—a goal they realized with the declaration of the Manchukuo Empire in 1934. At the same time, even when subordinated to the Guandong Army, the state still needed the cooperation of modern elements among the Japanese, the Han, and the minorities in order to become strong and modern.

This tension was particularly apparent after the Pacific War. The Concordia Association became increasingly involved in the war effort, and through the forties one of its most important function was to encourage unrealistic increases in factory production while ensuring that workers did not rebel under these harsh conditions. Japanese representatives were quite candid about their dissatisfaction with this impossible task, and one member wrote in the society's journal *Kyōwa Undō* that the fanatical need to increase production existed basically in the Japanese head alone!

But what was most aggravating was the policy from about 1942 of involving the religious or redemptive societies in this twin effort to increase production and reduce tension. As a representative wrote in the same journal, the various religious organizations appeared to have very little comprehension of the goals of the mobilization campaign and refused to cooperate in the least. The city authorities now planned to change the format and use seminars and lectures to teach the activists of the redemptive societies.[138]

Although we can find this tension in its distilled form in the Concordia Association, it characterized the state and society beyond it; we may think of it as the fault line in the ideology of this Asian fascist regime. The survival of the regime depended upon maintaining a balance between, on the one hand, constructing a traditionalist corporatism and supporting redemptive societies, and, on the other, developing a modernizing project that was compatible with its state-building goals. Support from significant, but mutually hostile, communities depended upon the commitment to attaining both aims. Both were also crucial to the sovereignty claims of a state that was increasingly being recognized by other states.[139] Thus the regime functions of fascist corporatism appealed to ideas of Asian essentialism, whereas the imperative of governmentality in this particular time and space called for a rhetoric of modernizing legitimation. While, as we have seen, this was a characteristic tension of the temporality of the modern nation-state, and was doubly intense for non-Western nations, in Manchukuo it was triply intense because Asianism was so central to its claim to sovereignty. Like several East Asian regimes around it, the Manchukuo state sought to resolve the tension by re-presenting the authentic tradition in such a way that it could exclude what it did not like. By so deploying the East Asian modern, the ideologists of the regime sought to contain the aporia of modern time and its particularly heavy political fallout. This containment effort often assumed—as we shall see below—the figure of the modernity-of-tradition.

In an effort to escape the judgment that forecloses or severely restricts so many studies of Manchukuo, I determined to de-compose the categories of political analysis so that we could arrive at a more differentiated understanding of the situation without at the same time losing sight of the power structure in the regime. The underlying question posed by this mode of analysis is whether the imperialist power structure implied by the terms puppet state, false Manzhouguo, and even informal empire played such an important role as to make the experience substantially comparable to a colonial one. Does the ability of power-holders to influence and manipulate institutions and rhetoric overwhelm the effects of new institutions and policies in the changed domestic and international circumstances after World War I?

There are many ways in which power-holders are able to manipulate institutions not necessarily designed for their benefit. We can see this not only in the reduction of the autonomy of Manchukuo and the decision to go to war in Asia, but perhaps more strikingly through informal attitudes and everyday practices. Two recent and excellent Japanese studies by Yamamuro Shinichi and Komagome Takeshi both point to this factor as pivotal. For Komagome, the racialist ideology of the consanguineous descent group (*ketsuzoku*), identified with a unique Japanese people, tended to prevail over whatever other sentiments of affinity, built through cultural and linguistic ties, the Japanese may have felt with the peoples they came to colonize or dominate. No matter how radically sympathetic a Japanese activist in Manchuria may have been towards Chinese and others, it was, more often than not, premised upon a presumption of the acceptability of a naturally superior Japanese leadership.[140] Yamamuro points to the apparatus of control and the arbitrary authority of the police and the army. But he finds that the Japanese failure in Manchukuo lies less in the institutions they designed than in their attitudes and practices. The rhetoric of concord was contradicted in everyday practices such as the discrimination against Chinese in the military school or the consumption of ethnically differentiated rationed items—rice for the Japanese, sorghum for Chinese—at the same table during the war.[141]

To be sure, there is evidence that there were forces working for autonomy even within the power structure in Manchukuo. There were several occasions when special Japanese rights were attacked by the Guandong Army, most notably in 1936, when extraterritorial rights for Japanese citizens were abolished and a series of very real privileges began to unravel. The Japanese government also raised tariffs against the overwhelming exports from Manchukuo.[142] More recent research by Han, Young, and others takes seriously the Guandong Army's autonomy from the despised civilian governments at home—at least until the war in Asia. Nonetheless, these tendencies towards autonomy pale in comparison to the growing subordination of Manchukuo to the growing Japanese war machine.

The novelty of Manchukuo emerges from the institutional consequences of imperial nationalism in an emergent postcolonial time of mobilization and identity politics. Whether it be corporatist governmentality or the development of the "yen bloc," Manchukuo was considerably different from the colonial "night watchman state" or previous patterns of economic relationships between metropole and colony. Its locus as the site of the most advanced forms of design, mobilization, and experimentation had as much to do with the changing climate, demands, and strategies of the globally ambitious military as with metropolitan Japanese discourses and attitudes towards Manchuria. For many reformers and radical militarists, reform here was the starting point for reform in Japan.[143] It was also different because of reasons "ex-centric" to the metropole. Because Manchukuo was created at a different time and space from the conquest of Taiwan and Korea, the Japanese military had to work with Chinese allies and employ Chinese political and ideological forms in the creation of the political system.

In a general sense, as an aspect of Japanese imperialism, Manchukuo was of a piece with Korea and Taiwan, and we shall explore their role in the East Asian modern in the concluding chapter. As Komagome has revealed, this imperialism contained tendencies toward assimilation and alliance on the one hand, and racial exclusivism and reproduction of difference on the other.[144] But Manchukuo as a multinational state was only conceivable after the March 1919 Korean anticolonial movement, when groups both within the colonial regime and outside began to rethink the nature of Japanese expansionism. The need to avoid the repercussions of nationalism by seeking to co-opt it came to be intertwined with pan-Asianism, particularly after anti-immigration legislation in the United States and other developments in the 1920s fueled the Japanese self-perception not only as imperialists, but as victims of Western imperialism.[145] Soon after World War I, elements in the military began to conceive of a "strategic autarky" within an economic defense perimeter. Thus, the logics of territory and economics, which fused into a new type of regional hegemony sought by the Japanese—justified in the language of an Asiatic Monroe Doctrine—found expression in Manchukuo.

In several ways, Manchukuo was more continuous with the informal empire in Manchuria before 1931 than with Korea and Taiwan. As Tak Matsusaka has pointed out, many of the projects and policies carried out in Manchukuo, such as defense-related industrialization, managed economy, utopianism, and "techno-national-ism"—had been undertaken by the SMR long before 1931. Moreover, the plan for strategic autarky could never have been carried out without the partnership of Zhang Zuolin in the 1920s.[146] When he withdrew from this alliance, those who founded Manchukuo had to find other, more malleable allies. While imperialism was certainly preserved in this hegemony, it also dictated relations between center and periphery different from those of the older colonies. The new program involved more alliance, autonomy, investment, development, identity, and competitiveness. In many ways, Manchukuo prefigured the phenomenon of a junior partner or a client state dominated by hegemonic states such as the United States and the Soviet Union in the postwar period.

What kind of nation was Manchukuo designed to be? Official writings insist upon the special character of Manchukuo nationality and its difference from the colonies well into the Pacific War. But it was clearly a weak sense of territorial nationality, emphasizing civilizational character, nationality policies, and, of course, the ties to Japan. Anonymous Hegelian dialecticians from the flagship Jiango University grappled with the relationship between nationality and the state.

All nationalities in their life-worlds (*seken seikatsu*) must progress from the simple to the complex, from the unenlightened to the enlightened. The organizations, institutions, and culture of the various people express the spirit of universal citizenship (read, state) in form; but it is the special national character that determines the content. The objective existence of spirit is not exhausted (by this content); but it is external and moves from the outside to the inside. In the process, the institutions, organizations, and culture accept spirit, and national culture becomes the basis for the realization of spirit.[147]

The state would shape nationality, even as nationality was the basis of the state.

In philosophy, mobilizational strategy, identity formation, the production of authenticity, and the representation of sovereignty, Manchukuo resembled the modern nation-state. These strategies drew upon circulating resources and the most sophisticated technologies in East Asia. But the goal or object of these techniques of producing authenticity and citizenship was open-ended, variable, and confused. Apart from loyalty to the state (*jianguo*), Manchukuo failed to settle upon a vision of community—ethnic nationality, civilization, Manchukuo nation or empire, Japanese empire—because of the imperialist power structure and differences within it. In some ways, the regime "overimagined" the nation, presenting itself as the custodian of whatever cultural practice could appear as authentic. By the same token, it gives us the opportunity to examine these processes, not only in Manchukuo but in East Asia.

Notes

1. I still use the term Northeast when I quote or cite authors who use that designation.

2. League of Nations Commission of Enquiry on Manchuria [Lytton Commission], *The Far Eastern Problem: Official Texts and Summary of the Lytton Report* (Worcester, Mass.: New York Carnegie Endowment for International Peace, Division of Intercourse and Education, 1933), 63.

3. Robert H. G. Lee, *The Manchurian Frontier in Ch'ing History* (Cambridge: Harvard University Press, 1970), 184.

4. Mark C. Elliott, "The Limits of Tartary: Manchuria in Imperial and National Geographies," *Journal of Asian Studies* 59 (August 2000): 614. See also Mark C. Elliott, *The Manchu Way: The Eight Banners and Ethnic Identity in Late Imperial China* (Stanford: Stanford University Press, 2001).

5. Caroline Humphrey, "Shamanic Practices and the State in Northern Asia: Views from the Center and Periphery," in *Shamanism, History, and the State,* ed. Nicholas Thomas and Caroline Humphrey (Ann Arbor: University of Michigan Press, 1994), 191–228.

6. Elliott, "The Limits of Tartary," 619–24.

7. Owen Lattimore, *Manchuria: Cradle of Conflict* (New York: Macmillan, 1935), 39–42.

8. Lattimore, *Manchuria*, 41.

9. Lattimore, *Manchuria*, 60–61, 70. Christopher Atwood has revealed that a good many of Lattimore's ideas, particularly relating to the Mongols, derived from the views of Merse, a Daur Mongol intellectual and progressive Mongol nationalist; see Atwood, *Young Mongols and Vigilantes in Inner Mongolia's Interregnum Decades, 1911–1931* (Leiden: Brill, forthcoming).

10. Thomas Gottschang, "Economic Change, Disasters, and Migration: The Historical Case of Manchuria," *Economic Development and Cultural Change* 35 (1987): 461.

11. R. Lee, *Manchurian Frontier*, 78.

12. R. Lee, *Manchurian Frontier*, 113.

13. G. William Skinner, "Marketing and Social Structure in Rural China," *Journal of Asian Studies* 24 (1964–65): 3–43, 195–228.

14. Yasutomi Ayumu, "Teikiichi to kenjō keizai—1930 nen zengo ni okeru Manshū

nōson shijō no tokuchō" (The rural marketing system in Manchuria around 1930: Periodic markets and the economy of the county town) (paper submitted to *Ajia Keizai* 2002), 1–9.

15. Yasutomi, "Teikiichi to kenjō keizai," 19.

16. R. Lee, *Manchurian Frontier*, 40–55, and Tessa Morris-Suzuki, "Through Ethnographic Eyes" (unpublished paper, n.d.), 6–7.

17. Akamatsu Chijō and Akiba Takashi, *Manmo no minzoku to shūkyō* (Peoples and religions of Manchuria and Mongolia) (Tokyo: n.p., 1939), 161–64.

18. V. K. Arseniev, *Dersu the Trapper*, trans. Malcolm Burr (1941; reprint, New York: McPherson, 1996), 72–73.

19. R. Lee, *Manchurian Frontier*, 123, and Lattimore, *Manchuria*, 132–45.

20. R. Lee, *Manchurian Frontier*, 138–40.

21. C. Walter Young, *The International Relations of Manchuria: A Digest and Analysis of Treaties, Agreements, and Negotiations Concerning the Three Eastern Provinces of China* (Chicago: University of Chicago Press, 1929), 136–52.

22. Kang Chao, *The Economic Development of Manchuria: The Rise of a Frontier Economy* (Ann Arbor: Center for Chinese Studies, 1982), 5. Chao believes that the reported population increase—from roughly 7 million to 17 million—is likely to be an exaggeration and probably represents a considerable underestimate of the population before that date.

23. Chao, *Economic Development of Manchuria*, 7.

24. F. C. Jones, *Manchuria since 1931* (New York: Oxford University Press, 1949), 7–8, and Gavan McCormack, *Chang Tso-lin in Northeast China, 1911–1928: China, Japan, and the Manchurian Idea* (Stanford: Stanford University Press, 1977), 7.

25. Chao, *Economic Development of Manchuria*, 10.

26. Lattimore, *Manchuria*, 260.

27. McCormack, *Chang Tso-lin*, 7.

28. Jones, *Manchuria since 1931*, 12.

29. McCormack, *Chang Tso-lin*, 7–8.

30. Jeremy Adelman and Stephen Aron, "From Borderlands to Borders: Empires, Nation-States and the Peoples in Between in North American History," *American Historical Review* 104 (June 1999).

31. McCormack, *Chang Tso-lin*, 16–18.

32. McCormack, *Chang Tso-lin*, 59–72.

33. See also the recent study by Ronald Suleski, *Civil Government in Warlord China: Tradition, Modernization, and Manchuria* (New York: Peter Lang, 2002). Suleski reveals just how much Zhang was indebted to Wang Yongjiang for developing the economic and fiscal base of the region. For details of administrative reform, see chaps. 3 and 4.

34. McCormack, *Chang Tso-lin*, 79.

35. McCormack, *Chang Tso-lin*, 223.

36. McCormack, *Chang Tso-lin*, 253.

37. Mitter, *Manchurian Myth*, 132–34, and *ZDLSG*, 54–56. For an excellent account of the making of Chinese nationalism and its growth during the 1920s, see James H. Carter, *Creating a Chinese Harbin: Nationalism in an International City, 1916–1932* (Ithaca: Cornell University Press, 2002). Albeit focused on the city of Harbin, Carter's discussion of the growth of nationalism and its subsequent unraveling after 1928, as the interests of radical nationalists and security-seeking merchants began to diverge, is also relevant more generally to the region. He finds that many of the officials who had promoted this nationalism in the 1920s also promoted the new nationalism of Manchukuo in the 1930s.

38. *ZDLSG*, 27–30, and Jones, *Manchuria since 1931*, 17–18.

39. Westel W. Willoughby, *The Sino-Japanese Controversy and the League of Nations* (Baltimore: Johns Hopkins University Press, 1935), 400.

40. See Yosuke Matsuoka, *The Manchurian Question: Japan's Case in the Sino-Japanese Dispute as Presented before the League of Nations*, Observations of the Japanese Government on the Report of the Commission of Inquiry, Memorandum of the Japanese Delegation (Geneva: League of Nations, 1933), 27–28.

41. League of Nations Commission of Inquiry, *Far Eastern Problem,* 60–63; Willoughby, *Sino-Japanese Controversy,* 385.

42. League of Nations Commission of Inquiry, cited in Willoughby, *Sino-Japanese Controversy,* 387.

43. This was also because it was an anticommunist report.

44. League of Nations Commission of Inquiry, *Far Eastern Problem*, 80; Willoughby, *Sino-Japanese Controversy,* 404.

45. League of Nations Commission of Inquiry, *Far Eastern Problem*, 81.

46. Willoughby, *Sino-Japanese Controversy,* 399.

47. Matsuoka, *Manchurian Question*, 25–26.

48. Matsuoka, *Manchurian Question*, 28.

49. Matsuoka, *Manchurian Question*, 47.

50. Matsuoka, *Manchurian Question*, 48.

51. Matsuoka, *Manchurian Question*, 65.

52. League of Nations Commission of Inquiry, *Far Eastern Problem*, 62. Matsuoka, *Manchurian Question*, 19–20.

53. Chih Meng, *China Speaks: On the Conflict between China and Japan* (New York: Macmillan, 1932), 4. For Willoughby see Hatsue Shinohara, "Forgotten Crusade: The Quest for a New International Law" (Ph.D. diss., University of Chicago, 1996), 61.

54. Chih Meng, *China Speaks*, 182.

55. Chih Meng, *China Speaks*, 5.

56. Chih Meng, *China Speaks*, 65.

57. Feng Jiasheng, "Wode yanjiu dongbei shidi de jihua" (My research plan of the history and geography of the Northeast) *Yugong* 1, no. 10 (1934): 2–6.

58. Wang Qingyu, *Dongbei wenti* (The problem of the Northeast) (Shanghai: shangwu chubanshe, 1931), and Hua Qiyun, *Manmeng wenti* (The problems of Manchuria and Mongolia) (Shanghai: Dadong shuju, 1931). Fu Sinian, *Dongbei Shigang* (Outline of Northeast History), 1932, in *The Complete Works of Fu Sinian*, vol. 5, 74–85. Taipei: Lianjing Press, 1980.

59. Gu Jiegang, "Qin-Han tongyide youlai he zhanguoren duiyu shijiede xiangxiang" (The origins of Qin-Han unification and the image of the world during the Warring States) (1926; reprint in *Gushibian*, ed. Gu Jiegang, vol. 2., no. 1, Beijing: Pu she, 1930), 1–6.

60. Wu Shangquan, *Dongbei dili yu minzu shengcunzhi guanxi* (The relationship of the geography of the Northeast and the survival of the nation) (Chongqing: Duli chubanshe, 1944), 57–68.

61. Soren Clausen and Stig Thogersen, *The Making of a Chinese City: History and Historiography in Harbin* (New York: Sharpe, 1996), 9.

62. See also Hatada Takashi, *Chūgoku sonraku to kyōdōtai riron* (Chinese villages and the theory of village community) (Tokyo: Iwanami shoten, 1976), and Nishimura Shigeo, *Chū-*

goku kindai tōhoku chiyushi kenkyū (A regional history of Northeast China) (Kyoto: Hōritsu bunkasha, 1984), 2, 234–54.

63. Naitō's views on Manchuria and Manchukuo were quite ambivalent. In 1922, he had written that Manchuria was under Chinese sovereignty, but he was of the opinion that it was so because Japan had wrested it back from Russia. He regarded Manchukuo as the realization of a multiethnic and nonmilitarist state, but believed strongly that it had to be a Sino-Japanese partnership, a cooperative venture nourished in its own national conditions. However, he came to fear and mistrust the Guandong Army and refused to provide his knowledge to the propagandists of wangdao; see Joshua Fogel, *Politics and Sinology: The Case of Naitō Konan, 1866–1934* (Cambridge: Harvard University Press, 1984), 252–60.

64. Chianbu keisatsushi (Law and Order Ministry, Police Department), ed., *Kōmin* (Citizen) (Shinkyō: Manshūkoku toshō kabushiki geisha, 1940), 2–4.

65. League of Nations Commission of Inquiry, *Far Eastern Problem*, 63.

66. Gu Jiegang, "Qin-Han tongyide youlai," 4–5.

67. Laurence A. Schneider, *Ku Chieh-kang and China's New History: Nationalism and the Quest for Alternative Traditions* (Berkeley: University of California Press, 1971), 293.

68. Recently, the views of younger Chinese scholars appear to be changing. In personal conversations at least, they are prepared to acknowledge the higher levels of achievement in aspects of modernization such as life expectancy and information gathering in Manchukuo and Taiwan as compared with mainland China during the Republic. Indeed, one scholar believes that censuses in Manchukuo were more comprehensive than those conducted on the mainland in 1990. He has, however, yet to publish these findings.

69. Mark Peattie has suggested that Ishiwara Kanji, the architect of Manchukuo, could be described as a "military fascist"; see Mark R. Peattie, *Ishiwara Kanji and Japan's Confrontation with the West* (Princeton: Princeton University Press, 1975), 253–54.

70. Yoshihisa Tak Matsusaka, *The Making of Japanese Manchuria, 1904–1932* (Cambridge: Harvard University Press, 2001), 214–23. The security argument was underpinned by the rising threat of communism in China and Korea and the expectation of inevitable confrontation with the Soviet Union. Note here the way in which the argument for territorial security becomes a rationale for territorial expansion, how nationalism and imperialism were inseparable in this thinking.

71. Komagome Takeshi suggests that this decision should be seen in the trajectory of Japanese failed experiments with the participation of the colonized in government, particularly in Korea; see *Shokuminchi Teikoku Nippon no Bunka Tōgō* (The cultural integration of the Japanese colonial empire) (Tokyo: Iwanami Shoten, 1996), 236–37.

72. Yamamuro Shinichi, *Kimera: Manshōkoku no shōzō* (Chimera: A portrait of Manzhouguo) (Tokyo: Chuō kōronsha, 1993), 42–48.

73. Peattie, *Ishiwara Kanji*, 167, 281, 335. Note, however, that the special privilege of Japan and the supreme power of the Guandong Army was preserved by the signing between Japan and Manchukuo of two treaties, secretly settled beforehand; see Yamamuro, *Kimera*, 162.

74. Tessa Morris-Suzuki, *Re-inventing Japan: Time, Space, Nation* (London: Sharpe, 1998), 97–101; L. Young, *Japan's Total Empire*, 203–5, 221–27. Many of these people were associated with the Showa Research group.

75. One of the old questions of the historiography on Japanese expansion into Asia after the Manchurian Incident of 1931 is the extent to which the civilian government and the

military headquarters in Japan were involved in its premeditation. While scholars like James Crowley (1966) emphasized the importance of autonomous actions by local military officers, especially of the Guandong Army, others, such as Gavan McCormack, have preferred to view Japanese expansionism as a long-term process that preceded such unilateral military action. Louise Young's recent work leaves no doubt of the many sectors of society—especially the mass media—involved in whipping up mass support and even hysteria within Japan for the intervention in Manchuria. See James B. Crowley, *Japan's Quest for Autonomy: National Security and Foreign Policy, 1930–1938* (Princeton: Princeton University Press, 1966); McCormack, *Chang Tso-lin*; and L. Young, *Japan's Total Empire*.

76. Yamamuro, *Kimera*, 14–15.

77. Yamamuro, *Kimera*, 99–101.

78. Gavan McCormack, "Manchukuo: Vision, Plan, and Reality" (unpublished paper, 1987), 4, and Yamamuro, *Kimera*, 94–95.

79. Lincoln Li, *The China Factor in Modern Japanese Thought: The Case of Tachibana Shiraki, 1991–1945* (Albany: State University of New York Press, 1996), 17.

80. Li, *China Factor*, 104, and Yamamuro, *Kimera*, 113–17.

81. Li, *China Factor*, 13.

82. Li, *China Factor*, 46.

83. Ito Takeo, *Life along the South Manchurian Railway: The Memoirs of Ito Takeo*, trans. Joshua A. Fogel (Armonk, N.Y.: Sharpe, 1988), 118–20; Kenichiro Hirano, "The Japanese in Manchuria 1906–1931: A Study of the Historical Background of Manchukuo" (Ph.D. diss., Harvard University, 1983), 400–403; and Li, *China Factor*, 49.

84. McCormack, "Manchukuo: Vision, Plan, and Reality," 4.

85. Hirano, "Japanese in Manchuria," 407; Komagome, *Shokuminchi Teikoku Nippon no Bunka Tōgō*, 251–52; and Jones, *Manchuria since 1931*, 172–74. For biographical sketches of some of the military men and Yu Chonghan and details of provincial administrative reforms, see Suleski, *Civil Government in Warlord China*, 10–20.

86. *ZDLSG*, 304.

87. Mitter, *Manchurian Myth*, 95; Hirano, "Japanese in Manchuria," 403–4; Li, *China Factor*, 57.

88. Hirano, "Japanese in Manchuria," 419.

89. Mitter, *Manchurian Myth*, 102–110. See also Suleski, *Civil Government in Warlord China*, 193–201, for the extent to which the warlord government had been dependent on local control over county officials and elites for their activities.

90. Yasutomi Ayumu and Fukui Chie, *Manshū no kenryūtsūken* (Manchuria and county currencies) (paper submitted to *Ajia Keizai*, 2002).

91. Yamamuro, *Kimera*, 228. Scholars have speculated about why Pu Yi was subsequently made emperor. Actually, Pu Yi himself was quite disappointed at not having been made emperor in 1932. Many of his Chinese supporters, led by Prime Minister Zheng Xiaoxu, sought to reinstate him as emperor, but were opposed by other Chinese republican groups as well as the Youth Alliance and the *Daiyūhōkai*; see Hirano, "Japanese in Manchuria," 409, and Yamamuro, *Kimera*, 151. His instatement as emperor in 1934 was, according to Yamamuro, due to pressure from other colonial administrators to make his position more consistent with the Japanese imperial system and thereby facilitate greater Japanese control of Manchukuo; see Yamamuro, *Kimera*, 226–27.

92. *ZDLSG*, 277–280, and Jones, *Manchuria since 1931*, 41–42.

93. Jones, *Manchuria since 1931*, 26.

94. Janis Mimura, "From 'Manchukuo' to Japan's 'New Order': Bureaucratic Visions of a Totalitarian State" (unpublished paper, 1999), 11–15.

95. *ZDLSG*, 95–97, and Jones, *Manchuria since 1931*, 25.

96. *ZDLSG*, 100.

97. Hirano, "Japanese in Manchuria," 419–23, and Jones, *Manchuria since 1931*, 26.

98. Chianbu keisatsushi, *Kōmin*, 41.

99. Chianbu keisatsushi, *Kōmin*, 54–55.

100. The rural sector remained sluggish through the period.

101. Kungtu C. Sun with Ralph W Huenemann, *The Economic Development of Manchuria in the First Half of the Twentieth Century* (Cambridge, Mass.: East Asian Research Center, Harvard University, 1969), 101–2.

102. Young, *Japan's Total Empire*, 183–84, 213–15; Jones, *Manchuria since 1931*, 139.

103. Although at the height of the campaign to encourage rural settlement it was hoped that as many as five million Japanese settlers would migrate to Manchukuo by the mid-1940s, the rural settler population from Japan never did exceed 250,000. Potential settlers appeared to have a good enough idea of the harsh conditions of settlement among a hostile Chinese population who had often lost land to these alien settlers, and of the difficulties of learning a new terrain and climate while also engaging in military defense. Obviously, this knowledge was sufficient to dampen their enthusiasm for the whipped-up patriotic campaign to settle in Manchukuo; see Young, *Japan's Total Empire*.

104. Gottschang, "Economic Change, Disasters, and Migration," 465; Jones, *Manchuria since 1931*, 169–70.

105. Young, *Japan's Total Empire*, 240.

106. Ito, *Life along the South Manchurian Railway*, 134–51.

107. Sun, *Economic Development of Manchuria*, 76–78. Lattimore observed early in the regime that the Guandong Army's vision was not to have direct colonialism, but to create an "economic bloc." This demanded the ruthless subordination of the Manchurian economy "to forms that will supplement but not compete with the interests of Japan; but it also demands the suppression of interests in Japan which have a natural appetite for exploiting a region like Manchuria by extracting its wealth and transferring it to Japan"; see Lattimore, *Manchuria*, 306.

108. Ito, *Life along the South Manchurian Railway*, 152–55, and Jones, *Manchuria since 1931*, 145–47.

109. Sun, *Economic Development of Manchuria*, 80–81, and Jones, *Manchuria since 1931*, 146–48.

110. Jones, *Manchuria since 1931*, 148, and *ZDLSG*, 313–19.

111. See Sun, *Economic Development of Manchuria*, for figures.

112. Compare Jones, *Manchuria since 1931*, 157, with Sun, *Economic Development of Manchuria*, 82.

113. Jones, *Manchuria since 1931*, 139. Jones believes that the cost of war to the people in Manchukuo was perhaps comparable (though not more than) to that borne by the people in Japan themselves.

114. *ZDLSG*, 300–304, Myers, "Creating a Modern Enclave Economy," 158, 155.

115. *ZDLSG*, 131–38, 317–20.

116. Gavan McCormack, "Manchukuo: Constructing the Past," *East Asian History* 2 (December 1991): 122.

117. *ZDLSG*, 304.

118. McCormack, "Manchukuo: Constructing the Past," 119–20.

119. *ZDLSG*, 60–76, 190–210.

120. See Lee Chong-sik, *Revolutionary Struggle in Manchuria: Chinese Communism and Soviet Interest, 1922–1945* (Berkeley: University of California Press, 1983); Nishimura, *Chūgoku kindai tōhoku chiyushi kenkyū*; and McCormack, "Manchukuo: Constructing the Past."

121. *ZDLSG*, 160–74; Lee, *Revolutionary Struggle in Manchuria*, 271.

122. *ZDLSG*, 380–84.

123. Clausen and Thogersen, *Making of a Chinese City*, 120. The brutality and ruthlessness of the Japanese military is not in question, as it may be for the Japanese right wing. The nationalist lenses through which we have approached the understanding of this brutality is, however, quite limiting. There is often an assumption that these kinds of acts were a product of Japanese national character or something intrinsic to the Japanese. This is no more provable than it is for any other systematic act of violence by any people. Moreover, this kind of essentialist allegation tends only to reproduce the cycle of hostile or resentful nationalist consciousness, obscuring the will to see these acts of barbarism in cross-nationally discursive, political, and institutional terms.

124. Beginning around 1935 we see the decline of the plunder function and a rise in the developmental function. This is reversed in 1937, and once again there is a rise in the developmental function in 1939. With the Pacific War in 1941, the developmental function begins to decline steeply. See Nishimura Shigeo, "Research in Japan on the History of North-East China: Present State and Problems," trans. Gavan McCormack (unpublished manuscript, 1992), 10–14.

125. Foucault, "Political Technology of Individuals," 147.

126. Foucault, "Political Technology of Individuals," 160.

127. David Vance Tucker, "Building 'Our Manchukuo': Japanese City Planning, Architecture, and Nation-Building in Occupied Northeast China" (Ph.D. diss., University of Iowa, 1999), 27–28. Tucker believes the Manchukuo state was the "metaphorical precursor" for a "people that existed only in a metaphorical sense." See also David D. Buck, "Railway City and National Capital: Two Faces of the Modern in Changchun," in *Remaking the Chinese City: Modernity and National Identity, 1900–1950*, ed. Joseph Esherick (Honolulu: University of Hawaii Press, 2000); Jones, *Manchuria since 1931*, 54, 157, 207–13; and Lattimore, *Manchuria*, 260, 264.

128. Han, "Puppet Sovereignty," esp. chaps. 3 and 4.

129. Han, "Puppet Sovereignty," 10.

130. Han, "Puppet Sovereignty," 122–30.

131. See, for instance, the authorless and limited circulation publication entitled *Soren no minzoku seisaku* (Soviet nationality policy) (Shinkyō: Kenkoku Daigaku kenkyūin kan, 1940). In Tachibana's original plan for a national assembly, later rejected by the Guandong Army, the apportionment of seats was to follow the ratio: Han 7, Manchu 3, Korean 2, Muslim 2, Mongol 2, Japanese 7, and white (Russian) 1. However, a general principle of representation was maintained within the bureaucracy and for mobilization purposes; see Komagome, *Shokuminchi Teikoku Nippon no Bunka Tōgō*, 262.

132. Peattie, *Ishiwara Kanji*, 171, 174.

133. Cited in *ZDLSG*, 180; Jones, *Manchuria since 1931*, 50.

134. McCormack, "Manchukuo: Constructing the Past," 5.

135. *ZDLSG*, 177.

136. Tachibana, quoted in Yamamuro, *Kimera*, 115–16.

137. James Holston, "Alternative Modernities: Statecraft and Religious Imagination in the Valley of the Dawn," *American Ethnologist* 26 (August 1999): 605.

138. Fujiwara Kazuo, "Hoten ni okeru shokuba kōjō undō no genjō" (The circumstances of the workplace labor movement in Fengtian [Mukden]), *Kyōwa undo* 5 (September 1943), 43–47.

139. Manchukuo was recognized by Japan, El Salvador, the Vatican, Italy, Germany, Poland, Rumania, Bulgaria, Finland, Hungary, and Thailand; see Tucker, "Building 'Our Manchukuo,'" 93–94, n. 33.

140. Komagome, introduction to *Shokuminchi Teikoku Nippon no Bunka Tōgō*. Mariko Tamanoi has written a sensitive study of different Japanese identities in Manchukuo, including peasant immigrants, students, and officials; see "Knowledge, Power, and Racial Classifications: The 'Japanese' in 'Manchuria,'" *Journal of Asian Studies* 59 (May 2000): 248–76.

141. Yamamuro, *Kimera*, 279–80.

142. Han, "Puppet Sovereignty," 257–58; Young, *Japan's Total Empire*, 205, 211.

143. Young, *Japan's Total Empire*, 227.

144. For Komagome, Japanese nationalism was, as is well known, at the heart of its imperialism. At the same time, he is more aware than most other critics of the different possibilities in the Japanese political system and of its integrative tendencies, based on assimilation (*dōka*) by language and culture. But whenever the question of incorporating a colony appeared, the exclusionary principle of blood descent raised its head by inventing new forms of institutional, legal, or even attitudinal exclusion of non-Japanese in the empire. Imperial ideology made for a powerful and efficacious nationalism within what came to be thought of as the national core or inner territories (naichi) of Japan, but was unable to find sufficient cultural resources within to negate or transcend itself when this nationalism became expansionist in the outer territories (gaichi). Komagome thus wants to investigate the hypothesis that "in the history of imperial Japan's colonial domination of other people, the opportunity for the self-negation of nationalism carries within it a clarification of the deepening contradiction within this nationalism"; see *Shokuminchi Teikoku Nippon no Bunka Tōgō*, 8.

145. See Oguma Eiji, "The Green of the Willow, the Flower's Scarlet: Public Debate on the U.S. Exclusion Movement and the Colonization of Korea under the Japanese Empire," trans. Joseph Murphy (unpublished paper).

146. Matsusaka, *Making of Japanese Manchuria*, 393–95, 403.

147. *Soren no minzoku seisaku*, 1–2.

PART TWO

~

CIVILIZATION AND SOVEREIGNTY

CHAPTER THREE

Asianism and the New Discourse of Civilization

Since the Japanese have occupied Liaoning, the people have been terrified. Every day, the planes belonging to the other side (the Japanese) fly over the counties to conduct surveillance exercises. The noise is deafening and makes the people still more afraid. Further, since the merchant militias and police have surrendered, bandits have arisen and occupied the railroads and stations, disrupting communications. The other side has posted notices announcing that they sent their army because our government officials had exploited and harmed the people. They say that if we honestly obey their benevolent government, it will be fine. Although they will continue armed activities, they will not harm the merchants and the people. This has pacified the people a bit.

In each place they have taken over the fine buildings. Since ours is old and decrepit, it has not been occupied, and as they have not entered the interior, the spirit of Laozi (*Laozi zhi ling*) is as it was before. We dare not stop our work. Yesterday, we provided relief to over 250 refugees who had come up the river. This time it was fine, but whether or not we will be able to continue our work without harassment in the future is still unknown.

—*Shijie Hongwanzihui Zhonghua zonghui dangan,*
September 29, 1931

So reported an anxious follower of the *Hongwanzihui* (Red Swastika Society) to his superiors in Beiping in the immediate aftermath of the Manchurian Incident in September 1931. Another report from the same branch says,

Before we were able to devise a plan for relief work in the war areas, the enemy had already assembled the gentry and the professions. The city government called a meeting of all the groups (*jie*) in the localities regarding the mobilization of relief funds and efforts. The moneys were determined by discussion among the groups and the leadership of each group bore the responsibility.

Again, the report ends with the fear that good charitable organizations might have to stop their independent activities.[1] These reports speak to many issues: the terrors of war, the constant threat to noncooperation with bombers close at hand, the desertion by existing authorities, the early start of corporatist organizing, the mobilization of the elite, and, not least, the concerns of our reporters. I am particularly struck by their twin concerns about the ability to continue the work of public salvation and the possible desecration of the spirit of Laozi, which animated all their activities.

Our reporters, it turned out, did not need to worry overly much about the survival of their society. Apparently around the same time, a rumor began to circulate among the Society's members and others that Laozi had prophesied the Incident as a new beginning. After what had been a disastrous period for these societies with the KMT's Northern Expedition, the launching of the antisuperstitious movement, and the ban on most "redemptive societies" between 1928 and 1931 (detailed below), many among them were prepared to welcome a new beginning.[2] Whatever the actual details of the fit, it was, as Takizawa Toshihiro pointed out, an unexpected and timely opportunity for the Japanese to garner support from these popular elements. Tachibana was prepared to seize it. The opening salvo of his volume on Daoism opposed the view of Christian missionaries that "there is no religion in China," declaring, "the Chinese nationality is a religious nationality."[3] The Japanese not only permitted organizations such as the Red Swastika or the Morality Society to continue their work, they emerged stronger after Manchukuo and the Japanese occupation of the mainland than they had ever been. They were at the forefront of relief work after the Nanjing massacre in 1937, and the Red Swastika Society in particular became the largest welfare organization in Shanghai during the transitional years 1945 to 1949. The religious passion informing their work has eluded many historians, but the Japanese-backed regime not only recognized it, they utilized it to the hilt.

While the Red Swastika Society cadres may have been concerned about their work of salvation, their mission would come to be folded into a discourse of civilization. Although the new regime was bent on modernization to secure its goals, the rhetoric of tradition and Eastern civilization was the most important means to secure local allies and sovereignty claims. "The Government derives its authority from Heaven, as mirrored in the Popular Will. . . . The essence of the Wang-tao Government exists in the realization of ideal government based on theocracy (the Unity of Gods and Man)" declared Prince Konoye, adapting Mencian ideas of Heaven's mandate.[4] Ishiwara had proclaimed the "righteous duty" (*seigi, zhengyi*) to save the East, and Tachibana had spoken of "Asian essence." They all recognized the power of the old cultural universe in the establishment of the new polity. The Manchukuo regime was forced, by the circumstance of being an imperialist power in a national form, to exaggerate the transnational, civilizational source of its ideals. But it is precisely this exaggeration that reveals to us the importance of civilizational discourse in the sovereignty claims of anti-imperialist nationalism generally.

A Genealogy of Civilization

It is perhaps not difficult to understand why the Manchukuo regime sought to transform older, but living, cultural ideals and processes into symbols of civilizational authenticity. As custodians (and interpreters) of this authenticity, it could claim sovereignty vis-à-vis the outside world while building alliances within and deploying "civilizational" groups to consolidate state and regime power. But why and how ideas of civilization developed a salience and authorizing power at this time requires understanding in a wider, global framework.

Like all social concepts, "civilization" has varied with time and place, and I can only define it minimally, as expressive of the relationship of Self to Other—particularly a relationship in which the civilized Self embodies the ideals of a macrosocietal order. Here I will undertake to reveal the salient differences, ultimately relevant to Manchukuo and East Asia, that emerged over the last century or so.

The relationship between nations and civilizations transformed sometime during or at the end of World War I. From the mid-nineteenth century until that time, the signifier Civilization had become established as a singular and universal phenomenon in much of the world. I capitalize the term in order to specify the European Enlightenment conception of civilization. During much of the nineteenth century, Western imperial nations invoked the signifier to justify their conquest as a civilizing mission. Whole continents were subjugated and held in thrall because they were not constituted as civilized nations (to be a nation was to be civilized, and vice versa). Of course, the idea that there were civilizations other than that of Europe or Christendom had been around from at least the late eighteenth century, but during the nineteenth century the singular conception of Civilization, based originally upon Christian and Enlightenment values, came not only to be dominant but to be the criterion whereby sovereignty could be claimed in the world. In this way, it also became clear that to be a nation was to belong to a higher, authorizing order of civilization.[5]

Arising in the context of European domination of the non-Western world, this conception could be specifically found in the legal language of various "unequal treaties" and its interpretation by the international lawyers of the time. At an explicit level, the term Civilization in these treaties and interpretations referred principally to the ability and willingness of states to protect life, property, and freedoms as rights (particularly for foreigners), but this usage necessarily also presupposed and demanded the institutions, goals, values, and practices of the modern European state, ranging from the pursuit of material progress to Civilized manners and clothing. By the late nineteenth century, international law and its standard of civilization became increasingly positivist, and reflected the social Darwinist conception that certain races were more civilized than others. While a hierarchy of races with different capacities to achieve civilization seemed natural, it should be noted that the notion of Civilization did not theoretically preclude the ability of a "race" to become civilized.[6]

At the same time, an alternative view of civilization—the beginnings of what Lucien Febvre called "the ethnographic conception"—had emerged in Europe of the 1820s and '30s, particularly in the ideas of Herder and Alexander von Humboldt.[7] During the latter half of the nineteenth century, this Germanic counter-evolutionary strain coexisted with several other discourses within the penumbra of the hegemonic conception of Civilization. Most significant among these discourses in Asia were the older imperial Chinese conception of *wenming*; the Christian, and particularly Jesuit, valorization of Chinese civilization; the tradition of Orientalist scholarship of Sir William Jones and others in Bengal; and the world Buddhist revival.[8] Douglas Howland has elegaically documented the death of the imperial Chinese notion of the civilized world, or *wenming*, when the exchanges between Chinese and Japanese diplomats conducted through "brush-talk"—signifying mastery, and thereby affirmation, of the world of the written character—became evidently irrelevant to the Japanese and the world around them. Nonetheless, even as Fukuzawa Yukichi was exhorting Japan to escape from Asia (*Datsua*) and become Civilized, both Japanese and Chinese were reworking vestigial expressions of the old Chinese notions of common civilization (*tongwen/dōbun, tongjiao/dōkyō*) and improvising upon these ideas under the influence of contemporary social Darwinism, as seen in the neologism *tongzhong/dōshu,* or common race.[9] While these efforts at the turn of the century may have been intended to create an alternative East Asian civilization, they were still closely associated with the European ideas underlying Civilization. At any rate they did not make much headway.

Also relevant to the transformation of the conception of civilization was the idea of a world religion. Heinz Bechert has identified the emergence of "Buddhist modernism" in the last quarter of the nineteenth century, beginning with the Christian–Buddhist debates in Sri Lanka, the initiatives taken by Sri Lankan Buddhists and their Western supporters in the Theosophical Society, and the forging of international links between Buddhists in Sri Lanka, Japan, and the West. Indeed, Sri Lankans and Japanese Buddhist thinkers have remained in the forefront of contributions to contemporary Buddhist thought.[10] James Ketelaar has demonstrated how Japanese Buddhism could survive the persecution of a new Shinto national cult during the Meiji period only by refashioning itself as a world religion. In all of these cases, the end product resembled much less any particular or lived experience of Buddhism or Hinduism than an abstract, rationalized, modernized, and, perhaps most of all, Christianized body of thought that served to represent the core of another civilization. Central to this development was the 1893 Chicago Congress of World Religions, in which these traditions first gained publicity—indeed, were publicly produced as world religions.[11]

By the time of World War I, the German counter-evolutionary intellectual tradition produced what may have been the most important statement of the new conception of civilization, Oswald Spengler's *Decline of the West.* Ironically, if not unexpectedly, Spengler does not refer to the entities of his world history as civilizations, but as Cultures, or *Kultur.* This is because he reserves the term civilization for the final, frozen stage of a dynamic, evolving Culture.[12] For our purposes, his cultures are equivalent to what we have been calling the alternative conception of civilization: multiple, spiritual, and—as the highest expression of a people's achievements, virtues, and authenticity—authorizing. At the moment of German defeat in war, the Germanic notion of *Kultur* gained a significant victory over the notion of a universal Civilization that measured value only according to certain Western standards of progress.

The triumph of the alternative civilization must be grasped in relation to that other triumph of the world system of nation-states and nationalism as a global ideology, which ironically required the conception of a transcendent civilization. But Spengler's notions are important partly because they were very influential in global discourse (relayed to the English speaking world by Arnold Toynbee) and thus constructive of this new discourse of civilization. They clarified the inchoate shapes that had hovered in the penumbra of Civilization. Moreover, I believe it is important to recognize that the new discourse of civilization—especially Eastern civilization—was affirmed in the West before it was confirmed in Asia. In this sense too, civilization remains a postcolonial concept.

In his sweeping vision of the new world history, Spengler lays out the basic features that have endured in our understanding of civilization to this day. First is the critique of linear history based on the ancient-medieval-modern division, which rigs the stage to make the rest of the world turn around the "little part-world" that is Europe.[13] In its place, Spengler traces many mighty Cultures developing upon the model of organisms, each undergoing its own temporal cycle of rise and decline in isolation from the others. Spengler not only presents Cultures as autochthonous, but by distinguishing the new history from science, he also confirms the irreducible authority of Culture/civilization.

For Spengler, each Culture is a fundamentally spiritual or ideal phenomenon, authoritatively distinct from other Cultures. This ideational quality would become, or perhaps already reflected, the most salient characteristic of the new conception of civilization. Ideas of Eastern versus Western civilizations, which increasingly accompanied the Great War, were premised upon this ideal of civilizational spirituality. In the West, the most influential scholar to propagate and develop these ideas was Arnold Toynbee. In the course of over forty years (1920s–1960s) he wrote the twelve volumes of *A Study of World History*, which broke with the vestigial progressivist vision of (essentially Western) civilization.[14] But perhaps most significant was Toynbee's conception of the role of religion in civilizations. In contrast to Gibbon and others who often associated Christianity with barbarism as the destroyer of Civilization, Toynbee, in his earlier volumes, already viewed religion as a kind of aid to civilization, as a chrysalis that preserved features of an older civilization. By the 1940s, he began to see the rise and fall of civilizations as subsidiary to the growth of religion.[15] In the final years of his life, Toynbee was drawn to ideas of a common global civilization originating in the technological achievements of the West, but spiritually regenerated by the major world civilizations. It is not surprising to find his ideas fall on fertile ground in Japan, where he was accepted as a major public thinker and conducted a series of dialogues with the leader of the Sōka Gakkai, a new religion nourished precisely on such ideas of the blending of Eastern and Western civilizations.[16]

What were the conditions for the emergence of this view of civilization? It surfaced in tandem with the disillusionment the Great War wrought on the idea of the "civilizing mission." "The nature of the battle on the Western Front made a mockery of the European conceit that discovery and invention were necessarily progressive and beneficial to humanity," writes Michael Adas.[17] Writer after writer denounced the materialism and destructiveness of Western Civilization. At the same time, the wider political forces produced by the end of the war and the new balance of power, namely, the beginnings of decolonization, the emergence of new nation-states, and the concomitant ascendancy of the ideology of anti-imperialism, found little use for Civilization. To many in these nascent movements, Civilization was increasingly seen not only as compatible with but as having furnished the moral ground for imperialism and war. The final triumph of nationalism or national self-determination over imperialism as the hegemonic global ideology was clinched by two political developments: the Soviet revolution and Woodrow Wilson's advocacy of the right to national self-determination in the aftermath of World War I.[18]

The philosophy of Spengler and Toynbee reflected the world as a newly unified theater of history.[19] Spengler's insistence on seeing Europe as just a bit player in the history of humanity (rather than its telos) was well suited to a changing world where other actors (nations) had learned the language through which they could demand to be heard. Not only were new nations beginning to emerge all over the world from the early part of the century, they were telling their histories in the same linear mode of emergent national subjects fathered by classical civilizations. To be sure, the new civilizational discourse was part and parcel of the challenge to the hegemons of global competition, but this is not all. Since nationalism was genetically linked to a moral universalism greater than itself, civilization would serve as an ultimate rationale for the sovereignty of these nations, just as it had for imperialist nations.

While nations saw themselves as deeply linked to civilizations, the territorial nation-states were not coextensive with these civilizations. Indeed, nations require this duality because they often need to move between the nationalist and civilizational positions. New nations, like old ones, seek the transnational conception of civilization because it is only as a transterritorial, universal ideal—say, Islam or Confucianism—with its potential to reveal the truth of the human condition and embrace all of humanity, that the (civilizational) Self can achieve recognition from the Other. At the heart of the critique of Civilization launched by both Western and non-Western intellectuals after the Great War was the universalizing promise of the "civilizing mission," which exemplified the desire not (simply) to conquer the Other, but to be desired by the Other. In this critique, Civilization had forfeited the right to represent the highest goals or ultimate values of humanity and was no longer worthy of being desired, or even recognized, by the Other. In so opposing the legally articulated notion of the good and valuable posed by Civilization, the alternative civilizational self had to counterpose a still higher good and a truth that was authentically universal. One might say that the transcendent authority of civilization derives from this dialectic.

Note here the close relationship, indeed mirroring, by civilization of the older Western conception of Civilization. The spiritual, moral, and universal core of civilizations furnishes new nations with the same kind of authenticating and authorizing function that Civilization furnished for Western imperialist nations and, as such, the similarity represents the "recognition function" of the global circulatory process. Note further that the gap between the territorial nation and civilization is not only territorial, but principled. Because the spiritual impulse of a civilization tends to be universalizing, national boundaries are ultimately artificial and limiting. The transcendent stance of civilization thus may permit a critique of the nation and, as we shall see, produce the problem of loyalties divided between the nation and civilization.

At the same time, there is no doubt that the territorial nation-state seeks to equate itself with or otherwise appropriate civilization. As the masthead in the regime of authenticity, where the noble virtues of civilization identify the abiding subject of a changing national history, civilization becomes the means of exercising national hegemony both within and without. One might argue that for nations such as China or India, just as for France or England, one can stretch the nation to fit the civilization—territorially, if not in principle. But how can smaller nations do so? I believe there are several narrative strategies within national historiography that can be deployed by nations to enable them to be the true representative or the leader of, if not equivalent to, a certain civilizational tradition. The most powerful of these, at least in terms of its impact on the domestic population, was the Japanese claim to have inherited the leadership of Asian civilization because of its success in mastering Western Civilization. Lee Kuan-yew of Singapore made a similar bid for leadership in Confucianism and Asian values more generally. One can think of how Sri Lankan intellectuals went about constructing a Buddhist civilization in a way that made their nation the leader of such a project. Consider also the promotion of pre-Columbian civilizations among the relevant Latin American nations or pre-Islamic civilizations among Middle Eastern nations. Civilization in the era of nation-states thus needs to both transcend and serve the territorial nation.

The duality between the national and transnational orientation of civilization is closely related to another ambiguity in the term: civilization as an achieved *state* and as a civilizing *process*. Norbert Elias pointed this out most effectively in contrasting the civilizing process as an unselfconscious process emanating from the court before it was transformed into a "concept" of national achievement and superiority in the nineteenth century. In Elias's view, the bourgeois classes of France and Germany championed this reified version of *civilisation* and *Kultur* when they articulated their role as leaders of these competing nations. Given the thrust, timing, and reference points of Elias's work, the reader may well be led to believe that this transmutation of civilization had much to do with the European wars that enveloped the world in the twentieth century.[20]

Thus, the new civilization opposes the Civilization of imperialism, but also depends on it in the way that it authorizes this opposition for nations. This is most evident in the way the new civilization selects elements and themes from its history and reconstructs them in a narrative that will enable it to perform this authorizing function. The basic approach involves establishing equivalence by identifying elements that are both identical to and the binary opposites of the constituents of Civilization. One strategy is to discover elements identical to Civilized society within the suppressed traditions of civilization: Confucian rationality, Buddhist humanism, Hindu logic, and so forth. The other strategy finds the opposite of the West in Asian civilizations, which are, for instance, peaceful as opposed to warlike, spiritual as opposed to material, ethical as opposed to decadent, natural as opposed to rational, timeless as opposed to temporal. Finally, the nation authorizes its opposition to imperialist Civilization by synthesizing or harmonizing the binaries after the equivalence has been established. Thus Western materialism will be balanced by Eastern spirituality, and modernity redeemed. Indeed, because the categories of civilization have to be translated into the new lexicon of modernity they are more meaningful to a contemporary sensibility than to the historical society they allegedly represent. In these ways, civilization is always remade in reference to Civilization. Contemporary analysts such as Samuel Huntington, whose notion of civilization presents relatively open historical formations as pure and closed ancient continuities, are, like contemporary nationalists, reifying a relatively recent construction.

Asian Civilization in Japan and China

The story of how non-Western societies, beginning with Japan, began to overhaul their entire society and cosmology in an effort to become Civilized and sovereign is a well-known one. The Meiji period represented the height of the effort to make Japan a Civilized nation in the name of *bunmei kaika* (Civilization and enlightenment). It is worth reiterating, however, that the roughly ten-year period—between 1894, when it signed the Aoki–Kimberley treaty with Great Britain, and the end of the Russo-Japanese War in 1905—during which Japan succeeded in reversing the unequal treaties and began to gain access to "Civilized society" was a period bounded by its two successful modern wars.[21] For equally well-known reasons detailed in histories of the modernization of China, it took nearly fifty more years for China to have its unequal treaties finally abrogated in 1943 and be granted Civilized status. Indeed, the European conception of Civilization did not penetrate Chinese discourses until the turn of the century.

The great reformer Liang Qichao was perhaps the most influential advocate of the necessity for China to become Civilized. Liang was most definitely aware of the legal dimensions of Civilization and sought to make China into a Civilized legal nation even before his exile in Japan upon the failure of the 1898 reforms. However, he acquired a fuller understanding of Civilization in Japan, where, influenced by the writings of Fukuzawa Yukichi and Katō Hiroyuki, among others, he perceived its significance in relation to the new ideas of History and progress. Nothing could have been further from the Confucian notion of *wenming* when he wrote, "Competition is the mother of Civilization."[22] Through the writings of Liang and others, Civilization became, in the words of Ishikawa Yoshihiro, a keyword in Chinese intellectual discourse by the first decade of the new century, as essays on topics such as a civilized revolution, civilized drama, and civilized races began to appear among the modern reading community.[23] Beginning with the late Qing reforms at the turn of the century (1902), and certainly by the Republican revolution of 1911, the Chinese regimes tried strenuously to make Chinese laws fully compatible with the general expectation of Civilized countries through, for instance, the Revised Law Codification Commission. But because the political situation was beyond real control, these regimes could not implement the kind of legal and political system that, according to the 1926 Commission on Extraterritoriality in China, would make it a Civilized nation.[24]

Even as the regimes in both countries embraced the standard of Civilization in order to become fully sovereign, this embrace by no means excluded the development of alternative conceptions of civilization, which, as we have seen, burgeoned particularly during World War I. For instance, Zhang Binglin and his admirer Lu Xun quickly saw through the universalist pretensions of Civilization when it was being fervently propagated in the early 1900s. In Japan the notion of an alternate civilization centered around the concept of Asia. Although it was a conception that the Japanese inherited from the Europeans only in the nineteenth century, it became a powerful if changing spatial representation in relation to which Japanese identity came to be repeatedly made and remade.[25] Among the sharpest critics of Civilization was Okakura Tenshin, who early on perceived the critical link between warfare and Civilization in Japan. Among the first bilingual and bicultural thinkers in Meiji Japan, Okakura was able to gain some distance from the frenzied effort to "escape Asia" in Japan and build upon emergent Western ideas of an alternative Asian civilization. The case of Okakura is indicative of the extent to which the rediscovery or production of an alternative Asian civilization entailed a deep familiarity with European modes of constructing the idea of a civilization. Indeed, Okakura's conversion to Asian civilization came during his first voyage to Europe, which turned out to be a voyage of self-discovery. To be sure, he was aware of differences between Asian civilizations, but he believed that they all differed from Western Civilization in principle—in their promotion of peace and beauty. Okakura saw Japan as the exhibition hall of all these Asian civilizations but did not advocate what would become commonplace in the aftermath of the Russo-Japanese War: that Japan become the leader of an Asian federation because it could harmonize the best of Asian civilization with that of Civilization. Rather, he urged the various Asian nations to look within their common traditions to produce an alternative to the aggressive and dominating Civilization of the West.[26]

As Hashikawa Bunso has revealed, pan-Asianism in Japan contained both of these trends: the solidarity-oriented, nondominating conception of Japan's role in reviving Asia, and the notion of Japan as what we might call the harmonizing or synthesizing leader. Pan-Asianism in Japan both fed and resisted the nascent imperialism of that nation.[27] Increasingly after the Russo-Japanese War, however, the view that Japan was the only Asian nation capable of rescuing Asia and harmonizing Eastern and Western civilizations began to take hold. This, then, became the characteristic Japanese response to the aporia of nationalism: to absorb civilization within the confines of the nation and to yet maintain its transcendence so it may continue to perform the authorizing function. Because it belonged to Asia, the Japanese nation could bring to modernity the timeless essence of Asia, and because it had mastered Western Civilization, it could bring material modernity to Asia. Popular educational journals from the 1910s reveal the production of this sense of belonging; they depict the peoples of Asia as having close cultural and racial ties with the Japanese but as being without nation-states or a sense of peoplehood. The message was clear: given the danger of Western colonization, it was imperative for Japan, as their leader, to bring them into the modern era without destroying their traditions. What is remarkable is how the idea of the closeness or intimacy with Asians—the eternal Asians—in the Japanese imagination was produced so rapidly during the 1910s. Indeed, the language of the Twenty-one Demands made upon the Chinese government in 1915 reflected this narrative.[28] It was a compelling narrative precisely because it made the familial relationship between Asian peoples appear so natural. It compelled an entire nation to pursue its destiny in Asia.

Another, more aggressive ideology based upon the confrontation of Eastern and Western civilizations appeared in the immediate post–World War I era. Fueled by the American racial exclusions of Chinese and Japanese, this ideology would reappear during the Pacific War as the theater of an East–West showdown. The tendency was best represented by the thinker Ōkawa Shūmei, and later by Ishiwara Kanji in Manchuria. Ōkawa (1886–1957), an activist, writer, student of Indian philosophy, and translator of the Koran, was significantly influenced by Okakura. Like the latter, Ōkawa saw an underlying unity among the different Asian societies—a spiritual, moral, and timeless essence—which he opposed to Western civilization. Unlike Okakura, however, Ōkawa did not believe in the value of peace and viewed history in Civilizational terms, as progress born out of conflict and war—most centrally, war between Asia and the West. The ultimate victory of Asia over the West would be led by Japan's victory over America, which would liberate Asia from the enslavement of Western colonialism, and which was Japan's moral duty despite the ingratitude of the Asian peoples. But the first task for Ōkawa was to combat the corruption and obstacles that he encountered in the Taishō state. He was implicated in several terrorist incidents, including one in which Prime Minster Inukai was assassinated.[29]

In 1920, various Japanese pan-Asianist groups, including those associated with the *Ōmotokyō* (discussed below), had sought to establish in northeast Asia their ideal polity, which was in some ways the blueprint for Manchukuo. The Japanese involved in this enterprise were stalwart Asianists from the 1911 Chinese revolution, like Suenaga Misao of the Genyōsha and far right political groups like the Black Dragon Society of Uchida Ryōhei. In alliance with disaffected Korean elites, the Japanese Asianists sought to create their own utopian, anti-Western polity called the Koryo (*Gaoli*) nation in the Jiandao region between Manchuria and Korea, which had been the heartland of the ancient Koguryo state. Several circumstances converged to produce this movement. The evacuation of the Russian presence in northeast Asia following the Soviet revolution allowed the expansion of Japanese power into the region. The erstwhile *yangban*—the Confucian elite—were disaffected because of their displacement by Japanese policies. About one million laboring Koreans in the Jiandao region of Manchuria were rendered vulnerable by their stateless condition. Finally, American immigration policies sparked off renewed anti-Western sentiments.

To create this utopian nation Uchida's group joined with nativist Korean societies in an alliance named Isshinkai. They even formulated a constitution,[30] in which Confucianism was to be the national religion; property was to be owned collectively; land was to be distributed according to the ancient Chinese well-field system; the system of governance was to be *wuwei* (noninterventionist) and its goal *Datong* (the Great Unity). Citizenship among Koreans, Japanese, Chinese, and Asian Russians was to be exercised without discrimination on the basis of ethnicity or race. If we are to believe the proclamations, the doctrine of equality was of particular significance because the Isshinkai was opposed to the Japanese state policies in Korea and viewed the annexation as an imperialist act that denied the equality of Asian peoples. Thus the Isshinkai's ideology contained elements of a return to East Asian traditions, self-consciously embedding an opposition to the modern Western or Westernized state; at the same time, it proclaimed modern notions of republicanism and equality. In these ways it prefigured some of the theoretically radical ideas of Manchukuo (1932–1945), such as that of Concordia. While we cannot but see the Isshinkai movement as an effort to expand Japanese (albeit nonstate) power on the mainland, at the same time we also see how the new *ideology* of civilization, with its roots in the utopian egalitarianism of nationalism, shaped the movement and its projected political forms.

In China the new civilizational discourse and its links to pan-Asianism have been largely neglected or dismissed in the historiography precisely because of their association with Japanese imperialism. However, from 1911 until 1945 the discourse of Eastern civilization, whether as superior to Western civilization or as necessary to redeem the latter, actually flourished in China as an intellectual, cultural, and social movement. To what extent Eastern civilization could be distinguished from Chinese civilization was a subject both of debate and of ambivalence. The ambivalence mirrored the structural ambiguity in the relationship between nationalism and civilization noted above. While the (Chinese) nationalist impulse sought to conflate civilization with the territorial nation, the spiritual impulses sustaining the formulation of civilization tended to seek a universal sphere of application, viewing national

boundaries as artificial walls. To some degree, as we shall see, the modern intellectu-
alist construction of civilization tended towards the conflation, whereas the more
popular social movements tended to view civilization transnationally.

Ishikawa has persuasively argued that the development of East–West civilizational
discourse among Chinese intellectuals during the 1910s was closely connected to
that in Japan, even though it would take distinctive shape in China. Through the
1910s and early 1920s, Japan continued to be the principal lens through which Chinese gained modern knowledge, and there was a steady influx of Japanese books and
magazines together with a continuing growth of translations from the Japanese.[31]
The new civilizational discourse also entered through the same routes and brought
with it the particular assumptions upon which it had been constructed or reconstructed in Japan: the geographical and environmental bases of civilizational differences, the role of linear progressive history, the binary construction, the synthesis
formulation, and the redemptive character of Eastern civilization, among others.

One of the more important Japanese influences on Chinese thinkers during
World War I was the middle-brow Japanese writer Kayahara Kazan (1880–1951).
He was popular with Chinese intellectuals because his Japanese writing was relatively
lucid and simple. Kayahara's philosophy sought to synthesize the thought of various
Western philosophers such as Hegel, Bergson, and Emerson, as well as the geographical determinism of Henry Buckle and Ratzel. Kayahara delineated his own stages of
civilization, posited the distinction between the dynamic northern civilizations of
the Europeans and the quiescent southern civilizations, and explained these in terms
of geography and environment. Like other Taishō intellectuals he arrived at the
necessity of synthesizing the two civilizations.[32] Kayahara's impact on Chinese intellectuals was considerable; one Communist Party member even wrote to Mao, urging
him to fulfill the world historical tasks of Lenin and Kayahara. Li Dazhao, founder
of the Communist Party and librarian at Beijing University, collected a large number of contemporary Japanese magazines that included the writings of Kayahara,
whose stamp is evident particularly in Li's *Spring Youth,* which is centrally concerned
with the renewal of ancient civilizations such as those of China and India. Although
Li was perfectly aware of Japanese expansionist designs embedded in these ideas,
Kayahara appears to have influenced his conception of history and his particular
mode of synthesizing East and West to create a new civilization in the aftermath of
the world war.[33] Incidentally, Li Dazhao believed that the Russian revolution also
derived its world significance from Russia's intermediate geographical and civilizational location and resultant ability to mediate between East and West.[34]

Another important channel for the introduction of civilizational discourse was
the popular Chinese journal *Dongfangzazhi* (Eastern miscellany). Its editor, Du
Yaquan, was a tireless promoter of the idea of the superiority of the still or quiet
civilization of the East, which was obliged to rescue the world from the restless civilization of the West, responsible for the terrible violence of the world war. The editorial essays of the journal frequently dwelt on this theme, especially towards the end
of the war, and the journal often translated Japanese essays on the problem. In 1919,

Dongfangzazhi published a translation of a Japanese article on the Chinese Spirit and the European Spirit. Ishikawa has followed the chain of writing from an alienated, diasporic Chinese, via Europe and Japan, back to China. The article discussed two essays translated from English into German by Gu Hongming, the Malay-born, British- and German-educated, classical Chinese scholar. One of Gu's essays was entitled, "Reasons for China's Opposition to European Concepts," and the Japanese article reported the reception of his essay by a group of disaffected German intellectuals.[35] In China the *Dongfangzazhi* essay led to a major debate on the question of Chinese civilization versus Western civilization, in which the giants of Chinese intellectual life, including Li Dazhao, Liang Qichao, Liang Shuming, Hu Shi, Feng Youlan, Chen Duxiu, Zhang Dongsun, and others took a position. Thus the new discourse of Chinese civilization entered China through a complex global loop. This route underscores not only the emergence of a global intellectual sphere, but how the acceptability of civilization was dependent upon its recognition by the Other.[36]

The debate in China was framed in terms of whether China's—and more broadly, Eastern—traditional civilization could redeem the West. Some, like Liang Shuming, believed in the superiority of Chinese civilization; others, such as Li Dazhao and Du Yaquan, favored a synthesis, though in different ways; and the mainstream of radical intellectuals rejected the value of Chinese civilization. Nonetheless, the debate underscored certain common assumptions: that the differences between East and West were civilizational, and that such differences posited holistic, isolated, and pure civilizations. This was assumed even when thinkers called for the synthesis of the best qualities of the two. Since the ideas of these intellectuals are well known, I shall not dwell on them. By the mid-1920s, however, the discourse began to appear in cultural, political, and social practices as well.[37]

Perhaps the least studied and the most successful realm in which the idea of an Eastern civilization was constructed was culture. We have a rough idea of how the notion of an essentialized Eastern civilization was constructed by interactions during the 1920s between Chinese intellectuals and a host of Western philosophers, such as Bertrand Russell, John Dewey, Henri Bergson, Rudolph Eucken, Irving Babbit, and the Indian poet Rabindranath Tagore. Emerging research in a wide range of cultural practices reveals that perhaps more significant were the Sino-Japanese exchanges in areas such as the revival or reconstruction of traditional medicine, the reconstructions of Buddhism and Confucianism, and the representation of literati and Buddhist art (among other kinds) as exemplary of Eastern civilization.[38] Developed with reference to modern Western forms, in that their significance emerged either in opposition to or as a prefiguration of the latter, these practices exemplified the East Asian modern.

The political moment of Eastern civilization in China is associated with the famous lecture by Sun Yat-sen in December 1924 in Kobe, Japan, entitled "Greater Asianism" (*Da Yaxiyazhuyi*). I have discussed this lecture elsewhere, so I will only note that its significance has often been minimized in the historical scholarship, perhaps because of the later record of Japanese actions in China. Yet Sun seems to have absorbed the Asian civilizational discourse quite deeply and spelled out its key political category of *wangdao,* or the way of the ethical monarchs and peaceful rulership—as opposed to the unethical and violent way (*badao*) of the hegemon (the way of the West). Sun was rhetorically skillful at drawing the Japanese into a discourse of solidarity while simultaneously retaining a Chinese centrality by invoking the imperial Chinese tribute system. *Wangdao* was based upon the recognition of the Chinese emperor through the hierarchical system of reciprocities of the tribute. Thus Sun appealed to the Japanese to renounce the Western methods of *badao* and return to the Asian method of peaceful solidarity. As we have seen, the Japanese military appropriated the language of *wangdao* and used it to rule China instead. The political interest in pan-Asianism in China is also indicated by the convening of two successive Asian People's conferences, in Nagasaki (1926) and Shanghai (1927). Yet these conferences hardly demonstrated much solidarity, because the Chinese and Korean delegates understandably used the forum to argue that the condition for Asian unity must be Japanese renunciation of imperialism.[39]

In any event, Sun's discourse of civilization developed in two directions that exemplify nationalism's dual relationship to the idea of civilization. On the one hand, by the 1930s the KMT actively propagated the binary of East and West, perhaps best expressed in the New Life movement, through which it sought to revitalize Western material modernity by means of an ascetic Confucian spirituality and morality. Chen Lifu, the theorist of the New Life movement, made a classic statement of the East–West synthesis. Creatively employing the framework of evolutionism, Chen outlined a parallel material and spiritual evolutionism. Without spiritual progress, the evolution of material civilization would inevitably lead to the enslavement of mankind by things. The role of the New Life movement was to infuse the moral qualities from the essence of Chinese civilization into the evolution of material life. Thus will history be propelled into the civilizational ideal of *Datong,* or the Great Unity.[40]

Note, however, that Chen's civilization is uniquely a Chinese civilization; it represents that aspect of the new doctrine of civilization that becomes tied to the nation-state. But for several reasons the KMT's equation of civilization and nationalism could not always work, even for its own statist purposes. Sun Yat-sen's conception of a pan-Asianism was also centered on Confucian virtues of the kingly way, but unlike Chen he saw these ethical and moral goals as more fully Asian. This strand of thought in the KMT was picked up by another leading KMT theorist and leader, Dai Jitao, who in 1930 created an institute and the journal *Xin Yaxiya* (New Asia) to keep alive Sun's ideas. The publication well expressed the tensions of the new civilizational discourse in its mission both to counter European materialist and imperialist civilization and to create a pan-Asianist ideology. An important function of this Asianism was to secure the allegiance of the minority populations who occupied the vast hinterland over which the nation-state sought to exercise its sovereignty. The rhetoric of Asian brotherhood was one of the civilizational narratives transcending the racial or ethnic nation that Chinese nationalists developed in order to integrate the populations of these vast outlying regions (constituting over half the present Chinese territory) into the Chinese nation.

Redemptive Societies and Civilizational Discourse

In order to see how the Japanese mobilized the discourse of eastern civilization to gain political support, we need to grasp the political history of the redemptive societies in China. Some of the more famous of these societies were the *Daodehui* (Morality Society); the *Daoyuan* (Society of the Way) and its philanthropic wing, the *Hongwanzihui* (Red Swastika Society); the *Tongshanshe* (Fellowship of Goodness); the *Zailijiao* (The Teaching of the Abiding Principle); the *Shijie Zongjiao Datonghui* (Society for the Great Unity of World Religions), first organized in Sichuan in 1915 as the *Wushanshe*; and the *Yiguandao* (Way of Pervading Unity). There were many others. A great deal of our knowledge of the contemporary spread of these societies comes from Japanese surveys of religious and charitable societies in China conducted in the 1930s and 1940s. According to Japanese researchers and officials of the puppet administrations in north China, these societies claimed to command enormous followings. The Fellowship of Goodness claimed a following of 30 million in 1929, and the Red Swastika Society a following of 7 to 10 million in 1937.[41] There are also some notable Chinese works on individual societies, such as the famous study of the *Yiguandao* by Professor Li Shiyu of Shandong University, who joined the society in order to study them. Wing-tsit Chan's study of Chinese religion tends to dismiss these societies. He regards them as "negative in outlook, utilitarian in purpose, and superstitious in belief," and cites a figure of merely 30,000 adherents for the Red Swastika Society in 1927, as opposed to Suemitsu's figure of 3 million followers in 1932. However, Chan does note that the Fellowship of Goodness (*Tongshanshe*) claimed more than a thousand branches in all parts of China proper and Manchuria in 1923.[42] A recent study by Shao Yong, while perhaps even more critical of these societies than Chan's, cites figures that are closer to the Japanese estimates.[43]

These societies have to be understood in terms of the complex interplay between the particular historical tradition of their derivation and the contemporary global context of the 1910s. The societies clearly emerged out of the Chinese historical tradition of sectarianism and syncretism. While some were closely associated with the sectarian tradition and involved the worship of Buddhist and folk deities like the Eternal Mother, they also represented the late imperial syncretic tradition (*sanjiaoheyi*) that combined the three religions of Confucianism, Buddhism, and Daoism into a single universal faith. Late imperial syncretism, which urged the extinguishing of worldly desires and engagement in moral action, gained popularity among the Confucian gentry and the Buddhist and Daoist laity in the sixteenth and seventeenth centuries.[44] The modern redemptive societies inherited the mission of universalism and moral self-transformation from this syncretism. At the same time, these societies also retained the association of the older syncretic societies with sectarian traditions, popular gods, and practices such as divination, planchette, and spirit writing.[45] In this way they continued to remain organically connected to Chinese popular society. Hence, while it might appear confused to associate these movements with secret societies, their connections to popular culture and local concerns indeed caused several of them to blur with secret societies at their rural edges.

The new global context of the twentieth century significantly transformed the meaning of the societies' project. A number of them—with a strong elite base—viewed themselves explicitly in the new civilizational discourse as representing an Eastern solution to the problems of the modern world. Many of them were formally established or saw rapid expansion during the period from World War I through the 1920s, when the discourse of Western civilization as overly materialist and violent began to emerge globally.[46] The societies sought to supplement and correct the material civilization of the West with the spiritual civilization of the East. The resultant synthesis they envisaged took the shape of a religious universalism that included not only Confucianism, Daoism, and Buddhism, but Islam and Christianity. Several of them claimed to represent the essential truth of the five world religions, and by spreading this truth to bring an end to religious partisanship and achieve world peace and personal salvation. Not only did the societies adapt their cosmology to the new geographical conception of the universe (to include Christianity and Islam), some of them also adapted to the temporal vision of a progressive history. The Morality Society, established in 1919, declared that it sought to synthesize the scientific view of the world with the religious and moral visions of Asian thought.[47] With the great reformer and constitutional monarchist Kang Youwei as its president from 1920 until his death in 1927, the Morality Society argued that without moral and spiritual regeneration, human evolution (*jinhua*) would stall and turn even more destructive because of the present trend toward hedonistic materialism.[48] Even the *Yiguandao*, perhaps the least "modern" or "this-worldly" of these societies, added the truths of Christianity and Islam to its earlier synthesis and cross-referenced its own esoteric temporal scheme with the modern chronology of dynastic and republican history.[49]

Their modern orientation is also revealed by their engagement in contemporary projects. Organized with charters and bylaws, armed with a strong this-worldly orientation and a rhetoric of worldly redemption, these societies resembled other modern religious and morality societies all over the world. The New Religion to Save the World (*Jiushi Xinjiao*) sought to do so not only through philanthropic activities such as hospitals, orphanages, and refugee centers,[50] but also through dissemination and publicity (schools, newspapers, libraries, lectures), through charitable enterprises such as factories and farms employing the poor, through savings and loan associations, and even through engineering projects such as road and bridge repair.[51] As for the "red swastika" of the society with that name, while this can, of course, be understood in Buddhist terms, it was clearly modeled upon—an Eastern equivalent of—the Red Cross Society. The Red Swastika society, like several others, not only developed traditional and modern charities, their projects included international activities, such as contributions to foreign relief efforts and the establishment of professors of Esperanto in Paris, London, and Tokyo.[52] The *Zailijiao*, which emerged in the very late Qing period, had established twenty-eight centers in Beijing and Tianjin in 1913, and appeared to have forty-eight centers in Tianjin alone by the late 1920s.[53] It was a strict disciplinarian movement and developed drug rehabilitation centers using herbal medicines and self-cultivation techniques (*zhengshen*) that were said to fully cure over two hundred opium addicts a year.[54] This outer or worldly dimension was matched by a strong inner dimension relating to moral and religious cultivation of the individual spirit and body, as will be discussed below.[55]

Some Japanese researchers tried to grasp the class character of these societies through loosely Marxist categories. Takizawa saw them as new religions characteristic of an early capitalist society; through them, incipient capitalist groups sought to bring the rich and poor together in a traditional idiom. For the rich they were a means of gaining popular support, while the poor welcomed both the philanthropy and the salvationism. At the same time, Japanese scholars were insistent in recognizing the religious passion and devotion of the adherents to their mission.[56] They suggest that those who sought to manipulate the societies could not always appropriate this passion for their own purposes. To the extent that we can sustain the class analysis, we are reminded of Elias's critique of the nineteenth-century European bourgeoisie's identification of civilization with the nation, transforming it from a process to an achieved condition. However, while it may have had the effect of muting class tensions, the religiosity of these societies continued to predispose them towards a universalism. The Japanese military would seek to transform this universalism into a doctrine of confrontation between East and West, particularly after the outbreak of the Pacific War.

Civilization in Popular Society

The groups that the Japanese would seek to mobilize with the rhetoric of upholding Asian values, both in Manchukuo and on the mainland, occupied a spectrum ranging from redemptive societies, other sectarians, and secret societies to those whose concerns were more purely local. Aside from the last, most groups could, to a greater or lesser degree, be associated with civilizational ideals and practices. Let us further explore this connection in the Chinese context.

It may be useful here to summarize the genealogy of civilization. I differentiated between the *singular* and *multiple* conceptions of civilization, which were, in scope, both *national* and *transnational.* Either could manifest as civilizing *process* or as achieved *state.* The core of Elias's book is concerned with the idea that the civilizing process is unselfconscious before it is transformed into a "concept" of national achievement. As achieved state, civilization tends to conflate with the nation, whereas as process, the urge towards transcendent universalism is deepened. As process, the civilizing imperative also develops advocates in popular society. Figure 3.1 tries to diagram some of the principal connections and exclusions in the discourse of civilization from the late nineteenth century.[57]

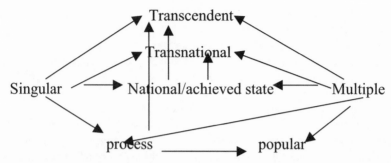

Figure 3.1. Principal Connections and Exclusions in the Discourse of Civilization

The imperial Chinese notion of *wenming* and the related idea of *jiaohua* express well the notion of civilization as process. *Wenming* means to enlighten with *wen,* which, at different moments in the long history of China, referred to the interpretation of heavenly signs or omens, and metonymically to writing or literature. Its practitioner potentially possessed a virtue that could fill or illumine the world.[58] *Jiaohua*—the use of teachings or doctrine to transform people's customs (*fengsu*)— may be thought of as a nonmilitarist means of spreading *wenming.* The *Hanyu Dacidian*'s definition of the premodern use of *wenming* includes the coupling *wenzhi jiaohua,* or "to morally transform (*jiaohua*) by means of virtuous rule (*wenzhi*)." The mode of moral transformation is explicated in the *Liji*: "Transformation through rites is subtle, one may nip the evil before it takes form."[59] Civilizing entailed the teaching of rites and obligations such as filiality, as well as the deeper cosmological truths of "heaven" and the Way. It was applied, moreover, to the barbarians as well as to "depraved" local customs. However, the process was not infinitely extendable; the circumstances of certain barbarians—such as the Xiongnu—might necessitate military subjugation alone.

The civilizing process as the relatively unbounded extension of a cosmologically sanctioned "way of life" also came to include a popular dimension insofar as many normative ideas were selectively absorbed in popular society.[60] This is one source of the "ethnographic" conception of civilization mentioned by Lucien Febvre. This popular dimension—whereby the populace, or a selection of the populace, was seen to represent the authentic civilization—became increasingly important through the twentieth century, as the idea of "multiple civilizations" gained ground. When the idea of civilization became somewhat freed from its ties to the cosmology of progress, intellectuals in both East and West sought to find the distinctive civilizational traditions among the people. The impetus for this ethnographic deepening of civilization came, of course, from the nationalist ideal of popular sovereignty, but it was also reinforced by the holistic conception of culture that was gaining ground globally.

This conception of culture is most closely associated in the scholarly world with

Franz Boas, who influenced American anthropology from his arrival in the United States in 1887 until and beyond his death in 1943.[61] We may see the holistic and relativistic Boasian notion of "culture" (also, of course, deriving from the German counter-evolutionary tradition) as an ethnographic parallel to Spengler's views of history and the philosophy of history. The two influences merged indistinguishably within many scholars, especially those studying non-Western societies in America, such as Ruth Benedict, Robert Redfield, Milton Singer, William McNeil, John K. Fairbank, Owen Lattimore, and many others. A pivotal figure, who synthesized the new ideas of culture and civilization conceptually and methodologically was Robert Redfield. Redfield, who ran the Comparative Civilizations Project for many years in Chicago, integrated the two notions into a multicivilizational ethnology; his efforts reflected the very multicultural sources of this new global discourse, and in the process lay the foundation for postwar American area studies.

Redfield was influenced deeply by the ideas of Toynbee and Spengler, and shared views of civilization with prominent Asian anthropologists like Fei Xiaotong and M. N. Srinivas.[62] Like Toynbee, Redfield sought to achieve lasting world peace by drawing from the various civilizational traditions, Eastern and Western. In order to do this, he had to first conceptualize the world as composed of different cultural wholes. Redfield's synthesis was quite remarkable. He brought the twin German counter-evolutionary traditions together in anthropology by treating civilization as a "sub-class of culture."[63] He sought to develop this anthropological synthesis as the foundation of area studies through the articulation of "great and little traditions," where the products of high Orientalism could be reconciled with peasant culture.

In China, we have seen how the idea of a holistic Chinese and East Asian civilization had its advocates among thinkers such as Liang Qichao, Liang Shuming, Du Yaquan, and many others. By the 1930s and 1940s, historians and anthropologists were also involved in the production of a pattern of Chinese civilization, in the conception, for instance, of "the Central Plains Confucian Culture of the Great Unity" (*Zhongyuan rujiao datong wenhua*). We will discuss this conception in a later chapter, but the ethnographic conception of civilization as one that pervaded even (or perhaps especially) the deepest reaches of rural culture was influential particularly among younger anthropologists such as Fei Xiaotong and Francis Hsu. Again, we will have occasion later to examine Fei's idea that Confucian norms and ideals (as opposed to legal or contractual relations) were most naturalistically preserved in peasant life. Although no romantic, Fei lamented precisely the erosion of these moral qualities and relationships brought on by Westernization.[64] I think Redfield betrays the influence of Fei—who lived in his home—when he writes about civilizations, "distinct in their total character," persisting for millennia in India and China. For Redfield, the unity of China, which "maintained its cultural integrity to modern times . . . was both made possible and exaggerated as the predominating Confucian view of life came to be cultivated and promulgated by the important scholarly elite."[65]

This mid-century, global, social scientific view was part of the new civilizational discourse furnishing—and reinforcing—a perspective on the ethnographic dimension of the "civilizing process," where elements in popular society could bring true and proper civilizational virtues to all. As we have seen, many religious societies articulated a redemptive vision that was continuous with their conception of the older moral order. David Ownby has identified a kind of "fundamentalism" among some of these societies, which were "both *against* and *from within* the mainstream." For example, some of them condemned the Buddhist church "for having abandoned its own mission of self-abnegation and transcendence."⁶⁶ Ownby's recent study of the apocalyptic Way of the Temple of the Heavenly Immortals illustrates how these societies fused deeply orthodox or "fundamental" values from Confucianism or Daoism with popular cultural traditions to reconstruct community along traditional, even utopian prescriptions.⁶⁷ These societies are civilizing in Redfield's sense: not only do they mediate between great and little traditions, they are a means "for communication between components that are universal, reflexive, and indoctrinating, and components which are local, unreflective and accepting."⁶⁸

Consonant with the inner, spiritual dimension emphasized in the new conception of civilization was the primacy of self-cultivation in the consciousness of these societies. A *Yiguandao* text composed sometime in the first half of the twentieth century declares that its purpose is to recover a person's true nature—the good mind (*liangxin*) of Confucianism and Buddha nature (*foxing*)—by drawing the truth of the universe into personal life. The technology of such a realization combines the self-cultivation techniques of the inner sage (*neisheng*) with the practical good deeds of the outer king (*waiwang*).⁶⁹ A similar statement was made by a leader of the *Dao-yuan* (the parent of the Red Swastika Society) to Japanese surveyor Suemitsu sometime before 1930.

> Q: What is the *Daoyuan* about?
> A: To simultaneously cultivate the inner and outer; the inner through meditation and the outer through philanthropy.
> Q: What is the *dao* of *Daoyuan*?
> A: It is the source of all things (*wanyou genyuan*). It is not a single religion; it has the power to clarify the good. . . . Actually the *dao* has no name, but we in the human world have to give it a name to show our reverence. So we revere the founders of the five religions. . . . We also respect nature and morality, and cultivate the self through charity.⁷⁰

Thus the cognitive map of these societies traced a path from the individual directly to the universal. True knowledge of the self came from self-cultivation practices sanctioned by cosmological ideas of heaven and the Way. Self-cultivation (*ziji xiuyang* or *xiushen*) ranged from practicing charity, to cultivating the habit of close moral and spiritual introspection, to the exercise of a strict disciplinary regimen. The disciplinary regimen in some societies emphasized strict vows of abstinence from drugs, meat, and alcohol, and sometimes involved the quasi renunciation of the family; in others, it provided detailed codes of moral behavior and bodily comportment.[71] Most societies combined all three: abstinence, renunciation, and morality. In the characteristic reciprocal movement from the self to the universal, these societies frequently defied political boundaries. For instance, the Yiguandao's construction of the genealogical transmission of the Way (*daotong*) begins with the Chinese sage kings, Yao and Shun, and follows the orthodox Confucian line until Mencius. Thereafter, the Confucian orthodoxy loses the way and the mantle is carried forth by Buddhists and Daoists. In its genealogical record of masters who continued to transmit the Way, Buddhist teachers from all over India and Central Asia are cited together with the classical Chinese place-names of their provenance.[72] The *Yiguandao* genealogy reveals how the geo-body of the nation was quite irrelevant to its principally spiritual mission. This is certainly one reason why the Chinese state has been relatively intolerant of these redemptive societies.

All the principal Chinese regimes of the twentieth century—the imperial, the KMT, and the communists—have banned these societies or sought to keep very strict control over them. The societies appear to have been caught in a pattern of relationship with the Chinese state, which made it hard for them to work together. The Chinese regimes appear to be especially threatened by the personal empowerment that allegedly emerged from tapping into cosmic forces. While direct traffic between the transcendent or cosmic power and the individual is hardly unique to China, historically, the Chinese state has tended to interpose itself between the two.[73] Whether because it claimed monopoly of access to the principle of the cosmos (the imperial state) or because it sought to guard forcefully the cosmological authority of science (modern states), the state has severely restricted religiosity to state-licensed organizations. Thus, even though they may have had orthodox and elitist elements within them, the redemptive societies often found themselves beyond the law. In turn, these groups tend to emphasize direct access to the cosmic principle not only as a means of self-empowerment for individuals, but as the only path to save the world.

It is in significant part for this reason that the KMT sought to prohibit all redemptive societies almost since it first came to power. In 1928, newspapers reported that the societies were banned not only because they were believed to have disseminated harmful superstition, but because they were regarded as incompatible with the spirit of progress. All provincial and city authorities were ordered to shut down these establishments and manage their properties for the public good.[74] In turn, the redemptive societies mobilized important figures to oppose this ban. A letter in the archives of the Red Swastika Society from Xiong Xiling, one-time prime minister during the preceding warlord era, written around 1929 and addressed to Chiang Kai-shek, makes several arguments to lift the ban on these societies and constitute a committee to reorder the role of religion in the new state. Xiong invokes the importance of religion in the cultural lives and morality of the people, and attributes to it the fundamental superiority of national morality to that of the West. He furnishes several practical reasons to preserve religion. Religion was the basis of the Qing unification of the empire, which the nation-state now seeks to inherit. Within this territory, he says, one-third are (the lands of) believers; and within the nation's population, two-thirds are believers. While the Chinese government attacks the "time-honored hearts of the people" (*guyou renxin*), foreign powers explore the great cultures of the East and are able to penetrate the hearts of the people both in the peripheries and inside China proper. He warns that the policy of banning redemptive societies will destroy the nation and strengthen the foreign powers. Xiong also emphasizes the functionalist role of all religious traditions—making people good, not through fear, but through their conscience (*liangxin*). Finally, with unexpected poignancy, he charges the government with turning its back on the very soldiers who had won its revolutionary war. Having witnessed the horrors of war, many of these revolutionary soldiers took the tonsure or otherwise turned to Buddhism. Does the government, at the very least, not owe those "wounded in the heart" (*shangxin*) the right to seek solace in religion?

Xiong closes his appeal by assimilating religious ideals to civilizational greatness. All the ancient religions take self-abnegation (*wusi, wuyü, wuwo*) as the principle whereby to redeem the self, humanity, and the world (*jiuji, jiuren, jiushi*). This is also the truth of *Datong*. But at the same time, he acknowledges the need for some reform.

> If religion becomes an obstacle to the progress of civilization, then it will lose its followers. If reform based on research of our ancient religious and philosophical truths can glorify them, then it will influence Europe and America and we may promote world unity (*shijie datong*) as well as our own national glory.[75]

The KMT did modify its interdiction of these groups following the reactions to its antireligious campaigns in the early 1930s.[76] Thus there was considerable discussion of what differentiated a religious society from a social welfare organization, and the Red Swastika Society was finally permitted to operate independently of the *Daoyuan*, as a philanthropic entity.[77] But even though the KMT sought to deploy the new civilizational discourse for its sovereignty claims, it was hardly prepared to adopt Xiong's synthesis of historical religions and civilization. Rather, it launched the extraordinarily ambitious New Life movement, by which it invoked classical Confucian ideals to produce a thoroughly modern and disciplinary transformation of the everyday lives of people. We shall discuss this movement in greater detail in the next chapter. In its effort to constitute a civilization selectively from Confucian ideals that were amenable to its state-centered vision, the regime ended up condemning even the relatively apolitical, gentry/merchant societies, such as the Morality Society and the *Tongshanshe,* as riven by superstitions and dominated by local bullies and warlords.[78] Behind this rhetoric, however, lay a strategic representation of modern religion and national civilization. In this strategy, the KMT produced a realm of legitimate spiritualism into which it incorporated modern, licensed religions as part of China's national civilization, while banning popular religious traditions as superstition.[79] As we have seen, many of the religious practices of these redemptive societies were, in fact, drawn from popular culture. But the regime was also threatened by the historical, subversive power of the societies deriving from their transcendent vision. The transnational spiritualism of the redemptive societies transgressed not only the KMT's definition of the modern, but its definition of the national boundaries of spiritual civilization. Certainly the cultural bonds of the societies to similar Japanese societies such as the *Ōmotokyo* made them susceptible to these attacks.

Redemptive Societies and the State in Manchukuo

The civilizational rhetoric upon which the sovereignty of Manchukuo rested, and which subsequently became the basis of the strategic alliances underlying Japanese control of the rest of China, was not simply initiated by the Guandong Army or Japanese political leadership. Redemptive societies in China and their equivalents in Japan had sought alternative, "Eastern" models of governance since at least the end of World War I.[80] Societies in Japan that championed Confucianism and Shinto as the spiritual alternative to excessive materialism and individualism, such as the *Shibunkai*, had begun to grow in strength from the 1920s, particularly as economic conditions worsened and social unrest grew. Asiatic moral systems emphasizing ethical responsibilities were celebrated as alternatives to capitalism and Marxism, both Western doctrines.[81] These new religious societies of the inter-war years numbered over a thousand in 1935, and some, such as the *Ōmotokyō* or the *Hitonomichi*, claimed adherents in the millions.[82] According to Sheldon Garon, these groups differed from the more established Shinto, Buddhist, and Christian societies not in their opposition to state goals, but in their resistance to manipulation within the framework of ideological orthodoxy devised by the state to utilize the religions as agencies of moral suasion (*kyōka, jiaohua*).[83] Thus, even though some of these societies may have supported the militant pan-Asianist vision of an imminent world war, the hardening of ideological orthodoxy in the 1930s led to ferocious state attacks that sought to destroy the societies. Interestingly, while similar attitudes and doubts dogged Japanese policy researchers in Manchukuo and occupied China, on the whole these regimes sought whenever possible to transform the societies into *jiaohua* agencies. Perhaps the need for constituencies of support in Manchuria, as well as the Guangdong Army officers' sympathy for some of these groups, such as the *Ōmotokyō* in Japan, led the Japanese in Manchuria to ally with groups similar to those that were attacked at home.

Founded in 1892 by Deguchi Nao, the *Ōmotokyō* had close ties with Chinese redemptive societies. It began as a regional sect responding to the erosion of community life generated by the new capitalist industrialization.[84] It rapidly evolved into a powerful, pan-Asianist spiritual movement in the 1920s under the leadership of Deguchi Ōnisaburō, boasting relations with other new world religious societies, such as the Baha'i and the *Daoyuan* (Red Swastika Society).[85] The arrival of the leaders of the *Daoyuan* in Japan to aid the Tokyo earthquake victims in 1924 apparently marked the beginning of an active program of cooperation with the *Ōmoto-kyō*.[86] The mission of the *Ōmotokyō* states,

> From the perspective of world history, it is clear that no single nation has the power to control other nations, that no one culture can have universal relevance, or that any one religion can assimilate all the people of the world. So we must strive to bring peace by love and faith in the Great Source (*Ōmoto*).[87]

The *Daoyuan* thus found a common basis in their pursuit of world peace through spirituality, morality, and humanitarianism.[88] But despite their rhetoric of universal love and world brotherhood, the Japanese "Eastern civilizational" societies, unlike the *Daoyuan* or *Daodehui*, had a violent and nationalist streak, as they had revealed in the past and would show again.[89]

In Manchukuo, the ideas of Japanese Sinologists like Tachibana and local researchers like Takizawa and Suemitsu were developed into an ideology and language that could forge an alliance with the redemptive societies. Tachibana had a unique perspective on Chinese religions. He not only believed the Chinese to be deeply religious, he felt that sectarians such as the *Zailijiao* and the *Daoyuan*, as distinct from secret societies, represented splendidly organized systems of faith whose authenticity (*shinjitsusei*) matched that of Christianity. Incidentally, he also viewed Christianity as one of the most influential forces in Chinese popular religion.[90] Indeed, Tachibana was inclined to highlight the nonsuperstitious character of redemptive societies, not only to counter intellectual or bureaucratic critics in both China and Japan, but because he wanted to showcase these groups as representing the East in the way that Christianity arguably did the West.

The East–West opposition furnished Tachibana with a way to draw what he called these "objectively valuable" groups into the Manchukuo regime. The state's doctrines of the Great Unity (*Datong*) and the "kingly way" (*wangdao*) represented the political symbols of this ideology of Eastern civilization. They became nodes in an ideological nexus of different groups, including political leaders of the old society, such as Yuan Jinkai, Zhang Jinghui, and Yu Chonghan; dyed-in-the-wool Confucian monarchists, such as Zheng Xiaoxu and his associates (who were the strongest advocates of imperial restoration); and, most numerously, the deeply religious and universalist redemptive societies. Tachibana said that they needed to deploy such groups as "the upper-class *Hongwanzihui* and *Jiushifotuan*, the middle-class *Daodehui*, and the lower-class *Zailijiao*," since they were much more amenable to mobilization as civic organizations (*jiaohua, kyōka*) than either purely community-defense organizations such as the Red Spears and Big Swords or the secret societies.[91] However, as we will see, doctrine was only one factor determining whether or not a religious or secretive group would support the Japanese military.

The Japanese ideologues of Manchukuo offered the redemptive societies an ideology and a space, however circumscribed, in which to pursue their goals. Given the history of their persecution, the societies must have found the opportunity very attractive. In the aftermath of the Manchurian Incident, a rumor suddenly floated among *Daoyuan* followers that Laozi had prophesied this apocalypse, and they welcomed it as a sign of their liberation.[92] The Morality Society (*Daodehui*) also embraced the regime, and, by one report, expanded its following to eight million adherents in 1936–1937 in Manchukuo alone (roughly one-fourth of the total population).[93] Founded in 1919 by the high literati of Shandong around a child prodigy who had once been a companion of the Xuantong emperor, the Society flourished until the establishment of KMT power and the antireligion campaign of 1928. It had developed a mass following within China and extensive networks around the world. Philosopher Kang Youwei, its president, believed that the ultimate significance of the nation arose from its self-transcendence in the universalist utopia of *Datong* (Great Unity), an ideal that meshed well with Manchukuo's rhetoric of civilization.

In Manchuria, the Morality Society expanded suddenly in the mid-1920s when the legendary Wang Fengyi (1864–1937) joined it, bringing with him a massive following and an extensive network of schools in Liaoning and Rehe.[94] Wang was a self-educated intellectual from a modest rural background in Chaoyang county, Rehe. His adoring followers referred to him as the righteous sage (*yisheng*), and he was popularly known as *shanren* (man who does good). His activities have been characterized as being in the tradition of *jiaohua* or advocating ethical transformation. Upon enlightenment of the *dao*, he threw himself into lecturing and doing good, urging filiality and the study of the sages and curing various ills with his theory of nature.[95] But perhaps the two most interesting dimensions of his civilizing program were his promotion of women's education and his theory of self-realization and self-reliance. We will elaborate on his program for women in the next chapter. His conception of self-knowledge was based upon a complex theory synthesizing the doctrine of the five conducts (based on the five elements) and *yinyang* cosmology with the teachings of the three religions.

In brief, the technical aspect of his theory sought to show how the five elements (*wuxing*)—wood, fire, earth, metal, and water—shape the five behavioral characteristics of a person (*wuxing*), not in a determinative way, but in combination with how the person cultivates (*xiudao*) these elements in the different circumstances of a life. On one level, his theory prescribed inner cultivation, but the self was ultimately realized in outward actions within a framework of changing circumstances. Self-exploration and self-reliance were the keynotes in Wang's philosophy.[96] We shall observe the practice of this philosophy in the next chapter.

Wang's technology of the self was rooted in the wider religious and philosophical movement of syncretism, or the religion of the "three-in-one" (*sanjiao heyi*). According to Lin Anwu, a contemporary follower and analyst of the philosophy, Wang affirmed the basic goodness of nature or natural dispositions (*tianxing*) and the three bonds (*sangang*) of Confucianism (father–son, ruler–subject, husband–wife). He found them compatible with the three treasures of Buddhism and the three transformations (the *hua* of *xing, xin*, and *shen*) of Daoism, all of which could be understood within the Buddhist realms of the three worlds.[97] Yet the goal of the philosophy, Lin writes, "is neither theoretical nor technical, but practically related to experiences in one's life; one can in this way find the roots of one's life. A person may thus return to the principles underlying the bonds between the world, heaven and humans."[98] In this cosmological foundation we may discern the civilizational agenda of the Morality Society.

Wang's commitment to "transform the world" (*huashi*) had been noted locally even before his association with the Morality Society. The Chaoyang county gazetteer observed that his efforts had led to an improvement of customs and the spread of education. Over a hundred segregated schools initiated by his son were eponymously called Wang Guohua schools.[99] A female devotee, Liu Shuquan, whom the senior Wang had deputed as the principal of a righteous girl's school in his hometown of Yangshan, was praised in her funerary inscription as having "enlightened (*kaiming*) our women's world, which had been steeped in darkness for thousands of years."[100] Wang himself appeared to be extremely energetic, traveling widely and establishing schools and branches of the society in what might be seen as a process of civilizing the frontier. He received the patronage of important politicians, such as the Manchu literatus Bai Yongzhen, who had been an important official before the Republic and later served as the speaker of the Fengtian provincial assembly (*Shengy-ihui jiangchang*).[101] It is Bai's calligraphy that adorns Wang's little book of teachings.

When Manchukuo was established, the Morality Society responded to Tachibana's formulation of *wangdao,* and became the most influential group aside from the Red Swastika Society. Wang sought government permission to organize a major summit in Xinjing and rapidly created branches all across the new state.[102] By 1934, the 312 branches of the Manchukuo Morality Society operated 235 "righteous" or "virtuous" schools, 226 lecture halls, and 124 clinics.[103] By 1936, a year before Wang's death, it boasted 13 head offices, 208 city and county branch offices, and 529 *zhen*-level branches.[104] Many of the top Chinese figures in the government, such as Yuan Jinkai and Zhang Jinghui, were associated with it. Its membership and officeholders included top officials, merchants, and landowners all the way from the major cities to the subcounty townships. The message of peace, morality, and spiritual salvation of the world by the East befitted these successors of the old gentry elite. As a *jiaohua* agency, the society revealed a strong propagandist urge. It put great stock by its cadres or activists (*shi*), who were characterized as benevolent and resolute.[105] Through their activities in schools, through lectures, through spreading *baihua* commentaries on classical morality, and through establishing popular enlightenment societies to "reform popular customs and rectify the people's minds and hearts," the society propounded a strong rhetoric of reaching out to all—the rich and poor, men and women.[106]

The effort to assimilate groups such as the Morality Society into the rhetoric of Eastern civilization reflected both the regime's concern for its sovereignty claims and its interest in transforming the societies to serve regime and state goals. The mechanism whereby it was able to bridge these two goals was the policy of *jiaohua* or *kyōka*. We have considered the role of *jiaohua*—to transform by teaching—in the civilizing process of imperial China. Like hundreds of words in the modern Japanese lexicon, *kyōka/jiaohua* was a paleonym from the classical Chinese that yielded a considerably different signification. Sheldon Garon, who has discussed the importance of *kyōka* in modern Japan, has translated it as "moral suasion": "Elaborate bureaucracies sprang up, devoted to running moral suasion campaigns, coordinating local moral suasion groups, disseminating 'social education,' and effecting 'spiritual mobilization.'"[107] We might say that in its modern incarnation, *kyōka* represented the state's institutionalized framework for guiding participation in governmentality.

Like the KMT based in Nanjing, the Manchukuo government censured the "superstitious" character of the redemptive societies, but instead of seeking to eradicate these societies it sought to transform them into *jiaohua* organizations—agencies engaged in welfare, enlightenment, and control of the people.[108] Japanese observers had long noted that religious groups and temple societies were the only agencies of social "welfare" (*kōsei*) in Manchuria, distributing food and providing shelter to the needy.[109] At the same time, they inevitably observed how, despite the strong this-worldly, social orientation, these same religious organizations were also rife with superstition and dangerous possibilities. The task facing the Manchukuo government was to reform the societies and make them usable while preserving their religious source of inspiration.

One significant institution developed to effect this transformation was the Federation of Social Enterprises (*Manzhou shehui shiye lianhehui*), established early in 1933 by the Department of Home Affairs (*Minzhengbu*, later *Minshengbu*); Prime Minister Zheng Xiaoxu, who was also minister of the Culture and Education Department (*Wenjiaobu*), served as an honorary member. The two departments often had different views of the role of religion in Manchukuo. The Federation, which brought out a regular publication of its activities, was expected to oversee relief provision, welfare enterprises, and improvement of the people's morality and spirit of citizenship. It was also charged with coordinating the activities of the various local government welfare departments with those of the redemptive societies and chambers of commerce.[110] On the one hand, the organization was an instrument of modern governmentality. Its agencies prepared meticulously detailed classifications of the needy and the means to help them, including factories for the poor, vocational training schools, and labor dormitories.[111] On the other, it actively sought to associate its welfare and relief programs with a traditionalist ideology. Food distribution, free clinics, lectures on hygiene and sanitation, management of schools, widows' homes and orphanages, and general relief work were often undertaken by redemptive groups such as the Buddhists, the Red Swastika Society, the *Zailijiao*, or the Morality Society. Whenever possible, philanthropy took place around temples and during religious festivals (such as for Niangniang, goddess of fertility, or Guandi, god of loyalty), and was inevitably accompanied by traditional imagery, drama, and propaganda heralding *wangdao* and *letu* (paradise).[112] Thus, under the rubric of *jiao-hua*—adding modern Japanese techniques to an old Chinese idea—the regime created a unique organizational structure integrating its rhetoric of civilization with modern welfare and political control.

Through the structural incorporation of these redemptive societies from the outside, the regime hoped to effect their internal transformation. The general idea was to model them upon Christian—especially Protestant—missionary societies under state supervision.[113] This meant ridding them of their extreme "superstitious" practices and further encouraging their educational, charitable, and civilizing functions. Their activities were to be closely scrutinized by officials. Records of the Morality Society indicate that officials of the Home and Education Departments constantly issued detailed rules and regulations and demanded strict accountability for finances and properties. Textbooks and even the daily schedule of the schools run by the Morality Society had to be in strict conformance with Education Department guidelines.[114] Before going on to examine the particular relationships between the different societies and the regime, let me indicate the extent to which this model of relations between popular societies and the Japanese-backed regime applied elsewhere in China.

The Japanese invasion of China south of the pass in 1937 produced a breakdown in the formal structures of control and authority, whether of the KMT or the warlords. Secret societies, sectarians, and redemptive societies were able to enlarge their influence in this vacuum. Indeed, in some cases the Chinese communists and Japanese forces often competed for their allegiance.[115] Unlike the KMT, which had earlier driven most groups of all three types underground, the Japanese military, drawing on their experience in Manchukuo, sought particularly to bring the redemptive societies under their wing. Researchers like Suemitsu believed that by forcing them underground, the KMT had actually increased the association of these societies with the violent secret societies and made them politically unreliable. The Japanese military hoped to appeal not only to the redemptive societies, but to secret societies that valued the traditional Confucian rhetoric of righteousness and loyalty.[116]

Occupation-era governments in north China at the county and city levels conducted investigations of religious societies in order both to identify opposition and to bring out and encourage the registration of sectarian and redemptive societies as *jiaohua* organizations. Records reveal the registration of, or petitions to register, a very large number of these societies between 1937 and 1945 with the Department of Police, the Department of Social Affairs, or the Department of Rites. In some places, these societies registered with the quasi-official Revive Asia Association (*Xingyayuan*) or the New Peoples Society (*Xinminhui*). The total figure for participants or followers of all societies within a single county or city often reached beyond tens of thousands. In one survey of several counties in Shanxi, of twenty-seven societies registered, only one was founded after 1941; twelve were founded from 1931 to 1941, and the rest predated the Japanese invasion. These were typically syncretic or

Buddhist societies that sought to uphold traditional Eastern morality, to salvage society, and more and more, to resist communism and uphold the East Asian new order. Many have the names we have encountered above, but there were also several Buddhist societies and some purely local ones. Of the societies registered only after 1937, some may have been created just to seize opportunities under an occupying regime, but the evidence points only to their registration as public bodies and not their founding.[117]

In central China under the Wang Jingwei regime the process of incorporating the societies into government projects came under the responsibility of the Social Movements Guidance Department (*Shehui yundong zhidao weiyuanhui*), which kept detailed records, including educational qualifications and other information about members of many societies. The groups included not only redemptive societies but secret brotherhoods (*banghui*), native-place associations, and professional groups (*tongye*), all of which the puppet Wang regime sought to control, mobilize, and transform into welfare agencies and propagators of the ideas of Eastern civilization.[118] The roster of one of these societies, the One Heart Heavenly Way Longhua Sagely Teaching (*Yixin tiandao longhua shengjiao*), which profiled its members in Tianjin and Nanjing, reveals that in 1943, of its sixty-five members in Tianjin, an overwhelming number (fifty-two) were educated in the traditional private schools (*sishu*). About five were teachers in such schools, a few were Chinese medicine doctors, and the remainder were merchants or farmers. Of the 420 members in the Nanjing branch, 118 had primary school degrees, about four or five had higher degrees, and most of the rest (312) had a traditional school education. Most of the members were merchants.[119] Records also include the distribution of the Morality Society in several provinces in 1942. There were about 130 branches in Hebei, 75 in Shandong, 7 in Anhui, 14 in Shanxi, and 7 in Inner Mongolia; the branches averaged about 150 members.[120]

Meanwhile, in Manchukuo, despite the relative success of the regime in working with these groups, the results were mixed. Most analysts, who usually conducted their surveys of them for the Home Department, continued to be suspicious of the societies. Takizawa was perhaps the most sympathetic, or perhaps the most cognizant of the importance of the religious inspiration behind social activism and loyalty. As part of general religious policy, he advocated the legal protection and expansion of temples and other religious properties, which he regarded as the most important collective property of the people. He recommended the reform of temples and monasteries and the education of priests and monks along the lines of both Christian missions and Japanese Buddhist missionaries. Finally, he called on his fellow Japanese to break with the idea of a pure national religion and promote the desegregation of the customarily separate worship in Chinese and Japanese temples and shrines, and the mixing of deities among them, in order to develop a composite Manchurian religion. "Religion," he concluded, "will be first and last in melding the spirits of Japan and Manchukuo."[121]

Others found this religiosity quite problematic. We noted the opposition by the

Concordia Association, which tended to be more interested in modernization. It preferred the other founding narrative of Manchukuo, as a new type of nation with equality between its nationalities and ethnicities.[122] Often the opposition to religion was spearheaded by the younger leadership of the different ethnic groups, such as the Mongols and the Daurs, who felt that too much emphasis on ethnic traditions would condemn them to backwardness. Most of all, the Japanese feared religious societies for security reasons. If religion could be said to be the opium that produces compliance and collaboration, it was equally a force that produced opposition to the regime in Manchukuo and north China. Manchukuo military and police often found religious societies, particularly in the rural areas, to be subversive. Christianity in particular afforded many of the Koreans in Manchukuo a means to resist the state, sometimes because Western pastors and the Christian church continued to be protected by extraterritorial rights.[123] Even such well-established elite societies as the Morality Society and the Red Swastika Society continued to have links with subversive secret societies in the countryside.[124] Ōtani Komei suggests that in smaller towns all over Manchukuo the larger societies were connected to violent secret societies whose politics were local and often directed against Japanese state penetration. In the hinterlands, the redemptive societies were hardly as cohesive as they appeared in the cities, and internal strife between pro- and anti-Japanese forces continued within them for a long time.[125]

Two societies about which the regime was most uncertain were the *Zaijiali* (or *Jiali*) and the *Zailijiao*, two different organizations, but both hybrid in their own ways and possessing secretive and public faces. In Suemitsu's survey, the *Zailijiao* was listed under the category of religious self-cultivation societies and the *Jiali* as a *bang* or secret society, but with strong syncretic, religious, and orthodox qualities.[126] The *Jiali* in Manchuria had evolved from a self-help organization among Shandong migrants and sometimes used the language of native-place associations. Indeed, by the 1930s it had produced a modern, legal charitable institution, the *Jiali tongxiang jiujihui* (Jiali Native Place Charitable Association), which operated under the laws of the state and appeared to cooperate with it.[127] At the same time, the association with rural self-help groups convinced surveyors that the regime would not be able to rid it of its subversive secretiveness.[128]

The *Zailijiao*, as we have seen, was a fiercely disciplinary and renunciatory redemptive society. It too never gave up its secretive dimension—keeping certain practices secret even from the adherent's family.[129] Ōtani gives us a glimpse into the state's effort to co-opt this society. According to secret police reports, the Harbin *Zailijiao*, which claimed to have about a thousand followers, actually commanded a much larger covert following and harbored "criminals and assassins."[130] When the Manchukuo regime was established, the group's leaders apparently affirmed the compatibility and sympathy of the new state with their own doctrine of righteousness (*yiqi*), thus supposedly coming into the open and conducting their activities lawfully. The number of their branches expanded rapidly, and they also set up many Japanese language schools. Yet the Harbin center appeared to have little control over the southern branches, and continued reports of opposition to the regime suggested that the results of its efforts were quite mixed. The regime continued to exercise strict surveillance of their activities.[131]

Surveys also found two other circumstances that contributed to the oppositional character of redemptive societies. First, in regions with ethnic diversity, such as Rehe—where over half the population was Mongol in many counties—there was often a tradition of communal hostility between Han and Mongol.[132] Religious societies here, including the Red Swastika and the *Jiali*, as much as the Red Spears and other communal societies, seemed to have a stronger Han consciousness, and were, according to Japanese surveyors, torn between loyalty to their ethnicity and to their faith.[133] Finally, the ecstatic and shamanistic aspects of these religious societies were viewed with genuine concern. In some areas, even seemingly pacific Buddhist societies could become inflammatory and oppose the regime. According to Ōtani, they were loyal to none but their own religious convictions centered around oracular authority.[134]

Despite these serious concerns, sectarian and redemptive societies were far too important to the regime's political projects to be abandoned. Bureaucrats from the Rituals Division (*Lijiaoke*) of the Education Department and other ideologues believed that it was necessary to stress the religious character of the various ethnic communities and associations in order to distinguish them from Western civilization. Religious societies could best exemplify the basically Asiatic characteristics of agrarian communitarianism (*nōhonshugi kyōdōtai*) that represented the essence of all the national and ethnic groups of East Asia. Fukunaga Tadashi, also author of *The Principle of Cultural War*, sought to deploy a transnational, civilizational argument about *kyōdōtai* nations in opposition to the individualistic civilization of the nations of the West. He argued that East Asian civilizational (and, more generally, Asian) qualities such as communitarianism and cooperativism were based upon a shared pantheistic view of the world. The shared qualities mandated a fundamental equality among the nationalities of the East and could thus also be distinguished from the German Nazi theory of pure blood.[135] Indeed, Fukunaga invoked the familiar Japanese historical narrative of Manchuria as the crossroads of many different peoples, starting with the Tungus groups and ending with the recent Han and Japanese settlers. While this narrative was used to make several claims, here it served to establish the region as the exemplary site of Asian cooperativeness. Manchukuo emerges as the state able to realize this essential quality in a new type of nationalism more in tune with the spirit of true egalitarianism than the nationalism of the West. Again, the discourse of civilization was essential to the rhetoric of the new nationalism.

Even as he sought to conjoin the modern egalitarian and timeless communitarian aspects of Asian civilization, Fukunaga firmly established Japan's role as the leader of these nations. Because Japan combined the superior Asiatic spiritual culture with the advantages of Western material culture, Japan had a responsibility to implant its culture in Manchukuo and other Asian societies in order to raise their civilizational level.[136] In other words, whereas the other peoples may have had some kind of pantheism and communitarianism that distinguished them from individualistic Western societies, this spirit was not as well developed as it was among the Japanese, where the people and the rulers were entirely one.[137]

Fukunaga's text returns us to the civilizational discourse with which we opened this chapter. It shows how the redemptive universalism of the sectarian and syncretic groups, an expression of an older civilizing process tied to new concerns, became assimilated into the hard doctrine of an exclusive civilization that underlay the principle of cultural war between East and West, especially after the outbreak of the Pacific War. Given the gaps between them, the only way this could be done was to subordinate the various societies to the state's ideology. Ōtani articulated this position most effectively. Noting that the secular philosophy of the Concordia Association did not appear to have much relevance to the lives of ordinary people, he had come to believe that religion was the more fundamentally motivating sentiment.[138] While many of the contemporary religious beliefs of the people in Manchukuo were decadent and backward, it was both necessary and possible to elevate this sentiment and bring the plurality of beliefs under a higher unified order, which he called *Datong weiyi shijie*, or the world of the Great Unity. Confucianism provided the moral and Buddhism the religious foundation for this transformation.[139] In this way, the state could channel the energies of the redemptive societies into productive and loyal activities as well as attain the civilizational goals of the Great Unity. Thus did the redemptive societies emerge from their hidden, secretive condition into a public world of state supervision and control. They were permitted to pursue their goal of redemptive universalism, but only under the watchful eye of a nonuniversal state.

The goal of this chapter has been to see how a global discourse of civilization worked within a particular political formation. Civilization in the twentieth century had come to represent the highest ideals of humanity, but, curiously, as embodied in distinctive national cultures. In other words, while each national project claimed its ultimate worth in its universal relevance or *scope*, their ideologues found it necessary to stress the *origins*, and hence the distinct authority, of their civilization. There were many groups emerging from the older Chinese society who found personal meaning and mission in the universalist aims and civilizing projects, but nationalists among the Chinese and Japanese—who valued such ideals largely for their authorizing function—sought to seize this universalism for the national or statist project.

Through the discourse of Asian civilization, state-builders in Manchukuo attempted to connect older conceptions of society, morality, and personhood to claims of sovereignty. In an age when this sovereignty was expected to conform to the identity (if not quite "will") of the people, the Manchukuo laboratory presents us with certain insights into how this dynamic worked more broadly in East Asia. On the one hand, the need to found sovereignty at least partially through the historical language and cultural imagery of older formations in East Asia was shared with the Chinese and Japanese nation-states, whether in the emperor system or the New Life movement, or, as we shall see, in the common conception of authentic womanhood. On the other hand, the state in all three societies had to transform or seriously modify the meanings and connotations of this historical language in order to achieve their goals of governmentality and the extension or stabilization of regime power. In all three nondemocratic regimes, the East Asian modern entailed a high degree of top-down reconstruction of tradition, enabling the state to lead modernization according to its own conception and interests. We have seen this in the KMT effort to define tradition and religion through its particular interpretation of Confucianism; in Japan, the cultural framework of *kyōka* furnished the mechanism to control the management of society within the larger ideology of the emperor system. Such top-down statist formulations frequently led to the exclusion from legitimate "tradition" of large groups of people who may have lived these traditions or who sought to embody their ideals.

Ironically, precisely because they lacked legitimacy as conationals or coethnics, Japanese power-holders in Manchukuo had few options but to ally with elements of these popular cultural traditions in order to stabilize their regime and achieve their goals. The rhetoric of Asian civilizational distinctiveness not only furnished a framework for this alliance and claim to sovereignty, it provided the opportunity to transform them for purposes of the state. Thus we may see the regime's use of redemptive societies as instrumental and ultimately uncommitted to the original ideals of these societies. We have also seen the incorporative process to have had mixed results, but it was more productive than the KMT's relationship with these societies.

Over the course of the anti-Japanese war, the KMT became increasingly aware of the Japanese co-optation of the redemptive societies and other religious and cultural groups that it deemed backward and lacking in education, culture, and national consciousness.[140] The KMT Central Committee's Bureau of Investigation and Statistics (*Zhongtongju*) was entrusted to investigate, penetrate, and countermobilize these societies, although it is not at all clear that they had much success. Judging from the classified reports of its investigations in Sichuan and other parts of south and west China in 1939–1940,[141] these societies were highly susceptible to the rhetoric and ideals of an older worldview, even when modern professionals were involved in them. An extensive report on the *Gelaohui*, an important secret society in Sichuan and the middle Yangzi provinces, reveals that the society had penetrated the civil and military administration—including bankers—of many cities and counties in these provinces. It points to the dangers of this infiltration by revealing how in 1940 a branch in Ba county, Sichuan, gathered followers and spread the message that China was destined to have an emperor.

Another report, about the *Hailufeng zhangtang* in Guangdong, also shows us the tensions generated by efforts to modernize these groups. Originally a branch of the White Lotus, the group became a formal and peaceful organization after the Republican revolution and even had important officials from the warlord government among its members. Although it remained vegetarian and sutra-reciting, it was neither political nor secretive. It was apparently in the forefront of the resistance against the Japanese occupation, attending to military preparedness and to the common people's needs. Soon after the failure of the resistance, the older leadership apparently regained control of the organization, restarted qigong practices, and turned the society into a militant Buddhist group whose loyalties appeared uncertain.[142]

While local factors—the perception of Japanese (or KMT, or warlord) threat to the community, local rivalries, and so on—played an indubitably important role in determining which side these groups would support, the KMT reports reveal a consistently negative view of these groups as backward and show little flexibility in accommodating their worldviews. Committed to a modernized Confucianism of its own kind, the KMT seemed unable to respond to the appeal of older, living practices and ideals. In this regard, although the Japanese military also often found them to be unusable for their purposes, it nonetheless developed the language and institutions of accommodation while it sought to transform them. Restoration of the imperial institution, which was pivotal to the historical cosmology, seemed very important to many of these groups and served the Japanese cause.[143]

By creating a framework for a working relationship, Manchukuo revealed a yawning gap that divided Chinese modernizing nationalists from the society they sought to modernize and nationalize. This society was linked in myriad practical, spatial, and material ways to conceptions of the cosmos and personhood that seemed hopelessly out-of-date to these modernizers. It would require a revolution to overhaul.

Notes

1. *SJHWZ*, case 143, October 8, 1931.

2. Takizawa Toshihiro, *Manshū no gaison shinkō* (Beliefs of Manchuria's towns and villages) (Shinkyo: Manshū jijo annaijo, 1940), 284.

3. Tachibana Shiraki, *Dōkyō to Shinwa Densetsu* (Daoism and myths and legends) (Tokyo: Kaizōsha, 1947), 1.

4. Fumimaro Konoye, "Manchoukuo, Precursor of Asiatic Renaissance and the Government by *Wang-tao* (Kingly Way) based on Theocracy," *Contemporary Manchuria* 2 (July 1937): 14–15.

5. Gerrit W. Gong, *The Standard of "Civilization" in International Society* (Oxford: Clarendon, 1984), 12, and Lucien P. V. Febvre, "Civilisation: Evolution of a Word and a Group of Ideas," in *A New Kind of History and Other Essays*, ed. Peter Burke (New York: Harper and Row, 1973), 229–47.

6. The embodiment of Civilization in legal form had the effect of universalizing it, or in other words of disassociating it from the particular soil or conditions of its emergence (such as Christianity) in the West. It was in this particular legal incarnation that countries like Japan (and Turkey) could aspire to the status of a Civilized nation and, indeed, sought very hard to do so.

7. Febvre, "Civilisation," 220, 236, and Matti Bunzl, "Franz Boas and the Humboldtian Tradition: From *Volksgeist* and *Nationalcharakter* to an Anthropological Concept of Culture," in *Volksgeist as Method and Ethic: Essays on Boasian Ethnography and the German Anthropological Tradition*, ed. George W. Stocking Jr. (Madison: University of Wisconsin Press, 1996).

8. James E. Ketelaar, *Of Heretics and Martyrs in Meiji Japan: Buddhism and Its Persecution* (Princeton: Princeton University Press, 1990); Heinz Bechert, "Buddhist Revival in East and West," in *The World of Buddhism: Buddhist Nuns and Monks in Society and Culture*, ed. Heinz Bechert and Richard Gombrich (London: Thames and Hudson, 1984); and Raymond Schwab, *Oriental Renaissance: Europe's Rediscovery of India and the East, 1680–1880*, trans. Gene Patterson-Black and Victor Reinking (New York: Columbia University Press, 1984).

9. Douglas Howland, *Borders of Chinese Civilization: Geography and History at Empire's End* (Durham, N.C.: Duke University Press, 1996), 262 n. 22, and Douglas R. Reynolds, *China, 1898–1912: The Xinzheng Revolution and Japan* (Cambridge, Mass.: Council on East Asian Studies, 1993), 22, 28.

10. Bechert, "Buddhist Revival in East and West," 274–75. The same reconstruction of Hinduism was taking place in India under the auspices of the Theosophical Society and thinkers like Sri Aurobindo and Swami Vivekananda.

11. Ketelaar, *Of Heretics and Martyrs*.

12. Oswald Spengler, *The Decline of the West,* abridged ed., ed. Helmut Werner (New York: Knopf, 1962), 5. One cannot but be reminded of the German association of the word civilization with an effete and superficial French cult of manners and courtesy; see Norbert Elias, *The Civilizing Process: The Development of Manners*, trans. Edmund Jephcott (New York: Urizen, 1978). But note that for Homboldt, writing in the early part of the nineteenth century, *Kultur* and *Zivilisation* were quite interchangeable; see Febvre, "Civilisation," 244.

13. Spengler, *Decline of the West,* 12.

14. William H. McNeill, *Arnold Toynbee: A Life* (New York: Oxford University Press, 1989), 103, 165, and Jerry H. Bentley, *Shapes of World History in Twentieth-Century Scholarship* (Washington, D.C.: American Historical Association, 1996), 7.

15. Toynbee, "Christianity and Civilization," 230–34.

16. McNeill, *Arnold Toynbee*, 269–73.

17. Michael Adas, "The Great War and the Decline of the Civilizing Mission," in *Autonomous Histories: Particular Truths*, ed. Laurie Sears. (Madison: University of Wisconsin Press, 1993), 109.

18. Barraclough, *Introduction to Contemporary History*, 118–22.

19. Bentley, *Shapes of World History*, 3.

20. Elias, *The Civilizing Process*, 3–4, 29–34, 38–40, 50. According to Elias, by civilization, "Western society seeks to describe what constitutes its special character and what it is proud of: the level of *its* technology, the nature of *its* manners, the development of *its* scientific knowledge or view of the world, and much more." Although Elias notes that this civilization allows Europeans to think of themselves transnationally as the "upper-class to large sections of the non-European world," he is much more concerned with its transformation within intra-European relationships into "national" civilizations. Note, however, that despite this transformation in the nineteenth century, the civilizing process does not disappear, as Raymond Williams points out; see *The Country and the City* (London: Chatto and Windus, 1973), 57–60. As we have seen, this is most evident in the "civilizing mission" idea.

21. Gong, *Standard of "Civilization,"* 190.

22. Liang, cited in Ishikawa Yoshihiro, "Bunmei, bunka, soshite Ryō Keichō" (Civilization, culture, and Liang Qichao) (unpublished manuscript, 1995), 8.

23. Ishikawa, "Bunmei, bunka, soshite Ryō Keichō," 9–10.

24. Gong, *Standard of "Civilization,"* 157.

25. Yamamuro Shinichi, "Ajia ninshiki no kijiku" (The axes of perceiving Asia), in *Kindai Nihon no Ajia ninshiki* (Modern Japan's perceptions of Asia), ed. Furuya Tetsuo (Kyoto: Kyōtō Daigaku Jinbun Kagaku Kenkyūjo, 1994), 3–41.

26. Ueda Makoto, "Okakura Tenshin—aru kyōkai no Ajia kan" (Okakura Tenshin: A view of Asia from a certain margin), *Kokusai kyōryu* 77 (1996): 56–58.

27. Bunso Hashikawa, "Japanese Perspectives on Asia: From Dissociation to Coprosperity," in *The Chinese and the Japanese: Essays in Political and Cultural Interactions*, ed. Akira Iriye (Princeton: Princeton University Press, 1980), 331–41.

28. Yamazaki Mugen, "Kyōiku zasshi ni miru Ajia ninshiki no tenkai" (The development of the perception of Asia as seen in educational journals), in *Kindai Nihon no Ajia ninshiki* (Modern Japan's perceptions of Asia), ed. Furuya Tetsuo (Kyoto: Jinbun kagaku kenkyūjo, 1994), 299–350.

29. Christopher W. A. Szpilman, "The Dream of One Asia: Ōkawa Shūmei and Japanese Pan-Asianism," in *The Japanese Empire and Its Legacy in East Asia*, ed. Harald Fuess (Munich: German Institute of Japanese Studies, 1988), 43–47, 50.

30. Hasegawa Yūichi, "Taishō chūki tairiku kokka e no imeiji—'Daikōraikoku' (Dagaoli, Koryo) kōsō to sono shūhen" (The image of a mainland nation in the mid-Taishō era: The conception of the "Great Koryo nation" and the area around it), *Kokusai Seiji* 71 (1982): 95.

31. Sanetō Keishū, *Nihon bunka no Shina e no eikyō* (The influence of Japanese culture on China) (Tokyo: Keisetsu shoin, 1940).

32. Ishikawa Yoshihiro, "Tōzai bunmeiron to Nihon no rondan" (The discourse of East–West civilization and the Sino-Japanese world of letters), in *Kindai Nihon no Ajia ninshiki* (Modern Japan's perceptions of Asia), ed. Furuya Tetsuo (Kyoto: Kyōtō Daigaku Jinbun Kagaku Kenkyūjo, 1994), 398–403.

33. Ishikawa, "Tōzai bunmeiron to Nihon no rondan," 430.

34. Ishikawa, "Tōzai bunmeiron to Nihon no rondan," 420.

35. Ishikawa, "Tōzai bunmeiron to Nihon no rondan," 415–16.

36. The ambivalence regarding the value of Chinese "civilization" continues to dominate Chinese intellectual discourse on the subject. Partly as a result, both the Enlightenment conception and the post–Great War conception of civilization continue to inform the Chinese signifier *wenming*. Thus it is by identifying the context of its use, as well as by differentiating the usages of "culture" (*wenhua*)—as in the German usage of *Kultur*—that we can grasp which sense of civilization is meant.

37. See Jerome B. Grieder, *Intellectuals and the State in Modern China* (New York: Free Press, 1981), and Guy S. Alitto, *The Last Confucian: Liang Shu-ming and the Chinese Dilemma of Modernity* (Berkeley: University of California Press, 1979).

38. Aida Yuen Wong, "In Search of the East: Art History and Sino-Japanese Relations" (Ph.D. diss., Columbia University, 1999).

39. Mizuno Naoki, "Senkyūhyaku nijū nendai Nihon, Chōsen, Chūgoku ni okeru Ajia ninshiki no ichidanmen—Ajia minzoku kaigi o meguru sankoku no ronchō" (An aspect of the perception of Asia in the three countries of Japan, Korea, and China during the 1920s: The arguments of the three countries surrounding the conference on Asian peoples), in *Kindai Nihon no Ajia ninshiki* (Modern Japan's perceptions of Asia), ed. Furuya Tetsuo (Kyoto: Kyōtō Daigaku Jinbun Kagaku Kenkyūjo, 1994), 509–44.

40. Chen Lifu, "Xin shenghuo yu minsheng shiguan" (New Life and the Minsheng conception of history), in *GWXSY*, 128, 133.

41. Takayoshi Suemitsu, *Shina no himitsu kessha to jizen kaisha* (China's secret societies and charitable societies) (Dalian: Manshū hyoronsha, 1932), 252; Takizawa, *Manshū no gaison shinkō*, 67.

42. Wing-tsit Chan, *Religious Trends in Modern China* (New York: Columbia University Press, 1953), 164–65, 167; cf. Suemitsu, *Shina no himitsu kessha to jizen kaisha*, 302.

43. Shao Yong does not furnish a systematic estimate of the membership of these societies, which he calls *huidaomen*. He supplies scattered figures of membership in different localities, drawn from various sources, including the societies' own statements. For instance, in one place he suggests that the *Tongshanshe* membership in Hunan province alone exceeded 20,000 in 1918. Again, for 1938 he claims that the societies had a combined membership of one million in the provinces of Henan, Shandong, and Anhui. Most astonishing is his revelation that membership of the Morality Society was as high as eight million in 1936–1937 in Manchukuo alone. See Shao Yong, *Zhongguo huidaomen* (China's religious societies) (Shanghai: Remmin chubanse, 1997), 174, 321, 325. Thanks to David Ownby for supplying me with this reference and his translated notes. I have since consulted the original and am fully responsible for any errors in transcription. While we can assume that the Japanese researchers may have wanted to exaggerate the numbers in these groups, there was also a concern for accuracy since the surveys were conducted principally to assess the potential for support and opposition to their rule. The figures cited above refer to the spread of religious societies all over China, largely before the Japanese occupation. Most of the surveys were marked secret or for internal consumption. Note that a similar mystery of exaggerated numbers accompanies the rise of such redemptive societies as the *Falungong* or the *Zhonggong* today. Given the climate of suppression and secrecy in which these societies had to operate during both periods, the resemblance is perhaps not accidental.

44. Kai-wing Chow, *The Rise of Confucian Ritualism in Late Imperial China: Ethics, Classics, and Lineage Discourse* (Stanford: Stanford University Press, 1994), 21–25.

45. Kai-wing Chow, *The Rise of Confucian Ritualism*, 22–27.

46. *MDNJ*, 4:1; Takizawa Toshihiro, *Shūkyō chōsa shiryō* (Materials from the survey of religions), vol. 3, *Minkan shinkō chōsa hōkokushō* (Report on the survey of popular beliefs) (Shinkyō: Minseibu, 1937), 67 ff ; and *HZN*, 505–57 ff.

47. *MDNJ*, 1:3–6.

48. *MDNJ*, 4:1, and Takizawa, *Shūkyō chōsa shiryō*, 67.

49. Li Shiyu, *Xianzai Huabei mimi zongjiao* (Secret religions in north China today) (1948; reprint, Taipei: Guding shuwu, 1975), 50–55.

50. *HZN*, 485–86.

51. *HZN*, 491–93.

52. Suemitsu, *Shina no himitsu kessha to jizen kaisha*, 292–305, 354.

53. *HZN*, 507–27.

54. Suemitsu, *Shina no himitsu kessha to jizen kaisha*, 262–63.

55. For the fullest reports on the social welfare activities of these societies, especially for the Red Swastika Society, see the reports of the Shanghai city social bureau's reports in *SSJYB*, 1930–1932, 1946.

56. Takizawa, *Manshū no gaison shinkō*, 282–84, and Suemitsu, *Shina no himitsu kessha to jizen kaisha*, 337–40.

57. Note that the four definitions of civilization in *Webster's II New College Dictionary* (1995) basically conform to the different dimensions I have identified: 1) advanced human

condition (conforms to singular/transnational); 2) nations showing advanced condition (conforms to national/transnational); 3) the type of culture of a group or society (conforms to *Kultur*/multiple); 4) the act or process of civilizing or reaching a civilized state (conforms to process and achieved state).

58. Hanyu Dacidian bianji weiyuanhui (Hanyu Dacidian editorial committee), ed., *Hanyu Dacidian* (Shanghai: Sanlian chuban, 1987), 6:1522.

59. Hanyu Dacidian bianji weiyuanhui, *Hanyu Dacidian*, 5:445.

60. These popular ideas may have still shared in a common cosmology, or "doxa," even if imperial orthodoxy regarded them as heterodox (*xiejiao*). According to a recent, well-researched historical study of the *Yiguandao* by Fu Zhong, a sympathizer, not only were the doctrinal differences between the redemptive (*jiushi*) societies—at least by the early twentieth century—not great, but popular Confucianism also incorporated a strong redemptive element. Most popular religious societies combined a strong salvationist ethic with the propagation of orthodox teachings of loyalty, filiality, charity, and social ethics (*daode lunli*); see Fu Zhong, ed., *Yiguandao Lishi* (Taipei: Zhengyi shanshu, 1997), 250. Note also how, although they may have advocated the overthrow of the dynasty, even secret societies valued these doxic teachings of righteousness (*zhongyi*) and so forth. Perhaps the most important difference was the presence or absence of an eschatological vision—of the imminence of apocalypse; however, it not only differentiated some of them from the state, but from other secret societies. We should note that Fu Zhong seeks to play down the apocalyptic element, claiming even the *Yiguandao* to be orthodox (*wulun, bade*) and restorative of classical values; see Fu, *Yiguandao Lishi*, 273–74, 280.

61. See George W. Stocking Jr., ed., *Volksgeist as Method and Ethic: Essays on Boasian Ethnography and the German Anthropological Tradition* (Madison: University of Wisconsin Press, 1996), 3–5.

62. Robert Redfield, *Human Nature and the Study of Society: The Papers of Robert Redfield*, ed. Margaret Park Redfield, vol. 1 (Chicago: University of Chicago Press, 1962–63), 373–77, 406–10.

63. Redfield, *Human Nature*, 402.

64. In postliberation China this ethnographic conception of civilization does not seem to have survived too well; *wenming* tends to refer to the Enlightenment ideal of material and moral progress. I believe this has a lot to do with the close affiliation of Marxism with Enlightenment ideals. Someone like Du Weiming, on the other hand, is clearly more representative of the idea of Confucian civilization.

65. Redfield, *Human Nature*, 413.

66. David Ownby, "Chinese Millenarian Traditions: The Formative Age," *American Historical Review* 104 (December 1999): 1528.

67. David Ownby, "Imperial Fantasies: The Chinese Communists and Peasant Rebellions," *Comparative Studies in Society and History* 43 (2001): 65–91.

68. Redfield, *Human Nature*, 394.

69. Fu, *Yiguandao Lishi*, 278, 280.

70. Fu, *Yiguandao Lishi*, 308–9.

71. Suemitsu, *Shina no himitsu kessha to jizen kaisha*, 266, 326–28; Takizawa, *Manshū no gaison shinkō*, 76–78; and Chan, *Religious Trends*, 164–67.

72. Li, *Xianzai Huabei mimi zongjiao*, 51–55.

73. By transcendent I do not refer to the philosophical idea of a *noumenon* beyond

knowledge and the realm of possible experience. Rather, in the Chinese or East Asian case, I use it to refer to the "other world" beyond mundane experience, but accessible by specialized techniques, faith, and other means.

74. *SJHWZ*, case 73, October 11, 1928; Ōtani Komme, *Shūkyō chōsa shiryō* (Materials from the survey of religions), vol. 2, *Kitsurin, Kantō, Hinkō, kakoshō shōkyō chōsa hōkoku* (Report on religious surveys of the various provinces of Jilin, Jiandao, and Binjiang) (Shinkyō: Minseibu, 1937), 69, 123; and Suemitsu, *Shina no himitsu kessha to jizen kaisha*, 251, 255.

75. *SJHWZ*, case 86, n.d.: 1–6.

76. Duara, *Rescuing History*, 109–10.

77. *SSJYB*, 1930: 251–54, 291–97; 1931: 296–300; and 1932: 101–9.

78. Suemitsu, *Shina no himitsu kessha to jizen kaisha*, 251.

79. Duara, *Rescuing History*, chap. 3.

80. Takizawa, *Manshū no gaison shinkō*, 283.

81. Warren H. Smith Jr., *Confucianism in Modern Japan: A Study of Conservatism in Japan's Intellectual History* (Tokyo: Hokuseido, 1959), 123–26.

82. Sheldon Garon, "Women's Groups and the Japanese State: Contending Approaches to Political Integration, 1890–1945," *Journal of Japanese Studies* 19 (1993): 5–41, 70–71.

83. Garon, "Women's Groups and the Japanese State," 85–86.

84. Hasegawa, "Taishō chūki tairiku kokka e no imeiji," 100.

85. Uchida Ryōhei, *Manmō no dokuritsu to Sekai Kōmanjikai no katsudō* (The independence of Manchuria-Mongolia and the activities of the World Red Swastika Society) (Tokyo: Senshinsha, 1932), 112, and Hasegawa, "Taishō chūki tairiku kokka e no imeiji," 100.

86. Uchida, *Manmō no dokuritsu to Sekai Kōmanjikai no katsudō*, 108–9.

87. Quoted in Suemitsu, *Shina no himitsu kessha to jizen kaisha*, 317.

88. Uchida, *Manmō no dokuritsu to Sekai Kōmanjikai no katsudō*, 112, 129, and Suemitsu, *Shina no himitsu kessha to jizen kaisha*, 310–20.

89. Hasegawa, "Taishō chūki tairiku kokka e no imeiji," 100. Uchida Ryōhei, himself a source for information on the relationship between these two groups, became the leader of the World Red Swastika Society (*Kōmanji*) and established many branches that exist to this day in Japan and Hawaii. When Uchida began to advocate violence in the 1930s, the Manchukuo Red Swastika Society disconnected itself from the Japanese groups and returned to a more universalist rather than pan-Asianist stance; see Takizawa, *Manshū no gaison shinkō*, 285.

90. Tachibana, *Dōkyō to Shinwa Densetsu*, 1–3, 13.

91. See Komagome, *Shokuminchi Teikoku Nippon no Bunka Tōgō*, 265.

92. Takizawa, *Manshū no gaison shinkō*, 284.

93. Shao, *Zhongguo huidaomen*, 321.

94. Shao, *Zhongguo huidaomen*, 306–7.

95. Lin Anwu, "Yin dao yi li jiao—yi Wang Fengyi 'shierzi xinchuan' wei gaixin zhankai" (Establishing "the Way" as religion: Explorations centered upon Wang Fengyi's "twelve character teachings"), in *Zhonghua minzu zongjiao xueshu huiyi lunwen fabiao* (Publication of the Conference on the Study of Chinese Religion) (Taipei: n.p., 1989), 12.

96. Lin Anwu, "Yin dao yi li jiao," 15–17.

97. Lin Anwu, "Yin dao yi li jiao," 13–15.

98. Lin Anwu, "Yin dao yi li jiao," 19.

99. *Chaoyang xianzhi* (Chaoyang County Gazetteer), comp. Zhou Tiejing and Sun Qingwei (1930), juan 19:14–16, juan 35:45–46; *MDNJ*, 8:23.

100. *Chaoyang xianzhi*, 1930, juan 35:46–47.

101. *Dongbei fangzhi renwu zhuanji ziliao suoyin: Liaoning juan* (Index of biographical materials from Northeast local gazetteers: Liaoning volume) (Shenyang: Liaoningsheng chubanshe, 1991), 10, 521.

102. Takizawa, *Manshū no gaison shinkō*, 293.

103. *MDNJ*, 1:21.

104. Shao, *Zhongguo huidaomen*, 321.

105. *MDNJ*, 4:2.

106. *MDNJ*, 2:36–42; 4:117, 118; 8:22–23.

107. Garon, "Women's Groups and the Japanese State," 7. See also Gluck, *Japan's Modern Myths*, 103.

108. Takizawa, *Manshū no gaison shinkō*, 82–86, 100–102.

109. Yamada Seizaburō, *Manshūkoku bunka kensetsuron* (The theory of cultural construction in Manchukuo) (Shinkyō: Geibun shobō, 1943), 91–92.

110. *MSSJ*, 1:1–5, 15, 51, 122; 2:55–56.

111. *MSSJ*, 1:1–5.

112. *MSSJ*, 1:12; 2:172–77, 191–95, and Yamada, *Manshūkoku bunka kensetsuron*, 91–92.

113. Takizawa, *Shūkyō chōsa shiryō*, 82–83.

114. *MDNJ*, 2:4–51. For example, the schedule for the tuition-free Pure World Girl's School in Fengtian showed 2 hours per week were spent on self-cultivation; 3 on classics; 5 on art, needlework, and music; 8 on Chinese; 2 on Japanese; 2 on history; 2 on geography; 6 on mathematics; and 2 on nature study. See *MDNJ*, 2:5–6.

115. Mitani Takeshi, "Senzenki Nihon no Chūgoku himitsu kessha ni tsuite no chōsa" (Surveys of Chinese secret societies in prewar Japan), in *Senzenki Chūgoku jittai chōsa shiryō no sōgoteki kenkyū* (Composite studies of prewar surveys of actual conditions in China), ed. Honjō Hisako (n.p., 1998), 104.

116. Suemitsu, *Shina no himitsu kessha to jizen kaisha*, 208–9.

117. *WWD*, Archive 2018.

118. *WWD*, Archive 2013: 303, 764, 767, 775.

119. *WWD*, Archive 2013: 773.

120. *WWD*, Archive 2013: 764.

121. Takizawa, *Shūkyō chōsa shiryō*, 102–3.

122. But as long as the new nation was based upon allegedly Asiatic qualities, the Concordia Association still needed a conception of Asiatic distinctiveness. As the "confrontation" thesis gained ground during the Pacific War, it became more difficult for the Concordia Association to play down Asiatic distinctiveness and sustain the original rhetoric of Manchukuo as a supramodern nation based on the synthesis of Eastern and Western civilizations.

123. Ōtani, *Shūkyō chōsa shiryō*, 27–32, 38, 46, and, on extraterritoriality, 58–60, 97 ff; and Takizawa, *Shūkyo chōsa shiryō*, 89–92.

124. Takizawa, *Shūkyō chōsa shiryō*, 95.

125. Ōtani, *Shūkyō chōsa shiryō*, 70, 132, 137.

126. Suemitsu, *Shina no himitsu kessha to jizen kaisha*, 259, 103.

127. Suemitsu, *Shina no himitsu kessha to jizen kaisha*, 109–12.

128. Suemitsu, *Shina no himitsu kessha to jizen kaisha*, 112, and Ōtani, *Shūkyō chōsa shiryō*, 44.

129. Suemitsu, *Shina no himitsu kessha to jizen kaisha*, 266–68.

130. This was, of course, precisely the kind of uncertainty the KMT feared.

131. Ōtani, *Shūkyō chōsa shiryō*, 104–8, and Shao, *Zhongguo huidaomen*, 323–24.

132. Yamazaki, *Nekka, Kinshū ryōsho shūkyō chōsa*, 98.

133. Yamazaki, *Nekka, Kinshū ryōsho shūkyō chōsa*, 54–58, and Ōtani, *Shūkyō chōsa shiryō*, 62, 64.

134. Ōtani, *Shūkyō chōsa shiryō*, 77, 145.

135. Fukunaga Tadashi, *Manshūkoku no minzoku mondai* (The nationalities problem of Manchukuo) (Shinkyō: Manshū Fukuyamabo, 1943), 91–92. He insisted that Japanese should not fear intermarriage because the Japanese stock would improve the lesser peoples (93).

136. Fukunaga, *Manshūkoku no minzoku mondai*, 88–90.

137. Fukunaga, *Manshūkoku no minzoku mondai*, 77–78.

138. Ōtani, *Shūkyō chōsa shiryō*, 140.

139. Ōtani, *Shūkyō chōsa shiryō*, 150.

140. *ZTJ*, Archive 11, case 1480, pp. 1–9.

141. *ZTJ*, Archive 11, cases 1442–48.

142. *ZTJ*, Archive 11, case 1446.

143. For instance, the leader of the banned *Tongshanshe*, Peng Ruzun, who was hiding in Sichuan, sent his son to Changchun in 1933 to tell the "emperor" Puyi that he wanted to train several hundred thousand spirit troops for him; see Shao, *Zhongguo huidaomen*, 286.

CHAPTER FOUR

~

Embodying Civilization: Women and the Figure of Tradition within Modernity

How did the new civilizational discourse affect individuals as a source of personal authenticity? I explore this problem among a group of women of the Morality Society in Manchukuo. These personal narratives, however, can only be grasped in the context of gender conceptions and roles in Manchukuo and more widely in China and Japan. This chapter is thus largely devoted to analyzing a patriarchal conception in the East Asia modern of woman as the figure of "tradition within modernity." In this conception, women were expected to embody "the truth" or "the Way" of the civilization. Whereas the search for authenticity is determined by the problem of time and identity, this chapter will probe more concretely how and why women come to represent this authenticity. What kinds of political forces create these representations? How do they become enmeshed in projects of sovereignty and governmentality? And how do the women negotiate these projects and their sense of personal truth?

In 1997, I had the opportunity to visit and interview one of these women, whom I shall call Mrs. Gu, in Taiwan. Born in 1915, Mrs. Gu lived in Manchuria until the communists took over the mainland; she then moved to Taipei. Here she reestablished the Morality Society and was its vice president at the time of our meeting. Today in Taiwan, although the *Wanguo Daodehui* still holds international conferences, imparts moral education, and owns some splendid property, it is much reduced in scope and has become primarily a day care provider and a women's recreation organization. Its role has been affected by changed ideas regarding the role of women and by the much more spiritually charismatic and socially active Buddhist societies.

Nonetheless, Mrs. Gu remained a highly dedicated and passionate activist for the cause. As she recounted the story of her life in the organization, surrounded by several

131

attentive younger members, her pride and reverence for this form of self-sacrificing activism, superior to any political loyalty, became evident. We will take up the political question later; here let me present some of her own words to sound out the ironies in the concept of "tradition within modernity":

In 1933, I joined the *Daodehui*, when I was eighteen years old. Since my childhood, I have had a strong and independent personality and did not want to suffer the restraints of the old family system. I believed that women should be independent (*zili*), not be dependent on parents, husbands, or children. I never wanted to marry.

At that time, my father was the village headman and since he had many connections with the KMT he was arrested by the Japanese. I was very anxious, but luckily there was a member of the *Daodehui* called Mr. Zheng Zhidong who knew a Mr. Ono in the military police (*xianbingdui*). Through him, we were able to secure my father's release and save his life. Upon his release, we all joined the *Daodehui*. After this event, I was sent to Shenyang, Fujiao Lane, to receive training for six months. During the day, we turned the mill, washed the floors, cultivated patience, and in the evenings we studied the lectures. We certainly did not believe the kind of talk about "virtue lay[ing] in women not having talents."

Once a group of seven of us (five girls, one man, and one leader) went out on a lecture tour and met some bandits on the way. We were terrified, and the young girls fled, but our leader lectured to them about Confucius's teachings, changed their hearts (*ganhuale*) and succeeded in getting them to give up their habits. In 1934 and 1935, every locality set up branches of the Society. I also resolved to set up ten lecture units. I already had a small reputation by then. When I was in Daxiguan, a scholar (*xiucai*) wrote a poem for me. I returned to Shenyang after spending three years in a humble store. I lectured so much that I lost my voice. . . .

In 1939, I was a lecture manager and lectured on the importance of female virtue (*fudao*), breast-feeding (*rudao*), women's education, and prenatal education (*taijiao*). I told my listeners that women should go out and suffer in order to be happy, should preserve the good heart in order to establish resolve and achieve great results. . . .

After Japan's defeat, I advocated the takeover of the Japanese shrine (*lingmiao*) for the Society as its Welfare Center and spent money to establish the management council. When the new government took over the shrine, I protested the confiscation daily, saying "those who want to make revolution may have their heads chopped and their blood may flow, but they will not abandon the Northeast." The committee to oversee the reconstruction of postwar northeast China had no choice but to return the shrine to us. Later, even Mrs. Chiang Kai-shek summoned (*zhaojian*) me in recognition of my efforts. . . . The Society was popular in Shandong and Huabei and there were fifty-eight units in the city of Shenyang alone. What it meant by *Datong* is world peace and opposition to struggle. It is a moral force (*wuxingde wuqi*, literally, a formless weapon). It cultivates the public heart (*gongxin*): to give up the private and preserve the public for the sake of the greater self and the masses. When people are old we realize that truth is in public service. Women should be wise mothers and virtuous wives.

To many contemporary readers this juxtaposing of the self-sacrificing and traditional against the fiercely independent and even revolutionary woman may sound a little incongruous, but it was an important model of womanhood in much of China and Japan in the first half of the century. It is the figure of woman as embodying tradition within modernity, or as the KMT leader Wang Jingwei put it, "inheriting the past to enlighten posterity." In a lecture delivered at a girls' school in 1924, Wang observed that the conflict between the old and the new in society could be seen as the clash between the school as the nucleus of the new thought and the family that preserved the old ways. In order for China to progress in this competitive world of nation-states, it was important for students to take control over society and reform its evil customs. He recognized that it was easy for girls to succumb to the control of the family and be assimilated into society, but he implored them not to take this path. It was particularly important for girls' schools to nourish a spirit of social reform among their students, since in their present state they stood as obstacles to national progress.[1]

Having framed his talk within the evolutionary discourse of modernity, Wang's second theme was the importance of choosing the right kind of education. Although Chinese tradition included a lot that was bad, it had one strength: the cultivation of a long tradition of willing self-sacrifice (*xisheng*) among females, whether for the sake of their parents in their natal home, of their husbands after marriage, or of their sons in old age. Doubtless, the old society often used blind self-sacrifice to bury women's freedom. But women should know that the responsibility of the individual was heavy and should not be exploited (*liyong*) by society. If they genuinely felt (*zhenzhende qinggan*) the spirit of sacrifice, then such conduct was proper, and, indeed, highly admirable. The spirit of self-sacrifice actually formed the indispensable basis of all morality—Confucian, Buddhist, and Christian.

> Chinese women are rich in the spirit of self-sacrifice. If we can properly direct this spirit towards [the collectivity] . . . and use it, then we can on the one hand perhaps preserve a little of the essence (*jingsui*) of the teachings of several thousand years, and on the other still plant the roots of modern liberatory thought. In seeking education for girls I hope we can uphold our mission of inheriting the past to enlighten posterity [*chengxian qihou*].[2]

The Chinese woman, for Wang, was both modern citizen and locus of unchanging authenticity. Nationalist patriarchy crafted the self-sacrificing woman as a symbol of national essence.

Compared to the writings on the emergence of the modern woman in China associated with the May Fourth movement (1917–1921)—widely regarded as China's Enlightenment—about the radically anti-Confucian, indeed antifamilial, nationalist woman, contemporary scholarly attention to the kind of woman Wang was trying to shape is still relatively rare. It is beyond the scope of this work to explore which model of the modern woman was more relevant to the middle classes in Republican China. Suffice it to say that the political establishment of the early twentieth century—including both the late Qing and the KMT regime—favored

Wang's model. This model of womanhood first emerged during the late Qing, when reformers and statesmen began to accept the importance of modern education for girls and a limited public role for them.

The Japanese influence on the emerging discourses and institutions of modern China during this period was particularly deep in this realm. During the middle years of the Meiji period (1868–1912), as the Japanese state consolidated and centralized its rule, it launched a series of laws denying women (together with other categories of people) political rights and barred them from joining political associations. Bureaucrats appealed to the Japanese ideal of the "good wife and wise mother," arguing that political involvement would only divert them from fulfilling these roles.[3] In this way, the historical ideal of the self-sacrificing and frugal samurai woman became generalized in the Meiji era as the model of feminine virtue for the nation as a whole. Women were represented as having to transcend petty politics in their role as "officials" of the household, which, in the emergent family-state ideology of the period, was seen as the microcosm of the nation-state.[4]

Recent work on late Qing education of girls in the first decade of the twentieth century has given us a detailed picture of how this Japanese model penetrated China among intellectuals and reformers as well as policy-makers. To be sure, this was a process of selective borrowing in China and had different consequences, but the ideology of the "good wife and wise mother" was enthusiastically received because, Joan Judge argues, as an amalgamation of East Asian and Western ideals, past and present values, ancient female ethics and contemporary nationalist concerns, Japan provided China with a most suitable gender ideology.[5] The Japanese model was also less threatening to a still largely patriarchal Chinese elite than the more radical models of female education in the West—even as it satisfied this elite that the model was acceptable to a nation as modern as Japan.

The Japanese influence was transmitted by returning Chinese students educated in Japan, and most especially through the widespread translation of Japanese texts and their dissemination through specialized educational journals and the wider press including the highly influential Japanese-owned newspapers such as *Shengjing Shibao* (from Mukden or Shenyang) and *Shuntian Shibao* (Beijing). There were also very great numbers of Japanese teacher trainers, educational advisors, and teachers active in schools in China, including those for female education.[6] Perhaps the most significant single figure behind the transfer of role models for women was the educator Shimoda Utako.

Shimoda was dedicated to the task of creating a pan-Asian modernity and worked closely with Japanese and Chinese politicians to create educational institutions to instill East Asian values. Working within the civilizational discourse of East versus West, she was determined to "strengthen Asia" by extending education to all women while at the same time preserving the Confucian conception of female virtue. Thus Shimoda's ideal East Asian woman would simultaneously practice feminine virtues and serve the nation; she would serve the nation, not by rejecting traditional virtues of self-sacrifice, but, in a move that was echoed by Wang Jingwei and countless others, by reorienting these virtues towards patriotism. Shimoda was very influential among both official and unofficial circles concerned with educational reform for girls. This influence was evident in the conservative proposal of 1904, "Memorial on Regulations for Early Training Schools and for Education on Household Matters," drafted by prominent statesmen such as Zhang Zhidong and others, and her ideas had a strong impact on the empress dowager, Cixi.[7] In 1908, Zhao Jingru, the principal of Fengtian (Shenyang) Normal Girls' School, visited Japan and paid her tribute to Shimoda, declaring, "Since the condition of women's education and the fate of the nation are intimately connected, the spirit of peace [in East Asia] rests on the shoulders of Shimoda."[8] Peace would turn out to be a distant dream, but the state in East Asia would find the controlled figure of woman as "tradition within modernity" a highly desirable means of penetrating society and shaping the nation.

Modern Patriarchy

Women have been represented as the embodiment of the essential truth of a nation or civilization, not only in China and Japan but in many parts of the modern world. Recent studies of gender histories in the West (and especially in Latin America) have shown how women and their bodies, systematically excluded from the public sphere during much of the modern period, have served as a crucial medium for the inscription and naturalization of power: "Explored, mapped, conquered, and raped, the female body and its metaphorical extension, the home, become the symbols of honor, loyalty, and purity, to be guarded by men."[9] Partha Chatterjee has drawn our attention to how modern nationalists in late-nineteenth-century India appropriated the middle-class production of a sphere that he calls the inner domain of sovereignty of nationalist ideology. Like Chinese nationalism, Indian nationalism was built upon a duality of the material versus the spiritual, and cultural. Thus, while the Indian nation had much to learn from the material and scientific civilization of the West, in spiritual matters India had the upper hand and a contribution to make to world civilization.[10]

Chatterjee's particular contribution is to show how this dualism was organized so as to create an inner realm of national life that could not be contested by the colonial power. Nineteenth-century Bengali middle-class intellectuals had reworked certain historical texts to define the "ideal woman" and distinguish her from depictions of the "traditional" (that is, recent historical, rather than quintessential) Bengali woman, from depictions of contemporary lower-class women, and from the figure of the Western, materialist, and masculinized woman. Modern Indian nationalism found this trope of the enlightened but quintessentially "traditional" woman highly congenial, and appropriated it as the core of the essential nation. Tradition thus came to mark a realm of inner sovereignty that was simultaneously demarcated as domestic, spiritual, and feminine. The Hindu nationalist representation of woman—educated and educating, but personifying the spiritual virtues of domesticity—gave body to this national essence. While on the one hand this lofty idealization of the Hindu woman provided new aspirations for some women, we can assume that it was patriarchal because it was an image shaped by men for women to follow.[11]

In East Asia, this representation of woman was less directly connected to colonialism, but it was decidedly a response on the part of a patriarchal elite to manage the shift to a more Westernized society and changing relations between the genders, and between the domestic and public spheres. In China, we can understand this phenomenon precisely as the nexus between a global process and historical institutions of gender relations. Most of the early nationalists and reformers emerged from the habitus of the gentry and inherited the patriarchal traditions of this society and its ideals of womanly virtue. The rhetoric of female virtue and sacrifice, exemplified most particularly in the cult of chaste widows and virtuous wives, was pervasive in late imperial China.[12] During the early twentieth century, when the increasing integration of China into global capitalism produced rapid change in gender relations among urban families, this patriarchal legacy surfaced in a novel context and was sustained in the heightened concern with preserving female virtues. "Virtuous and chaste girls' schools" (*zhennü yixue, baonü yixueyuan*) sprouted everywhere in this period, and the journals about women, such as the *Funü Zazhi* of the early 1920s, were filled with anxious essays about the problem of gender mixing.[13] Female virtue became a metonym for Chinese civilizational truths.

Nationalists made great efforts to improve the status of women, in order to attain the higher goal of national strengthening. Women's education, the abolition of footbinding, and the need for prenatal care became major issues in the reform movement of the turn of the century, led by Kang Youwei and his colleagues, because, as Kazuko Ono writes, these issues became "linked to the nation's survival or demise, its strength or weakness, through the education of children."[14] While there were some notable efforts by women writers themselves to undo the connection,[15] throughout most of the twentieth century the legitimacy of women's issues continued to remain dependent on the primacy of the national cause. As in many other early-twentieth-century patriarchal nationalisms, women were to be liberated for the nation. They were not to shape the nation in their own image, but rather to be shaped and protected by the nation in its image. This same primacy authorized nationalism to demand a self-sacrificing woman to incorporate its essence.

Women were doubtless hypostatized because of their institutionalized dependence on men in China, as in most other historical cultures. But they were also perceived as key to maintaining the stability of the family, that bedrock of Confucian society. Thus the figure of timelessness was also to serve as a performing role model. Needless to say, the pressures upon such a figure were enormous. As noted in chapter 1, the human embodiment of authenticity—mirrors of the enduring self—is susceptible to the inevitable failure of human lives to live up to idealized representations. Strains arose not only from the impact of outside influences and market forces on the family and gender relations, but also because the reformist, developmental side of Chinese nationalism itself channeled women into the public sphere, thus exposing them to transformation and "contamination." For instance, nationalists in both China and Japan were mindful that women should not only be involved with reproduction functions in the domestic sphere, but also contribute to production in the modern sector in order to strengthen the nation. Weikun Cheng writes that even the involvement of females as students and teachers in the segregated girls' schools and professional associations entailed a certain level of participation in the public sphere.[16]

Moreover, the alternative model of the progressive woman, backed by her increasingly acceptable status in the West, was readily available in the media and attracted many younger women. In Japan by the 1920s, the Modern Girl, active in the public sphere of work and politics, came to threaten "the patriarchal family and its ideological support, the deferring woman who was presented in state ideology as the 'Good Wife and Wise Mother.'"[17] According to Miriam Silverberg, she became the symbol of all that was non-Japanese and modern, in contrast to the Meiji image of the woman who served as "'the repository of the past,' standing for tradition when men were encouraged to change their way of politics and culture in all ways."[18] The Modern Girl of the 1920s became the target of conservatives appalled by rapid change all around them, but she became so only because she, no less than the Meiji woman, occupied a special place within the order of authenticity, a place she was beginning defiantly to transgress.

In China, the popularity of the model of the liberated woman reached its great height among educated young women in the May Fourth movement. Indeed, through the 1920s and beyond, perhaps the greatest threat to the conservative model of womanhood came from the May Fourth Westernized, antitraditional model of woman. The two models were intimately implicated in the political and ideological battles of the period, leading sometimes to a great deal of violence inflicted upon women. After the split between the KMT and CCP in 1927, thousands of "modern" women were killed by the KMT forces because they were accused of "free love," or sometimes simply because they had bobbed hair, unbound feet, or a local reputation for opposing familial authority.[19] While they were surely killed because they were marked by these signs as communist (whether or not they were), the causal logic worked in both directions. Communism itself was illegitimate significantly because such women and their behavior despoiled the innermost purity of Chinese culture.

Aside from such dramatically violent episodes, the tension in gender conceptions underlying these conflicting models was pervasive in urban, middle-class China. The great May Fourth writer Lu Xun reflected deeply on the gender issues of his time and directed some of his most acid writing at modern gentry patriarchs like Kang Youwei (who became president of the Morality Society in the 1920s), who, he believed, employed the language of traditional essences to ultimately exploit and dominate women.[20]

There is perhaps no better description of the tension than his story "Soap." Lu Xun's protagonist Simin has bought a cake of foreign, scented soap for his wife. His wife is pleased but also embarrassed by the coded message that she should make herself cleaner and more alluring. When Simin had insisted on opening the package of soap at the store to check its quality, he was taunted by some schoolgirls with bobbed hair using a foreign word he did not understand (it turns out to be "old fool"). Highly agitated, he now orders his school-going son to check its meaning and begins to rave and rant about the moral havoc that the new schools are wreaking on China, especially the schools for girls. He says,

> Just think, it is already in very poor taste the way women wander up and down the streets, and now they want to cut their hair as well. Nothing disgusts me as much as these short-haired schoolgirls. What I say is: There is some excuse for soldiers and bandits, but these girls are the ones who turn everything upside down. They ought to be very severely dealt with indeed.[21]

Simin then contrasts this behavior with that of a filial beggar girl of eighteen or nineteen, who turned over all the money she received begging outside a store to her blind grandmother. The crowds that gathered to watch the two not only did not give much money, but made jeering remarks about how the girl would not be bad at all if she were scrubbed up with two cakes of soap. Simin sees this as evidence of the catastrophic decline of morality in modern China. Later, at dinner, when Simin's wife can no longer take Simin's irritability, she hints that he secretly longs for the beggar girl and is trying to cover this up by exalting her filial and self-sacrificing conduct. In utter frustration, she exclaims, "If you buy her another cake and give her a good scrubbing, then worship her, the whole world will be at peace." Later she adds, "We women are much better than you men. If you men are not cursing eighteen- or nineteen-year-old girl students, you are praising eighteen- or nineteen-year-old girl beggars: such dirty minds you have."[22]

At this moment, Simin is rescued from this tirade by the arrival of some friends who have come to remind him about the urgent need to publicize an essay and poetry contest for their Moral Reform Literary Society (*Yifeng Wenshe*). The title for the essay had already been drafted as "To beg the President to issue an order for the promotion of the Confucian classics and the worship of the mother of Mencius, in order to revive this moribund world and preserve our national character." Thinking about the beggar woman, Simin suggests that the poem should be titled the "Filial Daughter," to eulogize her and criticize society. In the following exchange one of his friends laughs uproariously upon hearing the jeering comments about giving her a good scrubbing. Simin is acutely pained by his friend's laughter, because, as Lu Xun hints, it suggests to him the truth of his wife's words, which he had repressed.

Lu Xun sets up the duality between Chinese and foreign, East and West, old and new as the basic framework of the story. The foreign and new—schoolgirls, bobbed-hair, modern education, English words, the heavy sound of leather shoes worn by Simin's son—are an intrusive and disruptive presence for Simin. Lu focuses our attention on the power of a new (if seemingly insignificant) *commodity*, soap, to disturb his protagonist by its capacity to arouse desire and throw his world out of kilter. It is clear that what Simin finds most disturbing is the unmooring of gender and sexual norms by the changes he sees around him. He responds vituperatively, denying the need for girls to go to school (thus keeping them within the domestic sphere) and valorizing the conduct of the pure and filial beggar woman. For Simin she represents everything that is eternal and pure in Chinese tradition and he wants the poetry contest to immortalize her purity. This effort to restore the moral authenticity of the nation via the beggar woman thus has to exalt her poverty (filial even in desperate need) and desexualize her as the object of men's (especially his) desire.[23]

Although he satirizes it as a ridiculous failure, Lu Xun's jibe about the poem on the "Filial Daughter" incidentally reveals one of the means whereby the conservative model of woman sought to prevent her from "contamination" when she emerged from the home. Modern patriarchy permitted women's involvement outside the domestic space but sought to wrap the woman-in-public with the flag of civilizational authenticity represented by the historical rhetoric of self-sacrifice and virtue. We might try to imagine this strategy spatially, as one where women's bodies move within a larger public space in rhetorically encased units. This perspective permits us to see how such a protective strategy was continuous with the organizational strategy of segregation. Segregated organizations, such as virtuous girls' schools, women's professional associations, and even the women's wings of the redemptive societies, were the other way in which women's involvement in the public sphere was contained in signifying encasements. As we shall see, redemptive societies were for men extended means of monitoring and control; but for women this mode of involvement in the public sphere could also be empowering. Women in these societies often desired separate organizations.

Take the case of the Red Swastika Society. Reports and queries from separate women's groups within this society begin to appear in the records around 1932 from cities and towns in China and Manchukuo. The mother organization (*muyuan*) of the World Women's Red Swastika Society was created in Jinan in February of that year, and its headquarters later established in Beiping. A report from the women's group (*nüshe*) of the *Mouping Daoyuan* to the general assembly insisted on the clarification of the status of women's groups in the Society. It noted that while all the formal niceties of the new organization had been decided, the question of whether or not separate and parallel women's organizations should be established at each administrative level had not. The places for women to gather for self-cultivation and to conduct research and philanthropic activities were not ideal, since the women had to share these places with the original men's organization.[24] Separately, the southeast branches headquartered in Hangzhou reported the difficulties in the procedures for conducting women's worship when originally women had not made offerings at the same altars (*shenkan*). It also reported the need to expand the size of worship halls in order to accommodate the rising number of worshippers.[25]

The *Mouping* proposal strongly urged that the organizations and locations be separated and the constitution of the Society be amended to reflect these changes. The assembly resolved that preparatory offices (*choubeichu*) and committees formed of the leading women in the Beiping office and representatives from the localities be set up. They formulated the rules and bylaws for the seventy new women's branches that they hoped to set up. In addition to the general relief work and lectures that the women's organization shared with the men, its special philanthropic activities included managing schools, child care, and research, education, and mobilization around women's concerns.[26] Judging from the reports and the large number of proud photographs of women-only branches in the records, it would appear that women favored segregated organizations, perhaps not only as the appropriate means to enter public life, but also to limit the interference of men in the organization. It was their conditioned engagement in the public world that would shape their understanding and practice of the civilizational pedagogy that sought to mold their lives and self-conceptions. At the same time, these signifying "women's spaces" became targeted by regimes in Manchukuo, Japan, and China as the organizational means of penetrating and restructuring the family and redefining the relationship between private and public, though these efforts were hardly always successfully.

Governmentality and Modern Patriarchy

Michel Foucault has suggested that in the West the status of the family transformed from a model of governance—for instance, in the thought of Machiavelli—into an object and instrument of govenmentality.[27] Later work has elaborated this process:

> The everyday activities of living, the hygienic care of household members, the pre-viously trivial features of interactions between adults and children, were to be anato-mized by experts, rendered calculable in terms of norms and deviations, judged in terms of their social costs and consequences and subject to regimes of education and reformation. The family, then, was to be instrumentalized as a *social machine*—both *made* social and utilized to *create* sociality—implanting the techniques of responsible citizenship under the tutelage of experts and in relation to a variety of sanctions and rewards.[28]

State policies towards the family in inter-war East Asia followed a similar path, but the power of the historical representation of women in the domestic sphere ensured its conspicuousness in the ideology of state power, especially as the latter sought to penetrate, transform, and deploy the family as an instrument of governmentality.

Governmentality has the effect of nucleating, rationalizing, standardizing, and institutionalizing the family as a means to shape individual subject formation, whether to extend life, guide consumption, or channel political loyalty. In demo-cratic regimes this function is distributed between the state and relatively autono-mous societal associations, whereas in nondemocratic regimes of the inter-war years the autonomy of social organizations was much reduced.[29] Particularly noteworthy about the three regimes in Japan, KMT China, and Manchukuo were the common elements within the ideological and institutional means of this reshaping effort. The elements relevant to this chapter are the ideological figure of woman as the self-sacrificing representative of "tradition within modernity," the government-administered mass organizations for women, and related civic societies such as the *Daodehui*. These elements came together as the regimes sought to engage women activists in the transformation of family and society. Whether they were expected to embody the gendered ideology of womanhood or retain it in segregated organizations, these women were perceived as more susceptible to state directives than either the uneducated working woman or the Westernized Modern Girl.

We have noted how the model of "good wife, wise mother" came to stand for everything that the Modern Girl in 1920s Japan was not: Japaneseness and the past, as well as the new, enlightened domesticity.[30] Silverberg believes that it was the threatened militancy of the working woman that generated the image of the Modern Girl, relentlessly depicted in the press as promiscuous and non-national. In contrast, the 1920s state cult of domesticity targeted the "housewife" of the rapidly proliferating middle-class, nuclear family to implement its policies of improving domestic life, encouraging rational consumption, fostering scientific attitudes, thrift, and the like.[31] While women's associations were engaged in enhancing the public role for women, including the suffrage movement, the majority of these associations also appear to have voluntarily operated within the state's ideology of ideal womanhood. Indeed, women activists even argued that the Japanese women's movement was different from Western women's movements because the Japanese recognized the difference between men and women and the special role of the mother's love in social development.[32] In a context where motherhood was increasingly becoming the central image of the 1930s revival of the Meiji period family-state ideology,[33] such declarations indexed the extent to which the family had become the instrument of a state-driven governmentality.

Sheldon Garon has suggested that the Japanese state was able to penetrate the household to achieve its goals of resource extraction and hygiene improvement to an unprecedented degree after the 1920s because of the emergence of women as intermediaries in the project of social management.[34] Whether as housewives or in segregated associations, these women tended to conform to the ideology of womanhood contained and guided by the state-mandated demarcation of public and domestic as separate spheres for men and women. Although the KMT in China was a much weaker state, I believe we can see a similar strategy by this regime to utilize segregated women's organizations to extend the ideological roles and norms of domestic womanhood (nursing, educating, nurturing) into the public. Conversely, it sought to turn these women, contained ideologically in segregated organizations, back toward the family in order to achieve the goals of the state. Thus did the state seek to control the increasingly unstable boundaries between the public and the domestic.

To be sure, different women's groups and publications loosely affiliated with the KMT expressed radical and feminist points of view, but the dominant political tendency represented the view of a modern patriarchy. A recent study by Karl Gerth shows how the "national products" (*guohuo*) movement, led by the KMT to boycott foreign goods and encourage consumption of domestic products, spotlighted the authentic national woman, described as the *xianqi liangmu* (virtuous wife, good mother). She was a figure who promoted national consumption not only by her own consumer practices but by guiding household consumption of domestically produced goods and reproducing nationally minded consumers. New Life women's associations were critical to the promotion of the movement of national consumption in the family, and engaged in such tasks as organizing exhibits of national products for women in the provinces.[35] The obverse of this figure, like the Modern Girl in Japan at the same time, was bitterly attacked for selfishly consuming foreign products and neglecting the family and national duties. Underscoring the trope of authenticity and purity associated with the Chinese woman, these women were denounced as prostitutes who had sold out to the outsider.[36]

The KMT's New Life movement, launched in 1934, was a campaign to revive traditional values for the purposes of governmentality. It thus fits well the model of "tradition within modernity," which allowed the state to serve as the custodian of authentic tradition while deploying that tradition for the KMT's disciplinary project of modern subject formation. As Chiang Kai-shek put it, "Today we all recognize the important place of the (ancient) ideals of *li, yi, lian, chi* (propriety, justice, honesty, and shame/modesty) in revolutionary nation building (*geming jianguo*)."[37] And Madame Chiang Kai-shek, better known in China as Song Meiling, described these Confucian ideals as the inner counterpart of spiritual and moral renovation (*gexin*) to outer political and economic reform.[38] Founded initially to rehabilitate the communist-dominated region of Jiangxi, which the KMT had ravaged, the campaign was extended to the entire country, drawing on ideals of self-discipline and moral regulation—allegedly the factors behind China's historical greatness—to produce a new citizenry dedicated to the collective. As Arif Dirlik says, "Its basic intention was to substitute 'political mobilization' for social mobilization, thus replacing revolutionary change from the bottom (which threatened the social structure) with closely supervised change orchestrated from the top (which served the goals of the state)."[39] Like other fascistic regime-administered mass movements, its ideal of mobilization included the total transformation of the individual through reform of customs and everyday practices relating to personal hygiene and moral improvement.

Women were particularly important in the New Life movement because so much of individual transformation was expected to take place in the family. Before the outbreak of war in 1937, women were not particularly discouraged from working outside the home, but the overwhelming tone of the writings by political leaders and intellectuals celebrated the great contributions that women could make to the nation by focusing on their role as mothers. Song Meiling, the driving force behind the movement, recognized that "intelligent and educated" women should not have to restrict themselves to the home, but urged that the main task of women was to manage the household and the children's education. She appealed to them to infuse a spirit of self-sacrifice, extirpate the habits of ignorance and laziness, and manage the household in an orderly and scientific manner.[40] From 1937, when women were urged to come out of the home to participate in the war effort, Song clearly identified the patriotic and self-sacrificing woman—against both the comfort-seeking, parasitic, and unpatriotic women and the ignorant rural women—as one to target for productive service.[41]

Such New Life women's organizations as the Women's Service League (*Funü fuwutuan*) and Women's Life Improvement Society (*Funü shenghuo gaijinhui*) sought to play an important role in the institutionalization and standardization of domestic life. As the 1934 report on the Nanchang Women's Service League declared, the method for achieving the goals of the movement was first to develop professional (elite) women's organizations and then penetrate the domestic sphere (*tui zhi jiating shehui*) through them. New Life groups sought to establish standard family guidelines regarding clothing, diet, hygiene, production, child-rearing, education, economy, medication, and sociability (*zuoren*).[42] The movement hoped to be able to educate and exhibit 200–1,000 "standard families" as models to be followed. New Life organizations intervened to regulate marriage age and registration, the promotion of (economical) group weddings, the abolition of "superstitious" or "unhygienic" rituals, and even the standardization of the kind (domestically made) and length of the *qipao*, or Chinese women's dress.[43] The Women's Life Improvement Society also set up several subdivisions, such as the Domestic Affairs Study Society, handicraft cooperatives, the Women's Labor Service League, and others. During the war years, women's associations were expected to nurse wounded soldiers, attend to their families' needs, mobilize and train rural women in the production of various goods (especially textiles), and undertake educational and family improvement projects, as well as to educate and propagandize among local minority people in the wartime KMT regions.[44]

In Japan, as in China—and, as we shall see, in Manchukuo—the advent of war brought women out of the home in increasing numbers to fulfill the goals of the wartime state. But the fundamental conceptions of women and strategies for directing their role in society appear to have not so much changed as intensified, extended, and expanded to deal with the new circumstances. Women continued to be mobilized through segregated organizations and to serve in gendered roles and functions; and these services continued to be directed at the family and other women's communities, such as textile workers. Through these means, the regimes sought to protect the gendered ideology of women as embodied cultural assets.

Different ministries in Japan sponsored several different women's mass organizations in the 1920s and 1930s. The Greater Japan Federation of Women's Associations (*Dainihon rengō fujinkai*), sponsored by the Ministry of Education, flourished during the Great Depression as a means to promote the household economy, health, and morality. During the 1930s, it was gradually displaced by the Defense Ministry's National Defense Women's Association (*Kokubō fujinkai*), which advocated traditional morality and exhorted women to fight the "world economic war" and "world thought war" in the kitchen. As the war deepened, this defense association, which counted 7.5 million members by 1938,[45] brought the women out of the home to support the war effort through the segregated institutions that extended the modern ideology of domesticity into the public sphere. Women's associations were involved in the conscription effort through functions consonant with women's roles as nurturing wifes and, especially, as mothers.[46] Members provided comfort packages for troops, visited hospitals and graves, educated soldiers, inspected youth training, and celebrated the departure and return from battle of every soldier. They reinforced the symbolism of the home and ideals of self-sacrifice by wearing plain white aprons that, according to Kasza, were designed to avoid "kimono competition" and other signs of luxury consumption.[47] At the same time, they were expected to represent the state in resolving the crises of wartime families. They addressed family problems such as the not-unusual rape by the father-in-law of the absent soldier's wife and conflicts between the wife and the family of the dead soldier.[48]

Women in Manchukuo

The status of Chinese women in Manchuria into the early years of the twentieth century was greatly affected by the frontier circumstances of the settler population. Lattimore observed that among the older settlements in the southern regions of Liaoning province, the considerable influence of Manchu customs on Chinese women led to their being less dependent on the patriarchal system than in China proper. He cites as instances the early abandonment of bound feet among Chinese women and their relatively free interaction with men in this region.[49] In the other regions of Manchuria, where the process of Chinese settlement had begun more recently, the relative scarcity of women led both to a greater valuation of women and to widespread prostitution—prevalent even in villages of forty or fifty households.[50] The mushrooming of new towns and cities was, like the Western expansion in the United States, accompanied by a booming prostitution business. The city of Harbin, for instance, already a cosmopolitan city with an elegant downtown by the 1920s, had a flourishing prostitution trade divided by class and ethnicity, with separate quarters for Chinese, Korean, Russian, and Japanese prostitutes. Indeed, the Manchukuo government levied a progressive tax on brothels based on the class of their service and clientele.[51]

During the first few decades of the twentieth century, the formation of an urban middle-class cultural consciousness among the Chinese and the much smaller Japanese communities led to a discourse on womanhood and a civilizing project to erase the stigma of the frontier. This discourse followed to a considerable degree the model of the figure of tradition within modernity that permitted a controlled and limited reform of women's conditions. Records of the Morality Society give us a glimpse of the beginnings of this development. In the 1930s, the Society sought to honor those among its members and their forebears who, during the first two decades of the century, had made contributions to the Society's ideal social vision. Most were local elites who expressed their social commitments, not as they had traditionally, by building and maintaining temples, but by establishing, managing, and contributing money to the new "virtuous and chaste girls' schools."[52] Virtuous girls' schools in the Manchurian context were not merely a means of containing (and managing anxiety about) women in the public sphere; they represented a civilizing strategy for the frontier.[53] Segregation worked together with the application of a civilizing rhetoric upon the bodies of these women. Thus, one woman claimed that she only really understood what it meant to read after her father transferred her from a regular school to a virtuous school. Learning to read was not true learning unless such reading could shape the body and its conduct (*xing dao shenshang, na jiao shizi*).[54] The Morality Society, which honored the virtuous school–building elite, was thus also continuing the project of attaining civilized respectability.

The discourse of female virtue found here is clearly continuous with the cult of chaste widows and virtuous wives of late imperial times.[55] But inevitably, there was also a shift in its meaning. Just as nationalists like Wang Jingwei in the KMT reorganized the role and meaning of the ideal woman, so too in Manchuria we find a new awareness of women's issues and their role in the public realm. The most widely read Chinese newspaper in the region, the Japanese-owned *Shengjing Shibao*, established in 1906, registered this growing awareness. Coverage of women's education and their role in the family became frequent and systematic after 1916, and picked up significantly after the May Fourth movement in 1919. During this period, reports and editorials in the newspaper tended to the more conservative view of women, but favored some reform. While they frequently praised filial and self-sacrificing women as models of virtue, they also praised women's education insofar as it would strengthen and enlighten the family.[56]

Women's direct involvement in the public sphere frequently brought disapproval. The British American Tobacco Company, which employed hundreds of women workers, apparently attracted crowds of gawkers at the factory gate during shift changes. The paper found this most unseemly and recommended banning women's employment for the sake of public morals. Women walking around in bobbed hair and leather shoes invited the comment that the women's movement had only converted them into men. Opposition to women's involvement in politics, especially in the student's movements of the early 1920s, was particularly vociferous. A *Shengjing Shibao* editorial entitled "Beijing University and Women Students" opined that this trend was an overreaction to the earlier closeting of women in the inner chambers. The commentator believed that the reform of women's condition should be encouraged in the family and society, but their participation in politics should be discouraged.[57] These views were probably not inconsistent with those of the middle class elsewhere in China.

At the same time, the model of the modern, liberated woman also began to appear in the 1920s and 1930s. The Chinese intelligentsia in Harbin was deeply affected by Russian émigré culture. Writers such as the feminist Xiao Hong and her partner Xiao Jun, nourished on Gorky, Gogol, and other European writers, produced a radical literary culture that survived even after their departure from the region in 1934.[58] Cities like Dalian also produced independent Japanese women. Perhaps the best known of these was the editor of the *Dairen Women's Times* magazine and journalist with the *Manchuria Daily*, Hoshina Kiyoji, who wrote widely on women's conditions in Manchuria and advocated a greatly enhanced role for women in society.[59]

Until 1937, this variety of views on gender issues was represented in Manchukuo newspapers. While the *Shengjing Shibao* continued to be conservative, others were more progressive. The *Datongbao* discussed women's issues in the 1930s, initially in a section called *modeng* (modern), which later changed to *xiandai* (contemporary) and finally appeared in a specialized segment simply called *funü*, or women. Letters, essays, and editorials in this section reflect a range of concerns, from health issues to the problem of arranged marriage. Some essays emphasized the need for women to understand that it was acceptable to serve society and the nation by producing good sons, citing such exemplary historical figures as the mothers of Mencius and Yue Fei.[60] By and large, however, the editors denounced the traditional (*zongfa*) conception that women were to serve the extended family. A man who wondered if the upwardly mobile city girl he was considering marrying would be happy looking after his parents in the village received the firm response that marriage was not about the extended family, and that he should hire someone or look after his parents himself. The editors exulted in a letter from a fifteen-year-old girl who opposed her parents' decision to force a marriage, writing, "we cannot suppress our marvel at how advanced women's consciousness has developed when we hear a fifteen-year-old say things like 'deciding my fate is a critical issue' or 'my mother did not seek my agreement on the matter of my own marriage.'" When responding to this genre of letters, the editors remarkably and frequently emphasized the illegality of forced marriage by parents, recommending that the women take legal or quasi-legal action by sending their own letters to the man's side breaking the contract, and keeping copies of such letters as evidence.[61] A two-part article written in October 1936 evaluating the old family system came out strongly on the side of the nuclear family and individual choice of partner. Although it urged people not to overlook the advantages of the old system—particularly its usefulness in caring for the old parents—the advantages it lists for the new family are overwhelming. The paper continued to carry sympathetic essays about the struggle for women's rights in Europe and elsewhere.[62]

These views appeared to coexist with more conservative measures and policies undertaken by the Ministry of Culture and Education (*Wenjiaobu*). The Ministry pursued programs to honor filial children, virtuous wives, and chaste widows, although it also prescribed appropriate physical and athletic activities for schoolgirls to make them strong and healthy citizens.[63] The *Datongbao*, of course, reported the Ministry's promotion of traditional virtues, but it was able to discuss these programs without relinquishing its views on the importance of the ability of women and youth to make independent choices.[64] After 1937, and especially after 1941, the autonomy of the press in Manchukuo was severely curtailed, but even so, the regime's attitude toward women was by no means a mere return to the past. The ideal was not to confine women to the home, but to contain and deploy them in the public in a way that would serve state and regime interests. For the moment, I want to note that the conservative model of women—as the essence of tradition within modernity—was not the only one available in Manchukuo, even though the regime sought to cultivate it. The women we shall discuss in the Morality Society were surrounded by images, views, and the reality of women making decisions and life choices in relative independence. In terms of the extant models of womanhood, there is no reason to think that the situation for women in Manchukuo through the 1930s was significantly different than in other parts of China.

Although the May Fourth model of the Westernized woman certainly existed, middle-class society and the rural elites were prepared to tolerate only limited reform of women's conditions and involvement in the public realm. Whereas certain ministries, such as Social Welfare or Defense, and the Concordia Association may have favored the model of "tradition within modernity" so as to deploy women in governmentality, others, such as the Ministry of Culture and Education, emphasized the *ideology* of woman as the soul of East Asian civilization—in significant part because of the common cause that it had made with this elite. Thus this model of woman served the regime's sovereignty claims.

We can imagine the extent to which the historical image of woman as embodying a precious and violable cultural essence pervaded the middle classes when we encounter it in the writings of even progressive nationalists in Manchukuo. In a short story called "Children of Mixed Blood" (*Hunxie er*), written in 1943, Shi Jun reflects on the question of intercultural marriages in the region. His protagonist, a Chinese magistrate in a border town, helps out the Russian widow of a Chinese man and her children. Thinking about his conversations with her, the magistrate expresses his feelings about mixed marriage. He is gratified by the woman's praise of responsible Chinese men in contrast to drunkard Russian men. But a fury rages in his heart when she innocently inquires why it was alright for Chinese men to marry Russian women, but not for Chinese women to marry Russian men. The thought that the Han people, with their rich history and culture, could give up their women and progeny to such barbarians was deeply insulting to him. The Manchukuo police censors who regularly went through the writings of suspected Chinese nationalists by this time interpreted the story as a thinly veiled expression of anti-Japanese nationalism.[65] Neither censors nor the predominantly male literary establishment seemed at all struck by this mercantilist characterization of women as precious national resources to be taken and not given. Whereas this model of woman may well have been deployed in an anti-Japanese allegory, the Manchukuo government seems to have gambled on the strategy that supporting the conservative view of womanhood would yield more by way of a shared discourse than its occasional deployment for nationalist goals.

The writer Liang Shanding, whose career and novel, *Green Valley*, we will discuss in more detail in chapter 6, was a nationalist and radical whose images of the feminine nonetheless reflected some of the gender conceptions of the time. *Green Valley* is about bandit heroes tested by life in the deep forests of Manchuria, whose mystery and truth they also embodied. Although there are many women in the novel, few have believable characters. Instead, feminine imagery plays a crucial role in the novel's representational structures as a means of clarifying its ideals. Thus, for instance, the land and the forest are depicted as the true and eternal mother, in contrast to the protagonist's biological mother, who has abandoned the land and succumbed to the temptations of the alienated city. Similarly, a simple, suffering peasant girl represents the purity of an orchid from the deepest forest, again in contrast to cheaply made-up city girls. Perhaps the only credible and strong female character who complicates the simple dualism of women as either pure or contaminated is the protagonist's aunt. A paragon of self-sacrifice, she is named Shuzhen, which means virtuous and chaste. In order to maintain the honor of the lineage, she has refused to marry after the death of her fiancé, but at the same time she has been having a lifelong affair with the foreman of the estate. Curiously, while the novel is now hailed in contemporary critical circles in the Northeast, the one aspect that continues to be singled out for particular criticism is Shanding's (actually rather complex) admiration of this sacrificing woman, seen as betraying a residual feudalism.

The controversy over the short story "Blood Lineage" (*Xiezu*) by the woman writer Dan Di, published after the fall of Manchukuo in December 1945, reveals the extent to which the model of the self-sacrificing woman became implicated in the nationalist rhetoric of the period. The story is told from the point of view of a sickly younger sister who is forced by necessity to live with her impoverished and unhappy brother and his small family. The brother tries to improve their situation by raising chickens in the house, but without much success. In contrast, the chickens raised by their Japanese neighbors are plump and productive. As the hot-tempered brother becomes more and more frustrated, he vents his anger on the family and in a climactic scene beats his sister. She leaves the household and meets with her father, who advises her, even as she shows him her bleeding hand, not to let this sorrow enter her heart, because her brother is, after all, a blood relative (*xiezu*). It was the pressures of life that had made him so mean-spirited. When the brother shows up, she forgives him but resolves not to marry.[66]

Dan Di was educated in Japan and is said to have exercised an important influence on women's literature when she returned to Manchukuo during its last years. While it is hard to fathom her literary impact, Dan Di's fictional account is remarkably continuous with the kind of letters to the editor that one finds in the women's section of Manchukuo newspapers, protesting or airing grievances by women wronged by their families. Dan Di herself suffered repeatedly at the hands of men who abandoned her.[67] Here we glimpse how public writing by women across both genres was a mutually influential mode of self-expression and coping with modern patriarchy.[68] Critics from the Northeast consider her writing to be melancholic and individualist, taking the reader into a feminine world where "women's feelers (*nüxingde chujiao*) explore fantasies in a shattered reality."[69] They have recently also included her among the group of progressive writers in the region, a coded designation of her present (posthumous) acceptability.[70] But Dan Di may have been most representative of the tragedy that befell writers during the tumultuous years of regime change, as she was imprisoned by each of the regimes in Manchuria from the 1940s: the Japanese, the KMT, and the CCP.[71] Immediately upon publication, "Blood Lineage" was attacked in a mainland paper as reflecting the slavish mentality of the colonized for admiring the Japanese and speaking in the language of the *Xiehe* or Concordia. In response, Dan Di and a number of writers and readers from the Northeast defended the story as a critique of Japanese imperialism and an exposé of the miserable conditions for Chinese in Manchukuo. There were also angry responses protesting the spiteful nationalist tendency to charge as traitors those very people "who had suffered under the cold window."[72]

We will return to the problem of the literary production of Northeastern identity in our discussion of Shanding. I think we can safely agree with Dan Di and her defenders that the little story is more liable to be read as a critique of conditions in Manchukuo than a defense of Japanese imperial ideals. If so, might we be right in suspecting that the unmentioned eye of the storm in the story is none other than "blood lineage" itself? After all, the revelation of the cost of the blood tie could not have been comforting to a patriarchal nationalism. In *The Field of Life and Death*, the more famous Xiao Hong had also concluded her devastating critique of the violence in the Manchurian countryside—both of the animal struggle for existence and the brutal Japanese occupation—with a rape committed not by a Japanese soldier but by a Chinese man. Lydia Liu has shown how nationalists have tried to smooth over the tension between feminism and nationalism in the novel and to frame it entirely as a patriotic novel.[73] Dan Di's story can be seen as a critique of a patriarchy that was inherited by both Chinese nationalism and civilizational discourse in Manchukuo. It is a cruel irony that the nationalists attacked her for criticizing the very same patriarchal relationship that the Manchukuo regime had sought to utilize for its sovereignty claims.

State, Family, and Woman in Manchukuo

As in China and Japan, the model of woman as representing "tradition within modernity" was important to the regime in Manchukuo, both for its sovereignty claims and as a strategic lever to penetrate the family. Whether from the perspective of governmentality or the regime's immediate concern with its own stability, the family was of central importance in Manchukuo. The family-state imagery, derived from Japan, was pervasive, especially after the war in Asia, and the family became the root metaphor for loyalty to the state. Demands of unconditional loyalty to the nation-state were premised upon the unconditional loyalty of the individual to the family in official declarations.[74] While the family formed the basis of the political community, it was also clear that the nuclear family was the norm of modern society—and ought to be the norm in Manchukuo—whereas large families and lineages were characteristic of backward places without a modern nation-state.[75]

Indeed, the regime revealed an enormous appetite for knowledge about the family. Within a year of its establishment, the statistical department of the General Affairs Board of Manchukuo began its annual surveys of family structure and economic life known as the Household Statistical Survey Reports (*Jiaji diaocha baogao/ kakei chōsa hōkoku*). These were extraordinarily detailed statistical reports, largely from urban areas, collected by data gatherers dispatched by city and county government offices on a regular basis. After collection, meetings were held at different administrative levels to process the data into information.[76] The declared purpose of the surveys was to obtain information on household income and consumption in order to evaluate the degree of satisfaction of urban households and the possibilities for economic growth. The surveys were relatively complex and differentiated spending patterns by generation and household size, among other criteria. It is also easy for us to imagine how through these and other intrusive means the family could become the target of surveillance and restructured to be made more responsive to the needs of the regime and govenmentality. The main agencies for penetrating, mobilizing, and reforming the family were the Concordia Association and the redemptive societies. As in China and Japan, the new regime seized the ideal of self-sacrificing women for this task.

The Japanese military also tried to develop women's organization for its needs, although it was not very successful. Japanese women's groups in the leased territories appeared soon after the Manchurian Incident. Praised by the regime for their patriotic service toward their countrymen, soldiers, and even Koreans and Manchurians (meaning Chinese) affected by war, they became the core of the organization known as the All Manchukuo Women's Federation (*Zenman fujin dantai rengōkai*).[77] Modeled in role and function on Japanese women's organizations of the time, they appeared, however, to be less responsive to the needs of the army and regime. These concerns were addressed in 1933 in a letter to the federation by General Koiso Kuniaki, general chief of staff (*sambōchō*) of the Guandong Army and second in command of the Japanese military (*rikugun*). While thanking them deeply for their self-sacrificing service to society despite "their important and heavy burdens in the home as its managers, mothers, wives, and sisters," he pointed to divisions among these groups that prevented them from emerging as a united group and serving the new nation.[78]

It turned out that one of Koiso's principal problems was that Japanese women's groups resisted the effort to transform them into an organization serving all ethnic groups, which would make them into a national organization (under the military). Given the mainly Chinese personnel of the Manchukuo Army, the rhetoric of national service was clearly important. In building the new nation, he declared, the tasks of politics and economics naturally fell to the men; the role of women was to comfort and encourage them in these tasks. But Koiso recognized "the special role of women's kindness" in the task of melding the Japanese and Manchurians (*nichi-man yūwa*). He emphasized the role of women in social welfare, the true meaning of which could only be grasped as the "encompassing love of the mother towards humanity transcending national boundaries . . . something that a narrow nationalism cannot understand."[79] He said, "Without forgetting the [ethnic/national] self, there is no true spirit of self-sacrifice," and urged Japanese women's organizations to become the nurturing mother of the greater nationality (*daikokumin*) of Manchukuo.[80]

A consideration of the tasks of the Federation leads us to wonder if there were other reasons for the women's hesitation. The tasks included social work, comforting families of wounded and bereaved, managing mother's day, responding to women's public opinion, and managing soldiers' homes (*heisha hōmu*).[81] The federation report of 1933 discusses the soldiers' homes as places where women were expected to voluntarily take turns comforting Japanese soldiers as "mothers and sisters" did in their villages back home.[82] Although the report mentions only preparation of baths, playing mah-jong, and writing letters, these "homes" may have been among the notorious sexual "comfort" stations for Japanese soldiers that developed during the foreign occupation and war. A systematic study of "comfort women" in Manchukuo has yet to be done.

After the invasion of the Chinese mainland, the Defense Ministry in Manchukuo organized the National Defense Women's Association (*Manzhouguo guofang funüren hui*) in 1938. Modeled on the Japanese National Defense Women's Association and coordinated by the Concordia Association, it did not seem able to recruit Chinese women in very large numbers. Membership, including that of Chinese women, in each of the twenty-two provinces and several special cities and districts averaged only about six or seven thousand women in 1938.[83] By May 1939, the association's sixty-nine branches had a membership of only 150,000, among which the Japanese accounted for 70 percent, Chinese for 20 percent, and Koreans the remaining 10 percent.[84] Its most important function was, of course, to support the war. Dressed in white aprons, members were instructed to build a nucleus around women; reassure and calm the population; explain the goals of "self-defense"; disseminate information; attend to wounded soldiers; and comfort, guide, and help the families of the war dead. Once in place, however, the activities of the organization were not restricted to military functions. The women were also expected to turn toward non-military families, organizing local women and lecturing them about morality, improvement of domestic life, child rearing, health, frugality, and the need to increase production. Here again, women's associations were melded into the frame of governmentality.[85] Thus, even though Chinese women may not have been successfully recruited into these kinds of mass organizations, the organizations clarify the role of women's associations in the regime's effort to control the interface between the domestic and the public.

The story was quite different with the redemptive societies and their women's groups, which had a much closer relationship with the regime. Mrs. Gu, whose narrative opened this chapter, thought of the relationship more as a partnership. She noted that "the important judge Feng Hanqing introduced the *Daodehui* to the Japanese," and that the regime "supported the *Daodehui* and did not casually force women into labor service. They distributed food and supplies to us." In the remainder of this chapter, I examine more closely the relationship of the regime with the Morality Society, as a way to explore attitudes and policies towards gender, domesticity, and the public realm in Manchukuo. The Society not only focused a great deal of its activities on women, it had a large number of women activists whose views we have an opportunity to hear.

Recall Wang Fengyi's success in reviving the Morality Society in Manchukuo in his mission to restore Chinese civilizational values and "transform the world" (*huashi*). Women were particularly important to the new society that Wang conceived: one that would combine modern ideas with enduring Chinese ideals of selfhood and the world.[86] Wang had been at the forefront of the development of virtuous girls' schools, having established 270 of them by 1925; they all became part of the Morality Society when he joined it around that time.[87] While the importance of gender segregation doubtless derived from Wang's commitment to classical morality, he was also clearly committed to a conception of woman as linking the past to the future. He reported a conversation with a Christian pastor in which Wang exposes the insufficiency of historical religions. All religions certainly pointed to the same Way (*dao*), but they neglected or demeaned women in the education of the Way. He insisted that women be educated and independent (*liye*) so that they could understand the Way.[88] If women's education and limited participation in the public sphere were necessary to the redemptive mission of the Society, such a role was quite compatible with the needs of the fascist regime. The two parties converged on an image of woman as representing a pristine East Asian traditionalism while she was simultaneously inserted into a program of modernization.

The Manchukuo regime stressed the Society's role as a mediator between state and family. The summit meetings of the Society drew such high-level figures as Tachibana Shiraki, now leader of the Concordia Association, and other top officials. The Manchukuo police were closely associated with the project for moral renewal of the citizenry. The head of the Capital Police Bureau declared that in order to attain national goals and renew the people, it was first necessary to cleanse the people's hearts. While this was the indirect responsibility of the nation-state, it was more directly the responsibility of such *jiaohua* agencies as the Morality Society. These societies should bond the people to the state (*guanmin yizhi*) by nourishing ethical attitudes and duties toward the family, society, and the nation.[89] Employing an orthodox Confucian rhetoric, officials repeatedly emphasized the central importance of the five ethical relationships in constructing a chain of loyalty to the state.[90] This is how Tachibana formulated the logic:

> Superstition has no basis in morality, but morality is the basis of belief. The youth at home must believe in the elders, the wife in the husband, and the husband in the wife. If there is no harmony within the family, then there will be no harmony in society and no harmony in the nation. The Morality Society thus represents the progress (*jinbu*) of morality.[91]

It was through the representation of the family, and the special role of women within it as repositories of the essence of tradition, that the new middle-class patriarchy made common cause with the Manchukuo state. Woman became the upholder of the "new family," which was the basis of citizenship. The new family was morally pure, selfless, and committed to the moral regeneration of the world by adhering to the "kingly way" (*wangdao*).[92] Weddings were to be frugal and unostentatious, since the goal was to achieve love and righteousness among the couple.[93] Women (and, to a lesser extent, men) were encouraged to rid themselves of jewelry and other accoutrements so that they could come to know their inner selves.[94] The Morality Society not only conducted lectures and ran schools, it organized many "family research groups" (*jiating yanjiushe*) in which the roles of model wife and mother were investigated. It is from these research societies that the righteous girls' schools received the knowledge to improve women's service to the family and nation without necessarily having to leave the home.[95]

In this representation, the goals of the nation-state could only be fulfilled when the family was strong, when husbands were righteous and wives obedient. The oral records of the morality seminars of the Third Manchukuo Morality Society (*Disanjie Manzhouguo Daodehui daode jiangxi yulu*, or *DMDY*), which were held in 1936 in Xinjing (Changchun), are an extraordinarily revealing text of over 300 pages of personal narratives and testimonials from members of the society who taught in its righteous schools and traveled the country giving lectures on morality.[96] Participants in the seminar made presentations about how their lives were guided by the appropriate moral doctrines of the Society. We hear the life stories of about twenty-five women and an equal number of men, including government officials. Within the family, the ideal moral roles for men and women were very different. From the speeches and narratives of the officials and leaders of the Society, we learn that the masculine virtues were loyalty, incorruptibility, bravery, and self-restraint. On several occasions in their narratives, men recounted as virtue the self-control by which they restrained the urge to beat their wives. One of them indicated that in showing restraint he was expressing his filiality, because both his marriages had been arranged by his mother.[97] Director Feng (*Feng zhuren*) was once faced with a serious moral crisis when his youngest wife threw his baby son on the floor: seized by a desire to avenge his progeny, he was about to strike her when he recognized the virtue of self-restraint.[98] Female virtue often entailed following the three obediences (*sancong*). The locus classicus of this doctrine is the *Book of Rituals* (*Yili sangfuzhuan*), which holds that a woman should obey her father before marriage, her husband upon marriage, and her son upon the husband's death. But in the pedagogy of the Society, as we shall see, obedience on the part of women did not necessarily entail confinement to the household. Rather, the ideal woman was shaped (or regulated) by the virtues of the family and by the reproduction of these virtues in the righteous schools and the Morality Society itself.

Having outlined the ways in which the pedagogy of the regime and the Society constituted women as subjects, let me turn to the personal narratives of the women.

The bulk of their narratives is organized around the five conducts (*wuxing*) drawn from the classical tradition, discussed in chapter 3 in the context of Wang's philosophy. They are *zhiming* (to know your fate); *zhixing* (to know your nature); *jinxin* (to devote your heart and mind, to devote oneself); *lishen* (to establish your self or body), in turn divided into *lizhi* (to resolve your will) and *liye* (to fulfill an enterprise or profession); and finally *zhizhi* (to know your limits).[99]

My goal in retelling the stories of these women is to see them neither as unwilling victims of a fascist regime nor as collaborators with an alien power. Nationalism was clearly less important to them than being able to pursue their religious mission and personal goals, and there are also suggestions that they stopped cooperating when it became impossible to pursue their mission. Although it is difficult to evaluate their efficacy as agents of the state and the Society, they were clearly identified with the avowed goals of the regime. As a result, these women represented the relative success of an East Asian model of womanhood that became the means of ordering gender roles and domesticity. What interests me in their narratives is the extent to which these women fashioned their lives and actions in accordance with a pedagogy that sought to control them. To what extent is the technique of self-knowledge subordinated to the pedagogy of the three obediences? What was the nature of the gap between the constituted subject and the enunciating subject?[100] I am not suggesting that we can find, in this gap, some kind of subaltern agency or independence from the structures of domination. Rather, I will try to show how the self is fashioned not only by the dominant representations of truth and power, but by a range of practices outside their ambit as well.

Women and Techniques of the Self

Who were the women who joined these societies, particularly as lecturers? As lecturers, they must, at some level, have believed in the pedagogy. Like teachers everywhere, they expressed demoralization when few attended their lectures and were gratified by a large turnout. Many of them were women with much grief in their lives. There were those whose children had died young, those locked in loveless marriages, those who sought solace because a younger wife or concubine had been brought in to replace them, younger wives bullied by older wives and in-laws, and many others. Many were devout Buddhists and found the Society to be basically compatible with their Buddhist faith. These were women for whom the Morality Society offered a rationalization or justification of their fate, a means of coping with their difficult lives, a missionary sublimation, and spiritual solace. A woman named Tu declares that hers is the fate (*ming*) of a stepmother. Neither the old nor the children treated her well, no matter how hard she tried. But she had come to understand her fate and had resolved her will (*lizhi*). Whereas earlier she had been addicted to drugs, she had become a vegetarian and felt no need for drugs. Indeed, she had acquired such strength and influence in her household that no one there took drugs.[101] A Mrs. Zhao states simply that earlier she would be sad when people called her "wife number two" (*er taitai*). Now she had learned to live with her fate (*tianming*) and was happy.[102] Mrs. Liu's in-laws got a "little sister" (a concubine) for her husband who was filial and sisterly, and so she had to learn to be a good elder sister. She decided to make up to her in-laws and husband by performing service to society, and had done so for the past ten years.[103]

But resignation, coping, and solace from grief and mistreatment were not the only meanings that women derived from their participation in the Morality Society. The narratives also reveal various strategies whereby women were able to maneuver the goals of the Society to secure advantage for themselves and for other women. This was hardly easy, as many women must have experienced the pedagogy as a form of objectification. Counter-representations of the modern, Westernized woman were readily available to these women. Newspapers in Manchukuo, we have seen, debated the issue of women's liberation, and until 1941 at least often carried positive images of liberated, Western, and Westernized women. Indeed, it was the often unacknowledged irruption of elements of this discourse into their own that enabled some of their maneuvers. Yet it is also clear that they accepted the virtue of filiality and even obedience to patriarchs. Most of all, they appeared to derive their inspiration and strength from the spirit of devotion and self-sacrifice—from that space of authenticity sanctified by the pedagogy of the Society. How could they be true to their beliefs when they were surrounded by messages about their domination?

The first and perhaps most important difference between the discourse of these redemptive societies and the historical, Confucian, or patrilineal discourse on women was that the rhetoric of confining women to the home in these societies was balanced or countered by a valorization of public or social service.[104] Not only did these societies have an ideal of public service, they were themselves part of the new public sphere. As such, women who participated in them as members, as audience, or as lecturers were ipso facto involved in activities outside the home, albeit through segregated organizations. Recall that even in the official articulations of society's duty to create a nested hierarchy of moral obligation linking the individual to the state, the family was not directly linked to the state. The relationship was mediated by the need to fulfill a moral obligation to society. The realm of society or *shehui* as a positively evaluated sphere of human—male and female—interaction represented a significant, though not necessarily recognized, departure from earlier historical discourses containing women within the domestic sphere.[105] Mrs. Zhao was one who did recognize the significant difference:

> Those of you under the age of forty have had the benefit of a modern education and may work outside of the home. Those of us over forty are barely literate and we know little about affairs outside the home. Now this Society allows us to exchange knowledge. I can go to your home and you to mine; we are not restricted by being rich or poor. . . . From this it is clear that the future of women is bright. We can come and hear lectures every day; we can obtain morality. The young can be filial to the old and the old can be kind. I hope my sisters will strive to build the future.[106]

The realm of the social, however, was rife with ambiguity and a dangerous capacity to erode the virtues cultivated in domesticity. Even in Mrs. Zhao's comments, which reveal a deeply felt sense of liberation, moral development afforded by the emergence of the social was ultimately brought to bear to restore filiality. While many of the men acknowledged the importance of service to society, they believed that confining women (though not necessarily to the home) was the best possible way for society to develop. Just as the virtuous girls' school was the way to regulate the behavior of girls who were exposed to society, so too, for some of these men, women's participation in the Morality Society was itself an ideal way to control their activities outside the home. The director of the society, Mr. Feng, had four wives—all of whom, he claimed, were happily involved with the Morality Society and regularly *ketou* (kowtow) to its teachers.[107]

However, this mode of containing women in the public sphere did not necessarily result in the kind of abject dependence that Mr. Feng's words might lead us to believe. Takizawa Toshihiro, who investigated social welfare organizations in Manchukuo, reported an episode from one of the virtuous schools that he visited in 1937 in Liaoyuan county. The school and its dormitories were basically well maintained. The school derived its income from a wool-weaving workshop and a grain store. It had separate lecture halls for women citizens (*funü shimin*), appointed with a picture of the emperor Puyi and an altar to Confucius. On one of the days he was there, a vigorous discussion on the subject of "the spirit of nation-building and women in the family" (*jianguo jingshen he jiating funü*) followed a talk by a lecturer from Fengtian. Takizawa was impressed by the dedication of the students and teachers of the school to popular enlightenment, and the way they criticized the old-fashioned attitude of the lecturer. Takizawa recommended that rather than preach homilies to these children, the Society should emphasize the teaching of practical life skills. In this way, they would learn from the scienticization (*kagakuka*) of everyday life.[108]

The very involvement of girls and women in a public organization, however segregated, could transform domesticity and the self-image of the women. The positive evaluation of social or public service in modern discourse together with the ambivalence of the leaders (contrast Feng's behavior with Wang's comment on religions restricting women), created opportunities for these women, which they seized and utilized to the fullest extent. A Mrs. Bai decided to give up the life of the inner quarters because she realized that the world of women was a very grasping one in which one could not be ethical. By giving public lectures, she could make a living that permitted her to support both her mother and mother-in-law. Thus she could be filial and moral without being dependent on anyone, neither husband nor children.[109] A recently married woman described the foreordained nature of the daughter-in-law: to serve all in the family with devotion—to be filial to her in-laws, help her husband attain a Buddhist nation, be kind to her children—and rid herself of vain desire. At the same time, women could follow the men and devote themselves to social good. Indeed, once one had satisfactorily served the in-laws, it was incumbent in the next phase to serve the world.[110]

Mrs. Chen reveals the significance of public service and the independence that it can bring to women. She emphasizes the utility and value of women in the family and the importance of these qualities in purifying the world and resolving to do good for society. She begins her narrative with an account of how her father-in-law brought her into the household because the education she received from her mother would bring good values into their home. These were the qualities that permitted *lishen*, the ability to establish oneself. In earlier periods, *lishen*, to the extent that it referred to women, referred to feminine bodily comportment within the domestic sphere. In a booklet of moral instruction for women that circulated in the late imperial period, *lishen* is described as a

> way of being tranquil (*qing*) and chaste (*zhen*). Tranquillity brings purity (*jie*) and chastity brings honor (*rong*). While walking, do not turn back your head; while speaking, do not expose your teeth; while sitting, do not move your knees; while standing, do not raise your voice. . . . When of necessity you have to go out, be sure to veil your face. . . . Only when you establish your body in such proper and upright ways can you be a person (*lishen duanzheng fang ke weiren*).[111]

The close connection between personhood and bodily comportment has not disappeared in the time of the Morality Society: recall the comment of the woman who learned the true meaning of reading only after applying it to her bodily conduct. But this is not how Mrs. Chen uses *lishen*. Personhood for her is dependent on material independence; the best means of *lishen* is to set up a livelihood of one's own (*liye*). Now that Manchukuo has entered the era of *Datong* or the Great Unity, Mrs. Chen avers, women have plenty of opportunity to make a livelihood. Once they have set up a living, they can devote themselves to the task of purifying the world (*huozhe neng sheshen shijie*). In this way, because one would not be working for money or fame, one could rid oneself of greed. Was this not the best way to *lishen*?[112]

Several points in this personal narrative deserve attention. First, observe the ease with which the meaning of *lishen* in one context (home) is transferred to another (society), where it may be subversive of the original context. Crucial to this transfer (and subversiveness) is not simply the valorization of social service, but the corollary notion of financial autonomy. The notion of *liye*, often treated in these narratives as a subset of *lishen*, becomes one of the most important concerns of these women as they seek to establish a material base to enable their role as moral citizens of the Society and the world. Second, note the appropriation of the rhetoric of the Manchukuo state. Many women were purposeful in their use of state rhetoric and tended to seize any rhetorical openings to advance the condition of women. Finally, there is the conflation of service in the outside world and moral purification of it. This suggests that participation in the social world is subordinated to ethical and religious goals. These goals occupy the space of authenticity and inner meaning for the individual woman, but it is a space framed by the new patriarchy of the middle class and the state.

The interweaving of these three elements—appropriation of the rhetoric; carving out a space, role, and basis for independent social action; and employment of this autonomy to achieve the moral and religious goals of the Society—is, adjusting for individual details, a recurring pattern in the women's narratives. Note how grandmother Cai elides her unfiliality in an era when universal education has become an unquestioned value. At the age of thirty-three, grandmother Cai confesses, she defied the wishes of the elders and went off to study. Now it is her responsibility to devote herself (*jinxin*) to the education of her children and grandchildren. She closes with the comment that she is a vegetarian, is deeply religious, and has tried to rid herself of vain desires. Here the value of women's education in wider society, both in the modernist rhetoric of the Manchukuo state and in the vision of the Morality Society, allows her to justify an earlier act of unfilial behavior. She finesses filiality, however, with recourse to the superior values of universal education and devotion to spiritual virtues.[113]

The strategy in these "games of truth" is to detach oneself from one kind of pedagogical value but continue to derive meaning from the constitutive representation by emphasizing another of its qualities or values.[114] Thus Mrs. Li, like several others, uses filiality to trump unquestioned obedience to her husband. Ever since she heard how a leader of the Society cared for his own mother, Mrs. Li determined to set up her own source of livelihood (*liye*) to care for her ailing mother. Since she had to go out of the home, her husband yelled at her and accused her of being unfaithful. She says that she had never loved any man other than her husband. But now her loving heart had set.[115] Mrs. Sun had to care for her sick father and student brother. Her husband had problems at work and could not provide for all of them. She had been inspired by the wise words of Wang Fengyi—"In devoting herself, the woman must not weary the husband; rather she should be able to help the husband obtain virtue"—to set up an independent means of livelihood.[116]

The ideal of moral autonomy within *lishen* is sometimes interpreted in such a radical way that it subverts the very basis of the pedagogy: family values. Thus, one Ms. Liu declares that her understanding of *lishen* includes the philosophy of single living (*dushen zhuyi sixiang*)—the merits of remaining unmarried.[117] We also see a kind of feminist filiality overcoming patriarchy. A Mrs. Liu recalls that her mother was ordered back to her natal home. She and her brother were not permitted to visit her. Later she and her brother devoted themselves to restoring the family and she established a source of livelihood for her mother.[118] This woman goes on to challenge the sages, who

> ask us to follow the three male figures (*sancong*) and learn from our husbands. We listen to our husbands, but they do not hear us. My husband eats meat and is not very virtuous, whereas I have only eaten meat once and I am a filial daughter-in-law. Should I not be the one from whom he should learn the Way? But he has been formed early and I am incapable of helping him. Anyway, I am not much concerned about my marriage.[119]

Note, however, even in this last episode, the filial link to the mother, as much as enlightenment in the Way, appears to be the driving sentiment for Mrs. Liu.

Perhaps the episode that best reveals the inseparability of the search for autonomy and commitment to the moral values of the Society is narrated by the same Mrs. Chen who urged women to take advantage of the job opportunities for them in Manchukuo.

> I was once sent to Beijing to lecture, but my husband followed me and insisted that I return home. Why is it that men can bully women so? I asked the teacher (*shanren*) if I should return. He replied, "You may return. What do you have to fear? All you have to know is whether or not you have the will." I returned. In Tianjin I was asked whether I returned of my own will. I nearly wept. I had resolved to return because I remembered that I could not violate my parents' will (*ming*). The next time I left, I went away for four years. And so I am what I am today. The important thing is to know your own will (*zhi*). It is how and why people make up their minds that is important, not the decision itself. I believe it is important to be filial. . . . When you have an independent income you are not only, as the teacher says, the iron master (*tie caizhu*), you become the golden master (*jin caizhu*).[120]

I want to dwell on this complex narrative not because of the way in which these women have grasped the importance of outside service and financial independence, or because of the continued importance of filiality. Rather I am struck that the source of strength and resolve for this woman derives precisely from the very ideology that constrains her in so many other ways. It is by knowing her mind and cultivating her resolve (*lizhi*)—the Way—that she is able to establish her independence from her husband despite the constraints. The segment in the records of the proceedings of the conference that is most restricting for women is the one titled *zhizhi*, to know the limits. The doctrine that is invoked most often as a constraint, and indeed as self-constraint, is that of the three obediences, or *sancong*. When faced with such constraints, one as strong and gifted as Mrs. Chen can still pick her way around them, but that is not necessarily true for many other women. Mrs. Chen acknowledges the importance of the obediences but she does not dwell upon them at length. From our fathers, she says, we can know our nature, from our husbands our fate, and through our sons we can establish ourselves (*lishen*). She does not elaborate upon what she means by *lishen* here, but moves immediately to the differences between the ways in which her parents were "good people" and the way she can be a morally pure person. Her parents were good people of a village or county; she is a good citizen of the entire nation, and indeed the world.[121] Once again she invokes the expanded community of moral service to elude constraints.

But not all the women were as skillful as Mrs. Chen. Mrs. Zhao says that her greatest aspiration is to be a man, so much so that she sometimes forgets that she is a woman. But her nature is that of a woman, her mind is that of a woman, and her body is that of a woman. She needs to remind herself constantly about these constraints.[122] Another woman cites the sages to acknowledge to herself that a woman must recognize her limits in her duty to observe the three obediences.[123] Mrs. Liu believes that, having a woman's heart, she was not filial to her in-laws and did not obey her husband (*congfu*). Consequently, they brought a "sister" into the household. Now she has tried to be a good wife and obeys her husband dutifully. Although they are poor, they are pure inside.[124] Thus we are returned to the pedagogy of authenticity.

The figure of woman as the essence of "tradition within modernity" addresses most fundamentally the aporia of time, the anxiety faced by individuals and regimes in societies driven by a conception of historical time as the constancy of flux. As the anchor of an eternal, civilizational essence—guarded during her movement out of the home—woman was expected to function as the figure of authenticity for both individuals and the regime. I have tried to examine the relevance of the regime of authenticity in the lives of these mostly ordinary women of the Morality Society, and have found it to be quite complex. On the one hand, as our concluding passages indicate, the "truth" of the doctrine was a powerful source of the sense of the self and its mission. Even more, we have seen how the pedagogy did indeed shape the behavior of these women in ways that were intended. But a life is scarcely shaped by a pedagogy alone. Pedagogy is grasped in the environment of its performance, in the spaces and practices of everyday life. Both the Society and the regime conceived of a modern role for women in public spaces, but they also sought to contain and control them through segregated organizations and an ideology of domesticity. Even with this limited participation in the public world, women could garner sufficient moral and economic resources to conceive the Way "strategically" and fashion their lives at some distance from the pedagogy.[125] This is how they learned to live by the authentic and live in their time.

For the regime in Manchukuo, as much as in China and Japan, the figure of woman as authentic—developed as part of its sovereignty claim—became a significant constituent of the symbolic regime of authenticity. As its custodian, the state possessed the ability to deploy it for purposes both of governmentality and short-term regime goals. In particular, it sought to use segregated women's organizations to control and penetrate society, by manipulating the changing interface between domestic and public spaces—extending the domestic into the public and turning the domestic-in-public back toward re-forming the family. The sign of civilizational authenticity and the lever for state manipulation converged in the virtue of self-sacrifice. The historical discourse of the self-sacrificing woman was inherited by modern patriarchies in all of the modern states in East Asia and represented a paradigmatic model of individual self-sacrifice for the nation. A similar pattern of political participation, in which state power sought to control the relationship between personal authenticity and sovereignty, linked nation building, state penetration, and citizenship in the three societies.

Indeed, as the work of Meng Yue and others shows, this pattern remained paradigmatic for the communist state in China during much of the Maoist period.

According to Meng, in the literature of the People's Republic (PRC) before 1980, the triumph of class struggle was secured through the figure of woman as desexed, nonmaterial, and pure. Ideally, both men and women gained their sense of the authentic communist self (the self that realizes the abiding, if latent, collectivism and selflessness of the propertyless) through the model of the self-denying, sacrificing, sexless woman. Meng writes,

> On the one hand, the state's political discourse translated itself through women into the private context of desire, love, marriage, divorce and familial relations, and on the other, it turned woman into an agent politicizing desire, love, and family relations by delimiting and repressing sexuality, self and all private emotions.[126]

Meng Yue's analysis is not directly concerned with the problem of timeless authenticity, but we can see that not only did such a woman enshrine all that was pure and true in communist discourse, she also symbolized that unchanging core—the stillness of the true—whereby communism could recognize itself in the march of change. It thus appears that the Maoist regime shared with the evidently different prewar regimes in East Asia a historical, if subterranean, conception of women as lacking political agency specifically as women.[127] In both Maoist China and noncommunist East Asia, it was women's passivity, their being spoken for, that represented the political meaning of their gender.

I have deliberately stressed the common elements in the discourse of and policies toward gender, domesticity, and the public realm in Japan, China, and Manchukuo in order to show how shared nation-work belies the narratives of national distinctiveness that it produces. To be sure, there were several distinctive features regarding this cluster in Manchukuo, and others have begun to write about them. Perhaps most distinctive was the government's propaganda whereby cross-ethnic marriages and adoptions were seen as the expression of an ideal of ethnic harmony—contradicted in practice by the considerable separation and hierarchy among ethnic communities, especially in relation to the Japanese.[128] A more subtle expression of this duplicity was the phenomenon of the cross-ethnic actress Li Xianglan, or Ri Koran. Of Japanese parentage but born and raised as Chinese in Manchuria and Beijing, Li acted as a Chinese in Japanese-produced films promoting themes of pan-Asian womanhood, family values, and amity. Given her considerable popularity among Chinese audiences, who mostly did not know of her Japanese background, we are led to believe that national differences were probably not as salient as the common cultural and historical framework through which these films were viewed.[129] Perhaps just as distinctive of the gender–family complex in Manchukuo was the wide-ranging role played by women of the redemptive societies, particularly the Morality Society and the Red Swastika Society. In neither China nor Japan were such originally independent societal groups entrusted with such extensive functions of governmentality and loyalty building for the regime.

It is thus entirely possible to see the women's associations as collaborating with an unmitigated evil, the occupying enemy force. But such a view derives from a nationalist perspective, and few of these women saw themselves from this perspective at the time. Indeed, most important for them was the Way, knowledge and practice of which would lead to the salvation, not just of the nation, but of the world. The rhetoric of the "kingly way" and "Great Unity" promoted by the regime suited the worldview of the redemptive societies, and the Manchukuo government was the first in recent history to have created a legitimate space for them to function and flourish. They—the women in particular—responded with considerable enthusiasm to the opportunity to serve their cause in public; however this may have also served the regime. Mrs. Gu, with whom we began the chapter, tended in fact to see the Japanese as following the *Daodehui* rather than the other way around. She saw little contradiction in serving different regimes as long as she could continue her mission.

When after the Chinese war in 1937, and especially after the Pacific War in 1941, Manchukuo became increasingly subservient to the interests of the Japanese war machine, the regime became more oppressive and began to pose difficult choices for its allies like the redemptive societies. In this situation, many responded with noncooperation. We have pointed to instances of increasing suspicion about several of these societies or their branches by Japanese police. We also have complaints from the Concordia Association about members of redemptive societies refusing to take part in campaigns to increase production. Mrs. Gu notes that during the Pacific War the numbers of lecturers in her unit reduced from 140 to 20, although she was proud to be among those who did not shirk from the hardship.

However we view the politics of such an alliance—as collaboration or partnership—it is undeniable that, as in China and Japan, the regime used these women for its purposes. At the same time, note that the women were also able to use the resources of the regime—ideological and institutional—to fashion their lives in a way meaningful to themselves and their ideals. Indeed, the nationalist condemnation of such people poses a conundrum: Can a Chineseness be denied to those who seek their identity in their own cosmopolitan traditions? Ironically, as we will see in the next chapter, it is precisely the older, Confucian, cosmopolitan vision of Chineseness that nationalists would invoke to bring into the fold those who may have had other loyalties.

Notes

1. Wang Jingwei, "Duiyu nüjiede ganxiang" (Reflections on women's world), *Funü zazhi* 10 (1924): 106–7.

2. Wang Jingwei, "Duiyu nüjiede ganxiang," 108. The notion of self-sacrifice, of course, pervades this entire topic and deserves more discussion. Several scholars have argued that self-sacrifice is critical to establishing the claim to nationhood. See Renan, "What Is a Nation?"; Liisa H. Malkki, *Purity and Exile: Violence, Memory, and National Cosmology among Hutu Refugees in Tanzania* (Chicago: University of Chicago Press, 1995), 216–18; and John D. Kelly, "Diaspora and World War, Blood and Nation in Fiji and Hawai'i," *Public Culture*

7 (1995): 489. Martyrdom is the root sacrificial form that sanctions and sanctifies rights for the wronged. Historically, the sacrifice of the pure and authentic often redeemed the desire for wealth, lust, and power; see Richard Von Glahn, "The Enchantment of Wealth: The God Wutong in the Social History of Jiangnan," *Harvard Journal of Asiatic Studies* 51 (1991): 651–714. The same mechanism may perhaps be at work in the national martyr, but note that the sacrificial action also produces the authentic.

3. Sheldon Garon, *Molding Japanese Minds: The State in Everyday Life* (Princeton: Princeton University Press, 1997), 119.

4. Sharon H. Nolte and Sally Ann Hastings, "The Meiji State's Policy Toward Women, 1890–1910," in *Recreating Japanese Women, 1600–1945*, ed. Gail Lee Bernstein (Berkeley: University of California Press, 1991), 157, 171–72.

5. Joan Judge, "Talent, Virtue, and the Nation: Chinese Nationalisms and Female Subjectivities in the Early Twentieth Century," *American Historical Review* 106 (June 2001): 771.

6. Sanetō, *Nihon bunka no Shina e no eikyō*, 159–166, 260–4; Judge, "Talent, Virtue, and the Nation," 773–83; Weikun Cheng, "Going Public through Education: Female Reformers and Girls' Schools in Late Qing Beijing," *Late Imperial China* 21 (2000): 110–12, 117 n. 40; and Reynolds, *China, 1898–1912*, chap. 5.

7. Judge, "Talent, Virtue, and the Nation," 15–16; Cheng, "Going Public through Education," 120; Kazuko Ono, *Chinese Women in a Century of Revolution, 1850–1950*, trans. and ed. Joshua Fogel (Stanford: Stanford University Press, 1989), 54–59; and Reynolds, *China, 1898–1912*, 58–59. Judge discusses at some length the experience of Chinese women in Shimoda's school for them in Tokyo. Ironically, many of these women rejected much of Shimoda's pedagogy of traditional virtues and were more impressed by Japanese women's high levels of education.

8. Zhao Jingru, quoted in Sanetō, *Nihon bunka no Shina e no eikyō*, 264.

9. Jennifer Schirmer, "The Claiming of Space and the Body Politic within National-Security States: The Plaza de Mayo Madres and the Greenham Common Women," in *Remapping Memory: The Politics of Timespace*, ed. Jonathan Boyarin (Minneapolis: University of Minnesota Press, 1994), 196. See also Ana Maria Alonso, "Gender, Power, and Historical Memory: Discourses of Serrano Resistance," in *Feminists Theorize the Political*, ed. Judith Butler and Joan Scott (New York: Routledge, 1992), 404–25, and Joan Landes, *Women and the Public Sphere in the Age of the French Revolution* (Ithaca: Cornell University Press, 1988).

10. Partha Chatterjee, *The Nation and Its Fragments: Colonial and Postcolonial Histories* (Princeton: Princeton University Press, 1993), chap. 6.

11. Chatterjee, *Nation and Its Fragments*, chaps. 6 and 7.

12. Katherine Carlitz, "Desire, Danger, and the Body: Stories of Women's Virtue in Late Ming China," in *Engendering China: Women, Culture and the State*, ed. Christina Gilmartin et al. (Cambridge: Harvard University Press, 1994), 101–24; Susan Mann, *Precious Records: Women in China's Long Eighteenth Century* (Stanford: Stanford University Press, 1997), 37–56; and Mark Elvin, "Female Virtue and the State in China," *Past and Present* 104 (1984): 111–52.

13. Yan Shi, "Nannü tongxue yu lian'ai shang de zhidao" (Coeducation and guidance on amorous relationships), *Funü zazhi* 9, no. 10 (1923) 18–19; and Wang Zhuomin, "Lun wuguo daxue shang buyi nannü tongxiao" (On the inappropriateness of coeducation in our universities), *Funü zazhi* 4, no. 5 (1918) 1–8.

14. Ono, *Chinese Women in a Century of Revolution*, 27.

15. Li Youning and Zhang Yufa, eds., *Jindai Zhongguo nuquan yundong shiliao, 1842–1911* (Documents on feminist movements in modern China, 1842–1911) (Taibei: Zhuanji wenxueshe, 1975), 463–67.

16. Cheng, "Going Public through Education," 132.

17. Miriam Silverberg, "The Modern Girl as Militant," in *Recreating Japanese Women, 1600–1945*, ed. Gail Lee Bernstein (Berkeley: University of California Press, 1991), 263.

18. Silverberg, "Modern Girl as Militant," 264.

19. Norma Diamond, "Women under Kuomintang Rule: Variations on the Feminine Mystique," *Modern China* 1 (1975): 6–7.

20. Lu Xun, "Wozhi jielieguan" (My views on chastity), in *Fen, Lu Xun Quanji* (1918; reprint, Taipei: Tangshan, 1989), 1:101–13.

21. Lu Hsün [Lu Xun], "Soap," in *Selected Stories of Lu Hsün*, trans. Yang Hsien-yi and Gladys Yang (New York: Norton, 1960), 167.

22. Lu, "Soap," 171.

23. I would like to acknowledge my debt to Carolyn Brown's reading of "Soap," which inspired my own analysis; see Brown, "Woman as Trope: Gender and Power in Lu Xun's 'Soap,'" in *Gender Politics in Modern China*, ed. Tani E. Barlow (Durham: Duke University Press, 1993), 74–89. Brown points out that the one person in "Soap" who is able to see through this trope of woman is none other than the only woman unrepresented by the male characters—Simin's wife. Brown writes, "with the character Mrs Sumin, he (Lu) empowers a semi-traditional woman with speech and the capacity to 're-read the male text,' making her the locus of his own value" (77). Thus, with characteristic irony, Lu Xun suggests a robust skepticism towards the project of authenticity among those, like Mrs. Simin, who could well have been objectified by this project. The reader will not miss the final irony of Mrs. Simin being given voice by Lu Xun, the man.

24. Jinan Daoyuan, ed., *Li Daodayuan yishilu* (Record of the virtuous events of the establishment of the Great Dao Yuan) (Jinan, 1932), 74–78.

25. Tongshihui zhiyin (Management committee printed), *Wansi Chungshantang zhuankan* (Pamphlet of the Wansi Chungshan Lodge) (Hangzhou, 1935), 1–2.

26. Jinan Daoyuan, *Li Daodayuan yishilu*, 77.

27. Foucault, "Governmentality," 92.

28. Nikolas Rose, "Governing 'Advanced' Liberal Democracies," in *Foucault and Political Reason: Liberalism, Neo-liberalism, and Rationalities of Government*, ed. Barry Andrew, Thomas Osborne, Nikolas Rose (Chicago: University of Chicago Press, 1996), 49.

29. The neo-Foucauldian view tends to minimize the relative autonomy of civil society and the importance of liberalism's critique of state power as a short-lived moment in the nineteenth century. It emphasizes the interdependence of state and social organizations in governmentality (albeit mostly in the post–World War II era). See Barry Andrew, Thomas Osborne, and Nikolas Rose, eds., *Foucault and Political Reason: Liberalism, Neo-liberalism, and Rationalities of Government* (Chicago: University of Chicago Press, 1996), 8–10. In my view, the relative autonomy of societal organizations clearly had a different impact on people's lives than did governmentalities where regimes controlled mass organizations.

30. Silverberg, "Modern Girl as Militant," 263–64, and Garon, *Molding Japanese Minds*, 120.

31. Garon, *Molding Japanese Minds*, 126.

32. Garon, *Molding Japanese Minds*, 131, and Yoshiko Miyake, "Doubling Expectations:

Motherhood and Women's Factory Work under State Management in Japan in the 1930s and 1940s," in *Engendering China: Women, Culture and the State*, ed. Christina Gilmartin et al. (Cambridge: Harvard University Press, 1991), 274–76.

33. Miyake, "Doubling Expectations," 271.

34. Garon, *Molding Japanese Minds*, 144–45.

35. Yan Pinzao, "Nanchang mofan laodong fuwutuan fangwenji" (Record of a visit to Nanchang's model labor service team), in *XYDB*, 5 and 6 (April 1937), 114.

36. Karl Gerth, *Nationalizing Consumer Culture in Modern China* (Cambridge: Harvard University Asia Center, forthcoming), 356, 366, 372.

37. Chiang Kai-shek (Huizhang), "Xinshenghuo yundong qizhounian jinian xunci" (Exhortation speech commemorating the seventh anniversary of the New Life movement) (1940), in *GWXSY*, 84. See also Kirby, *Germany and Republican China*, 176–81.

38. Song Meiling, "Xinshenghuo yundong" (New Life movement) (1936), in *GWXSY*, 112.

39. Arif Dirlik, "The Ideological Foundations of the New Life Movement: A Study in Counterrevolution," *Journal of Asian Studies* 34 (August 1975): 947.

40. Song Meiling, "Xinshenghuo yundong," 110–11.

41. Song Meiling, "Funü xinshenghuo yingyoude jingshen" (The spirit that women's new life ought to have) (1938), in *GWXSY*, 114–17.

42. *MQX*, 269–70.

43. *MQX*, 193, 197; Fujiansheng xinyunhui (Fujian province New Life committee), "Fujian Lianjiang, Jiangyue xian hunsang lisu tiaocha" (Survey of wedding and funeral customs in Fujian's Lianjiang and Jiangyue counties), in *XYDB*, 5 and 6 (April 1937), 58–59; Guangdongsheng xinyunhui (Guangdong province New Life committee), "Guangdongsheng Renhua deng xian lisu diaocha" (Survey of customs in Guangdong's Renhua and other counties), in *XYDB*, 5 and 6 (April 1937), 60–64; Yan Pinzao, "Nanchang mofan laodong fuwutuan fangwenji" (Record of a visit to Nanchang's model labor service team), *XYDB*, 5 and 6 (April 1937), 106–8; and *XSY*, 12–17.

44. *MQX*, 585; *GWXSY*, 298–303, 303–10; and *XSY*, 24–28.

45. Kasza, *Conscription Society*, 89.

46. Miyake, "Doubling Expectations," 277.

47. Kasza, *Conscription Society*, 90–91; See also Garon, *Molding Japanese Minds*, 142–43.

48. Kasza, *Conscription Society*, 99–100.

49. Lattimore, *Manchuria*, 268–69.

50. Lattimore, *Manchuria*, 269, and Lee, *Manchurian Frontier*, 86–91.

51. Clausen and Thogersen, *Making of a Chinese City*, 103–6.

52. *DMDY*, 1:10–58.

53. *MDNJ*, 7:10–48, 8:23.

54. *DMDY*, 4:142.

55. Elvin, "Female Virtue," 104; and Dorothy Ko, *Teachers of the Inner Chambers: Women and Culture in Seventeenth-Century China* (Stanford: Stanford University Press, 1994).

56. In praise of self-sacrificing women, see *SJSB*, March 19, 1918; January 15, 16, and 24, 1919; February 29, 1920. On women's education, see *SJSB*, February 12, 1920.

57. *SJSB*, January 11, 1919; February 6 and 25, and March 20, 1920.

58. Lü Qinwen, "Dongbei lunxianqude wailai wenxue yu xiangtu wenxue" (Foreign and

native-place literature in the literature of occupied northeast China), in *Zhongri zhanzheng yu wenxue*, ed. Yamada Keizō and Lü Yuanming (Changchun: Dongbei shifandaxue chubanshe, 1992), 129–30.

59. Hoshina Kiyoji, *Josei yo Manshū yo* (To women and Manchuria) (Dairen: Dairen Fujin Taimuzu sha, 1931–34).

60. *DTB*, March 23, 25, 28, 1933; October 2, 4, and 10, 1936.

61. *DTB*, March 4, 10, and 15, 1933.

62. *DTB*, October 8 and 15, 1936.

63. *WJYK*, June 1934, 51, 53, 66.

64. *DTB*, March 21–23, 1933.

65. Mita Masao, "Shukei tokuhihatsu" (Capital police special secret publication), no. 3650, November 29 (n.p.), submitted to the police headquarters (Jing wu zongjü), 1943. I am very grateful to Howard Goldblatt for supplying me with these police reports on Manchukuo writings.

66. Dan Di, "Xiezu" (Blood lineage), *Dongbei Wenxue* 1, no. 1 (1945): 4–31.

67. Dan Di's real name was Tian Lin. For an account of her life, see Tian Lin, "Yiwei baojing fengshuang de zuojia—fang nüzuojia Tian Lin" (A weather-beaten writer: An interview with Tian Lin), interview by Feng Weiqun and Li Chunyan in *Dongbei lunxian shiqi wenxue xinlun* (New interpretations of the literature of occupied Dongbei) (Changchun: Jilin daxue chubanshe, 1991), 244–48.

68. Observe, for instance, how one woman presents herself as caught between patriarchal values and her own future. "My family is truly representative of this transitional era. My father is a reputable merchant who is half-for and half-against a modern-style relationship between men and women. Once my father introduced me to the son of a friend from his hometown. Later the boy wrote me an admiring letter and invited me to visit his school. My parents encouraged me to go, saying that there was no harm nowadays in a girl meeting a boy. Although we initially developed a friendship, I later realized how shallow he was and wanted to break it off. But my parents refused to let me, because we had already formed a relationship, and, besides, he has a picture of the two of us together. They say this can bring shame on us. Dear Editors: Our earlier age was a lot better. If I follow [my parents], my future is finished; if I don't, they will suffer. I feel I am riding a tiger I cannot get off"; *DTB*, March 21, 1933.

69. Huang Wanhua, preface to *Dongbei xiandai wenxue daxi, 1919–1949* (Northeast Modern Literature Series), vol. 11, ed. Zhang Yumao (Shenyang: Shenyang chubanshe, 1996), 12. See also Wu Ying, "Manzhou nüxing wenxuede ren yu zuopin" (Female writers and their works in Manchuria) (1944), in *Dongbei xiandai wenxue daxi, 1919–1949* (Northeast Modern Literature Series), ed. Zhang Yumao (Shenyang: Shenyang chubanshe, 1996), 1:347–48.

70. Bai Changqing, preface to *Dongbei xiandai wenxue daxi, 1919–1949* (Northeast Modern Literature Series), ed. Zhang Yumao (Shenyang: Shenyang chubanshe, 1996), 2:9.

71. Tian Lin, "Yiwei baojing fengshuang de zuojia," 246–48.

72. Hua Min, "Guangfu yu wenren" (Recovery and writers) *Dongbei Wenxue* 1, no. 2 (1946): 13. See also Dan Di, "Guanyu nuhua sixiang ji weiman zuojia" (Regarding slavish thought and writers in puppet Manchukuo), *Dongbei Wenxue* 1, no. 2 (1946): 6–8, and other contributions to the same issue: Shao Ge, "Yougan yiti" (The topic of feeling), and Jin Hua, "Bushi pian" (Not literature).

73. Lydia Liu, "The Female Body and Nationalist Discourse: The Field of Life and Death Revisited," in *Scattered Hegemonies: Postmodernity and Transnational Feminist Practices*, ed. Inderpal Grewal and Caren Kaplan (Minneapolis: University of Minnesota Press, 1995), 37–62.

74. Chianbu keisatsushi, *Kōmin*, 41. Moreover, the same text says, "Just as a family can adopt a member, so too a nation can naturalize a citizen" (43).

75. Chianbu keisatsushi, *Kōmin*, 5–6.

76. *JTB*; *MSSJ*, 2:50–56.

77. Ishikawa Shinobu, ed., *Zenman fujin dantai rengōkai hōkokusho* (Report of the All Manchukuo Women's Federation) (Dairen: Zenman fujin dantai rengōkai, 1933); *DTB*, October 10, 1936, 4.

78. Koiso Kuniaki, "Zenman fujin dantai rengōkai kai'in shoshi ni tsugeru no sho" (Letter to all our sisters of the All Manchukuo Women's Federation), in *Zenman fujin dantai rengōkai hōkokusho* (Report of the All Manchukuo Women's Federation), ed. Ishikawa Shinobu (Dairen: Zenman fujin dantai rengōkai, 1933), 5. Koiso, who would become prime minister of Japan during World War II, was, according to Tak Matsusaka, the chief architect of the idea of "strategic autarky"; see Matsusaka, *Making of Japanese Manchuria*, 214–23.

79. Koiso, "Zenman fujin dantai rengōkai kai'in shoshi ni tsugeru no sho," 6.

80. Koiso, "Zenman fujin dantai rengōkai kai'in shoshi ni tsugeru no sho," 7.

81. Ishikawa, *Zenman fujin dantai rengōkai hōkokusho*, 8–9.

82. Ishikawa, *Zenman fujin dantai rengōkai hōkokusho*, 11.

83. *MGFH*, 1–20.

84. Shen Jie, "Japanese Women and Their War Responsibility: Regarding Fascist Female Organizations in the Spurious Manchuria Country," paper presented to the International Federation of Women's Historians Conference, University of Melbourne, 1997, 4.

85. *MGFH*, 13–20; Shen, "Japanese Women and Their War Responsibility," 4–5.

86. In some ways, Wang's ideas were remarkably similar to those of the earlier nationalist reformers. He believed that if women did not understand the Way, they would give birth to ignorant children, ignorance being handed on to ignorance, so that the whole world would end up ignorant; see Shao Yong, *Zhongguo huidaomen* (China's religious societies) (Shanghai: Remmin chubanse, 1997), 307. Note here how the language is close to that of the early nationalist reformers, but where the cause for them was the nation, for Wang it is the world.

87. Shao Yong, *Zhongguo huidaomen*, 306–7.

88. *DMDY*, 4:207. The gazetteer recorded how his female devotees went to hear him lecture on the way of "ordering the home and managing the country"; see *Chaoyang xianzhi* (Chaoyang County Gazetteer), comp. Zhou Tiejing and Sun Qingwei (1930), juan 35:47a.

89. *DMDY*, 3:4–5, 38.

90. Three of these relationships—between father and son, older and younger brothers, husband and wife—concern stabilizing family ties; the fourth relationship, between friends, connects horizontally across families; and the fifth, between subject and monarch, links the family to the state.

91. *MDNJ*, 11:29.

92. *DMDY*, 4:134.

93. *MDNJ*, 10:6, 12:24.

94. *DMDY*, 4:151.

95. *MDNJ*, 2:41, 4:27.

96. Note that these materials are from a time (1936) before the war on the mainland.

97. *DMDY*, 4:221–23.

98. *DMDY*, 4:97.

99. The *Hanyu Da Cidian* quotes passages from the representative texts in which these categories occur: the first can be found in the *Yijing*, the second and third in the *Mengzi*, the fourth in the *Xiaojing*, *lizhi* in the *Hou Hanshu*, *liye* in the *Hanji*, and *zhizhi* in the *Liji*.

100. See Homi Bhabha on enunciation: "The reason a cultural text or system of meaning cannot be sufficient unto itself is that the act of cultural enunciation—the *place of utterance*—is crossed by the difference of writing. . . . It is this difference in the process of language that is crucial to the production of meaning and ensures, at the same time, that meaning is never simply mimetic or transparent"; *The Location of Culture* (London: Routledge, 1994), 36.

101. *DMDY*, 4:90.

102. *DMDY*, 4:94.

103. *DMDY*, 4:138.

104. For patrilineal discourse, see Charlotte Furth, "The Patriarch's Legacy: Household Instructions and the Transmission of Orthodox Values," in *Orthodoxy in Late Imperial China*, ed. Kwang-ching Liu (Berkeley: University of California Press, 1990), 187–211, and Mann, *Precious Records*. To be sure, the recent work of Susan Mann and others has shown that the high moralism confining women to the home was a consequence of the Confucian "classical revival" of the eighteenth century and should not be viewed as an eternal feature of imperial society; see Mann, *Precious Records*, 22–31. This work has also shown that despite all the rhetoric and measures designed to confine women to the home, there was still a great deal of physical mobility among women in late imperial society.

105. Furth, "Patriarch's Legacy."

106. *MDNJ*, 11:30.

107. *DMDY*, 4:53.

108. Takizawa, *Shūkyō chōsa shiryō*, 94–95.

109. *DMDY*, 4:185.

110. *DMDY*, 4:134–35.

111. Song Ruohua, *Nü Lunyu* (The analects of women) (ca. 780; Shanghai: Shanghai dazhong shuju, 1936).

112. *DMDY*, 4:181.

113. *DMDY*, 4:137.

114. Michel Foucault introduces the idea of "games of truth": "what I have tried to maintain for many years, is the effort to isolate some of the elements that might be useful for a history of truth. Not a history that would be concerned with what might be true in the fields of learning, but an analysis of the 'games of truth,' the games of truth and error through which being is historically constituted as experience"; see *The Use of Pleasure*, in *The History of Sexuality*, vol. 2., trans. Robert Hurley (New York: Vintage, 1990), 6–7.

115. *DMDY*, 4:140.

116. *DMDY*, 4:139. A Mrs. Zhu recalled being so driven by anxiety when her stepmother arrived after her mother's death that she wore out fifteen pairs of shoes. Later she realized that her stepmother was not unkind and she herself had been unfilial. So in order to make up, she set up a business together with her stepmother and her selfish feelings have dissolved; *DMDY*, 4:130.

117. *DMDY*, 4:188.

118. *DMDY*, 4:231.

119. *DMDY*, 4:231.

120. *DMDY*, 4:181–82.

121. *DMDY*, 4:227–28.

122. *DMDY*, 4:219.

123. *DMDY*, 4:220.

124. *DMDY*, 4:236.

125. "Strategically," that is, in Foucault's sense of the "games of truth."

126. Meng Yue, "Female Images and National Myth," in *Gender Politics in Modern China*, ed. Tani E. Barlow (Durham, N.C.: Duke University Press, 1993), 118.

127. Mayfair Mei-hui Yang, "From Gender Erasure to Gender Difference: State Feminism, Consumer Sexuality, and Women's Public Sphere in China," in *Spaces of Their Own: Women's Public Sphere in Transnational China*, ed. Mayfair Mei-hui Yang (Minneapolis: University of Minnesota Press, 1999), 44–46.

128. Shao Dan, "Gender in the Construction and Deconstruction of Manchoukuo," (unpublished paper, 2001), 5–6.

129. Shelley Stephenson, "The Occupied Screen: Star, Fan, and Nation in Shanghai Cinema, 1937–1945" (Ph.D. diss., University of Chicago, 2000), chaps. 6 and 7.

PART THREE

THE AUTHENTICITY OF SPACES

The complex of time, identity, and sovereignty that I have sought to analyze in this book comes to be rooted in Manchuria, as a space and place.[1] The next two chapters focus on certain spatial practices and symbolizations of the region that represent another war—for the loyalties and identities of the people with the land. These chapters show how political forces, especially the Manchukuo regime, but also others, seek to produce and mobilize, and in turn are mobilized by, spatial representations that embed claims upon places and people, or peopled-places. We know how the depiction of places, such as the Holy Land, *Heimat*, or lands claimed through Manifest Destiny, can fire the passions, steel the will, and demand life itself. Spatial representations can also negate or preempt claims; thus the idea of the dreamtime among the Australian aborigines produced a discourse among settlers alleging the aborigines' unreal connection with the land and sanctioning their brutal dispossession.[2] If the authenticity of civilization discussed in part II was designed to appeal to the principally Chinese population of Manchuria, the Japanese representation of the region as a natural place sought to limit the claims of this population. Chinese counter-representations of the region as both frontier and homeland did not take long to appear.

Images of authenticity typically occupy the heart of spatial representations. They can nourish sentiments of nostalgia and loyalty that political forces try to channel to their goals, whether to win a war or produce a claim to sovereignty. But the contest over the authentic—or, more accurately, over the production of the authentic as a political resource—is not fixed. In Manchuria, as the key players changed over time, the authenticity of the region came to serve other political projects and visions. However, the representation of the region, whether as frontier or heartland, frequently concealed the violence whereby the land was depleted and indigenous people were decimated.

As we have seen, the distinct identity of Manchuria in the eighteenth century was to a great extent fostered by the Manchus, but the region itself was scarcely homogeneous. Manchuria was constituted by several different spaces: by grasslands

171

and nomadic life in the west, settled agriculture in the southern valleys, and the forests and mountains in much of the rest. Despite the Qing effort to freeze it, the relationship between these spaces was quite dynamic. Imperialism by the railroad from the second half of the nineteenth century so radically re-spatialized the entire region that we can hardly grasp major internal events and changes without reference to developments outside Manchuria. World market prices for lumber or soya beans, the plague and other diseases, imperialist rivalries, and warlord politics in China were merely some of the obvious factors affecting demographic movements, land use patterns, and political relationships in the area. By dint of Manchuria's rapid integration with the outside world, differences within became increasingly effaced, as agriculture and industry replaced the forest and grasslands. *Green Valley* applies a microscope to the impact of this re-spatialization upon a community where we can still glimpse patterns of earlier relationships. Shanding, author of the novel, uses the motif of the railroad as the central force penetrating the valley and forest. Although it is not surprising that it would have such an unprecedented transforming effect upon a landscape, the railroad was particularly significant in Manchuria, as a largely landlocked region made relatively impenetrable by physical, climactic, and political factors. Penetration by the railroad was not only a technical breakthrough, it was an imperialist action. It was designed to open up a closed land, exploit its resources, and change the economic landscape for the benefit mostly of others. As it turned out, the railroads enabled the settlement of the Chinese agricultural community, which became the major force reshaping the environment. But many of the intellectual representatives of this community, such as Shanding, were quite ambivalent about the railroad, because in the form of the South Manchurian Railroad it represented Japanese imperialism. They also believed that by sucking out the resources of the region, the railway destroyed livelihood and landscape.

The network of railroads built around the two major trunk lines, the Russian Chinese Eastern Railroad (CER) and the Japanese South Manchurian Railroad, produced enormous changes simply by their own consumption needs. Forests were felled for the wood to construct the lines, provide fuel for the trains, and supply the towns that grew around them. According to a CER report warning of the need for rational management of forests, railroads themselves consumed from 40 to 70 percent of the total estimated output of the forest regions after 1922.[3] By 1937, export of lumber from Manchukuo outstripped that of Canada, which had been the second largest exporter (after the United States) in the world.[4] But of course the effects of railroads were more extensive and deeper. Railroads brought with them towns, commerce, industry, new rhythms of life, the promise of progress, and the threat of destruction. They also led to less visible changes, such as in the spatial foundations of political power. We saw how the pattern of agricultural settlement of the hinterland enabled by the railroad made Manchuria a different place from the Chinese mainland. While language and customs, temples and schools made the villages culturally much like those in north China, the coextensiveness of economic and political spheres enhanced the technology of administrative control and produced new types of regimes.[5] In "Railway of Annihilation," the avant-garde poet from Dalian, Kitagawa Fuyuhiko, had already linked the railroad directly with the military state in 1929.

> The military state's railway progressed through the frozen
> desert planting numberless teeth, numberless teeth that sprouted
> spikes.
> . . .
> The railway will only be completed with pain to human beings.
> Human arms change shape beneath the railroad ties. More readily
> than a rotting leaf separating from a tree.
> . . .
> In the end, the military state, wearing away this one scab,
> extends its arm.
> Toward ruin.[6]

The novel spatial practices, relationships, and modes of power that came with the railroad bore an oblique relationship to the simultaneously emergent representations of the landscape and people. Despite the new and myriad linkages to the outside world, these representations tended, first of all, to view the region as a distinctive space. Such distinctiveness appears to have served as a precondition for identifying the sites and narratives of authenticity. But each representation was differently contoured and bounded, whether for the Japanese, the Chinese, or the Koreans. Early-twentieth-century Korean nationalist writings depicted Manchuria and present-day Korea as the stage of Korean history—the land of Tangun.[7] This territory was centered on Changbai Mountain, the putative ancestral birthplace of the Korean nation that nationalists like Ch'oe Namson wanted to sacralize by "reviving" a religion of the "Way of the Park." Ch'oe's concept of a "northeast Asian cultural sphere" incorporating Manchuria stressed Korean—as opposed to Japanese or Chinese—leadership of this sphere.[8] Even today, Andre Schmid argues, such ideas foster an irredentism among Korean nationalists.[9] Recently, official anthropology in the PRC, which has denied a Korean ethnic link with the ancient kingdom of Koguryo in Manchuria, has revised the understanding of the Koguryo heritage to confirm China's rights to those territories, and has limited Korean access to the physical remains of that heritage.[10] My goal in these chapters is to see how narratives of authenticity relate to the contesting Japanese and Chinese spatial projects, and how the authenticity of a place and/or its people came to serve a succession of regimes.

We have already examined the spatial representation woven into the Japanese historical narrative sketched by Naitō Konan. To some extent this was selectively developed in relation to the eighteenth-century Manchu narrative of the distinctiveness of the region and the autonomy of Manchu imperial traditions. This narrative portrayed a land with three thousand years of history developing outside agricultural civilization and around grasslands and primeval forests and mountains. In the Japanese popular imagination, Manchuria in this period emerged as a romance of "endless sky canopying a land inhabited by bandits, horse thieves, rebels and mysterious heroes," a land of danger and opportunity like the Wild West.[11] Japanese *rōnin* wandered this land, aiding bands of revolutionaries in 1911 or leading bandit gangs who fought the Chinese settlers.[12] In Manchukuo, Japanese visual or literary depictions of the land and people tend to erase or marginalize the role of agriculture and the Han agricultural population. The vigorous film industry (*Man'ei*), the hundreds of picture books, and other propaganda materials that its many institutions churned out in several languages portrayed the grasslands and herdsmen; aboriginals and the forest; the variety of ethnic communities, including Japanese agricultural settlers; traditions and religions; modern cities and industrial power. The innocent observer might hardly be aware that over 80 percent of the population consisted of Chinese agriculturists.[13] Even the radical poet Kitagawa, quoted above, participated in the myth of Manchuria as an unpopulated frontier when he depicted the vast lands— much of which was already converted into agricultural fields—as the "frozen desert."

As an institutional condensation of the historical and spatial nation, the National Manchukuo Central Museum (*Manshūkoku kokuritsu chuō hakubutsukan*) revealed a vision consistent with the marginalization of the Chinese. Established in 1938, the museum coordinated the activities of all museums in the country and housed a major collection. It was recognized as the pioneer of the "new museum" and subsequently became the model for postwar Japanese museums. Designed not simply for viewing, it engaged in research and extension activities, including teaching, performances, film viewing, special exhibitions, friendship societies for science education, and so forth. The museum reflected a split vision of the nation and the world: on the one hand, the collections, publications, and programs of the museum and its branches were concerned with the natural resources, indigenous peoples, and historical kingdoms of Manchuria; on the other, the artifacts and materials linked Manchukuo to a pan-Asian civilization, deriving particularly from non-Han sources of Chinese empires, such as the Mongols or Turfan in the Tang Dynasty.[14] As a new type of museum, it sought to integrate this vision with the public and society to a much greater degree than previously. Thus, the museum was not only a simulacrum of civilization guiding recognition and self-location,[15] it sought to be an active force in the remaking of society according to a wartime vision of pan-Asianism.

The driving force and spirit behind the museum was its prolific deputy director, Fujiyama Kazuo. Fujiyama, among the more visionary of Manchukuo bureaucrats, sought to reconcile his original adherence to Shingon Buddhism with his adoption of Christianity. A naturalist by training, he was deeply influenced by Emerson and Thoreau, by Danish theories of agriculture and German romantic philosophy of the forest. As a public figure and museum official, Fujiyama sought to initiate several projects. He envisioned a separate folkways museum (*minzoku hakubutsukan*) as an open-air, recreational theme park to showcase the cultures of the many different people in Manchukuo and the ways they had adapted to the natural landscape and environment. Museum construction had barely begun before it ran into wartime financial problems, but Fujiyama sought to install scale reproductions of scenes from everyday life and architectural forms, such as a Mongolian yurt, a Chinese temple, an Oroqen tent, or a Russian church. His goal, which the regime opposed, was to encourage the Japanese rural settler community to learn ways of adapting to the environment from the indigenous communities.[16] Fujiyama also launched a campaign for the greening of Manchuria. His ideas and advocacy of a rational forest management policy reflected both his religious sentiments and awareness of the currents of environmental thinking in the West. As environmental policy and critique of the lumber industry, his ideas were perfectly consonant with progressive thought.[17]

However, the narrative and rhetorical dimensions of his environmental policy reveal its political implications; they tell a story about the production of a landscape in which the forest has far greater value and visibility than the farm. Even the folkways museum plan presented as representative of Manchukuo lifestyles that were rapidly disappearing under the pressures of urbanization and Chinese settlement. The environmental story pits not merely the Chinese farmer, but a whole culture that is allegedly grossly insensitive to the natural environment and its treasure, the forest, against both the aboriginal and the civilized modern nations (read, Germany and Japan). Fujiyama warned that Manchuria was rapidly on its way to suffering the same fate as the loess belt of north China, whose dry plains and bare hills, he claimed, were covered by dense forests less than a thousand years ago. Unless the forest and the ways of the indigenous people who live in it are protected, Manchukuo would be overtaken by the Gobi Desert creeping in from the west.[18] In this way, even while the SMR and other Japanese interests were practically involved in its destruction, the receding forest stood at the center of the moral landscape of Manchukuo ideology.

If the Japanese representation of the true Manchuria centered on the forest was implicated in an ideological attack upon the Chinese agriculturalist, Chinese depictions of the land erased the vestiges and memory of tribal cultures. Shanding's *Green Valley*, which derives its strength from the author's quasi-mystical search for a balance between agriculture and the primeval forest, is nonetheless remarkably silent about the people who were there when the Chinese peasant, merchant, fortune-seeker, and bandit arrived on the scene, subjected them to chattel slavery, and drove them to oblivion. To simplify somewhat, it is possible to see these two representations of the land and people as embodying the authenticity of two kinds of spaces, both important components of the nation but also problematic for it: 1) the frontiers and peripheries of the national territory, and 2) the locality or the countryside, in which the "native place" possesses a special "structure of feeling." In the gaze of the modern city, both spaces are timeless, or at least belong to a different temporality from that of the city. Whereas the "primitive" in the periphery is frequently romanticized to represent a lost human *nature*, the peasants occupying the timeless heartlands often embody ancient civilizational values that the modern nation is in the process of losing. The deeply contested nature of the Manchurian landscape, however, meant that the disappearing primitive would come to represent a lost *Japanese* nature, and the description in Shanding's novel of Manchuria as a repository of (threatened) Chinese heartland traditions was itself a complex displacement of the region as a frontier zone or borderland.

These chapters also attend to the modes of producing knowledge about—and policies towards—the spaces and people of this region. The institutionalized production of modern knowledge in/through/of history, literature, anthropology, geography, and folklore (and touching on geology, archaeology, eugenics, and journalism) in East Asia mostly derived its methods and objects of study from globally circulating sources and the nation-state system. To be sure, these disciplines necessarily interacted with highly developed historical modes of knowledge production, such as Confucian evidential and historical scholarship or Tokugawa ethnographical and geographical writings, and these mediations set the region apart from much of the rest of the world. At the same time, the global stimuli and resources that shaped social scientific and humanistic knowledge in this period were also appropriated into categories that tended to view trends, processes, and effects as immanent. Perhaps among the most prominent of these categories was the bounded notion of "culture" and "civilization," which bore a distinct, if complex, relationship with the space of the nation and empire. Culture as a field of knowledge was where the quest for identity, authenticity, and their custodianship was situated. The cultural investment of the place as the locus of authenticity turned out to be more enduring than the regimes that staked their claims of sovereignty and control upon it. It continues to shape subjectivity and identity to this day.

Notes

1. By space, I refer to the mutual determination of the environment and social relationships. This includes the determinative role of spatial representations as well as the role of geographical or built relationships in the reproduction or transformation of social relations. By place, I refer to the particularization of this mutual determination within a geographical area.

2. Patrick Wolfe, "The Dreamtime in Anthropology and in Australian Settler Culture," *Comparative Studies in Society and History* 33 (1991): 197.

3. I. A. Mihailoff, ed., *North Manchuria and the Chinese Eastern Railway* (Harbin: CER Printing Office, 1924), 197.

4. Fujiyama Kazuo, *Manshū no shinrin to bunka* (Shinkyō: Tōhō Kokumin Bunko, 1937), 139.

5. Yasutomi Ayumu, "Teikiichi to kenjō keizai—1930 nen zengo ni okeru Manshū nōson shijō no tokuchō" (The rural marketing system in Manchuria around 1930: Periodic markets and the economy of the county town) (paper submitted to *Ajia Keizai*, 2002), 1–9.

6. Kitagawa Fuyuhiko, "Railway to Annihilation," quoted in William O. Gardener, "Colonialism and the Avant-Garde: Kitagawa Fuyuhiko's Manchurian Railway," *Stanford Humanities Review* 7 (1999): 16–17. The translation is Gardener's.

7. Andre Schmid, "Rediscovering Manchuria: Sin Ch'aeho and the Politics of Territorial History in Korea," *Journal of Asian Studies* 56 (1997): 34.

8. Chizuko T. Allen, "Northeast Asia Centered around Korea: Ch'oe Namson's View of History," *Journal of Asian Studies* 49 (1990): 796, 799, 800–803.

9. Schmid, "Rediscovering Manchuria," 42.

10. Mark E. Byington, "Claiming the Koguryo Heritage: Territorial Issues in the Management of Koguryo Archaelogical Sites in Northeast China" (paper presented at the Second Worldwide Conference of the Society for East Asian Archaeology, Durham, England, 2000), 18–19.

11. Faye Yuan Kleeman, "Mysticism and Corporeality: Re-envisioning Manchuria in a Postcolonial Japan" (paper presented at the conference on Contemporary Japanese Popular and Mass Culture, Montreal, Canada, 1999), 2.

12. Kleeman, "Mysticism and Corporeality," 2–3.

13. The representation was consistent with the active policy of the Manchukuo government to discourage Chinese rural immigration; see Jones, *Manchuria since 1931*, 167–69.

14. *SHT*, 63–67, 90–91, 114–15.

15. Timothy Mitchell, *Colonising Egypt* (Berkeley: University of California Press, 1991).

16. Kawamura Minato, *Manshū Hōkai: "Daitōa bungaku" to sakkatachi* (The collapse of Manchukuo: Writers and "Greater East Asia literature") (Tokyo: Bungei shunjū, 1998), 77–79. Even earlier, Fujiyama ran afoul of the military government because he objected to its Japanese settler policies. He was transferred for his views; see *SHT*, 83–84.

17. Fujiyama, *Manshū no shinrin to bunka*, 5–6.

18. Fujiyama, *Manshū no shinrin to bunka*, 137–41.

CHAPTER FIVE

Imperial Nationalism and the Frontier

The system of modern—and perhaps early modern—states is built on the imperative that *all* global resources be controlled by territorially sovereign polities, whether
nations or empires. It was this logic that transformed the fuzzy frontier zones of the
historical empires into the militarized boundaries of the modern "geo-body."[1] The
rulers of modern empires, such as the British, the French, or the Japanese, were
obsessed by the need to maximize their territories and militarize their boundaries,
often in remote, unprofitable regions. Their actions provided the impetus for emergent nation-states like China, India, and Thailand to maximize and militarize their
territories. Such massive investment of state resources in these areas often contrasted
markedly with the informal arrangements, multiple sovereignties, forbidden lands,
and imagery of barbarian wildernesses that had characterized them in the old
empires. Modern states have tended to incorporate contiguous, alien territories and
peoples wherever possible, thereby blurring the practical distinction between imperialism and nationalism in these areas.

At the same time, the vision and interests of the dominant power shaped the
particular image and institutions of frontier integration. Indeed, the Japanese integration of Manchukuo as a national space sought to retain or reproduce the representation of the natural frontier, as exemplified by the incorporation of the Oroqen,
studied below. Further, by studying the Chinese nation-state's response to this mode
of integration, in its approach to other frontier peoples and regions, we can gain a
historical understanding of the spatial formation of the nation in East Asia.

If in this era imperialism was forced to adopt nationalist rhetoric and technologies to accommodate its expansionism, nationalism also had to develop other strategies to deploy its territorial imperative. The impact of the new rules on latecomers
to the old imperialist game, such as Germany and Japan, as well as on emergent
nation-states in the twentieth century led not simply to a new language designed to
conceal expansionism, but to new spatio-political forms to channel this territorial
imperative. These forms, such as the "multicultural/multinational" or the "anthropogenetic" nation (discussed below), were premised upon a representational princi-

ple different from that of old-style colonialism: they sought to transform the difference between "primitive" and "civilized" into a commonality of co-nationals. Three elements, not always separable, comprised these forms: the ethnological—or ethno-historical—discourse of ethnographers, historians, bureaucrats, and nationalist intellectuals, which produced the fundamental assumptions regarding "primitives" and their environment; administrative technologies to incorporate the "primitive" and the borderlands; and cultural technologies to naturalize and subjectivize the claim to them among the citizens of the national core. These forms did have consequences that were different from those of old-style colonialism, but the encapsulation of "peripheral" peoples, cultures, and regions by both the Japanese and Chinese state-builders also produced the (imperialistic) domination of the periphery by the center, or, frequently, peripherialized once-autonomous regions.

Ethnology and the Oroqen in Manchukuo

The Oroqen (*Elunchun* in Chinese, and *Oronjon* or *Orochon* in Japanese) appear at the center of a broad ethnological discourse of Japanese racial-cultural origins in which not only professional anthropologists but self-styled folklorists, journalists, and even security officers took part. The Oroqen were a hunting tribe that lived in the forests of the Xing'an mountains in northern Manchuria. Estimates of their population over the last hundred years indicate a high of 18,000 in 1895, declining to about 4,000 in 1917 and to approximately 3,000 by the 1930s. In the early 1950s, their numbers stood at 2,000.[2] Despite these small numbers, the works on the Oroqen in Japanese exceeded twenty, testifying to their significance in the Japanese narrative of Manchukuo.[3]

Before analyzing the role of the Oroqen in Japanese narratives of Manchukuo, I will attempt to extract a history of them from precisely those Chinese and Japanese sources that have framed them within their interested narratives. Before the seventeenth century, the Oroqen were hunters who occupied both banks of the Heilongjiang River. Tsarist expansion into this area pushed them mostly to the southern bank of the river, and by the mid-seventeenth century they came under the control of the Qing in the Xing'an Mountains.[4] In Qing times (1644–1911) the Oroqen were organized into banner forces and in 1875 they were trained in gunfire by the government of Heilongjiang to fight bandits. They were also used to suppress the Boxers in 1900 and the mutinies of the 1911 Republican revolution.[5] The Qing representative who dealt with them was known as the *yinda* or *anda*. He was responsible for the collection of fur as tribute to the Qing, and by the nineteenth century was notorious for his cruel exploitation of the Oroqen.[6]

The most significant element of Oroqen history in the modern period, since the domination of Manchuria by the Russian, Chinese, and Japanese powers in the 1880s, is the rapid decline in their population as seen in the figures above. All accounts point to exploitation by the foreign powers and the Han population, who denuded the forests that were their principal source of existence, and the spread of opium addiction and of diseases as the chief reasons for this decline.[7] Hunting was increasingly commercialized as Manchuria became settled by the Han population and the Oroqen came under the control of Han merchants, referred to in Chinese communist sources as *jianshang*, or dishonest merchants, merchants whose exploitation had both a class and an ethnic (*minzu*) character.[8] In these accounts, the merchants first made "friends" with the Oroqen, giving them wine, food, and gifts. Subsequently, they trapped them in debt bondage by depressing the prices of skin and fur and depleted the community by depriving them of their guns—their chief means of livelihood—and women.[9] Opium addiction played a role in the depopulation and it was no coincidence that the name for opium in their language, *honokata*, was the same as for the Han people who purveyed it to them.[10]

During the 1920s, the warlord government of Manchuria sought to organize them into a border security force to fight the Russians and to serve as guides to the forests and mines. This reorganization appears to have worsened their condition, because while on the one hand they were forced to abandon hunting, their salaries as soldiers were inadequate and much of it never reached them.[11] However, it is not at all clear how successfully the warlord regime was able to implement the reorganization; many of the Oroqen appear to have avoided military service, retained their old banner structure, and continued hunting.[12] In 1924, the Oroqen, led by a banner leader called Gang Tong in the Chinese sources, rose against the merchants, killed several dozen of them, and disappeared into the forests with their grain. The government bureau established and run for four years after the uprising, ostensibly to address the special problems of the Oroqen, actually turned out to provide a way for the warlord bureaucrats and merchants to further monopolize and exploit Oroqen business.[13]

Japanese imperialism contributed to the depopulation and decline through the deforestation caused by the Japanese lumber and mining industries and by the monopsonistic purchase of furs under the Manchukuo regime (1931–1945).[14] The Manchukuo government also continued the practice of using the Oroqen in the border forces (*shanlindui*), and they were forced to undergo two months of military training each year. This military training was a great hardship for the Oroqen because it coincided with the hunting season and contributed to a decline in their income from that source.[15] They were also forced to work as spies for the Manchukuo government in the Soviet Union, although the Japanese army suspected them of counterespionage.[16] Most significantly, state intrusion in the lives of the Oroqen was much more far-reaching under Japanese occupation than it had been under the warlord regime; and ironically, this intrusion took place in the name of preserving their original culture.

The basic strategy of the Manchukuo state was to isolate and concentrate the various tribes. In 1934, they overhauled the administrative system: Heilongjiang and Inner Mongolia were subdivided into fourteen provinces, and two of which, the Eastern Xing'an and Western Xing'an provinces, were to be the homeland of the Oroqen. When the ethnographer Akiba Takashi visited the Xing'an provinces, he found the Oroqen to be concentrated in about fifteen camps running east–west along the Xingan range.[17] Morever, their banner structure was dismantled and they were brought under the direct rule of an administration staffed by Oroqen, Han, and Japanese officials.[18]

The aim of the new dispensation was to prevent the assimilation of Oroqen into the wider Han agrarian population and to restore their old modes of life by sequestering them. These arrangements also conformed to Manchukuo's ideology of the Concordia of Nationalities (*minzu xiehe, minzoku kyōwa*), which involved organizing ethnic groups into separate collectivities. PRC researchers claim that the new dispensation was a particularly regressive step because, by the 1930s, many Oroqen had become partial agriculturists under the influence of the surrounding Han and other peoples. By forcibly moving them off farmland and forbidding the practice of agriculture and marriage with other peoples, Japanese policy must have been at the least a terribly wrenching process.[19] In effect, this policy not only isolated them, it sought to return them to their "primitive" status. The strategic ideology of harmony among the races thus required the state to reverse the pervasive process of Sinicization among minorities and construct "pure" races in order to implement the very program of racial harmony. But in addition to this factor and the need for spies, the incorporative technology of the Manchukuo state has to be understood in terms of a Japanese discourse of race and culture in Manchuria.

In the Japanese ethnic classifications prevalent in Manchuria, the Oroqen represented the most primitive and ancient subgroup of the Tungusic people. In this scheme, which was not without variations, the Japanese and Koreans represented the Southern Tungus; the Daurs, the Solons, the Yellow River Tungus, and the original Shandong peoples represented the Mongol Tungus; the Manchus, the Goldi (the Fishskin Tartars), represented the Manchurian Tungus; and the Oroqen represented the Siberian Tungus.[20] The idea of a Tungusic or pan–North Asian people, as a great Asiatic people constructed as the mirror image of the Indo-European people, was derived from the "Ural-Altaic thesis," popular first in Europe and Russia in the nineteenth century and then in Japan by the turn of the twentieth. Fragments of language and religious practices were systematized into a theory of common racial/ ethnic origins for a vast group of peoples including the Turks, the Mongols, and the Tungus. Historian Shiratori Kurakichi appealed to the Ural-Altaic thesis as early as the 1890s to demonstrate Japan's roots in northeast Asia even while constructing Japan's superiority over other members of this family.[21]

The Ural-Altaic thesis was paradigmatic of Japanese ethnological discourse in the early twentieth century. In contrast to Western colonial anthropology, which self-confidently took the colonized Other to be the object of its analysis, Japanese anthropology did not clearly demarcate colonial from national concerns. As Shimizu Akitoshi has suggested, Japanese ethnography emerged at a time when Japanese membership in the club of nation-states was still uncertain and Japan was itself an object of ethnographic analysis. It was perhaps due to this circumstance that despite a highly developed Tokugawa tradition of ethnography, Japanese anthropology was basically shaped by Western concerns. Although the pioneering Japanese ethnographers, among them Tsuboi Shōgorō and Torii Ryūzō, did not always acknowledge this inheritance, in terms of method, classification systems, and object of analysis the research problematic was heavily indebted to European and, even more, to Russian scholarship.[22] We may see in this process the nationalization of a global discourse.

The first sustained debate that fundamentally shaped Japanese anthropology was triggered by Edwin Morse's 1877 discovery of the "Ōmori shell mounds," and concerned the origins of the Japanese among cannibals who came from outside the islands.[23] Tsuboi, Torii, and others continued to search out these origins in their researches on the Ainu of Japan and the tribes of Siberia, northeast Asia, and the South Seas. Japanese anthropology remained tied to the search for Japanese origins in "racial contact, migration and assimilation in Asia,"[24] and in places as far afield as Okinawa, Hokkaido, Indonesia, Korea, and elsewhere. But notably these were also places of Japanese expansion and colonialism. Despite the diversity within it, and whatever its relationship to global systems of knowledge production, Japanese anthropology succeeded in displacing the quest for the barbarian or primitive origins of the Japanese onto zones that the state either controlled or sought to control. In this way, Japanese ethnology contributed to a peculiarly nationalist claim upon peopled-places at the borders of and beyond the national territory.[25]

Torii, whose work tended to follow the northward expansion of Japan, subscribed to the view that northeast Asia was the ancient meeting ground of all the Far Eastern races. Following Russian ethnic/racial categorizations, he and others believed that the indigenous inhabitants of the Siberian-Manchurian region had remained basically unchanged since "prehistoric times."[26] Torii hoped to develop an integrated view of Asia with Japan at the center, and suggested that shamanism had provided a common feature and source for the indigenous religions in northeast Asia, including those of Korea and Japan.[27] But the principal architect of the Ural-Altaic theory in the Japanese context was Torii's associate and coadvocate of a Japanese field of Oriental studies (*Ajia Gakkai*), the historian Shiratori Kurakichi. According to Stefan Tanaka, the theory permitted Shiratori to construct a new philosophy of history that saw the Altaic peoples of Asia, especially the Mongols, as "key to the unfolding of world history."[28] At the same time, by connecting the Japanese to the Turks, Tungus, and Mongols, Shiratori's version of the theory "separated Japanese essence and spirit from China."[29]

In Manchukuo, the theory also had the effect of furnishing Japan with a special link to and role toward the indigenous people. The notion of a common or closely related family and social structure among the Tungusic peoples was frequently invoked to suggest a unified cultural foundation for Manchukuo. Writer after writer, and not only those writing in an official or semiofficial capacity, stressed the commonality of the Tungusic race and the place of Manchuria as the original homeland of the Tungusic peoples.[30] Given that the Japanese regarded themselves as the southern branch of the Tungusic peoples, the obvious effect of this argument was, by means of a racial logic, to give Japanese rule an anthropogenetic claim in Manchuria.

The discursive landscape in which Japanese ethnographers elaborated their depictions of peoples in Manchuria called for the imbrication of race and culture. Where the racial principle could not be stretched adequately to frame the community, an allegedly common culture was invoked as a supplement to race. The various non-Han peoples were classified as Tungusic and their cultural practices were compared not only with each other, showing various degrees of relationship, but also with Japanese practices. For instance, the Koreans were said to be linguistically and culturally very close to the Japanese, especially to the "ancient Japanese culture," and although the Chinese influence on the elite was very strong, the ordinary people had strong Tungusic traditions in their family structure and traditions. [31]

Some scholars, such as Ōyama Hiko'ichi, a professor of Jianguo University in Xinjing, focused on the *gemeinschaft* character of Manchu families, based upon the authority structure of the lineage, its collective traditions, and, most importantly, shamanism, which emerged as the symbol of racial-cultural unity transcending language roots and physical type. Many studies of this practice in Manchuria were conducted, comprising thousands of pages and often accompanied by detailed photographs. They depicted such forms as Siberian shamanism, Mongol Lamaist shamanism, Manchu family shamanism, professional shamanism, high and primitive shamanism, female shamanism, and others. This great variety reflected the different levels of cultural evolution of the different peoples, but at the same time shamanism also represented the distinctiveness of the culture of northeast Asia. Indeed, the culture of Man-Mo (Manchuria and Mongolia) was said to serve as the point of contact between the culture of north Asia (Japan and Korea) and that of China and southeast Asia. [32]

Turning specifically to the Oroqen, the definitive scholarly work was that of S. M. Shirokogoroff, *Social Organization of the Northern Tungus*, first published in 1933 and translated into Japanese. [33] It was the major inspiration for the ethnographic work of Akamatsu Chijō and Akiba Takashi known as *Manmō no minzoku to shūkyō* (The peoples and religion of Man-Mo). Akamatsu and Akiba were at Seoul Imperial University and had been active in research on folk religion and shamanism in Korea. [34] In turn, the work of these two ethnographers became the most important reference point for writers in Manchukuo. The actual fieldwork on the Oroqen was done by Akiba Takashi in 1935, and it is instructive to pause for a moment on the narrative structure through which he presents his materials. The diary form of Akiba's account dramatizes his travel to the Oroqen camps: it is a dangerous and awe-filled journey into a different timespace—the depths of the primeval Xing'an forests—in search of the primitive, indeed primeval, Oroqen, the living ancestors of the Tungus peoples. He happens to travel with a Japanese forest ranger, his wife, and their young children, who keep their courage in the dangerous forests by their Christian faith. The first vision of the Oroqen appears as in a dream, when Akiba sees their campfire in the dim light of dawn. The mixture of awe and terror remains as he describes the blood-stained clothes and the game of a hunter who was reputed to have also killed seven men. Everywhere he is attentive to the exotic details of

Oroqen mythology, customs, and personality. The romance of a journey of discovery highlights the exotic quality of primitivity.

But in additon to the exotic, Akiba presents us with a complex account of the Oroqen's contemporary situation, their material life, and their relations with outsiders. He declares,

> While we may think of the Xing'an mountains as an enchanted fairyland, cut off from the human world, it is a place where many peoples have come into contact and a composite culture has emerged. Now the Oroqen are in the process of losing their primitivity. What the shape of their nonprimitivity will be in the future is a major question facing all of the peoples of Man-Mo.[35]

Thus, in addition to the exotic quality of Oroqen primitivism, Akiba is particularly attentive to the question of a composite culture—to the way in which details of Oroqen culture, especially shamanism, are related to a wider culture of various Tungus communities. The names and functions of the gods are related to the Mongol's and especially the Korean's gods; the clothes of the shaman (*mukunda*) are like the Daur's, his drums and bells like the Manchu's; the community deity inhabits the house of the shaman as it does the house of the Korean *madang*; the structure of the tent with indwelling divinity is like the Japanese *jinja*; and the great shamanic ceremony devoted to the Protector of Horses every three to five years resembles the Japanese communal fox prayer.[36]

To be sure, Akamatsu and Akiba's preoccupation with shamanism signaled something wider than the political, and they engaged the topic in scholarly terms that were too wide to accommodate an overt political agenda. For instance, in their view shamanism was also prevalent among the Han peoples in the Northeast, and thus it transcended the purely racial. But on closer reading it is apparent that Han shamanism was considered to be a Manchu influence on the Han, first appearing among the Han bannermen or Hanjun.[37] The authors were torn between two separate conclusions: to the extent that they were influenced by Japanese imperialist discourse, they concluded that shamanism was distinctive to the race and culture of northeast Asia; attending to global, especially Russian, scholarship, they were forced to conclude that shamanism could hardly be so confined by race or area. They resolved their dilemma thus: "Shamanism has a specific, local meaning among the North Asian peoples, but also a wider scientific meaning that incorporates the cultures of other Asian and non-Asian peoples."[38]

Another influential ethnography of the Oroqen was, however, much more clearly subordinated to the political imperatives of the state. As chief investigator of the Security Bureau of the Manchukuo General Staff, Nagata Uzumaro's researches on the Oroqen, conducted from 1937 to 1938, dealt, of course, with administrative and security issues. But they also went far beyond these topics to include a full-fledged ethnography embedded within the ethnological discourse we have alluded to above. In addition to administrative history and current social and medical problems, the ethnography includes the detailed analysis of physical type, psychological nature, social structure, customs and ceremonies, and, not least, shamanism. Shamanism reflects Oroqen primitivity, but is also among their most distinctive Tungusic features. Indeed, Nagata cites recent Japanese research to the effect that the very word "shaman" derives not from the Sanskrit *sramana*, as the standard etymology alleged, but from the Tungus language.

Nagata also elaborates on the Oroqen's extraordinarily strong primitive sense of community cooperation (*kyōdōteki*), egalitarianism, and respect for elders, which ironically and amazingly make them resemble the civilized peoples—doubtless the Japanese.[39] At various points, he draws attention to the practices among the Oroqen that resemble those of the Japanese: the role of the women in the management of the home where the division of labor is very strict; their family structure and respect for elders; the absolute power of the family head; and their strong sense of individual honor combined with a cooperative spirit.[40] And yet, of course, this urge to see the Self in the primitive Other is countered and contained by the dominant narrative of evolutionism, in which Oroqen family life is regarded as having been frozen for over two thousand years (this despite considerable discussion of historical change). Nagata writes, "we can see the true form of the life of the Tungus race only among the Oroqen, and we can imagine the lives of the ancestors of the Japanese from this."[41] Japanese evolutionist discourse had mastered the trope whereby one could be advanced, but still claim the privilege of primordiality.

Nagata's ethnology is closely tied to the Japanese state program for the Oroqen. He justifies the state policy of separating and isolating the Oroqen, the ban on their practice of agriculture, the prohibition of opium, and the rejection of a "life of dependence" (on commercialized Han society) in favor of a "self-sufficient, independent life."[42] In addition to recounting the history of their exploitation by outsiders, he invokes the incompatibility of modern laws with their customs and ways. He cites the case of a quarrel between two Oroqen youth over a mere *mantou* (steamed bread roll), which led to a brawl in which one youth killed the other. The surviving youth casually returned home and the families concluded the matter among themselves. But the police, exercising the law of the state, arrested the youth and charged him with murder. According to Nagata, this law of civilized society, which left the family of the killer without its breadwinner, was viewed as terrifying by the Oroqen. Isolating the Oroqen was a means of protecting them from the ravages of modernity.

Nagata also urges isolation and the return to self-sufficiency as a way to reverse the decline in numbers of the Oroqen. As the forest disappeared and they came increasingly into contact with others, opium and new civilized (*bunmeiteki*) diseases, particularly eye and venereal infections, had afflicted the entire population: "Earlier the Oroqen were proud of their health and boasted that they lived in heaven. They hated the city and complained of headaches and nausea whenever they went there. Now the civilized and cultured diseases are attacking their virgin lands (*shojochi*) with their germs."[43] Finally, Nagata reports a decline in school attendance since the establishment of Manchukuo. Before 1931, there were eighty Oroqen students enrolled in primary school and twenty in high school. Now there were only twenty-seven students in all. But Nagata does not apologize for this decline. He believes that the schools were ineffective and the youth learned much more from their homes in the forest environment where the elders taught the youth under a very strict regimen.[44]

Nagata's strategy for returning the Oroqen to the forest—their virgin lands—recalls the representation of the forest in the Japanese historical accounts of Manchuria by Inaba and others. Fujiyama Kazuo also staked the Japanese duty to preserve the forest upon a non-Chinese history of the region. The historical kingdoms and empires of Manchuria, such as the Koguryo, Bohai, Khitan, Jurchen, and Manchu, ruled communities for whom the forest was cradle, grave, and soul. But the agricultural Chinese population had, in a short period, torched the primeval forests and violently forced the aboriginal peoples off their lands.[45]

Fujiyama derived his logic of the deep physical and spiritual influence of forests upon a nation from German romanticism, particularly Goethe, finding the strength of German character in the resilience and resources of the natural environment and German attitudes to it. He claimed to be able to identify similar links between indigenous and aboriginal religion and the Manchurian forest. Manchu shrines and gravesites were surrounded by pine groves; Lamaist temples were enveloped by thick forests. Fujiyama invokes Manchu legends and myth, including the myth of Manchu origin in Lake Tianchi by Changbai Mountain (also claimed as the place of origin of the Korean people), where a divine maiden gave birth to Aisin Gioro after a bird placed a fruit in her mouth.[46] He attributes the Manchu interdiction on the felling of trees to this spiritual connection (ignoring the economic and political dimensions of this ban).[47] Among his practical projects, he advocated reforestation, botanical research, and tree-planting festivals that would take place during regular memorial services around monuments, shrines, and graves of loyal soldiers and heroes. In this way, Fujiyama sought to develop a cult of the forest with the state as guardian of its true spirit.

The representation of the sacred forest and the ethnological discourse of a common Tungusic race and culture come together in the life of the Oroqen. They emerge at this point of intersection as the embodiment of a "primitive authenticity." This authenticity was not only useful for the Manchukuo state, it shaped the realities of Oroqen life. The "authenticity" refers, of course, less to the primitive, than to the colonizer himself—to a yearning to see his true self in the primitive, through a glass darkly. As such, "primitive authenticity" was a technique that linked the self to the primitive even while it distanced itself in the security of civilized status—a technique enabled by the narrative of History.[48] This technique is different from the detached gaze of the colonialist with which we are familiar from nineteenth-century North–South colonialism, and grants the colonizer a different kind of right, a right to make a claim on the basis of shared race and culture.[49] It was a technique consistent with the decline of imperialist justifications of alien rule and with the new administrative technologies to encapsulate alien territories and communities. The

Oroqen were no longer primitive in the manner of an anachronism to be done away with; rather, they represented a valued part of *our* lost selves, to be protected and preserved. The technique grants *us* the sovereign's charge to protect and preserve.

That this political form did little to alleviate the exploitation of the Oroqen during the Manchukuo years has been plain to see. Indeed, their status as authentic primitives forced a radical reorganization of their society and a forced uprooting of the people. But if this was an undeniably instrumentalist policy, the arguments presented by such state representatives as Nagata, promoting, in effect, the idea of a reservation for aboriginals, was hardly unique to Manchukuo. We can find some recognizable form of it all the way from the United States to independent India. Ethnological discourse in the era of nationalism enabled the state to make claims on alien peoples and territories by producing the latter as primordial objects of care-taking.

The Ethnology and History of the Chinese Geo-body

The Japanese conquest of Manchuria and the mode of incorporating peripheral spaces and indigenous people discussed above fundamentally reshaped Chinese ideas, practices, and policies regarding the formation of national space. Older conceptions of unwelcoming, barbarian frontier regions, whether in the Northeast, West or Southwest—and covering over half the Qing empire—were transformed, and the regions produced anew as vital national territories. Anthropology, history, and geography, as academic disciplines and as popular discourse, became engaged in the production of these places and people within the national narrative. In the remainder of this chapter, I fold the study of Manchuria into a discussion of the Chinese response to imperialist, particularly Japanese, penetration of the Qing imperial peripheries more generally.[50]

Scholars and administrators became preoccupied with transforming the empire into the national geo-body soon after the ascendancy of the KMT in 1927, but the process became more urgent after the Japanese invasion of 1937. While the idea that the territory of the modern nation would be coextensive with the limits of the Qing empire was taken for granted by the nationalists, the problems of dealing with the peoples, loyalties, and powers in the vast regions of the empire turned out to be much more complex. As Fang Qiuwei put it, "historical change—the changing of space with time (*shijian tong kongjian de bianhua*)—demonstrates the mistake of disregarding the border regions, an enormous mistake that cannot be erased from history."[51] Nation-builders enumerated and lamented the causes of the frontier regions' neglect, which had permitted imperialists to encroach upon the territory from all sides: There was no Chinese military presence in these regions and officials used to be sent there as a kind of banishment. There was no awareness or study of the peoples, customs, languages, geography, and economies of these areas. Indeed, to travel from China to Yunnan, it was best to take a boat to Vietnam and cross back into Yunnan on the French railroad; to travel to Xinjiang one had best take the trans-Siberian railroad and go through Soviet territory; Tibet was most accessible via India; and so on.[52] The spatial ideal of the homogeneous national territory was symbolized on the jacket of *Borderlands Newsletter* (*Bianjiang tongxun*), where a blank map of China was covered by communication lines radiating directly from Nanjing to the boundaries.

The establishment of the KMT regime led to the institutionalization of the new forms of knowledge production. In 1927, a group of prestigious scholars, closely associated with Chiang Kai-shek and influenced by the French educational model, established Academia Sinica as the premier research institution of the nation-state.[53] Designed as much to legitimate state power as to institutionalize scholarship, the institution contributed much to the production of modern knowledge for the nation. Chiang himself became acutely aware of the teaching of "Chinese History" and "Chinese Geography" as a means to produce "a citizen who loves his country more than his own life."[54] KMT leader Chen Yifu wrote in his introduction to the work of noted geographer Wu Meiji that geography was none other than the mother of the nation, its politics and its livelihood. Wu himself linked the future progress of China to the development of systematic knowledge of its geographical evolution.[55]

Unlike Japan where anthropology had had a history of several decades by the 1930s, anthropology in China had barely made an appearance. But by the mid-1930s, responding in great part to the Japanese military and discursive thrust, anthropology burgeoned and rallied to the national cause in both the academic and the political establishments. The study of the primitive peoples of the world suddenly became relevant to understanding and reclaiming the primitive peoples on China's peripheries who were being lured by Japanese propaganda.

The founding of anthropology in China was most closely associated with the name of Cai Yuanpei, president of Beijing University and an academic trained in aesthetics and ethnology in Germany. But apart from a few courses that Cai himself offered at Beida, anthropology had no institutional presence in China until 1927, when Cai, the leading scholar responsible for the establishment of Academia Sinica, incorporated an ethnology section in its Institute of Social Sciences.[56] Cai served as director of the institution from 1928 until 1940,[57] and doubtless associated the establishment of anthropology with nation building. Indeed, he chose to follow the Japanese practice of naming the subject *minzuxue*, translating *ethno-* (<*ethnos*) with *minzu* and *-logy* (<*logos*) with *xue*.[58] He preferred the term to *renzhongxue* or *renleixue* (also extant Japanese terms), which he believed referred to the study of the physical and mental qualities of humans as a species, or to *minsuxue*, which was folklore. *Minzuxue* was to be the branch of anthropology that compared differences in human cultures, or, in other words, cultural anthropology.[59] Note that *minzu* was also the term for nation or nationality, and the subliminal association of culture with nationality was unavoidable and telling.

Cai's conception of anthropology emerged in his discussion of its relation to sociology. Sociology was the study of contemporary society; but it was clear that contemporary society could not be understood apart from its evolution, and the historiography of civilized society yielded a very poor understanding of its prehistorical past. What was needed was anthropology in all its branches. Naturally, archaeology was important, but so was the study of contemporary uncivilized societies (*weikaihua minzu*). Cai furnished several examples to show how the study of primitive cultures both in and outside China could deepen the understanding of ancient Chinese practices such as totemism or matriarchy.[60] At the same time, the study of primitive cultures could also help distinguish the signs of evolved civilization among the Europeans, Japanese, and Chinese.[61]

Cai's anthropology, still firmly in the grip of an evolutionism, was classically allochronic with regard to its object of study: the primitive as a survival from another time.[62] As such, at this stage—Cai lectured mostly in the 1920s—the novel dimension of nationalist ethnology, namely the desire to produce a sense of national oneness, had not yet emerged with clarity. The goal was to study the non-Han peoples in order to reflect on the Han. By the mid- to late 1930s, with the onset of the Sino-Japanese war, anthropology in China took on a new urgency and the study of primitive peoples within China was undertaken increasingly in order to make a claim upon the frontier territories that these peoples had historically occupied. In 1934, academic anthropologists under the guidance of Cai formed the Chinese Ethnological Association (*Zhongguo minzuxuehui*), and in 1936 launched their professional journal, *Ethnological Research* (*Minzuxue Yanjiu jikan*). Two prominent academic anthropologists, Huang Wenshan and Wei Huilin, served as its editors.[63]

The political concerns of this professional journal were evident in the first issue. Huang Wenshan perceived a nationalist role for anthropology that went beyond Cai's vision. To be sure, *minzuxue* was for Huang the science of the natural presence (*ziran biaoxiang*) of the lives of the people outside the civilized areas of Europe and Asia; it was the study of nonliterate cultures.[64] But it was a colonial discipline for a national project.[65] Citing Sun Yat-sen's Three People's Principles, Huang identified the national problem of the peripheral peoples, who, having been beguiled (*youhuo*) by Western influences and (Japanese) imperialism, had continuously embraced separatist movements (*lixin yundong*).[66] In his survey of ethnographic research in Manchuria, Huang discussed various works, including that of Shirokogoroff and Japanese researchers. Commenting on the extensive research of the SMR, he concluded that Japanese intentions in China were long-term and sinister.[67] Huang, who was trained in America as a Boasian and sought to adapt ideas of cultural and historical particularism, believed that it was up to anthropologists, using the theory and practice of ethnology, to renew the belief of these peoples in the idea of *zhonghua minzu* or a China of different nationalities.[68]

But the extent to which academic ethnology, such as represented by Huang, participated in the ethnological discourse emanating from the political center is quite remarkable. The journal *Xinyaxiya*, or *New Asia*, perhaps best exemplified such a center of discursive production. It was begun in 1930 by Dai Jitao, a KMT leader and theorist, and one-time socialist. Dai and his group viewed the mission of the journal from a pan-Asiatic perspective and Dai was among the few Chinese leaders who believed that the Chinese had much to learn from studying Japan for its own sake, and not simply to learn about the West.

The relationship between Dai's pan-Asianism, nationalism, and the ethnological project was a complex one, as can be seen from the mission of the journal. The mission statement joined the goal of the liberation and revival of the nations of the East with the reconstruction of China and study of its border regions. "In order to reconstruct China it is necessary to develop China's border areas; in order to liberate the nationalities (*minzu*) of Zhonghua, it is necessary to liberate the nationalities of the East in the same stroke."[69] Pan-Asianism meant a great number of things to the writers in the journal. The inspiration for the journal came from the speech on Great Asianism that Sun delivered in Japan in 1924, calling for the unity of the Asian peoples. Sun, who had acknowledged the influence of both Wilsonian and Soviet ideas of self-determination, grounded Asian unity in the common circumstance of oppression by Western imperialism, an allegedly common culture, and a common bond of race or coloredness (*yousede minzu*).[70] Similarly, the many essays promoting this Asianism ranged from careful studies of anti-imperialism in India or Vietnam to fanciful narratives of the shared cultural and racial origins of the various Asian societies, to the celebration of the anti-imperialist, racial fraternity with the Chinese overseas.

The nationalist interest of the journal was evident in two ways. First was the manner in which several of the framing essays, including Sun's own, depicted Chinese ideals or ideas, such as *wangdao* (the "kingly way") or the Three People's Principles, as the guiding means of saving or liberating the rest of Asia.[71] Second, and not dissimilar to the Japanese case, pan-Asianism furnished a framework to incorporate the peripheral peoples of the borderlands into the newly territorialized nation-state in a way that utilized the vagueness of the discourse. Early Chinese nationalism, as during the Republican revolution of 1911, was built securely upon global, social Darwinist ideas of a racially cohesive nation that would triumph over inferior and mixed races that lacked history; by the 1920s, however, nationalism drew upon the new global discourse, which reflected an unstable mix of racialist ideas and an anti-imperialism that validated a unity based upon a shared culture and history (of anti-imperialism). This new nationalism ironically needed more than ever a wider transnational redemptive model—redeeming ancient Asiatic goals—to ground its authority.[72] At the same time, however, the nation-state could deploy incorporative notions of shared history and culture (avoiding overt reference to race) among the "primitive peoples" without abandoning the premise of assimilation to create the cohesive nation.

This volatile combination of different political principles underlying the national idea fed an ethnological discourse that functioned to produce the "border areas" and "frontier peoples" as a marked but inalienable part of the nation. By supplementing—or even displacing—race with culture, nationalists could more easily justify the incorporation of these people and territories. Not only did such a discourse undergird the ideas of professional anthropologists like Huang Wenshan, but it informed the various journals about the border regions that proliferated in the 1930s, such as *Bianzheng gonglun* (*Frontier Affairs*), *Yu gong* (*Tribute to Yu*), and the more popularly oriented *Bianjiang tongxun* (*Borders Newsletter*) or *Zhibian Yuekan* (*Frontier Settlement Monthly*).

These writings were rife with the tension between extending a measure of respect for the cultures of fellow Asiatics within China's boundaries on the one hand, and assimilation on the other. A prolific reporter of the Northwest, Ma Hongtian, tended towards the aggressively assimilationist strategy, although even he could be disarmingly naive about this project. In his discussion of the founding of the China Border Regions Institute, a group established in Nanjing to study the problems of border areas and which included many of the editors and contributors to *New Asia*, Ma commented that the original name chosen for the institute was the China Settlement and Colonization Institute (*Zhongguo Tuozhisuo*).

> [The Chinese character] *tuo* suggested opening up, and *zhi*, cultivation. Since both words suggested something natural, it was felt that it would be a good name. But then some feared that this name would lead to misunderstanding among the local peoples of these areas, who might resist. So it was decided that the name be changed to the China Border Regions Institute.[73]

But despite the change of nomenclature, Ma saw the Northwest as a land of "desolation and wilderness" that would have to be colonized by the Han people, who could bring progress to the area and also relieve the problem of overpopulation in the hinterland of China. For Ma, the Tibetans, Mongols, and other primitive peoples had "not been able to escape a life from antiquity and the Middle Ages; they are so backward that they shame us Chinese."[74] He believed that the policy of improving their lives had not been successful in the past because only vagrants, soldiers, and bandits had been sent to these peripheries. He urged that

> solid, honest working families and enterprising people be sent to plan for progress. Up until now, only bad types have gone over there and have cheated and exploited the border peoples, who have resisted them. If we send good people to these regions and educate the border peoples, we can reform their old customs and restore their basic nature (*fuxing benxing*). We love the people of the Northwest and want to benefit them. We also want to solve our internal and external problems; we hope our brothers (*tongbao*) will understand.[75]

Indeed, the contradictions were apparent at the very heights of the KMT regime. Although the Republic of 1912 was founded upon the unity of China as a Republic of Five Peoples, the KMT abandoned the commitment to the autonomy of the "five nationalities" soon after the outbreak of the Sino-Japanese War. In 1939, a KMT ordinance asserted that "in our country, the racial, cultural, and blood fusion (*hunhe*) among different groups has long been completed and should not be arbitrarily analyzed."[76] In 1943, Chiang Kai-shek declared in *China's Destiny* that "the

Chunghua nation . . . has grown by the gradual amalgamation of various stocks into a harmonious and organic whole."[77] By the 1947 edition, the idea had been added that these various stocks were "originally of one race and lineage" and that "the distinction between the five stocks is territorial as well as religious, but not ethnological."[78] Certainly, KMT military administration in these regions tried to assimilate (*tonghua*) the "frontier peoples" by Sinicizing language, customs, and even clothing and hairstyles.[79] However, even in the Southwest, where the KMT was headquartered during the war, the practical policies of nation building and assimilation did not succeed in Sinicization, but rather in forcing the people back into the poorer lands.[80] Owen Lattimore, who served as personal advisor to Chiang for over a year from 1941, was severely critical of the "frontier policy," but his advice was roundly ignored.[81] The fuller integration of these vast peripheries would have to await the PRC, although here too the process was hardly without tensions.

Among professional anthropologists there was some difference regarding technologies of incorporation. An associate editor of *Ethnological Research*, Wei Huilin, recommending a postwar policy for the nationalist government toward the border regions and cultures in 1944, revealed a most liberal position.[82] He proposed revising the assimilationist *tonghua* policy to a more multicultural *ronghe* one. He advocated regional autonomy and self-government, a dual-language policy, respect for the culture or region's original nature (*yuanshi tezhi*), and the pursuit of industrial and immigration policies in the area for the benefit of the region, among other measures.[83] By and large, however, such policy prescriptions did not appear frequently in *Ethnological Research*, and a policy essay from 1948, by Ma Zhangshou, appeared to fully endorse the project of assimilation. Ma's position contrasts in almost every respect with Wei Huilin's. Ma recommends the deployment of the military capacities of the border areas for the sake of national defense (*bianjiang wuli de guofanghua*); the rapid assimilation of the minorities (who, he believes, welcome assimilation); the exclusive implementation of the Chinese national language in education and government; and a rational, uniform bureaucratic structure, or in other words a strong state presence.[84] Huang Wenshan too backed the policy of "assimilating (*tonghua*) the backward peoples (*qianhua minzu*) with the relatively advanced Han peoples," but, aware of the sensitivities in this regard, he called for each culture to absorb Han elements "at its own level"(*sic*).[85]

We need to grasp the importance of both the theory and practice of frontier incorporation. Given the imperialist connotations of the idea of race, there was a transition, however complex, to the "culture" idea in the understanding of the national community. This transition should not be dismissed as merely rhetorical, since it would produce changes in assumptions and expectations of citizenship rights over the long term.[86] The Chinese national project (like the Japanese imperial project) would have to diminish the difference between the dominant population and the indigenous or ethnic populations so that they could all be seen to belong to the same national community. But the transition did not immediately affect the practical efforts to produce a homogenized nation by military-administrative and other nonvoluntary means of incorporation. Where Japanese expansionism had used both cultural pan-Asianism and the common origins/race ideas of the Ural-Altaic theory to incorporate the lesser Others, a Chinese *theory* of incorporation was still at the experimental stage before the war. When it did emerge more fully, the narrative was put together from the vast storehouse of Chinese historiography, and anthropologists and other social scientists came to locate their understandings of culture within this historical narrative.

The only major Chinese ethnographic study of Manchuria before 1945 dealt with a Tungusic people along the rivers of northern Manchuria called the Goldi, known in China since the end of the nineteenth century as the Hezhezu, and by Westerners as the Fishskin Tartars. The study was conducted by Ling Chunsheng, who had been trained at the University of Paris and served as the head of the ethnology section of Academia Sinica's History and Philology Institute.[87] Undertaken in 1930 but published in 1934, the study represented a model for ethnographic research and writing in the profession. Although Shirokogoroff had reported in 1915 that there were 10,000 Hezhezu in Siberia and 8,000 in Manchuria, and that their numbers had declined by 25 percent since 1897, Ling could only find about 1,200 Hezhe individuals scattered along the Sungari River in the 1930s.[88] Ling's analysis of the decline does not sound the note of pretentious paternalism that we found in Nagata with regard to the Oroqen. Nor does he sound particularly sympathetic. He declares that the Hezhezu have no discipline and are promiscuous and unhygienic. They squander their money on drink and opium in which even the women and children indulge. They have a high child mortality rate, and since many of their women are married to the Han, the procreative level of the people has presumably declined.[89]

The most striking aspect of the study is the extensive historical analysis that frames the ethnography. The history draws from classical Chinese texts, but also refers to contemporary historical research and controversies. Ling denies the claim of the nineteenth-century German *Volksgeist* scholar Heyman Steinthal that anthropology is the study of a people without history. A people, he argues, do not live apart from neighbors, and if the culture of the neighbor is high and literate, then the scholar can find some fragments of their history in the neighbor's.[90] Ling seeks to understand the Hezhezu in the context of Chinese and Tungus historical relations, and his ethnological conclusions are significantly driven by the historical narrative he constructs.

Ling's immediate goal is to distinguish the Donghu of the ancient Chinese texts from the Tungus. He attributes the mistaken conflation of the two to Western Sinologists and takes on a number of them, from Abel Remusat to Otto Franke, to Shirokogoroff. More importantly, he challenges the Japanese scholars, Shiratori and Torii.[91] But despite the length and complexity of these arguments, what impresses the present-day reader of this debate is the utterly fragmentary and inconclusive nature of the textual evidence that Ling and the Japanese scholars cite from the ancient Chinese historical records. Huang Wenshan, although committed to historical particularism, had once admonished scholars to eschew dubious historical allusions and promote ethnographic research.[92] But the actual ethnographic tradition continued to rely heavily on history in the representation of the "primitive peoples."[93] One suspects that other issues were involved in the convoluted and passionate debate as to whether the Donghu are the same as the Tungus. Indeed, Ling seeks to distinguish the Donghu from the Tungus for the same reason, perhaps, that Shiratori sought to conflate them. By identifying the Donghu and the Xiongnu with the Tungus (who according to Ling appear later in the Northeast), Shiratori could presumably show that the Tungus were continuously dominant in the Northeast.[94]

Ling's argument proceeds by exploding several other myths as well. He follows the new research of historians like Gu Jiegang and Feng Jiasheng, who deny that the Chinese have a single origin.[95] Evidence shows that the Shang and the Zhou had different ancestors, and the idea that the Shang came from the west was merely a Jesuit myth. The Shang were really among the autochthonous eastern people that included the Hui and the Mo of Manchuria and the Koryo of the Korean Peninsula. Here he attacks Torii, who in 1915 declared the Hui, Mo, and Koryo to be Tungus. Rather, these were the ancient Asians (guyazhouren) who lived in Manchuria, Korea, and the Bohai Bay area or in mainland northeast Asia (excluding therefore the Japanese archipelago), and were all one people and covered by the ancient appellation Dongyi.[96] The Tungus came from elsewhere.[97] The Chinese people call themselves the descendants of Huangdi or the Yellow Emperor, but they do not know that Huangdi was also a Dongyi. The true Chinese people who created Chinese culture in pre-Shang times were the people who lived in the east and were the ones whom the Zhou called the eastern barbarians, or Dongyi. In this way, Ling excludes the Tungus and connects the origins of Chinese culture to the northeastern region.[98]

Ling's ultimate argument depended not on an overt notion of racial unity or commonality among the peoples in China, but rather on the idea of an evolving historical culture that was compatible with both anti-imperialism and pan-Asianism as much as with Anglo-American ideals. It presented nationalists with an alternative to the history of China as a preconstituted unity. The most articulate statement of this perspective that I have found was by Yao Congwu, a historian renowned for his work on the Chinese Northeast. Yao, who had studied in Germany, presented his views in a series of lectures to the Society of the Friends of the United Nation in Taipei in 1947 (lianheguo tongzhihui), even though the idea appears to have been around for a couple of decades.[99] Thus, his ideas are also significant as a justification of the principle underlying Chinese nationhood in the late Republic, and are consistent with the new principle of nationhood attending the rise of the United States and the defeat of racist nationalism in World War II. Indeed, Yao's interpretation of the evolving history of China as a cultural unity is reminiscent of the American "melting pot," an expression explicitly used by Chiang Kai-shek in China's Destiny.[100]

According to Yao, the modern Chinese nation (zhonghua minzu) should not be thought of as a racial nation or the territory of a single nationality. Rather, it was the cultural unity of various tributary cultures of the minorities, which could be subsumed under the rubric of "The Central Plains Confucian Culture of the Great Unity" (*zhongyuan rujiao datong wenhua*), or Great Unity for short. Confucianism had the ability to civilize and induce the voluntary absorption of peripheral peoples because of its universal acceptance of outsiders. Indeed, according to Yao, even such stalwart Chinese dynasties as the Ming and the southern Song could not be considered representative of the culture of Great Unity, precisely because they emphasized Han nationalism. The Qin-Han, the Mongols, and the Manchus were more pure expressions of this unity, since their own traditions were absorbed by the evolving culture.

Yao's narrative was premised upon a core territorial space shaping this culture—the central plain. History became closely intertwined with geography as the new authority of spatial knowledge. I have alluded to the geography that linked the rivers and mountains of Manchuria to those of the mainland, and Wu Shangquan's claim that the Northeast had been a part of the "nine *zhou*" since the time of the Yellow Emperor (Huangdi, 2,698 B.C.). This position was consistent with Chiang Kai-shek's view that the physical configuration of mountains and rivers, including the Pamir Plateau and the Amur River valley, formed one integral and inseparable system.[101] But the principal physiographical factor shaping the culture of the Chinese nationality (*zhongguo minzu*), according to professional geographers of the time, was the central plain (*zhongyuan*), the birthplace of the Han. The Chinese nationality—or even its principal constituent, the Han—ought not to be seen as a blood group, but as a cultural formation that had been historically assimilating a variety of other races such as the Tungus, the Mongols, and the Tibetans. The primary force behind this continuing formation was the environment of the great plain and its rivers, which nourished a peace-loving agricultural people forced by political and economic circumstances to spread outward, to the south, northwest, and northeast, thus either absorbing other people or pushing them to the mountains.[102]

It was from this perspective that Zhang Qiyun declared that Manchuria had long represented the natural (*tianliu*) granaries and lifeline (*shengmingxian*) of north China, an argument that was remarkably parallel to the Japanese "lifeline" argument.[103] Moreover, just as Japanese ideologues denied the Chinese a sense of territorial nationhood, geographer Wu Shangquan believed that the indigenous inhabitants had no sense of territorial belonging, since they were nomadic, lacked a literate culture, and identified only with a "banner." The Tungus, he states, started to become a nation only after contact with the Han. But by that time they had already become Sinicized and the region thoroughly integrated with China. The true national subject is presented as a spatial formation, but it nonetheless completes Yao's theory of a cultural nation by sanctioning assimilation as the historical destiny of the people surrounding it.[104]

Yao's historical narrative also drew from the ideas of his German mentor, the Sinologist Otto Franke, and his son Wolfgang Franke. But his ingenuity is evident when the narrative is placed in the context of the extant historiography of China's general history (*tongshi*). Yao was able to resolve the narratological problems faced by such writers as Fu Sinian and Lei Haizong (as well as the Japanese historian Fu was responding to, Kuwabara Jitsuzo) in one fell stroke.[105] Fu and Lei had developed their histories of China as the history of the Han *race* (even as late as 1937); when faced with the glories of the non-Han dynasties, they were often forced to elaborate textual strategies that would allow them to smooth over the narrative impediment.[106] Instead, Yao was able to constitute the history of China as a seeded geo-body: an expanding, absorbing subject that could still acknowledge contributions of other people. While this cultural narrative was compatible with Chiang Kai-shek's formulation of an "enduring and all-embracing culture," by 1947 Chiang had added that a common ancestry "can be traced as far back as to Huang-ti."[107] Perhaps race was still a supplement to culture.

For anthropologists like Ling, the narrative of the Central Plains Confucian Culture of Great Unity addresses the dilemma outlined above: it permits the idea of contributions from different historical sources, but at the same time directs these contributions into the overarching Greater Confucian Unity. Thus one could have incorporation and at the same time show respect for different peoples' histories in China. The important device enabling this strategy is the notion of "historical assimilation." Confucianism engaged in a civilizing project; because it offered a higher ideal, it historically attracted lesser peoples to assimilate voluntarily. The task of the anthropologist in this regard was to show how, despite their wholeness as peoples, these groups had historically assimilated various Chinese practices and traits.[108]

In the ethnography itself, the anthropologist took great care to show the assimilation of Chinese practices among the neighboring peoples. In the folktales of the Hezhezu, for instance, the storytelling methods were like those in north and south China, where both singing and talking without accompaniment were practiced. Ling writes that "since they live within China's borders their relations with the Chinese are close . . . and they have mostly absorbed Chinese culture through the Manchus."[109] Ling also speculates that since some of the stories and practices that show a commonality with Chinese stories (such as those involving fox fairies) may be found in Chinese histories as well as among the Chinese people (*minjian*), it is possible that their stories emerged from the "womb" (*tai*) of Chinese culture.[110] The fox fairy stories were also precisely the ones that Japanese ethnographers used to draw links to the Tungus. Indeed, the procedure of exposing connections between the cultural practices of different peoples was, as we have seen, a common Japanese practice. Whereas in the Japanese case it revealed an allegedly primordial connection, in the Chinese, the alleged linkage revealed a process of voluntary absorption of Chinese culture since ancient times.

Whence the importance of culture? Culture, expressed in cultural nationality, introduced an element of porousness, voluntarism, and volition that gained importance because it was tied to a global discourse of nationality rights. Yao's formulation, made in the context of the Friends of the United Nation, ensured the compatibility of his narrative with the organization's purpose. Many of the scholars,

especially the anthropologists we have considered, were educated in the metropolitan centers of the West and accepted the premise that the objects of their study were
culturally bounded communities. What distinguished these anthropologists from a
Boas or a Radcliffe Brown was their perception that the ultimate "culture area" that
shaped these communities happened to be coextensive with the national geo-body.
This discourse presumed two levels of culture: one was that of the individual nationalities, whether these be small, such as the Goldi or the Yi, or numerous, such as
Tibetans or Mongols; the other, a wider, even civilizational conception covering the
nation-state and expressed in the nomenclature of *zhonghua minzu*. In a way, the
historians had reconstructed an old Confucian civilizing discourse (again, not without interactions with global, especially Germanic, Sinology) for the purposes of the
modern territorial nation-state. The parallel between this civilizing strategy and
kyōka, like the parallel between Japanese and Chinese pan-Asianism—of *New Asia*,
for instance—suggests a repertoire of strategies that may be classified in the East
Asian modern.

Finally, the granting of a measure of rhetorical autonomy to national cultures was
necessitated by the reality of many antigovernment movements with nationalistic
aspirations, produced at least in part by the spreading ideology of nationality rights.
Soon after the establishment of the Republic the Mongols had claimed independence, based on the idea that their relation with the last Manchu empire—the pure
embodiment of the Great Unity—had been a relationship of ritual suzerainty within
a Central Asian empire, and not a submission to the sovereignty of China.[111] During
the Republic, wars, uprisings, movements, or incidents occurred in virtually every
part of what was Qing central Asia and the Southwest.[112] From the perspective of
the peripheries, the narrative of the Great Confucian Unity must have still sounded
a great deal like subjugation, since the practical problem of assimilation and what
the "frontier peoples" actually felt and wanted, remained.

Thus, while it was important to educate the indigenous peoples in the ways of
the Chinese nation, in the meanwhile, nationalists had to develop technologies of
territorial incorporation that could bypass the will of the peoples in these territories.
One such means was evident in the strategy of journals like *New Asia*, which gave
new meaning to the peripheries. The goal was to invest these territories with a certain cultural and psychic density in the landscape of the national imaginary and
thus produce the geo-body within the subjectivity of the citizen inside China proper
(*neidi*).[113] These modes of incorporation did not involve construing the local peoples
as embodying authenticity, at least not at this time. Rather, they represented an
institutional effort by nationalists to create the cultural infrastructure for such an
imaginative cathexis.

The building of this infrastructure could be divided, according to Fang Qiuwei,
into two parts. First is the development of scholarly and research enterprises—
particularly by agencies like Academia Sinica—to enhance knowledge of the history,
people, and resources of the regions. Second, Fang calls for a wider, more popular
mode of dissemination designed to stimulate interest in and feelings for these spaces.

Textbooks at every level of the school system were required to contain materials about the problems of the border regions, and Fang encourages the development of popular media, such as the cinema and slide shows, with the customs and conditions of the local people as the subject matter.[114]

In the third volume of *New Asia*, editorial commentary called upon readers to transform their view of the peripheries from the clichéd imagery of desolation to an appreciation of their "limitless mysteries" and "inexhaustible treasures." It called for photographs of the landscapes and peoples of those regions, so that readers could become more familiar with them.[115] Apart from the many ethnographic and descriptive essays that already filled its pages, the journal called for a special type of fiction writing not found elsewhere, concerned with recording the customs of the peripheries or travels to Asian lands: "What we need is the 'travelog-ization of fiction' (*youjihuade xiaoshuo*) or 'the fictionalization of travel writing' (*xiaoshuohuade youji*)."[116] Although some readers were mystified by this new genre, there was no shortage of the kind of writing and photography that the editors desired.[117]

Take, for instance, the travel diary of a journey through Guizhou undertaken by a team from the biology department of Sun Yat-sen University in Canton (of which Dai Jitao was the president). Melding nature and culture, the travelogue recorded ethnographic and botanical details of this frontier region. It compared the physical resources and social customs of Guizhou and the team's native Guangdong, noting in particular the extent of Sinicization among Guizhou's many non-Han groups. Vaguely reminiscent of Akiba's account, the travelogue mixed the exotic with the recognizable in a way that gave the region its unique place within the national landscape. And not least, it was animated by the drama and adventures of journeying through bandit-infested forests.[118] This was perhaps the kind of personal investment in the production of the geo-body that the editors desired.

The moral authority of new nation-states has often been built upon the distinction between "imperialism" and "nationalism" as discrete and oppositional forces representing "alien rule by conquerors" versus "self-rule." While acknowledging the historical role that nationalism has played in opposition to imperialism, it is just as important to reveal the territorial imperative underlying the modern state form common to both. Nowhere is this more visible than in the frontiers and borderlands and the fate of peoples who inhabit them.

In East Asia, as in many other parts of the world, these regions and their inhabitants typically became subject to the modern state's program of territorial administration and surveillance. They were brought under the jurisdiction of civil, military, or special administration, and were integrated into the state by modern means of communication and institutions of survey, classification, enumeration, education, and other forms of governmentality. But because territorial incorporation was a response to or simultaneous with their emergence as contested borderlands, these regions were transformed from dark frontiers into hot spots. They became political spaces where the effort to invest sovereignty and defend it was most densely concentrated.

At the same time, the circumstances under which the state sought to bring these regions and people under its control reproduced their subordination. The relatively disadvantaged indigenous or local populations were subject to the practically assimilative, exploitative, and imperialistic attitudes of the dominant group, whether the Japanese in Manchukuo or the Han Chinese in the peripheries. Despite the tacit promise contained in the concept of nationality, incorporation often confronted them directly with new conditions of inequality and endangerment.

Although the logic of frontier transformation has systemic features, each place, of course, is distinctive, and none more so than Manchuria. We have described its complexity in the "frontier as reservoir" formulation. The Japanese, who had extended the territorial basis of their control through the railroad even before creating Manchukuo, sought to conserve the spatial image of the area as a nonagricultural frontier—a virginal forest land, a frontier of the modern—at the very heart of the national imaginary. Such an imaginary also well suited the Concordia doctrine of equal nationality rights, enabling them to ignore the numerical preponderance of the Chinese and the reality of Japanese control. At the same time, the discourse of the primitive, even primordial authenticity of the Oroqen enabled a technology of cultural investment among Japanese that tied Manchukuo back to Japan. The authenticity of Manchukuo as a frontier nation was produced in a way that required Japanese custodianship.

After 1931, the Chinese nationalists, of course, no longer had the political capacity to institutionalize the national imaginary of the Northeast within Manchuria. Instead, I have considered the intertwined historical, ethnographic, and geographical narrative transfiguring the Qing frontier regions and peoples into a national space. Manchuria was understood as the original homeland of the Chinese and as the natural extension, outlet, and lifeline for Chinese agricultural society. These ideas were developed in tandem with a narrative in which the assimilation of frontier peoples by a civilizing Confucianism became their historical destiny. In the next chapter we will see how Shanding sought to integrate the distinctiveness of the region with agrarianism and popular Chinese values.

Although the civilizing narrative was developed out of the resources of Chinese historiography, it was a response to Japanese modes of claiming territories and people, and both understandings were conditioned by globally derived knowledge of such people and spaces. The new anthropology, geography, or progressive history had vast and varied epistemological effects, but this knowledge was also mobilized for the nation, often through representations of a distinctive space or culture area. Ancestral shamanism or the folkways of agrarian civilization, for instance, came to identify and symbolize the authenticity of culture.

These cultural projects also sought to produce the frontier anew within the national imaginary. Japanese and Chinese citizens would have to learn to see these contested territories as inalienable parts of their national being. The technique of "primitive authenticity" and the cultural investment of the border landscape produced a psychic value for these areas that continues to have important consequences. The relentless drive to extend, "stabilize," and militarize modern state boundaries in these remote, often unprofitable regions entails massive investments of state resources, as for instance in Xinjiang or Tibet (or Kashmir).[119] Ironically, not only do the projected economic gains from these investments frequently go unrealized, but the strategic defensive considerations driving border buildup between states are governed by a mutually reflexive and self-perpetuating process. In other words, the impact of territorial loss in these frontier zones is often not principally economic but psychic. The cost of allaying these psychic fears, which in this recursive mode actually amounts to feeding them, is not only high economically and militarily, but continues to have human and cultural consequences for the peoples who live in these peripheries.

And what of the "primitive," who has appeared in this chapter only as the effect of another's narrative strategy and policy? To be sure, there are some accounts remarkable for their sympathy and understanding.[120] At the same time, there is no denying that our historical knowledge of them is inevitably conditioned by the larger forces of state building and incorporation. I have pointed to a difference between the Japanese and the Chinese modes of incorporation. The romanticization of the authentic primitive in the manner of the Japanese attitude toward the Oroqen— which also appears, for instance, among the French avant-garde in relation to Africans—appears, with a few notable exceptions, to be absent in Republican China.[121] Revealingly, this romanticization begins to appear with the consolidation of state power in the Chinese periphery in the writings and films about the primitive beginning in the 1960s. In this context, we will touch upon the Oroqen stories of Zheng Wanlong in the next chapter. The trend gets fully underway in the spate of writing and films after the ravages of the Cultural Revolution (1966–1976), when the primitive is depicted as having a purity that is beyond, or held hostage by, the horrors of modern totalitarianism.[122] Interestingly, this is also the period when the "primitives" themselves become incorporated as citizens and try (against considerable odds) to take advantage of the rights of citizenship promised by the new political forms. Thus it is that the voice of the primitive is heard as the cry of our redemption, but only at the moment of her disappearance.

Notes

1. See chap. 1, n. 38.

2. *EJB*, 3.

3. Nagata Uzumaro, *Manshū ni okeru Oronjon no kenkyū* (Studies of the Oroqen in Manchuria), vol. 1 (Shinkyō: Chianbu Samboshi chōsaka [Investigative Division of the Security Bureau of the General Staff], 1939), 89–91, and Sasaki Tōru, "Nihon ni okeru Orochon in kansuru minzokugakuteki hōkoku no hikaku kenkyū—'Orochon no jissō' o chūshin to shite" (A comparative study of Japanese ethnological reports regarding the Orochon, with

particular reference to "The Real Facts about the Orochon"), *Hokkaidoritsu Hoppō Minzoku Hakubutsu Kenkyū kiyō* 3 (1994): 94.

4. Lu Kuangbin, Han Youfeng, and Du Yongji, eds., *Elunchunzu sishinian, 1953–1993* (Forty years of the Oroqen nationality) (Beijing: Zhongyang minzu daxue chubanshe, 1994), 6–8.

5. Nagata, *Manshū ni okeru Oronjon no kenkyū*, 8–10.

6. Lu, Han, and Du, *Elunchunzu sishinian*, 7, 11–12.

7. *EJB*, 4; Akamatsu Chijō and Akiba Takashi, *Manmō no minzoku to shūkyō* (Peoples and religions of Manchuria and Mongolia) (Tokyo: n.p., 1939), 90, 97.

8. *EJB*, 93–95.

9. Lu, Han, and Du, *Elunchunzu sishinian*, 12–13.

10. Akamatsu and Akiba, *Manmō no minzoku to shūkyō*, 96–97.

11. *EJB*, 81–85.

12. *EJB*, 84.

13. *EJB*, 95–97; Lu, Han, and Du, *Elunchunzu sishinian*, 12–14, 26–27.

14. *EJB*, 128.

15. *EJB*, 126–28.

16. Nakao Katsumi, "Shokuminchishugi to Nihon minzokugaku," *Chūgoku—Shakai to Bunka* 8 (June 1993): 234–35, and Sasaki, "Nihon ni okeru Orochon in kansuru minzokugakuteki hōkoku no hikaku kenkyū," 123–25.

17. Akamatsu and Akiba, *Manmō no minzoku to shūkyō*, 102.

18. *EJB*, 121–24.

19. Lu, Han, and Du, *Elunchunzu sishinian*, 9–10.

20. Nagata, *Manshū ni okeru Oronjon no kenkyū*, 4.

21. See Ōtsuka Kazuyoshi, "Shiberia—Nihon ni okeru minzoku kenkyū," in *Nihon minzokugaku no genzai*, ed. Joseph Kriner (Tokyo: Shin'yōsha, 1996); Kawamura Minato, *"Daitōa minzokugaku" no kyojitsu* (The truths and falsehoods of "Great East Asian folklore") (Tokyo: Kōdansha, 1996), 76; Hyung-il Pai, "Japanese Anthropology and the Discovery of Prehistoric 'Korea,'" *Journal of East Asian Archaeology* 1 (1999): 366; and Tanaka, *Japan's Orient*, 84–93.

22. Akitoshi Shimizu, "Colonialism and the Development of Modern Anthropology in Japan," in *Anthropology and Colonialism in Asia and Oceania*, ed. Jan van Bremen and Akitoshi Shimizu (Surrey, England: Curzon Press, 1999), 125–26; Tessa Morris-Suzuki, "Through Ethnographic Eyes" (unpublished paper, n.d.), 11–12; and Paul Barclay, "A Tale of Two Meiji Ethnologists: Inō Kanori and Torii Ryūzō in Taiwan" (paper presented to the Association of Asian Studies, San Diego, Calif., 2000, 8–9). See also Paul Barclay, "An Historian among the Anthropologists: Inō Kanori and the Legacy of Japanese Ethnography in Taiwan," *Japanese Studies* 21 (2001): 117–37.

23. Shimizu, "Colonialism and the Development of Modern Anthropology in Japan," 122–25.

24. Barclay, "Tale of Two Meiji Ethnologists," 8.

25. However, the "native ethnology" of Yanagita Kunio and others, which has been identified with a specific concern with the question of origins and tradition within Japan, cannot be confined to this formulation. As Kawamura Minato has demonstrated, despite the official stance of this movement and Yanagita himself, there were plentiful links between "native" ethnology and colonial, and even officially sponsored, ethnography. By the time of the Pacific

War, and perhaps even before, a far-flung network of researchers linked the peripheries of the empire to Yanagita's research center in Tokyo. Moreover, the research in these areas was not really for the self-understanding of the indigenous culture, as Yanagita had stressed for Japan itself. Rather, these cultures came to be judged by how close they were to Japanese culture. See Kawamura, *"Daitōa minzokugaku" no kyojitsu*, 10–11, 74–85.

26. Pai, "Japanese Anthropology and the Discovery of Prehistoric 'Korea,'" 355, and Morris-Suzuki, "Through Ethnographic Eyes."

27. Allen, "Northeast Asia Centered around Korea," 795; Shimizu, "Colonialism and the Development of Modern Anthropology in Japan," 130–33; Ōtsuka, "Shiberia"; and Sasaki, "Nihon ni okeru Orochon in kansuru minzokugakuteki hōkoku no hikaku kenkyū."

28. Tanaka, *Japan's Orient*, 88.

29. Tanaka, *Japan's Orient*, 88–93. For details of the "Ural-Altaic hypothesis" in the nineteenth and early twentieth centuries, and a devastating critique of its assumed relationships between linguistic and racial origins, see S. M. Shirokogoroff, "Ethnological and Linguistic Aspects of the Ural-Altaic Hypothesis," *Qinghua Xuebao* (*Tsinghua Journal*) 6, no. 3 (1931): 199–396. Shirokogoroff tellingly remarks how the centrality of this whole discussion in Japan diverted attention from another source of the Japanese lexic complex, the Chinese language (389). It is evident that the Japanese researchers in Manchuria who so admired Shirokogoroff were ignorant of, or chose to ignore, this piece. Incidentally, the idea of Japanese and Korean descent from ancestors in Manchuria persisted. As recently as 1964, Egami Namio sought to demonstrate that horsemen from northeast Asia (by way of Korea), related to the Koguryo and Donghu, conquered Japan, spread their culture, and unified the state; see "The Formation of the People and the Origin of the State in Japan," *Memoirs of the Research Department of the Tōyō Bunko*, no. 23 (1964): 49–50.

30. Fukunaga Tadashi, *Manshūkoku no minzoku mondai* (The nationality question of Manchukuo) (Shinkyō: Manshō Tomoyamabō, 1944), 60–65.

31. Fukunaga, *Manshūkoku no minzoku mondai*, 58–60. In Korea the Ural-Altaic thesis may have acquired even greater power as the foundation of a national myth. Ch'oe Namson, who taught in Manchukuo's Jianguo University, also developed his ideas about a "northeast Asian cultural sphere" from notions of a common Altaic language and the practice of shamanism (see below). Whereas most Japanese accounts stressed Korean subordination to Manchuria or Japan within this northeast Asian sphere, Korean, and especially Ch'oe's, narrative located Korea at the center, and thus as the leader of a tradition that was independent of both the Chinese and Indo-European traditions. See Allen, "Northeast Asia Centered around Korea," 788, 800–803, and Roger L. Janelli, "The Origins of Korean Folklore Scholarship," *Journal of American Folklore* 99 (1986): 31–32. Together with some Japanese ethnographers in Korea, Korean folklorists distinguished the "northern" shamanism associated with the culture of pastoral and hunting societies of the Northeast from the "southern" (Japanese) shamanism; see Kawamura, *"Daitōa minzokugaku" no kyojitsu*, 76. Another folklorist who studied shamanism, Yi Nung-hwa, also emphasized Korea's connection with Manchuria rather than Japan, arguing that ancient Choson was an enormous territory encompassing much of present-day Manchuria; see Janelli, "Origins of Korean Folklore Scholarship," 33.

32. Akamatsu and Akiba, *Manmō no minzoku to shūkyō*, 22–40; Ōyama Hikoichi, *Samankyō to Manshuzoku no kazoku seido* (Xinjing: Jianguo daxue yanjiuyuan, 1942), 3–4; Nagata, *Manshū ni okeru Oronjon no kenkyū*, 61–64.

33. Although Shirokogoroff's book was only translated into Japanese in 1941, Japanese

scholars were familiar with the original. Incidentally, Shirokogoroff, who taught at Beijing's Qinghua University, was widely respected by many of the Chinese anthropologists who studied with him. His most famous student was probably Fei Xiaotong, who admired him greatly. However, Francis Hsu, who also studied with him, believed that Shirokogoroff "was obsessed with the Tungus and knew nothing else." See Gregory E. Guldin, *The Saga of Anthropology in China: From Malinowski to Moscow to Mao* (New York: Sharpe, 1994), 45–46.

34. See Shimizu, "Colonialism and the Development of Modern Anthropology in Japan," 136–37.

35. Akamatsu and Akiba, *Manmō no minzoku to shūkyō*, 126.

36. Akamatsu and Akiba, *Manmō no minzoku to shūkyō*, 103–11.

37. Akamatsu and Akiba, *Manmō no minzoku to shūkyō*, 367.

38. Akamatsu and Akiba, *Manmō no minzoku to shūkyō*, 22–29.

39. Nagata, *Manshū ni okeru Oronjon no kenkyū*, 61–65.

40. Nagata, *Manshū ni okeru Oronjon no kenkyū*, 44, 54, 64–66.

41. Nagata, *Manshū ni okeru Oronjon no kenkyū*, 53.

42. Nagata, *Manshū ni okeru Oronjon no kenkyū*, 39.

43. Nagata, *Manshū ni okeru Oronjon no kenkyū*, 57–58.

44. Nagata, *Manshū ni okeru Oronjon no kenkyū*, 78.

45. Fujiyama Kazuo. *Manshū no shinrin to bunka* (Shinkyō: Tōhō Kokumin Bunshō, 1937), 32–33.

46. For a more detailed and different version of Manchukuo's origins, see Mark C. Elliott, *The Manchu Way: The Eight Banners and Ethnic Identity in Late Imperial China* (Stanford: Stanford University Press, 2001), 44.

47. Fujiyama, *Manshū no shinrin to bunka*, 88–89.

48. Duara, *Rescuing History*.

49. The technique is tied to the persistent dualistic description of the Oroqen as noble or even refined, on the one hand, and childlike—egotistical and temperamental—on the other. Note for instance Akiba's description of the childlike reaction of Oroqen to the guns and uniforms supplied by the Japanese; Akamatsu and Akiba, *Manmō no minzoku to shūkyō*, 97. It is an ironic representation that mandates paternalistic control and guidance (over the "ancestors") and denies the Oroqen any agency.

50. Given that the Chinese state and professionals could not directly control or access the region, their efforts were largely discursive and are best understood in a comparative context.

51. Fang Qiuwei, *Feichang shiqizhi bianwu* (Frontier affairs during the emergency period) (Hong Kong: Zhonghua shuju, 1937–38), 2.

52. Fang, *Feichang shiqizhi bianwu*, 10

53. Chen Shiwei, "Legitimizing the State: Politics and the Founding of Academia Sinica in 1927," *Papers on Chinese History* 6 (1997): 36–38.

54. Chiang Kai-shek, quoted in Richard Wilson, *Learning to be Chinese: The Political Socialization of Children in Taiwan* (Cambridge: MIT Press, 1970), 276.

55. Wu Meiji, *Zhongguo renwen dili* (Human geography in China) (Nanjing: Nanjing Zhongshan shuju, 1929), 2–3.

56. He Liankai, "Sishinianlaizhi Zhongguo minzuxue" (Forty years of ethnology in China), *Zhongguo minzuxuebao* 1 (1955): 6.

57. He Liankai, "Cai Jiemin xiansheng duiyu minzuxuezhi gongxian" (The contributions of Mr. Cai Yuanpei to ethnology) (1959), introduction to *Cai Yuanpei minzuxue lunzhu*

(Cai Yuanpei discourses on ethnology), ed. Zhongguo minzu xuehui (Taipei: Zhonghua Shuju, 1962), 2.

58. Cai Yuanpei, "Shuo minzuxue" (On ethnology) (1926), in *Cai Yuanpei minzuxue lunzhu* (Cai Yuanpei discourses on ethnology), ed. Zhongguo Minzu Xuehui (Taipei: Zhonghua Shuju, 1962), 1.

59. Cai, "Shuo minzuxue," 7

60. Cai Yuanpei, "Shehuixue yu minzuxue" (Sociology and ethnology) (1930), in *Cai Yuanpei minzuxue lunzhu* (Cai Yuanpei discourses on ethnology), ed. Zhongguo Minzu Xuehui (Taipei: Zhonghua Shuju, 1962), 12–13.

61. Cai, "Shehuixue yu minzuxue," 22; Huang Wenshan, "Minzuxue yu Zhongguo minzu yanjiu" (Ethnology and the study of China's peoples), *Minzuxue Yanjiu jikan* 1 (1936): 1.

62. On the term allochronic, see Johannes Fabian, *Time and the Other: How Anthropology Makes Its Object* (New York: Columbia University Press, 1983).

63. He Liankai, "Jieshao Zhongguo minzuxuede wenxian yu gongzuo" (Introduction to materials and works in Chinese ethnology), in *Minzuwenhua yanjiu* (Research of nationality cultures), selected by He Liankai (n.p., 1951), 108–9. See also He Liankai, "Sishinianlaizhi Zhongguo minzuxue."

64. Huang, "Minzuxue yu Zhongguo minzu yanjiu," 2.

65. In 1944 a bibiliography of hundreds of items of ethnographic research in Chinese since the beginning of the war with Japan listed only about twelve entries on the Han peoples, most of which had to do with "folk customs" (*minsu*) or language; see Gu Jinshi, ed., "Kangzhanyilai woguo minzuxue xuanmu," *Minzuxue Yanjiu jikan* 4 (1944): 129–69.

66. Huang, "Minzuxue yu Zhongguo minzu yanjiu," 22.

67. Huang, "Minzuxue yu Zhongguo minzu yanjiu," 14

68. Huang, "Minzuxue yu Zhongguo minzu yanjiu," 22–23, and Guldin, *Saga of Anthropology in China*, 61.

69. "Xinyaxiyazhi shiming" (The mission of New Asia), preface to *Xinyaxiya* (New Asia) 1, no. 1 (1930).

70. Sun Yat-sen, "Da Yaxiyazhuyi" (Great Asianism), *Xinyaxiya* 1, no. 1 (1930): 1–7. See also David M. Deal, "Policy towards Ethnic Minorities in Southwest China, 1927–1965," in *Nationalism and the Crises of Ethnic Minorities in Asia*, ed. Tai S. Kang (Westport, Conn.: Greenwood, 1979), 33.

71. Prasenjit Duara, "Transnationalism and the Predicament of Sovereignty, China 1900–1945," *American Historical Review* 102 (October 1997): 1030–51. The editors of the journal also had to contain the ambiguity embedded in the title of Sun's original speech in Japan, which was called not "Xin Yaxiya," or New Asia, but "Da Yaxiya," or Great Asia. According to one of the editors, some people had misconstrued the title as suggesting that China should recover most of Asia as its historical territory. The editor pointed out that this was not at all Sun's intent, because he spoke of such moral values as benevolence and the "kingly way." Thus, in order to avoid such misunderstandings, the editors chose to name the journal *New Asia*. See Ma Hongtian, "Guanyu 'Dayaxiya' yu 'Xinyaxiya' timingde huiyi" (Remembering the titles of Great Asia and New Asia), *Xinyaxiya* 1, no. 1 (1930), 139.

72. Duara, "Transnationalism and the Predicament of Sovereignty."

73. Ma Hongtian, "Zhongguo tuozhi xuehui yu Zhongguo biandi xuehuizhi taolun yu shoubei" (The planning and discussion of the China Settlement and Colonization Institute and the China Border Regions Institute), *Xinyaxiya* 1, no. 1 (1930): 141.

74. Ma Hongtian, "Kaifa xibei shi jiejue Zhongguo shehui minsheng wentide genben fangfa" (Opening up the Northwest is a basic means of solving the problem of livelihood in Chinese society), *Xinyaxiya* 1, no. 1 (1930): 37.

75. Ma Hongtian, "Kaifa xibei shi jiejue Zhongguo shehui minsheng wentide genben fangfa," 38–39.

76. Quoted in Liu Xiaoyuan, "The Chinese Communist Party and the 'Nationality Question,' 1921–1945" (unpublished paper, 1999), 38 n. 2.

77. Jiang Zhongzheng (Chiang Kai-shek), *Zhongguozhi mingyun* (China's destiny) (n.p.: Zhengzhong shuju, 1943), 2.

78. Chiang, *China's Destiny*, trans. Wang Chung-hui (New York: Macmillan, 1947), 4, 12, 239 n. 1.

79. Fang, *Feichang shiqizhi bianwu*, 63–74; Siu-woo Cheung, "Subject and Representation: Identity Politics in Southeast Guizhou" (Ph.D. diss., University of Washington, Seattle, 1996), 108–20.

80. Deal, "Policy towards Ethnic Minorities in Southwest China," 34.

81. Liu Xiaoyuan, "The Kuomintang and the 'Mongolian Question' in the Chinese Civil War, 1945–1949," *Inner Asia* 1 (1999): 174–76.

82. Wei Huilin, "Zhanhou Zhongguo minzu zhengce yu bianjiang jianshe," *Minzuxue Yanjiu jikan* 4 (1944): 1–6.

83. Wei Huilin, "Zhanhou Zhongguo minzu zhengce yu bianjiang jianshe".

84. Ma Zhangshou, "Shaoshu minzu wenti," *Minzuxue Yanjiu jikan* 6 (1948): 20–21, 23.

85. Huang, "Minzuxue yu Zhongguo minzu yanjiu," 22.

86. Clearly, the goal of assimilating different peoples into a single national ideal dominated by the most advanced race/nationality (*minzu*), the Han, suggests a continuity with the social Darwinist ideal of "one nation, one race." The repeated references to "brotherhood" (*tongbao*), for instance, point to vestiges of this construct.

87. See Guldin, *Saga of Anthropology in China*, 31.

88. Ling Chunsheng, *Sonhuajiang xiayoude Hezhezu* (The Hezhe people downstream on the Sunghua river) (Nanjing: Guoli zhongyang yanjiuyuan lishi yuyan yanjiusuo, 1934), 60.

89. Ling, *Sonhuajiang xiayoude Hezhezu*, 61–62.

90. Ling, *Sonhuajiang xiayoude Hezhezu*, 281.

91. Ling disagrees with Shirokogoroff's idea that proto-Tungus occupied the central plain of China itself in 4,000 B.C. and were gradually pushed into Manchuria.

92. See Huang, "Minzuxue yu Zhongguo minzu yanjiu," 1936.

93. Huang Wenshan sought to displace or limit the hegemonic role of history in national governance. He notes that China has had a very powerful historical tradition, which it has used to govern the world (*tianxia*). Previously, historians had evoked the principle of "grasp[-ing] the past to understand the present" (*xian tonggu hou tongjin*), but at the time of Huang's writing it was clear that there were too many gaps and deficiencies in the historical records to do this adequately. More recently, anthropologists had reversed the slogan, to say one must "grasp the present to understand the past" through the methods of anthropology. By rereading ancient histories, discovering ancient artifacts, and researching contemporary primitive culture, the nation could gain a much better understanding of the evolution of its people than previous historians ever imagined. See Huang, "Minzuxue yu Zhongguo minzu yanjiu," 1.

94. Curiously, Ling even chooses to draw evidence from Huangdi and Yu, figures that

his contemporary Gu Jiegang had established were mythical figures; see Ling, *Sonhuajiang xiayoude Hezhezu*, 9–11.

95. Ling, *Sonhuajiang xiayoude Hezhezu*, 2–7.

96. Ling, *Sonhuajiang xiayoude Hezhezu*, 41.

97. According to Ling, these ancient Asiatic peoples came to be oppressed by the Zhou, the Tungus, and the Mongols. One part of them was assimilated by these invaders, while another part was pushed into the extreme northeast corner of Asia and are recognizable as the Chuckchee, the Koryak, Eskimo, Kamchedal, Ainu, and others. Ling, *Sonhuajiang xiayoude Hezhezu*, 34.

98. Cf. Li Changdan, who develops a complicated argument to prove the racial mixing of the peoples of north and northeast China since ancient times. Li's strategy is to show that since the Zhou dynasty, every time there was major warfare in north China, military and refugee movements took large numbers of people to the Northeast and Korea, where they mixed with the people there. Indeed, whether because of the nature of the sources or a desire to make claims on Korea, Li makes his argument for the Northeast largely in the process of showing how Korea was settled by Han Chinese. Choosing between two conflicting accounts from the *Shiji* and the *Shangshu*, Li suggests that Jizi (Kija in Korean), a loyal courtier of the Yin (the late Shang, ca. twelfth century B.C.), fled the Zhou conquest, taking with him five thousand people of Yin across the Liao River to Korea. Li prefers the *Shangshu* account, which suggests that Jizi was enfeoffed by the Zhou after he had set up rule in Korea with his people, and did not merely administer a colonial outpost of the Zhou as suggested in the *Shiji*. It was also in the process of moving to Korea that the Yin peoples were melded together with the Eastern barbarians in the Liaodong area through their common opposition and resistance to the Zhou. Similarly, the violent Qin–Han transition (third century B.C.) also saw the king of Yan fleeing to Liaodong. Sensing the need to strengthen these claims, Li appeals to archaelogical finds in Liaoning, including skeletal remains that he says were the same as those of the ancestors of the Han on the mainland. However, the Japanese archaeologists he cites claim only that while these discoveries show some relation to present-day Chinese and Koreans, they are much closer to neolithic man. See Li Changdan, "Dongbei yuanshi minzu he zhongguo benbuminzu zai renzhongshangde guanxi" (Racial relationships between the primitive peoples of the Northeast and the peoples of China proper), *Xinyaxiya* 11, no. 4 (1936): 31–35.

99. Yao Congwu, *Dongbei shi lun cong*, (Collection of historical essays on the Northeast) vol. 1 (Taipei: Zhengzhong shuju, 1959), 26.

100. Chiang, *China's Destiny* (1947), 6.

101. Chiang, *China's Destiny* (1947), 8–9; Wu Shangquan, *Dongbei dili yu minzu shengcunzhi guanxi*, 2–3.

102. Zhang Qiyun, *Zhongguo rendi guanxi gailun* (An introduction to relations between humans and land in China) (Shanghai: Dadong shuju, 1947), 1–4.

103. Zhang Qiyun, *Zhongguo rendi guanxi gailun*, 2.

104. See Wu Shangquan, *Dongbei dili yu minzu shengcunzhi guanxi*, 25–26.

105. Yao, *Dongbei shi lun cong*, 16–17. See also Duara, *Rescuing History*, chap. 1.

106. Duara, *Rescuing History*, 36–42.

107. Chiang, *China's Destiny* (1947), 13.

108. Cheung, "Subject and Representation: Identity Politics in Southeast Guizhou," 78–83.

109. Ling, *Sonhuajiang xiayoude Hezhezu*, 288.

110. Ling, *Sonhuajiang xiayoude Hezhezu*, 289.

111. Tatsuo Nakami, "A Protest against the Concept of the 'Middle Kingdom': The Mongols and the 1911 Revolution," in *The 1911 Revolution in China*, ed. Eto Shinkichi and Harold Z. Schiffrin (Tokyo: University of Tokyo Press, 1984), 146–47.

112. Liu Xiaoyuan, "The Chinese Communist Party and the 'Nationality Question,' 1921–1945" (unpublished paper, 1999), 41 n. 22; Cheung, "Subject and Representation," 119; and Nakami, "A Protest against the Concept of the 'Middle Kingdom.'"

113. Fang, *Feichang shiqizhi bianwu*, 73.

114. Fang, *Feichang shiqizhi bianwu*, 70–74.

115. Postscript to *Xinyaxiya* (New Asia) 1, no. 3 (1930): 15.

116. Postscript to *Xinyaxiya* (New Asia) 1, no. 3 (1930): 16.

117. Chen Yin, "'Xiaoshuo youjihua' de jieshi" (Explanation of the conversion of fiction into travel writing), *Xinyaxiya* 1, no. 6 (1931): 151–52.

118. He Guanzhou, "You Qian zaji" (Random notes on travels in Guizhou), *Xinyaxiya* 5, no. 5 (1933): 135–48.

119. Solomon M. Karmel, "Ethnic Nationalism in Mainland China," in *Asian Nationalism: China, Taiwan, Japan, India, Pakistan, Indonesia, The Philippines*, ed. Michael Leifer (New York: Routledge, 2000), 47–50.

120. V. K. Arseniev's story of the Goldi trapper Dersu is perhaps the most remarkable.

121. See Marie Denis-Shelton, "Primitive Self: Colonial Impulses in Michel Leiris's 'L'Afrique fantome,'" in *Prehistories of the Future: The Primitivist Project and the Culture of Modernism*, ed. Elazar Barkan and Ronald Bush (Stanford: Stanford University Press, 1995), 326–38. The most conspicuous exception from Republican China is the writer Shen Congwen.

122. See, for instance, the writings of novelists Bai Hua and Han Shaogong and the film *Sacrificed Youth*.

CHAPTER SIX

~

Local Worlds: The Poetics and Politics of the Native Place

A "native-place literature" fever that raged all over China following the Mao era has continued unabated in the Northeast. In response to my inquiries about this fever, the most prominent literary expert on the native place in the Northeast, Professor Sun Zhongtian, described it as a reaction to the dry and formulaic writings of the Maoist period and reflected a long-buried yearning among readers for community, whether of the hometown or home regions (*jiaxiang he diyu*). It occurred to me that the fever represented another moment in the expression of attachment to the local or regional that I had been studying in Manchukuo. While the area had seen several different regimes and the nature of regional representation had doubtless also changed, what had endured was the production of the local as sentiment and object of identity.

The preoccupation with the "hometown" or "native place" (*guxiang, xiangtu* in Chinese; *kyōdo, furusato* in Japanese) was a significant component—often symbolic or metonymic—of the modern representation of the local or the regional (Chinese *difang, diyu*; Japanese *chihō, chiiki*)) not only in Manchuria, but in twentieth-century East Asia more generally. As in many other parts of the world, this sense of the local was pervasively represented as a site of authentic values of a larger formation, such as the nation or civilization, frequently threatened by ascendant capitalist, modern, and urban values. As such, nationalists or the state were moved to protect this site of authenticity from the corrosive and homogenizing forces of capitalism, as much as to reform it.

As the local became (globally) a focus of cultural authenticity, its discourse appeared through a variety of media. In East Asia, the local as repository of the heartland traditions was produced through folklore studies, geography, local histories, and native-place literature; in such visual representations as the woodblock print, landscape art, the postcard, or the calendar; in social trends such as the folk art and ecotourism movements in Japan; and to some extent in political practices, such as

209

the rural reconstruction movements and Maoist populism, which posited a primordial community estranged by class conflict. These disciplines and practices temporalize the local space as belonging to another time than the reader or viewer, consistent with the cycles of nature or with a civilization enduring from antiquity. In this genre of knowledge, the local becomes an authentic and (heretofore) enduring object to be investigated, restored, and/or reformed.

The local is therefore subject to a politics that I will try to grasp by examining its production and reception historically in Manchukuo. First, what was the nature of the local that was being produced? The Japanese representations of Manchuria as native place and region were continuous with the image of the virginal and natural frontier that we have already seen. For the Chinese, representation of it would have to transform a frontier into the heartland. Thus, Manchukuo presented the paradox of a spatial representation that had to serve both as frontier and heartland. Second, while the production of the local generates sentiment and identity, the case of Manchuria reveals that the relationship of this spatial identity to a wider polity—as nation, part of nation, civilization, empire, or even transnational region—is neither given nor fixed.

The local or regional in modern China has typically been seen as politically and culturally part of the national. As Bryna Goodman's work shows, local consciousness at the turn of the century—in native-place associations, for instance—reveals a relatively novel if strong sense of national loyalty.[1] Although national incorporation of the local is undeniable, I prefer to see it as one factor or phase in a wider process of the formation of the local. The local may best be viewed in a field of multiple forces—nationalism, imperialism, transnational cultural ideologies, social networks, capital, and local forces themselves—contending to appropriate its meaning and resources. This view releases the local from a naturalistic fixity within the nation, so that it can be treated as *process*. The local is not a reality fully distinct from the different forces that seek to stabilize its meaning at any time, nor is its meaning unchanging over time.

The Native Place in Sino-Japanese Discourse

What was the historical understanding of the local in late imperial China, and what kind of relationship can we expect between the historical and the contemporary (1900–1949)? There is astonishingly little written about late imperial perceptions of the locality. However, we are lucky to have a recent, insightful introduction to the problem by Kishimoto Mio. Examining the notion of *fengsu* (local custom) during the Ming–Qing transition (sixteenth–seventeenth centuries), she notes that statesmen like Gu Yanwu and Wang Fuzhi, who had different views on the problem of local autonomy (the *fengjian–junxian* debate), shared the notion of a locality as having distinctive characteristics and customs. But the distinctiveness of the locality did not yield a conception of irreducible value embedded in the modern notion of culture or *Kultur*, or, as we shall see, in heartland writings. Instead, whether by means of state leadership (for Wang) or of the local Confucian elite (for Gu), the *su* (customs) of the locality had to be transformed (*jiaohua*) and revitalized by the moral leadership (*feng*) of upright men. Good *fengsu* was represented by people who led simple and honest lives, though neither ignorance nor poverty was acceptable in the name of simplicity. For both Gu and Wang, *fengsu* had declined terribly in their times (the seventeenth century), when urbanization, social division, and commodification had eroded the simple but stable life of village society. In Gu's view, the decline of *fengsu*, which was comparable to the moral decline during the barbarian invasions of the Wei-Jin period, represented the decline not simply of a dynasty but of a civilizational order (*wang tianxia*).[2]

Thus, in an orthodox Confucian view, locality was seen less as a source of value than as the index of this value and object of cultivation. We need to supplement this orthodox view with the view from vernacular popular culture, which celebrated the local upholders of justice—the *jianghu or lülin*—against corrupt bureaucrats and elites. This countertradition, while thoroughly interwoven with popular and subaltern ideas and imagery, likely did not refer to a distinct place or locality as a source of value, but rather to a utopian space also defined by orthodox moral values (*zhongyi*). Nonetheless, the twentieth-century historical and literary celebration of the locality derived, as we shall see, great inspiration from it.

If tradition provided the vocabulary and symbolism for modern Chinese writing about the locality, this writing also drew from a number of global sources to reinterpret historical conceptions and sentiments of the local. Among these sources were nineteenth-century Russian writers such as Chekhov and Turgenev (see their impact on Shen Congwen);[3] the anthropological writings of James Frazer, Andrew Lang, and others; and the Germanic literature of the homeland. The Japanese influence was also very significant. Chinese and Japanese have the same ideographs for the signifiers "native-place studies or literature," (Japanese *kyōdo kenkyū*; Chinese *xiangtu yanjiu, xiangtu wenxue*) and "folklore studies," (Japanese *minzokugaku*; Chinese *minsuxue*). The Japanese influence—and that of Japanese translations of Western sources—was especially profound upon the two great writers of the Chinese Republic, the brothers Lu Xun and Zhou Zuoren. The two had, in very different ways, an enormous impact upon the genre (both literary and nonliterary) of the local.

The status of Yanagita Kunio in Japanese folklore and native-place studies is much larger than life and the movement he spawned was extremely influential in China as well. Yanagita had begun the study of the native place in order to salvage a people and a locality's way of life from the pulverizing onslaught of commodification, modernity, and state building. It has been suggested that the study of the native place gradually changed to folklore studies among Yanagita and his cohorts around the 1930s and the "native place" became a metonym for Japan as a whole.[4] Thus the irreducibility of the local (in the face of state building) metamorphosed into the irreducibility of the national. Some believe that in this way Yanagita distinguished and rescued Japanese folklore from the dominant, imperialistic folklore studies pursued in the West by scholars like Frazer and Lang, which emphasized evolutionism and the comparative method. For Yanagita, the purpose of investigating the folklore of a society was not to probe the survival of barbarisms (and thus participate in an evolutionary scheme for cultures), but to understand the history of a people's cultural ethos in order to solve their present problems. He thus employed folklore to critique the notion of civilizational progress embedded in History. The emphasis on spiritual, subjective cultural traditions—the search for a nation's "collective doubt lurking beneath their hearts"—thus led him to focus on the special characteristics of each country's folklore as a manifestation of its interior and authentic life.[5]

During the early 1920s, when he was involved in the folklore studies journal *Geyao*, Zhou Zuoren was perhaps more impressed by the evolutionism of Frazer than by Yanagita, whose work became much more important for him later (even though he was well aware of it and had acquired all of Yanagita's work and every volume of *Kyōdo Kenkyū* since its appearance in 1914). He believed that much of contemporary folklore was a barbaric remainder from ancient times and drew upon Frazer's notion of primitive magic to criticize both the Confucian tradition, and especially Daoism, as a survival from primitive thought.[6] Yanagita's work began to dominate his ideas from the second half of the 1920s, particularly upon witnessing the violence of national revolution (1925–1927). As he turned more and more to Yanagita's writings, Zhou came to see in folklore the spirit of a people that existed outside the orthodox historical records and state forms. During this later phase, he explored such themes as the popular cult of the Unbegotten Venerable Mother, or Wushenglaomu, and the Daoist doctrine of forgiveness and understanding, *liangjie*, which he understood as an aspect of *renqing*, the popular and historical Chinese conception of human sentiment underpinning the social order. Zhou began to perceive folklore from a sympathetic perspective akin to cultural anthropology and to understand it as a history of a people's spiritual life.[7] Just as Yanagita critiqued state Shinto and regarded village shrines as the true basis of national culture, so too Zhou modeled the idea of popular Daoism and shamanism as the cultural foundation of the nation and an alternative to Confucianism, the culture of the elite and bureaucracy.

As early as 1923, in the essay "Locality and Literature," Zhou urged contemporary writers not to yield to the abstract and homogenizing tendency in literature, but to retain the plurality and creative energy inherent in local traditions and history.[8] Citing Nietzsche, he urged the new generation of writers, especially in his native Zhejiang, to be "loyal to the land," because the locality (*fengtu*) had the power to nourish the character of the "sons of the land": "Only when the breath of the soil and the flavor of the earth penetrates their veins and finds expression in their writing can we have authentic thought and literature."[9] We also see in Zhou a particularly clear expression of the articulation of locality with tradition or history. Zhou rejected the accusation that his was a conservative view of "national essence." He believed that there were two parts to "national essence": one was a living essence that flowed in the veins—our inherited flavor (*quwei*)—which we are powerless to determine, but which naturally reveals itself in all our words and actions and has no need to be conserved; the other, dead part comprised those morals and customs of the past inappropriate and unnecessary to the present. He hoped that a new national literature could have the capaciousness to give play to the special, historical character of the region.[10]

However, just as with Yanagita, it is also possible to interpret Zhou's concern with the local as effectively preserving existing power relationships. According to Harry Harootunian, Yanagita's "native ethnology" became a means "to preserve older forms of relationships and practice before their elimination (amidst rural ruin) as a necessary condition for seeking a solution to the question of division, fragmentation and conflict."[11] Japanese folklore studies sought to combat conflict by offering an image of naturalized folk custom tied to a timeless place beyond mere history. Zhou Zuoren's New Village movement of the 1920s, inspired by Japanese utopian socialism, had sought to build a community based on indigenous notions of self-help and personal ethical cultivation. Through this movement, Zhou sought to avoid the struggles and bloodshed associated with revolutionary, particularly communist, movements. According to Ozaki Fumiaki, the New Village movement advocated by Zhou initially appealed to youth, but the practical difficulties of implementing its goals, together with the growing attractiveness of bolshevism and eugenics, made such a movement appear impractical and retrograde, and it lost favor.[12] Both Yanagita and Zhou sought to find in the local a source of authentic value and to protect it (Zhou's "living essence") from the depredations of capitalist modernity and state building; at the same time, however, this very identitarian project—the search for an alternative, indigenous order—was susceptible to appropriation by national and imperialist ideologies.

Manchukuo also served as a space for several Japanese idealists and community activists to realize their projects. We have referred to Fujiyama Kazuo's vision of transforming the Japanese settler community's relationship to the land and environment through his folkways museum. As a Christian, he was particularly drawn to the faith-based village community built around the Russian log cabin church—the only model that he felt could give spiritual and social sustenance to the new settler communities.[13] Many Japanese leftists forced to flee Japan in the 1930s also sought to realize their ideals in rural Manchukuo, working with impoverished Chinese peasants in the Northern Manchuria Cooperative Society movement. Those for whom the locality carried a special meaning were activists like Satō Daishirō, inspired by Tachibana and pan-Asianist ideals of agrarian socialism as much as by Marxism. They believed that by organizing poor peasants into credit and marketing cooperatives and challenging the economic stranglehold of merchants from below they could achieve the ideals of the kingly way and Concordia.[14] The poet and activist Nogawa Takashi drifted away from these ideals as he became more interested in understanding the peasants than teaching them. He collected and adapted the Chinese folk songs of the area and wrote poetry whose sources and inspiration lay in peasant life. The ideals of these activists did not sit well with the wartime regime's notions of idyllic village communities (kyōdōtai), as we shall see. Satō and Nogawa were among the twenty-six Japanese leftists imprisoned by the increasingly intolerant and anticommunist regime in the early 1940s. Both died in prison.[15]

The trend to understand the local as a site of enduring value was not confined to utopian, conservative, folkloric, literary, or historical practices; it was secured just as much by the modern scientific disciplines. We have seen how anthropology, archeology, geography, and other fields contributed to the knowledge of national space. To some extent, disciplines such as sociology, anthropology, and geography in Japan and China also became involved during the 1930s in scientifically explaining the reproduction of enduring values in the village or locality (*xiangtu*).

The global emergence during the inter-war era of a scientific, geographical determinism was tied to German ideas of *Lebensraum* and "geopolitics." While both expressions had been associated since the end of the nineteenth century with the names of Friedrich Ratzel and the Swedish journalist Rudolf Kjellen, it was the defeat of Germany in World War I that stimulated a popular explosion of geopolitical thought. The critical notion of *raum*, denoting space or area in German but piled with "thick layers of nearly mystical connotations," combined topography, climate, and other physical elements with a specific people, or *Volk*, to create a mystical unity that produced the state. The idea of *Lebensraum* came to be associated with the necessity of an eternal struggle for a space sufficient for the autarkic existence of the German state both in central Europe and overseas.[16]

Geopolitical ideas rapidly became part of Japanese geographical knowledge—both academic and military-bureaucratic—between the 1920s and 1940s. Geographical determinism was employed to produce a timeless rural authenticity in the "battle against urbanism in modern capitalist civilization."[17] The rhetoric of the native place, long important in Japanese geographical pedagogy for, among other purposes, the development of nationalist identity, intensified during the rural crisis of the late twenties and thirties, leading to a kind of cult of the native place (*furusato*) as the moral alternative to modern capitalism.[18] After the establishment of Manchukuo, some leaders spoke of Asia as the theater of a kind of Japanese *Lebensraum*, and during the Pacific War geographical determinism was freely employed to describe occupied territories. Leading sociologists, economists, and legal scholars adapted the ideas of Karl Wittfogel to discover mythological Chinese villages embodying the pristine Asiatic values of cooperation (*kyōdōtai*).[19]

Although he criticized the relationship between geopolitics and the totalitarian state, the philosopher Watsuji Tetsurō produced in *Climate and Culture* (1935) perhaps the most influential geographical determinist argument of the time.[20] According to Susan Daruvala, Watsuji's understanding of *fūdo* or *fengtu* (a historical Chinese expression referring to the character of a place, shaped by both natural and social conditions) influenced Zhou Zuoren's idea of *mingyun* (destiny) through which the latter viewed the relationship between heredity and environment dialectically. Zhou found in Watsuji an important foundation for his own ideas about place and self-understanding.[21]

The geographical determinism of the local or regional also appeared in geographical knowledge in China during the 1930s and 1940s. Jin Qisan elaborated upon the geologist Baron von Richtofen's division of China into two distinct geological formations, in the north and the south. Jin marshalled geographical as well as racial and linguistic evidence to argue for enduring cultural differences between the two regions and explain history by means of geography.[22] In turn this north–south division became the basis of scholarly and popular understandings of culture, such as Lin Yutang's *My Country and My People*. Note that geographical determinism of the region or locality did not automatically yield to national determination, although nationalists did not find it difficult to frame the local within the national. A goal of this chapter is to show how the local was susceptible to framing within different scales of identity.

More strictly geographical education also contributed to the understanding of the local as productive of abiding values. An introductory text entitled "The Research Methods of Community Geography" (*Xiangtu Dili Yanjiufa*) was published by a professional geographer, Ge Suicheng, in 1939. Ge acknowledged his indebtedness to American, German, and Japanese geographers, particularly Sasaki Seiji. Indeed, the Japanese title of Sasaki's work is virtually identical to Ge's Chinese. It is no small irony that Ge wrote this work biding time in his home village, to which he had fled to escape the Japanese occupation of Shanghai. Ge uses *xiangtu* to translate the expressions "region," "home geography," and "*Heimat*." His goal was to transform the old geography of the locality, which described the various items of climate, soil, settlement, and so on discretely, in isolation from each other, into an analysis of the dynamic engagement between the environment and human culture in a place. The significance of "community geography" is its comprehensive understanding of the "cultural traits" (a term he deploys originally in English) produced by a village society living under particular environmental conditions.[23] Although Ge is more concerned with identifying the ways in which the environment shapes the positive and negative features of a community, the weighty role in his study of the environmental determination of rural space contributed to the constitution of this space as an enduring object.[24] We shall see how the novelist Liang Shanding employs scientific geography and geological conceptions of time to naturalize the local community.

The noted sociologist and anthropologist Fei Xiaotong also wrote a number of popular essays in the 1940s about the locality and native place that reflected the ways in which the discourse of the local spoke through him. The first essay in *Xiangtu Zhongguo* (Village China) is entitled "xiangtu bense," which may be translated as "the 'true color' of rural society." The notion of *bense* is also very important in Zhou Zuoren, and according to Daruvala refers to the natural color one finds, for instance, upon wiping off makeup.[25] The expression distinctly partakes of authenticity. Fei points to the deep-rooted relationship that the Chinese peasant—whom he often refers to as *laogen*, or "old roots"—has to the soil, revealed for instance in the universal worship of the earth god in China and the reluctance to move out of the isolated group or village. Everywhere Fei uses the metaphor of a tree or plant that continues to grow in one place, likening even forced migration (the only kind) because of disaster or famine to the "seeds blown from the old tree."[26]

The second half of Fei's essay is designed to show how rootedness and isolation, which he also sees as the richness of *difangxing*, or localness,[27] produce those enduring habits and values that, while they can be understood in terms of the sociological distinctions between *Gemeinschaft* and *Gesellschaft* and between Durkheimean mechanical and organic solidarity, are perhaps best understood in Confucian terms. He says, "in our own language, it is the difference between the society of rites and custom (*lisu shehui*) and the society of law (*falu shehui*)."[28] Familiarity develops through a closeness refined through enduring patterns of everyday interactions. According to Fei, this process is expressed in the word for practice (*xi*) in the first sentence of the *Analects* of Confucius. In a society steeped in familiarity, we are able to gain a level of freedom in which desire arises from the heart and flows with the norms—without violating them. This is very different from the society where freedom is guaranteed by law. Norms are not laws; they are rites and customs that arise from practice. And since they arise from practice, they arise from the heart. In other words, here the society and the individual develop an intimate understanding.[29]

Fei frequently invokes Confucius in the instances he cites of traditional practices, habits, values, and mentalities among the rural folk. In this way, it is clear that while the social sciences may, in part, be applied to understand them, the peasants represent the "old roots" of a distinctively Chinese tradition that can best be understood through an age-old conceptual language. This is possible precisely because of an enduring relation between a people and their space. Fei concludes the essay by decrying the loss and abuse of these authentic values by modern developments, a lament consonant with his well-known call to reverse the erosion of rural communities.

The curious part of it all is that in most of his work, Fei did not find it necessary to either maintain or reject Confucianism as the repository of authentic value, as it may have been for Liang Shuming. Nor, as he indicates in the essay and elsewhere, did he necessarily find these rural values to be virtues that should be preserved. Yet he depicted the peasant, and especially his relationship to the soil, in a distinctly timeless way. Fei certainly overstated the isolation and rootedness of the peasants, as the later research of G. W. Skinner and others has shown. Even more significantly, Fei's biographer, David Arkush, has pointed out that Fei's own research did not reveal Chinese villages as radically isolated communities.[30] Perhaps the discursive need to find authentic Chinese civilizational values in the people may have compelled Fei to overemphasize the abiding, almost timeless relationship between the old roots and their environment.

Fei Xiaotong's writings reveal that whether or not the objective conditions for the production of the local as a site of enduring values actually exist, such a notion is ultimately determined discursively and, most specifically, through its writing. Literary writing of the native place, then, is not only a significant means of its production, but together with the criticism and debates that accompany this writing reveals the fault lines of the local as a site of authenticity most sharply. Current writing on the history of native-place literature in the People's Republic of China identifies three trends: the "conservative romanticist" writings of Shen Congwen and the *jing-pai* school associated with Zhou Zuoren; the radical tradition pioneered by Lu Xun; and the nationalist tradition associated with the resistance to the Japanese occupation of China.

I will take up the "national resistance" strain—perhaps the one most productive of the local as authentic—in an analysis of Liang Shanding's *Green Valley* in the next section. I have touched on the ideas of the leader of the allegedly conservative and romantic school, Zhou Zuoren, and a great deal of commentary exists on these writers, especially Zhou and Shen Congwen. This school has been criticized, as Yanagita was, for depoliticizing the locality or countryside, and at worst enabling collaboration with the occupying forces. But there is also a more sympathetic judgement, which emphasizes their resistance to the pulverizing effects of modern state- and nation-making and their effort to discover, recover, or recreate the local as a different way of constructing the self and its relation to the nation or civilization.[31]

I find that I cannot disagree strongly with either of these readings of native-place literature. Both Zhou and Yanagita may have wanted to preserve the value of the local, but Yanagita also spoke of the local place as a metonym for Japan, and Zhou never lost sight of the locality's belonging in the nation. At the same time, Zhou also collaborated with the Japanese imperialists and the evidence of Yanagita's involvement is growing. The scales framing the locality's meaning were not consistent over their lifetimes, nor was there much consistency within the groups they allegedly represented.[32] My concern here is less with their politics, or even with the politics of the genre per se, as with the wider political struggle over the local as authentic object. I wish to examine how the writing of these individuals contributed to the discourse of the authenticity of the local, to the sentimental investment of the village as the bedrock of abiding values. Different forces—national, regional, transnational—working for different conceptions of political community as much as for different interests, sought to seize the object of this writing to pitch their claims on the authentic.

Lu Xun and Native-Place Writing

Lu Xun has arguably written more deeply and interestingly about native-place writing than any other writer in China. PRC writers often cite Lu's introduction to a 1935 collection of essays as proof of his view of the native place, in opposition to the nostalgic one, as a site for reforming superstition and backwardness. This is undoubtedly true. But despite his prescient critique of native-place *writing*, Lu Xun too could not be disassociated from the sentimental investment of the native place. I want to trace Lu's argument and the historical route to his conclusion, in order to suggest that his is a most complex and productive view of the native place.

Lu's 1935 introduction discusses a group of writers from the early 1920s, such as Jian Xian'ai, Pei Wenzhong, Xu Qinwen, and Wang Luyan, whose stories he identifies as "native-place writings" (*xiangtu wenxue*).[33] Lu identifies two types of writing about the native place, and he is extremely critical of one style, which is immersed in nostalgia, loss, and indeed death. Lu suggests that the absence of these authors, writing in Beijing, from their native places often causes them to dwell on darkly nostalgic memories. Some writers seek to retreat into childhood memories or into the mother's bosom, and others abhor the city—especially Beijing—and indulge themselves in a useless nihilism. Driven out of his village by circumstances, Xu Qinwen can only recall his father's garden and mourn the things that do not exist anymore. Xu consoles himself with the memory of things that are gone, rather than things that clearly exist but that he cannot approach. Lu is sharply critical of writing that is obsessed with memories and incapable of action. These writers have a certain cold detachment (*lengjing*) that produces a worrying laughter and seeks characters full, not of opinions and life, but of death.[34]

While Lu Xun's impatience toward this nostalgic brand of native-place writing sharpened during the last, radical phase of his life, it is not inconsistent with his earlier reflections on loss and death in the native-place stories, such as "My Old Home" (*Guxiang*), "In the Wine Shop" (*Zai Jiuloushang*), "The New Year's Sacrifice" (*Zhufu*), and "Village Opera" (*Shexi*), that he wrote between 1921 and 1924. I will not engage a detailed treatment of these stories, but while one can read a message similar to that of his 1935 essay in the conclusions to some of them, these stories are by no means univocal. Taken together, the stories examine memory as the medium of apprehending the native place and explore its preoccupation with loss and death. Lu Xun is well aware of the deception and tricks played by memory—particularly when "dawn blossoms [are] plucked at dusk."[35] This is clear at the start of some of the stories: the narrator, upon returning to the childhood scene, finds it to be different from the way he remembered it, only to realize that it is he who has changed. "Village Opera" is actually structured around the tricks of memory. The adult narrator thinks that he remembers liking the open-air village opera he went to see as a child. As it turns out, what he really enjoyed was not the opera but the adventure of his outing with his country cousins. For Lu Xun, writing is the means to both play and reveal the tricks of memory.

"In the Wine Shop" and "New Year's Sacrifice," written one week apart in 1924, probe the nexus of memory, death, and ritual mourning. In "New Year's Sacrifice," the story of Xianglin's widow, a miserable wretch driven to death by misfortune and the systemic victimization of unprotected women, is narrated by a modern, urban outsider. In part because of her victimhood, Xianglin's widow is cruelly rejected by the village, and Lu treats her death metaphorically as a communal sacrifice during the New Year celebrations. The ritual cleanses the community of the memory of its inhumanity and erases the narrator's nagging existential uncertainty. Although "Sacrifice" is an enormously complex story in many ways, its view of (ritual) sacrifice as erasure of bad memory is relatively straightforward, and Lu appears to want it to serve an edifying purpose.

Mourning ritual in "In the Wine Shop" appears in a more dialogical mode. The narrator, who decides to stay overnight in a sad, rural town from his youth, runs into an old friend, Wei-fu, who is also visiting the town. Over drinks at the wine shop, Wei-fu tells him the story of his life since they last met and it is one of disappointments and failures. He reveals that the purpose of his visit is to satisfy his mother's wish to rebury the corpse of his brother, who died aged three. Upon unearthing the old grave, Wei-fu encountered an utterly empty, rotting coffin, but decided to go ahead with the reburial ritual, "to deceive my mother and put her mind to rest."[36] The experience of loss is heightened by Wei-fu's second encounter with death in the same visit, that of a suffering young girl for whom he had brought some artificial flowers that she had longed for. At the heart of this story is the question of what we do when we come face to face with (the absolute loss of) death. Ritual presents us with a deception, but our only source of solace. We cannot but feel deeply empathetic toward this man in his encounter with death and loss, and sympathize with his gestures. Yet as the story comes to a close, Lu Xun shows Wei-fu as one sunk in his past and his failures, with no hope for/in the future. When the two part company, the narrator is refreshed by the snow beating upon his face as he walks away from the scene of the town that is becoming enveloped in snow. The simplicity of the story's conclusion belies the complexity of understanding the narrator has deposited, that is, as Derrida has said, posited and provisionally abandoned.

For Lu in 1935, the local is not the place to encounter the past, particularly not in the mode of nostalgic dwelling or mourning its loss. He has been there and he knows writing's memory tricks and the deceiving rituals that cause us to linger there. So how does Lu want us to see the local? Not as the lost past to be restored or preserved, but as the past to be reformed and transformed. The local is where today's peasants and gentry, mired in feudalism, must become tomorrow's modern citizens. In the 1935 introduction, Lu writes admiringly of two native-place authors, Jian Xian'ai and Tai Jingnong. Jian gives us a full view of cruel village customs in Guizhou, but he is able to show how the greatness of motherly love issues out from within this cruelty. Lu is also full of praise for Tai, who is able to transfer the subject of "death and *life* in the village, the breath of the soil (*nitude qixi*) onto paper. There are no better, no more industrious writers than this one."[37] These writers are good precisely because they do not wallow in nostalgia, because they work hard to interest and engage us with the misery of rural life.

But we might ask, Why write about the local? Why is the native place important at all? I am convinced that Lu Xun experimented sufficiently with memory and mourning for the native place to know that the kind of power exercised by the native place was generated less by the place itself than by the desire among writers and readers to (re) connect with it. Lu Xun recognized that, whether because of the tricks of memory or the reader's alienation, the power of this attachment was generated and mobilizable by the technology of *writing* about the native place. No matter how distant, good writing about a particular timespace can cathect universally. Lu says that Jian Xian'ai's story about motherly love shows us that "although Guizhou is a faraway land, the human condition is everywhere the same."[38] As in the cultural investment of the frontier, evocative writing about a native place can produce empathy in the reader by generating a desire to (re)connect with the timespace, to recognize oneself in the place. For Lu, the native-place story becomes a means of imagining a community of sentiment as much as one of purpose.

Lu's project of the local is thus twofold. First, it must depict the sorrow and the misery so that reform can be implemented and the nation strengthened. But in order to motivate his compatriots to engage in this task, the writing of the local also has to cathect the imagined community of the nation via the locality. It is through the particularity of the locality—in the sympathy and nostalgia for it—that an empathetic identification is built in the reader. If this emotional power is to be mobilized for the sake of nation building, Lu Xun tells us, we have to resist mourning, that overpowering urge to be absorbed by our loss. Mourning, however, is not the only problem Lu Xun's project encounters. For this mode of writing to work, the writer must also be able to identify or redeem some primordial worth from a locality that is otherwise covered in misery—perhaps something like the mother's love amidst pervasive cruelty in a Guizhou village. Yet, a couple of pages later in the same essay, Lu is critical of the writing of Wang Luyan, who seeks to become human by returning his heart to his mother and shutting out the rest of the world.

The danger in seeking out the source of attachment, the primordial worth, is that this worth can become an end in itself and subvert the program of action on behalf of other forces, such as the nation. We are reminded of the leftist activist and poet, Nogawa Takashi, who decided that it was better to learn from the peasants than to teach them. Note also how Lu's own stories exemplify this difficulty. At the end of the hometown stories, the protagonist is often relieved or refreshed as he walks away from the place of the past, but the power of these stories lies less in the endings than in the images of the past that haunt us. The writer who follows Lu Xun's project has to walk a very fine line to transform this attachment into improvement, because improvement will involve transformation of the object of attachment.

Thus, while there are real differences between the nostalgic or romantic mode of native-place writing and Lu Xun's demand for a grim realism, it is also important to recognize that both use writing to generate a desire for attachment and identification. Indeed, given the status of the discourse of the local in the modern world, it cannot but be so. Let us recall that in our analysis the local is the site of tension between market and modernizing forces (which transform or erode it) and nationalism (which needs, in part, to preserve it as authentic identity). Some scholars have recently demonstrated that the logic of nostalgia resembles the Freudian analysis of the fetish: it represents an effort to make whole by a substitute representation of the lost object, even as the representation signifies that the lack perdures.[39] However, the fetishization of the local itself has to be understood within the problem of time constitutive of modern nations and the demands of the regime of authenticity. Lu Xun's project of native-place writing reproduces the aporia in which the local must embody some abiding worth, but is in need of urgent renovation to serve as the basis of the modern nation. It seeks a new and difficult transformation of the local without eroding it; or, in other words, the ability to recognize the self in the local without preserving it.

Liang Shanding's *Green Valley*

Liang Shanding (pen name, Shanding) wrote his only novel, *Green Valley* (*Lüsede Gu*), in Manchukuo in 1942.[40] It is a classic native-place novel that dramatizes the tension I have probed in the discussion of Lu Xun and others above. While the novel succeeded admirably in producing the local as an abiding source of value, the great unasked question that haunted its afterlife came to be: of what did it represent the truth? Unasked, because each successive reading of the novel by regimes and intellectuals, including the author himself, presupposed a different answer, and in this way appropriated the meaning and affect of the native place. The novel, its historical background, and its contentious reception will serve as our guide in exploring the locality as product and process.

The principal plot of the novel revolves around the youthful heir to the Lin family estate, Lin Xiaobiao, and his movements between the village in the valley of Langgou, the city of Nanmanzhan (South Manchurian station, a likely play on the SMR Company), and the primeval forests of the mountains and valleys of Manchuria, which I shall refer to as primeval forests (*yuanshi lin*). The entire novel takes place in these three spaces, viewed topographically at the beginnings and endings of their respective descriptions and also throughout the novel. Sometimes the topographical view is achieved from the narrator's location on a mountaintop and sometimes from the air. In the underlying structure of the novel, each of the spaces acts upon the other, producing profound moral and political consequences that are woven together into a complex narrative of corruption and redemption. Relationships of class, community, and gender shaped by these spaces serve as motivating ideals or forces, driving the characters to actions that transform the spaces and the relations between them. In other words, each of the spaces generates or sustains a temporality, a mode of production, a lifestyle, and a morality, and during the time covered by the novel (roughly 1914 to 1931) the equilibrium between the three spaces is threatened with impending collapse.

Lin Xiaobiao has to leave the estate in Langgou Valley for the city (Nanmanzhan) when his father, a modern military officer in the army of the warlord of Manchuria, Zhang Zuolin, is killed in the Fengzhi wars of the mid-1920s. Xiaobiao's mother is forced by her own father to remarry a comprador, or agent of a Japanese company in the city, Qian Rulong, and the eleven-year-old Xiaobiao has to move with them. Xiaobiao reveals an early and stubborn hatred toward this decision to leave Langgou and for his mother's remarriage, especially to a greedy and power-hungry man. Despite an early revelation of the strength of his character, in the city Xiaobiao becomes an idealistic, dreamy intellectual with a tendency to lapse into an effete dandyism and cowardliness, especially in regard to women. Thus, on a visit back to Langgou, he falls in love and has a relationship with a poor tenant girl, Xiaolian. He likens her to the purest orchid in the heart of the forest and contrasts her with the cheaply made-up city girls, but at the time of her greatest need he abandons her.

When Xiaobiao returns after graduating from high school, he considers staying on as lord of the estate, which in the meantime had been managed by his aunt Lin Shuzhen and the foreman of the estate, Huofeng, who is also her not-so-secret lover. He feels a certain paternalism towards the peasants and regards the valley as his true mother against the one who remarried and left for the artificial and corrupt city. But despite the beauty of the land and authenticity of the people, he is also stifled by its feudal insularity. The time is the late 1920s and there is a property issue fomenting unease in the valley. Xiaobiao's stepfather Qian wishes to sell some of Langgou's barren, stony lands by the river to his Continental Company so that a railroad may be built in the area. From the perspective of the landlords of the region, such a development would catapult the value of the land, and each lobbies for the railroad to be built through their lands. Lin Shuzhen is keen on the sale so as to pay for Xiaobiao's higher education, but the tenants and Huofeng are opposed because it would deprive them of their livelihood. Xiaobiao, who views the land less as his patrimony than as his true mother, is confused.

At this point Xiaobiao decides to marry Yoshiko, a modern, idealistic Sinophile and the daughter of his stepfather's boss, the Japanese manager of the Continental Company. The boss has lived in Manchuria for thirty years and is devoted to things Chinese. Xiaobiao resolves to return to his beloved Langgou together with Yoshiko once he has completed his higher studies in Japan. The couple plan a farewell trip to Langgou before leaving for Japan, but unbeknownst to them the stepfather Qian and his investment partner are visiting Langgou at the same time to clinch the sale of the land. Before the young couple arrive, Qian and his coinvestor are witness to a great show of communal solidarity in Langgou when, upon a threatened bandit attack on the estate and the valley, Huofeng persuades Shuzhen to permit the tenants and their families to seek refuge in the estate compound while their men defend the estate. In the meantime, the hunter-bandit gang, led by Big Bear Paw, find an opportunity in kidnapping Xiaobiao and Yoshiko and demanding a huge ransom. Yoshiko is released but there is no news of Xiaobiao for several months. Xiaobiao's biological mother and Shuzhen seek to raise money for his ransom, and Qian Rulong hits upon the fiendish plan to do so by selling the barren land. Railway construction begins in the valley. Meanwhile, Big Bear Paw has a change of heart and helps Xiaobiao escape; together they spend several weeks seeking an uncharted way through the primeval forests. The ordeal, during which Xiaobiao develops an immense respect and fondness for Big Bear Paw, emerges as the ultimate test of Xiaobiao's endurance and his true learning of the secret power of the forest and the secret societies that live in it. When they finally find their way back to Nanmanzhan, the Qian house is locked up, most of the key players are ruined or imprisoned, and the city has been devastated by economic and moral collapse. Xiaobiao decides to return to Langgou, give up all his remaining property to the tenants, and embrace the valley, his true mother.

From the moment of its publication, most readings of the novel have located its ultimate significance outside the locality. This is even true of Liang Shanding's own reading of it in an 1987 postscript, written in light of having suffered twenty-two years of incarceration (from 1957 to 1979), in great part because the novel had been translated into Japanese. Indeed, the salient features of Shanding's life present us with the strongest evidence of the novel's historical reception. Born in 1914 (the same year as the fictional Xiaobiao), Shanding grew up in Harbin—a city he has called the "hometown of literature"—and was part of its thriving literary culture, profoundly shaped by modern Russian literature.[41] Together with his more famous and older colleagues Xiao Jun and Xiao Hong, he joined the anti-Japanese literary movement in Harbin after the Japanese occupation of Manchuria. While most of the important members of this resistance movement had fled south of the pass by 1934, Shanding continued to write in Manchukuo till 1943. Shanding wrote *Green Valley* in 1942 and the following year it was translated into Japanese. However, the Manchukuo government censored passages in the novel that implied criticism of the government and its extraction of rural resources conducted under the cover of Manchukuo political pieties. He was also harassed politically by the police after its publication and ultimately had to flee Manchuria for the interior. In the People's Republic, Shanding was charged in the antirightist campaign of 1957 as a traitor (*hanjian*) because of the Japanese translation and recognition of his work, and as a "rightist" he was subject to labor reform.[42] He was rehabilitated in 1979 and *Green Valley* was included in a Contemporary Chinese Literature reprint series undertaken by the Institute of Contemporary Literature of the Chinese Academy of Social Sciences.[43]

Green Valley in History

The study of the native place was initially fostered in Manchukuo for Japanese schoolchildren, but was ultimately extended to the wider school system. A middle school textbook in Japanese-language education published in Dalian in 1935 praised the pedagogy of the native place as a means of cultivating love for the region by describing the beauty of the land and its "natural peoples" (*shizen ningen*). Two strains of identity construction run through the textbook essays. One emphasized the identity of Japan and Manchuria, or rather an effort to comprehend the differences within a common framework of understanding. Thus an essay on the four seasons of Manchuria compares the sounds, sights, and feelings of each season with those in Japan, framing center and periphery in familiar categories of knowledge.

A contrapuntal theme in the textbook stressed the utopian and essentially natural character of Manchuria. A traveler strikes up a conversation with a young Japanese boy at Fengtian station. When asked if he would ever go back to live in Japan, the boy replies that he could not bear the dirty and crowded cities, the narrow streets and homes of Japan. He also claims to get along well with Chinese boys at school. This triggers a wellspring of emotions (and tears) in the interlocutor, whose mind roams over the vast and unspoiled wilderness that once was Japan and the good fortune of those who could continue to live so naturally in Manchuria. As the train speeds by a Lamaist tower soaring into the clouds, he envisions the young boy as a mountain goat roaming the vastness of nature. The images of vastness and freedom established the authenticity of a natural place continuous with the representation of the frontier space. Despite the common emphasis on nature, this was certainly a different kind of native place than that depicted by Shanding. But as an exemplary production of the native place, *Green Valley* could hardly escape the attention of the state.

Cultural control in Manchukuo intensified dramatically after September 1940, when Japan allied militarily with Germany and Italy and the Pacific War became imminent. Until then, cultural control had been relatively lax and did not intrude into all dimensions of cultural production. In March 1941, the Hongbaochu (or Hongbao office), which reported directly to the General Affairs Board, brought out the "Summary of Guidelines to Art and Literature," fundamentally transforming the role of arts and culture in the state.[44] The Hongbao was originally a propaganda organ, but its office soon became the principal instrument of cultural control in Manchukuo, monitoring publications, broadcasts, libraries, news agencies, film, and the arts, among other activities. After 1940, its control tightened and began to extend through local governments. The older, voluntarily organized associations of writers (many of them leftists), journalists, and other professionals came to be replaced by new organizations controlled by the Hongbao office, such as the Manchukuo Writers and Artists Concordia (*Manzhou wenyixiehui*) created in 1941.[45]

One goal of the Guidelines to Art and Literature was to centralize surveillance of all the arts, including cinema and radio. Another, more proactive goal was to provide direction to the arts and thus coordinate the "project of spiritual construction with the more advanced material construction of the nation."[46] These goals were, of course, consonant with the fascist military state's wartime needs, but also spelled a more active role for the state in the production of culture and, ultimately, identity. A core dimension of this cultural production was the depiction of the land through the independent native traditions of Manchuria. Whereas, in a debate with Shanding as late as 1937, well-known pro-Manchukuo writers like Ōtani Takeo and Gu Ding had ridiculed native-place writing as simplistic and limited, by 1943 the regime was aggressively promoting the native-soil literature of Manchukuo, publicizing it in the newspapers and incorporating the study of "independent" Manchuria's native traditions, simplicity, vigor, and natural beauty in school textbooks.[47]

The military fascists' new activism in culture entailed the sponsorship of several literary and arts (*wenyi*) conferences, including those encompassing the Greater East Asian Co-prosperity Sphere. Two Greater East Asian literature conferences were held in Tokyo (1942 and 1943) and one in Nanjing (1944). The fourth, planned for Manchukuo in 1945, needless to say, did not materialize.[48] But Manchukuo had no shortage of various national conferences, including a 1944 seminar on native-place literature called "How to Write about Manchuria?" (*Zenme xie Manzhou?*).[49] The participants celebrated the "spirit of blood and soil" promoted by German and Italian fascists in native-place literature. In this conception, critical realism was valued far less than the portrayal of the land as the source of a distinctive people. The identification of the author with the particular place, it urged, was absolutely essential to the production of a genuinely creative literature capable of generating such great symbols of the land as Japan's Mount Fuji.[50]

Shanding's work was appropriated in the context of this new activism. PRC scholars have noted that the Manchukuo state sought to assimilate Shanding's work and native-soil literature within a trajectory that extended from the locality to the nation-state, to a pan-Asianist cosmopolitanism.[51] In the official conception of the native place, the question of identity with the Chinese nation was bypassed, even as this conception established the superiority of the Japanese in Manchukuo. The Guidelines had declared,

> In order to establish the spirit of nation building, we have to embody the great spirit of [the phrase] "the world is one family" (*hakkō-ichiu*). We use the transplanted Japanese literature as the warp and the literature of the several original peoples as the weft, thus achieving a cosmopolitan cultural transformation and creating a pure and independent literature.[52]

One of the most important China experts in the cultural sphere was Ōuchi Takayoshi, a 1929 graduate of Tōa Dōbun shoin (the East Asian Culture Academy) in Shanghai, who wrote extensive surveys of literary and cultural trends in Manchukuo that incorporated information about the participants in literary circles and debates. Ōuchi held powerful positions in the cultural bureaucracy, including head of the section on literature and art in Man'ei, chief editor of the *Manchuria Journal*, and chief of the government's editorial office.[53] His detailed surveys were clearly important for surveillance and censorial agencies such as the Hongbaochu. Ōuchi quoted extensively from Shanding's work and covered the debates he had provoked on native-place writing. Distinctly aware that under the melancholic and sentimental mood of native-place literature lay a left-wing and nationalist tone, Ōuchi nonetheless found much merit and a strong nativist sensibility in Shanding's work. Most significantly, Ōuchi translated *Green Valley* into Japanese in 1943.[54]

While cultural bureaucrats like Ōuchi found value in Shanding's depiction of the Manchurian landscape from a discursive perspective, politically Shanding remained under surveillance. He was among nine writers, including Dan Di and Shi Jun, whose works were singled out in 1943 for censorship and surveillance. They were often forced to rewrite their views.[55] Just before he fled Manchukuo in 1943, Shanding published a poem celebrating pan-Asianism. In all likelihood he was compelled to write this (given that he had been under close surveillance since 1942) to demonstrate his loyalty to the official cosmpolitanism.[56] Small wonder that he fled Manchukuo. He shared a discourse of local authenticity with his political enemy. If the gap between his politics and discourse became too obvious, the regime would surely get him to bridge it on its terms.

In the 1987 postscript to the novel and in his later writings, Shanding depicts *Green Valley* as an anti-Japanese, nationalist novel written during the darkest period of Japanese rule in 1942. He points to the censorship and harassment by Manchukuo authorities. The communist authorities in the PRC had critiqued the novel along class as well as nationalist lines. According to Huang Wanhua, the peasants are depicted in the novel as feudal because they side with the landlord against the anti-Japanese bandits of the *yiyongjun*, or the resistance army.[57] In the postscript, Shanding seeks to persuade the reader that the novel does attend to the oppression of the peasants, but as the work was constrained by its time and circumstances the peasants could not be shown to stand up for their rights, particularly because there was no Communist Party in the Manchuria of the 1920s. In other words, Shanding provides alibis for the absent nationalism and class consciousness in the novel.[58]

Despite Shanding's enduring involvement in the anti-Japanese literary movement, nationalism is for whatever reasons not a major concern of the novel, in my reading of it. On the other hand, the conflict between capital and community is central to it. To be sure, the critique of capitalism implies a criticism of Japanese capital—the *zaibatsu* are occasionally named; the chief villain, Qian Rulong, is a comprador (*maiban*) of a Japanese company; and the Continental Company is very probably the (Japanese) South Manchurian Railroad Company—but it is capital that is attacked as a destructive mode of being, and no particular form of national or imperialist capital is singled out. Indeed, virtually all the unsavory rich people are Chinese and the two Japanese figures (Yoshiko and her father) are extremely sympathetic Sinophiles. Most importantly, the drama of class conflict does not unfold according to the standard communist narrative; rather, it emerges from a deeper anchoring of relations of production and class in sharply conflicting modes of timespace and moral ethos—between urban capitalism, whose temporality destroys a sense of belonging, and a place whose naturally rooted culture governs the experience of time.

Within the discursive terrain of the novel, class conflict is expressed through the activities of the bandit heroes of the primeval forest (*lülin haohan*), as Shanding himself attests in the postscript. For these bandit heroes, however, the fight against social injustice is associated not necessarily with class position, but with personal rectitude, resolve, and loyalty. This is dramatized in the final episode of the novel, during which a bond of loyalty is forged between Big Bear Paw and the heir to the land, Xiaobiao, during their escape through the forest. These values are associated with the moral ethos, not of a mode of production, but of a mode of being in relation to nature.

A nationalist reading of the novel is favored by the current literary establishment of the Northeast, or erstwhile Manchukuo. It is this establishment that worked for the rehabilitation of Shanding's reputation, and in the case they make for native-place literature they reveal a complex relationship between nationalism and regionalist sentiment. These scholars tend to emphasize the distinctiveness of native-place writing in the Northeast, which followed neither the romantic school of Zhou

Zuoren and Shen Congwen nor only Lu Xun's hard prescription of the analysis of internal social contradictions. It represented, rather, a deliberate and programmatic opposition to Japanese imperialism, and *Green Valley* is the exemplar. This nationalist tradition of native-place writing resembles that of colonies and occupied nations all over the world, but especially the native-place writing of Taiwan and East Europe under foreign control. Naturally, this nationalism could not be expressed directly, but was covert and disguised. A proper reading of this writing calls for a decoding of the text.[59]

According to these present-day authors, opposition to colonial rule is expressed in the realist techniques and unadorned writing through which Shanding exposes the grim realities of life under colonialism. We have seen how the regime heightened repression of cultural producers and others after 1941. We have also noted the evidence that Liang Shanding was strongly opposed to Japanese rule. After 1934 he was among the few literary figures remaining in Manchuria who kept up the spirit of the Harbin resistance literature in the newsletter *Manzhou Wenxue*. In 1937 an antitraditional group of Chinese writers joined with Japanese writers (born or settled) in Manchuria to advocate a new literature, creating a split among Chinese writers.[60] Those who joined with Japanese writers, the Literary Records group (*yiwenzhipai*), were bitterly criticized by Shanding. He satirized them for currying favor with the Japanese, saying that they cherished the writers of another country but not the rural folk of their own land, or even the newly settled Japanese villagers in Manchuria. He urged writers to write about the land, which would survive the Japanese occupation.[61]

Professor Sun Zhongtian of Northeast Normal University has argued that the real spirit of native-place literature is nationalism and patriotism. The commitment to the locality cannot but entail patriotism, because the concern of this form with traditional literature and the very embeddedness of language in a common culture produces an inseparability of the native and the national: "one cannot cut the veins of the culture of the fatherland."[62] A similar kind of automaticity is assumed by another authority from the Northeast, Lü Qinwen. In Lü's view, the native-place literature of the Northeast written by Xiao Jun and Shanding was deeply influenced by the Russian writings of Gogol and Gorky, communicated through the emigrant community in Harbin.[63] In Russian, he observes, the word for native place and the fatherland (in Chinese, *xiangtu* and *zuguo*, respectively) is the same, and thus the nation is embedded in the very signifier of the locality.[64] Such a view tends to naturalize the relationship between locality and nation, which is by no means given.

While I acknowledge that Shanding was politically a nationalist, it is hard to prove that the novel is overtly or covertly nationalist. One might say that exposing the grim realities of rural life could yield a critique of whatever power structure existed, not only of colonial power (indeed, such a critique became a dominant trend in mainland literature in the 1920s and after). As far as whether the critique of power in the novel is anticolonial or nationalist, I do not believe Shanding reveals a particular point of view. Whether or not this is because he had no means of political expression, from a literary and philosophical perspective these larger political identifications seem irrelevant in the work. More particularly, even if the novel is nationalist, Shanding's use of certain popular cultural traditions defies modern nationalist conceptions advocated by May Fourth activists and the CCP. This gap between his vision and modern nationalist ones returns us to the predicament of native-place writing that we encountered with Lu Xun.

Professor Sun has suggested that the power of the novel derives from an aesthetic that lends a mythic power to the valley and people. The evocation of the "ancestral memory" is crucially important for the nationalist argument that PRC critics today need to make,[65] not only in response to the party's critique of 1957, but also as a reaction to the reception of the novel in Manchukuo, where its significance was extended beyond the nation to a civilizational mission. Yet this evocation cannot be allowed to go too far. In invoking and idealizing the "ancestral memory," Professor Sun notes that Shanding sometimes slips into a "feudal" mode of writing. Shamanism and magic may be part and parcel of the mythic power of the valley, but when Shuzhen is praised for preserving her chastity a nativist cathexis has gone too far.[66] Indeed, a fuller version of this nativism—emphasizing ancestral, popular cultural elements—yields many associations with Eastern civilizational ideals emphasized by the Manchukuo regime, which the PRC scholars have to de-emphasize. The predicament of native-place writing (which has to be both evocative and reformist) for nationalism becomes especially acute and untenable for present-day PRC writers.

PRC scholars focus their critical ire on the Literary Records group, led by Gu Ding. This group is identified as clearly collaborationist, and scholars today particularly point to their attack on Shanding and native-place literature as parochial, regionalist, and lacking in cosmopolitanism.[67] We will recall Shanding's criticism of the Literary Records group for their lack of interest in rural society. The personal careers of these writers offer evidence that many of them engaged in opportunistic collaborationism.[68] At the same time, the leading Japanese authority on literature in Manchukuo, Okada Hideki, reveals that their writings were often stridently reformist and their critique of rural society had more in common with the May Fourth tradition than with writings that sought to find an authenticity within the locality.[69] We are thus faced with a complex irony: while the group had collaborationist elements but was intellectually autonomous from the dominant paradigms of Japanese and Manchukuo writing of the native place, Shanding, who once had a clear political position, was intellectually and discursively much more part of the world of this writing. The predicament of native-place writing would generate tortuous consequences.[70]

The Representational Structures of the Local

Most readings of *Green Valley* have sought to identify the overt or alleged covert political references in the novel (such as those objected to by the Manchukuo censors) as the anchors of their interpretations. Also important, especially for the Maoists, is the novel's translation into the Japanese—its textual form. At the referential level of event and description alone, the meaning of the novel is necessarily open to different contemporary and historical appropriations, because Shanding offers no coherent or programmatic politics. Rather, the significance of the novel derives from the way in which it produces the local as an object of identification and hence as an object of political desire by the powerful. In order to fully grasp it as such, we need to attend to three levels: the representational structures of the novel (the point of view and spatiotemporal schemes that structure the narrative), its descriptive and referential aspects, and the different political readings it has received. All three are part of the historical process of the production of local space.

The principal representational structures of the novel are constituted by its three chronotopes. The primeval forest is governed by a natural, cyclical time outside of linear history. It is a time of life, decay, and renewal—a return to childhood, to the mysterious and eternal source of life, and to the fount of justice and loyalty. We have seen the spiritual and political significance of the forest in Manchu understandings, and its tropic significance in the Japanese accounts of Inaba, Nagata, Fujiyama, and others. It has also been important for other Chinese authors from the Northeast, like Xiao Jun and the contemporary writer Zheng Wanlong.

In *Green Valley*, the fertilizing decay of the forest emits a vaporous, mysterious fog that shrouds the secret pact between bandit heroes (*lülin haohan*). They are its human agents, who live outside of social time but are necessary to justice in the community, to the forces renewing life against those corrupting and destroying it. This timespace also has a distinct gender profile: it is the realm of strong, loyal, and resolute men whose physique microsmically reproduces the attributes of the primeval forest. Xiaobiao's test of endurance in the forest teaches him more about living than any university can. Women are excluded from this realm. Big Bear Paw's wife, who is the liaison, always leaves it when dramatic things are about to happen. But the land itself is repeatedly figured as the mother: the eternal producer of life and one in whose bosom a child feels limitless warmth. Thus, in its representational scheme the novel reveals the truth of nature, and to the extent that human life in the valley or locality accords with the timeless cycles of nature it is an authentic life. We may also deduce that it finds truth in the often suppressed philosophical tradition of Daoism and the folk heroes of the "rivers and marshes" who celebrate this accordance.

Langgou Valley, the second chronotope, carries within it a class fracture that is visualized spatially as the division between the Lin family compound at the top of the ridge (*shangkan*) and the shantytown shacks of the Lin estate's tenants and hired hands at the bottom of the ridge (*xiakan*). This spatial visualization of social stratification is repeatedly invoked, particularly when exploring the feelings of liminal figures like the foreman, Huofeng, who as servant and lover is torn between these two spaces. For Shanding, the poor folk at the bottom of the ridge lead a life built around the natural, agricultural rhythms, and this mode of life has a close relationship with that of the primeval forest; they depend on the power and virtue of the forest for justice and renewal. The ridge-bottom community is, however, also tied to the city by the cash nexus, upon which it depends for the sale of its harvest and the purchase of its necessities.

The gentry residents of the Lin family compound—who own all the land in the valley—have, over the last 150 years or so since they settled the land, had a dual orientation: as paternalistic landlords, they have looked toward their estate and home in the valley, and, as elites who have served in the bureaucracy and the military from the Qing through the early Republic, they have looked toward the centers of national power. Xiaobiao's father's name, Guowei, means "national prestige," whereas the name of his villainous brother Guorong means "national glory." When the narrator tells us the history of the locality from the lives of this elite—about their roles in the Republican revolution of 1911, the Yuan Shikai presidency, the various warlord wars—the locality is brought into the linear time of the nation. But those at the bottom of the ridge neither understand nor care about these momentous matters; they can only remember the panicked evacuations during the Russo-Japanese War and are dejected by news of the continuing fall of the local currency under the warlords. When Xiaobiao decides all of a sudden to leave the valley for a second time to pursue his studies at the university, he addresses the disappointed young hired hands and tenants, who have developed a fondness and gratitude for him, with a halting and confused speech. The speech is full of such "foreign," temporal phrases as "historically speaking" and "in the present stage," and as Xiaobiao utters them he sees the tenderness of the laborers toward him suddenly evaporate. He wonders if they suspect and hate these words; he hastens to conclude by saying that "the land is our life; no matter who you are, to leave the land is to commit suicide."[71]

This passage not only attests to the two kinds of time that increasingly separate the two classes within the valley, it also contains the central tension that governs relations between the two parts: the tension between community and class. It is perhaps here, in the highly complex and contradictory feelings and consciousness of the two classes with respect to each other, and the even more elaborated attitudes of those class and gender fragments in between, that Liang Shanding delivers his most penetrating *social* insights, in marked contrast, as we shall see, to his depiction of urban society. These relations are explored in the direct encounter between the classes, in the romance of Xiaobiao with the tenant girl Xiaolian: in his callous treatment of her and the unresolved, violent swings in her attitude toward him and his family; in the uncompromising self-sacrifice of the aunt for the sake of the honor and wealth of the patriarchal lineage, even as she develops a shame-filled relationship with her servant.

Shanding seems to be saying that the best of the landed classes take their paternalism to heart and even when they scheme and deceive, they may be forced to act in the interests of their community. As for the poor, they can love and need their lord, even though they may know exactly what schemes he may be up to. Once the railroad line has been established and part of the land has been sold through chicanery to the railroad company, the tenants are outraged and feel greatly betrayed. The Mongol Huang says of the landlords,

> ["]We depend on them, we depend on the land; how can we live without the land? . . . We have nourished the land as we have our children; we have even transformed barren lands into ripe fields, and now we have been cast aside."
>
> Huofeng felt a bottomless sympathy for these sincere (*chengshi*) peasants, but he also felt that sincerity was nothing but a symbol of a kind of servility (*xunfu*). Having served and obeyed for several generations, they had suffered on account of this sincerity and also been deluded for several generations by the promise of the "future world," which they could never cast off. Their fatalism and sincerity appeared to be destined for each other. Suddenly, Huofeng realized that he too was such a person and it made him feel extremely uneasy.[72]

This is clearly no pastoral idyll, nor is it simply a case of false consciousness, because for Shanding, as for Huofeng, the sincerity of the peasants has value despite its susceptibility to abuse. It is the quality that Fei Xiaotong called *bense*, and that he tied so insistently to the rootedness of the people in land and place. Shanding gives us several instances of its liability to appropriation. When the comprador Qian Rulong devises a cunning plan to mortgage the land in order to borrow the hostage money for Xiaobiao's release (thereby releasing the land for his purposes), he plays up the virtues of the peasants of Langgou to the Japanese manager—precisely those qualities of simplicity, honesty, patience, communal solidarity, and landlord paternalism.[73] And yet this sincerity—the *bense*—for Shanding is perhaps the only resource with which to build and rebuild the community, as revealed by the episodes in which the peasants resist the bandits and stand steadfastly for the community. It is in the quality of their sincerity, the tension between its virtue and susceptibility to abuse, that the contradiction in native-place writing that we observed in Lu Xun is concentrated. The true color has to be both preserved and superseded.

The third chronotope is that of the city, Nanmanzhan. Shanding's social and psychological depiction of characters that belong to the city is perhaps the weakest part of the novel. They are, for the most part, stereotypes of cigar-puffing, scheming businessmen and their obsequious hangers-on; of languorous ladies playing cards and smoking opium late into the night; of back-street brothels and the like. But the spatial description of the city is quite striking. Chapter 5, where the city is first described, opens with an account from a bird's-eye view of the network of roads, electrical and telegraph lines, and nodes of business activity and speculation. In between these urban nodes, the unconnected places are like silted-up spaces, noisy but without purposeful conversation. Thereafter, the spatial description itself tends to become de-spatialized, as the author follows the course of electrical and telegraph lines all the way north to the borderless wilds and south to the harbor. From the harbor, information can be communicated to the dealers and speculators in a single minute.

This insight into the loss of place as a site of reference, generated by the accelerating pace of capitalist change (or what is now called time–space compression), is dramatized by Shanding's observation of the city's preoccupation with speculatory capital, the market in agricultural futures. Manchuria had become a most important agricultural supplier for the Japanese market, and the futures market included not only brokers and speculators, but landlords and property dealers who drove up property prices with the promise of increased access by the extension of the railroad to such lands. In this market where speculators and futures traders "buy and sell no thing" (*maikong maikong*), people live neither in the past nor the present, but in the future. For such people, the time of the present and the past (which for the author is the time of community and authenticity) is irrelevant.

The ultimate drama in *Green Valley* is played out at the level of its representational structures, by moralized representatives of the chronotopes. Authenticity inheres among the people of the valley, whose life hews closely to the rhythms of nature in the timespace of the primeval forest. It is an authenticity that emerges from the acceptance of the cyclical time of natural regeneration, and is recognizable in simplicity and a capacity for suffering. This time of the locality is directly opposed to the linear time of capitalist, urban modernity, and the novel tracks the corrosive and destructive power of the latter upon both the valley and the forest. But this force is also self-destructive, as the market collapses and Nanmanzhan is left a ghost town. In the last scene, our protagonists celebrate the victory of the valley's rebirth and the natural principle of regeneration.

Although the novel is a moral narrative told through its representational structures, its importance derives from the way Shanding creatively refashions historical discourses of the region, including events, processes, and popular imagery, to his purposes.[74] The Chinese pioneer and bandit played a major role in the settlement of Manchuria and an even more overwhelming role in popular historical consciousness. Through much of the nineteenth century, Chinese woodsmen, goldminers, ginseng diggers, and others had crossed the mountains and rivers as far as the distant banks of the Ussuri in search of the forest's wealth. Given the imperial ban on their activities, they were as much bandits as entrepreneurs, forming fugitive communities in the remote forests and ruling satellite settlements in the valleys by the code of the forest.[75] Even as late as 1887, the area around the Manchu's ancestral Changbaishan continued to remain out of bounds for Chinese. Here H. E. M. James found such outlaw "little republics," fully self-governing, with presidents and councils that possessed "the power of life and death."[76] Perhaps the most famous of these was the "little forest kingdom" founded by Han Bianwai, or "Han of the frontier," which expired after fifty years in 1925.[77]

In general, by the late nineteenth century, many of these outlawed communities were in the process of becoming recognized settlements controlled by the bandit-turned-landlord, who sometimes cooperated with or operated within the shell of the extending Qing administration.[78] As an early-twentieth-century observer wrote, "a man is sometimes bandit, merchant, and magistrate all at once."[79] Certainly banditry also offered military-political careers in this unsettled borderland, where even apex warlords like Zhang Zuolin carved a career by playing off contesting powers and building upon the deadly politics of sworn brotherhood.[80] Nonetheless, the figure of the Manchurian bandit, or Red Beard (*honghuzi*), continued to be legendary not only within Manchuria and China, but in Japan as well. Indeed, Lattimore still saw the Manchurian bandit as "the true frontiersman" whose independence was pitted against powerful propertied interests.[81]

Quite apart from the pioneer bandits, the war-torn and frequently anarchic history of this contested borderland in the twentieth century more commonly produced desperate and ruthless bandit gangs. Their vast numbers included railroad coolies, demobilized soldiers, and ordinary peasants confronted with a highly unequal land-ownership system. Alice Tisdale wrote in 1917, "In the early fall in Manchuria, there is a sort of presto change from farmer into bandit. It seems a trifle of a psychological somersault—one day a plodding farmer, the next a highwayman."[82] Their ranks, though, swelled in years of chaos and difficulty, such as during the many local and international wars, the fall of the Qing, and the annexation of Korea.[83]

Given the severe effects of the worldwide depression of the 1930s on the commercialized rural economy of Manchuria, many peasant-bandits, including secret societies such as the Red Spears and the Big Swords, were mobilized to oppose the Japanese. The Korean border regions of Manchukuo, including Tonghua and Jiandao Provinces, had long been hotbeds of bandit and rebel activity, and the anti-Japanese movement—both Chinese and Korean—flourished there through the early 1930s.[84] However, many of these patriotic resistance bands became alienated from the population, not only because of Japanese counterinsurgency measures, but also because most were not disciplined revolutionary forces. Their demands on the local communities were arbitrary and heavy, and their behavior often rapacious.[85] Nonetheless, the romantic image of the bandit grew during this period.

Several Chinese writers before Shanding had already transfigured the Manchurian bandit into a symbol of the region's authenticity. Xiao Jun and Duanmu Hongliang found in the bandit the incarnation of the vital forces of the region: wild, ruthless, but innately good. In their stories, it is often through the nationalist narrative of selfless service in the patriotic cause that the gangster is ultimately redeemed and his inner virtue restored. Note that both these authors left Manchukuo soon after its establishment, and so wrote about the resistance from afar.[86] To whatever extent the Manchurian bandit may have retained a spirit of resistance and independence, Shanding's imaginative deployment of this historical background did not utilize an explicitly nationalist narrative. While the bandit gang is romanticized, the romance derives from the authenticity of the forest and valley in opposition to capitalism and the city. Shanding invests the bandit myth with the legendary values of the vernacular novel, *Water Margin*—which we might note is set in Shandong, the homeland of most immigrants.[87] The "knight-errant" tradition celebrated in this novel also dominated Chinese popular culture, and remarkably, the self-perceptions of secret societies since Ming and Qing times. By investing the Manchurian landscape with the core ideals of popular Chinese culture, he brings it into the Chinese world. At the same time, by depicting the bandits as embodiments of the natural and timeless authenticity of the primeval forests, he seeks to capture the difference of Manchuria.[88]

What is lost in Shanding is an older history. The Russian surveyer and naturalist Arseniev, who with the Goldi guide Dersu explored the region around the Ussuri at the turn of the twentieth century, has left behind a remarkable travelogue. *Dersu the Trapper*—and the film version, *Dersu Uzala*, made by Akira Kurosawa—whose fuller exploration must await another occasion, is perhaps one of the most haunting accounts of the "authentic primitive" I have encountered. But *Dersu* is also a valuable record of the relations between the tribespeople and the Chinese. To be sure, Arseniev provides vivid descriptions of exploitation and culture loss, and there is evidence of tribal resistance and the plundering of Chinese settlements. But Arseniev also describes the interpenetration of cultures, as the animistic cults of the tiger or the mountain enter the lives of Chinese forest-dwellers.[89] The early pioneers often attached themselves to Mongol, Manchu, or other non-Chinese tribes, and bandit heroes such as the famed Chan-bao commanded bands of mixed ethnicity, with equal influence and authority over Chinese and aboriginal alike.[90] Shanding regarded Manchuria as something of a wasteland before the Chinese settlers brought history and literature to the region.[91] The principal traces of the indigenous people in his story are of a disappearing culture, expressed in occasional references to their malevolent shamans.

The production of the local in the form of the pastoral—of idylls threatened by encroaching modernity—has been described for many parts of the world.[92] In evoking the vernacular tradition of the "rivers and lakes," the author is able to infuse this global concern and form with meaning from the moral narratives and symbolism of Chinese popular culture. In this respect, it is interesting to compare *Green Valley* with the pastoralism of Shen Congwen, who wrote about his native western Hunan and the Miao. Shen deployed the figure of the primitive Miao (the Miao woman, in particular) to revitalize mainstream Chinese society with the energy of the frontier, even as the idyllic landscape was being ravaged. Despite the European provenance of Shen's pastoral trope, Timothy Oakes has suggested that the meaning of Shen's literary work has to be understood in the context of the transformation of the Confucian anxiety about the frontier.[93] But if Shen sought to vitalize Chinese culture with the primitive authenticity of the Miao, *Green Valley* identifies not the primitive but the Chinese bandit as possessing the life-giving power of the primeval forests. If in Shen the frontier will save the heartland, in *Green Valley*, the frontier was already none other than the heartland.

We are accustomed to think of regions as evolving naturalistically within the formation of states. While there are certainly historical forces that tie regions and localities to higher centers and larger formations for extended periods, there is nothing deterministic about these relationships, nor is it predetermined as to what kinds of political formations—nations, empires, civilizations—may attach to the region. During much of the twentieth century, the locality, which occasionally symbolized an entire region, would have to be produced as part of a sovereign formation through metropolitan cultural discourses and practices. The contradictory imperatives for identitarian states to modernize and simultaneously produce an authentic, timeless essence drove them and cultural producers to treat the locality as objects both of development and of identity. Thus, even when Lu Xun or Fei Xiaotong sought to employ native-place writing for reformist goals, they could not avoid a nativist cathexis, a poetics of identity.

My study of Shanding's *Green Valley* shows us how the local as space and sentiment is created through the relationship between a novel's representational structures, its re-figuration of historical imagery, and the politics of its reception. Through this procedure, we also see the stakes involved in the production of authenticity. The competing claims on the locality—as the metonym for Manchuria—by various political forces derived from the logic of controlling a place by controlling its representation. In the identity-based polities of the modern era, control of territory is critically dependent on the subjective production of its space as an object of identification. Of course, Shanding could never fully control the sentiment for the local that he helped generate; the particular representation of the locality would be shaped, among other factors, by a regime with a particular constituency and ideology. Despite the author's projection of heartland traditions into the frontier, the celebration of nature permitted the novel's absorption by Japanese authorities into the regime's representation of Manchukuo as a natural space. Even more, in its celebration of folk countertraditions, the "ancestral aesthetic" could come to serve the non-national, East Asian civilizational traditions so important to Manchukuo ideology.

Manchuria continues to occupy an important place in the Japanese cultural imagination. It remains an important icon for contemporary writers such as Murakami Haruki and Nakagami Kenji.[94] Tourist sites in the Northeast are still crowded with Japanese visitors, although those with personal memories of the place are obviously dwindling. But to return to where we began this chapter, in the Northeast itself the region's identity is being produced in a complex dialectic with the memory of Manchukuo. In the current rage of native-place writing, readers avidly consume writings both contemporary and from the Manchukuo period. The republications of his work reveals that interest in Shanding, while not as great as in Xiao Hong or Xiao Jun, is considerable. Let us consider, briefly and finally, the writings of one of the most popular contemporary writers of the Northeast within this framework of landscape and identity.

Among the most celebrated *xungen* or "searching for roots" writers of the 1980s, Zheng Wanlong, hails from Heilongjiang and, interestingly enough, writes about the Oroqen. His stories have been reprinted in many anthologies of contemporary fiction. In the introduction to the translated collection called *Strange Tales from Strange Lands* (*Yixiang yiwen*), Kam Louie argues that Zheng is really writing, like all *xungen* writers, about the truth of the self, the nation, and the human condition. In particular, Zheng, a Han who left the Northeast at the age of eight, utilizes the practices and rituals of the Oroqen and the landscape of the region to discuss themes of alienation centered on the masculinist ethos of rugged loners in the wilderness. Countering PRC critics who argue that Zheng represents the authenticity of the primitive in his descriptions of their passion and immersion in nature, Louie believes that Zheng finds fatalism and despair in savage society and a still greater alienation among these individuals, whose lives frequently end in senseless savagery.[95]

One cannot doubt that Zheng's intellectual message contains ironic, critical, and even dystopic elements. However, the dominant representational structure of the stories emphasizes the landscape and the individuals who live and die by it. The physical features of the region are massively foregrounded and the stories of individuals gain meaning from the precarious life that they fashion within this environment. Deep ancient forests, mighty rivers (alternately frozen and torrential), and volcanic mountains (both icy and fiery) produce a space that overwhelms the time of history. We can only guess from stray references that the stories are set sometime in the first half of the twentieth century. From this perspective, the stories are not principally about tribals or Han, but about the meaning of a landscape. No one knows whether the terrifying Three Kick Chen, who drapes a large leopard skin around his shoulders, is a Han Chinese or a Daur. He returns to die in Xiaosu Gully, where the snow will seal him in for the long winter. On his way, however, he passes on his dog-faced ring to a steely-eyed village boy who vows to honor his debts.[96]

Savagery (of different kinds, to be sure) exists on both sides, Han and non-Han. Vengeful shamans, tribal victimization of women, exploitative merchants all occupy the canvas, but the landscape and the individuals who are locked in it—fugitives and exiles, bandits and adventurers, miners and woodsmen—have a special place in these stories. In "The Gorge," a certain Shenken has been banished from the Oroqen tribe because he laughed at the exposed buttocks of a shaman during a ritual performance. When he encounters a couple of city-struck Oroqen youth in the mountain, he refuses to let them use their guns to kill a pregnant bear. Suddenly attacked by the bear, he dies in her embrace as he kills her with a knife. When the youths carrying the stretcher bearing Shenken and parts of the bear emerge from the mountain, they feel an incredible lightness and recognize that the souls of Shenken and the bear—totem of the Oroqen—have been left behind on the mountain.[97]

The stories reveal an evolution in the national incorporation of Manchuria since *Green Valley*. Zheng draws from older Chinese representational structures: the legends of the pioneers, the vows of secret brotherhood, the upholding of righteousness. At the same time, there is a greater self-confidence in incorporating tribal cultural elements such as shamanism, totemism, and animism—in particular the worship of mountain and animal spirits—even if they are processed through social scientific understandings. On the referential level, the preeminent theme in the stories concerns nature's challenge to culture—a composite culture of Han and non-Han—in which culture fails miserably. However, in the process of depicting this challenge, where loyalty, brotherhood, righteousness, and animism yield to nature—dying heroically in the embrace of the bear, or passing on one's honor before being swallowed by the snow—nature itself is made meaningful by a set of cultural categories that continue the project of region making exemplified by Shanding.

Whence the continuing search for regional identity? Many complicated factors have contributed to this brew of regional sentiment, including several historical ones. Among them is a persistent sense of the cultural backwardness of a recently settled frontier; the memory of the region as having been abandoned by the nationalists and world powers; and the lingering resentment that exploitation by the Japanese and the rampaging Soviet occupation was followed by victimization and allegations of collaboration and contamination. The loyalty of the Northeast to the nation was questioned even in the 1950s, when Gao Gang, the top party leader from the Northeast, was accused by the 1955 National Party Conference of the CCP of attempting "to make an independent kingdom."[98] But common history alone does not make a region. The distinctiveness of regional society and culture in the Northeast builds upon the successive, even if contestatory, representations of the region, from Manchu ideas and policies to the historical reception of Shanding and Zheng Wanlong.

The state response to this welling up of sentiment for community and place in the aftermath of the Mao era was almost immediate.[99] Soon after he became deputy director of Liaoning Party Cultural Department, Zhang Yumao, a one-time professor of literature and deputy mayor of Shenyang, invited the recently rehabilitated Shanding to edit the first collection of Manchukuo literature. Zhang subsequently sponsored the publication of the canonical fourteen-volume series "Modern Literature of the Northeast, 1919–1949." In his introduction to the series, Zhang underscores the regional quality of the literature. In particular, he regards native-place literature not only as the dominant genre, but as the most significant, since it is what makes the region a region. In a gesture designed to heal festering wounds, Zhang reaches out to the writers of the time, declaring that there were only a handful of real collaborators among them. Most had a complex attitude, being opposed to Japanese colonial literature but also deeply indebted to progressive Japanese writers and their translations of literature about the oppressed around the world.[100] Through efforts like Zhang's, the divisive politics of the past have ceased to haunt the literary public of the Northeast. What remains, however, is a sense of the land as brimming with sentiment, a continuing source of attachment and authenticity.

Notes

1. Bryna Goodman, *Native Place, City and Nation: Regional Networks and Identities* (Berkeley: University of California Press, 1995). While the Republican era (1912–1949) was dominated by the growing ideological hegemony of nationalism, it was characterized by the reality of weak political control. The nation-state was thus not only forced to grant substantial de facto autonomy politically and economically, but also to tolerate alternative discursive and

ideological defenses of the local against the nation, such as the rural education movement of Liang Shuming and others, or the federalist movement.

2. See Kishimoto Mio, " 'Fengsu' to Jidaikan—Minmatsu Shinsho no keiseironsha kara mita Sō, Gen, Minsho" (Chinese history in *"fengsu"* perspective: The Song-Yuan-Ming transition and statecraft discourse in the sixteenth century) (paper presented to the Song-Yuan-Ming Transition in Chinese History Conference, Lake Arrowhead, Calif., June 5–11, 1997).

3. David Der-wei Wang, *Fictional Realism in Twentieth-Century China: Mao Dun, Lao She, Shen Congwen* (New York: Columbia University Press, 1992), 281.

4. H. D. Harootunian, "Disciplinizing Native Knowledge and Producing Place: Yanagita Kunio, Origuchi Shinobu, Takata Yasuma," in *Culture and Identity: Japanese Intellectuals during the Interwar Years*, ed. J. Thomas Rimer (Princeton: Princeton University Press, 1988), 104.

5. See Zhao Jinghua, "Shū Sakujin (Zhou Zuoren) to Yanagita Kunio: Koyū shinkō o chūshin to suru minzokugaku" (Zhou Zuoren and Yanagita Kunio: Folklore centered on traditional beliefs), *Nihon Chūgoku gakkaihō* 47 (1995): 196–97.

6. Zhao, "Shū Sakujin (Zhou Zuoren) to Yanagita Kunio," 198.

7. Zhao, "Shū Sakujin (Zhou Zuoren) to Yanagita Kunio," 200–204.

8. Zhou Zuoren, "Difang yu wenyi" (Locality and literature) (1923), in *Zhou Zuoren zaoqi sanwenxuan,* (Shanghai: Shanghai wenyi chubanshe, 1984), 308–9.

9. Zhou Zuoren, "Difang yu wenyi," 310.

10. Zhou Zuoren, "Difang yu wenyi," 311.

11. Harootunian, "Disciplinizing Native Knowledge and Producing Place," 101.

12. Ozaki Fumiaki, "Shū Sakujin (Zhou Zuoren) no shinson teishō to sono hamon" (Zhou Zuoren's advocacy of the New Village movement and its ripples), in *Meiji Daigaku Kyōyō Ronshū* 207 (1988): 119–36; 237 (1991): 67–85.

13. See Kawamura Minato, *Manshū Hōkai: "Daitōa bungaku" to sakkadachi* (The collapse of Manchukuo: Writers and "Greater East Asia literature") (Tokyo: Bungei shunjū, 1998), 85–86.

14. Kawamura Minato, *Manshū Hōkai,* 45–48.

15. Kawamura Minato, *Manshū Hōkai,* 53–67.

16. David T. Murphey, "Space, Race, and Geopolitical Necessity: Geopolitical Rhetoric in German Colonial Revanchism, 1919–1933," in *Geography and Empire*, ed. Anne Godlewska and Neil Smith (Oxord: Blackwell, 1994), 177–78.

17. Keiichi Takeuchi, "The Japanese Imperial Tradition, Western Imperialism and Modern Japanese Geography," in *Geography and Empire*, ed. Anne Godlewska and Neil Smith (Oxford: Blackwell, 1994), 195.

18. Karen Wigen, "Teaching about Home: Geography at Work in the Prewar Nagano Classroom," *Journal of Asian Studies* 59 (2000): 561.

19. Hatada, *Chūgoku sonraku to kyōdōtai riron.* Japanese folklorists and ethnographers in different parts of the empire, inspired by Yanagita, coined the expression *Daitōa minzokugaku,* or Greater East Asian Folklore Studies (Asian Folklore, for short), which became a part of the larger ideology of pan-Asianism and its official counterpart, the Greater East Asian Co-prosperity Sphere. Pan-Asian Folklore employed the historical framework of the imperial Chinese *huayi* order underlying the imperial tribute system; see Kawamura Minato, *"Daitōa minzokugaku" no kyojitsu* (The truths and falsehoods of "Great East Asian folklore") (Tokyo: Kōdansha, 1996), 12–13. Its chief methodology was to establish Chinese civilizational cul-

tures—Chinese, Japanese, and Korean—at the core and locate other cultures beyond it in concentric circles. Needless to say, the center of the core was no longer China, but Japan. The idea was to intensify the study of the folklore of the core so as to radiate the ethos of the center to the peripheries. To be sure, Asian Folklore continued to distinguish itself from the Western methodology of comparative folklore studies. In theory, each of the cultures of Greater East Asia was to reflect its own distinctiveness even as each revealed its connections with Greater East Asia. But a hierarchy was also built in to the idea of distinctiveness, because each nationality's individual folklore was tied to its stage of evolution and hence dependent on the leadership of Japan. The characteristic Japanese formulation of combining uniqueness with evolutionary hierarchy was thus extended to folklore studies in order to secure Japan's special superiority.

20. Watsuji Tetsurō, *Climate and Culture: A Philosophical Study*, trans. Geoffrey Bownas (1935; reprint, New York: Greenwood Press in cooperation with Yushodo Co., 1988). See also Takeuchi, "The Japanese Imperial Tradition," 200.

21. Susan Daruvala, *Zhou Zuoren and an Alternative Chinese Response to Modernity* (Cambridge: Harvard University Press, 2000), 105, 106.

22. Jin Qisan, "Woguo nanbei zhi dili guandian" (Geographical perspectives on the north and south of our nation), *Fangzhi Yuekan* 8 (1935).

23. Ge Suicheng, *Xiangtu Dili Yanjiufa* (The research methods of community geography) (Shanghai: Zhonghua shuju, 1939), 3–4.

24. Ge Suicheng, *Xiangtu Dili Yanjiufa*, 8–10.

25. Daruvala, *Zhou Zuoren*, 152–54.

26. Fei Xiaotong, "Xiangtu bense," in *Xiangtu Zhongguo* (Rural China) (Shanghai: Guanchashe, 1947), 3. The essay has been translated by Gary Hamilton and Wang Zheng, but the translators tend to ignore the poetics that is critical to it. Thus for instance, Hamilton and Wang translate *bense* as "special characteristics." See Fei Xiaotong, "Special Characteristics of Rural Society," in *From the Soil: The Foundations of Chinese Society—A Translation of Fei Xiaotong's "Xiangtu Zhongguo,"* trans. Gary G. Hamilton and Wang Zheng (Berkeley: University of California Press, 1992), 37–44.

27. Hamilton and Wang's translation of *difangxing* as "parochialism" imparts a negative feeling; see Fei, "Special Characteristics of Rural Society," 41. It is interesting that English has no positive term for local orientation.

28. Fei, "Xiangtu bense," 5.

29. Fei, "Xiangtu bense," 6–7.

30. R. David Arkush, *Fei Xiaotong and Sociology in Revolutionary China* (Cambridge, Mass.: Council on East Asian Studies, 1981), 145–46.

31. Daruvala, *Zhou Zuoren*, and Wang, *Fictional Realism in Twentieth-Century China*. In addition, drawing attention to the textual dimension in Shen or Yanagita, scholars like David Wang have noted that the nostalgic writing of the native place hinges on the simultaneous "(re)discovery and erasure of the treasured image of the homeland." David Wang also finds value in Shen Congwen's native-place fiction which by means of displacement "makes possible the (re)definition of something either irretrievable or unspeakable" and thus enriches what is impoverished in memory. See Wang, *Fictional Realism in Twentieth-Century China*, 250, 252, 276. For Yanagita, see Ivy, *Discourses of the Vanishing*, 1995.

32. Christy, "Representing the Rural."

33. Lu Xun, introduction to *Xiaoshuo erji* (Second collection of fiction), ed. Lu Xun (Shanghai: Liangyou gongsi, 1935), 9.

34. Lu, introduction to *Xiaoshuo erji*, 9–10.

35. This refers to the collection of Lu Xun's [Lu Hsün] writings, *Dawn Blossoms Plucked at Dusk*, trans. Yang Hsien-yi and Gladys Yang (Beijing: Foreign Languages Press, 1976).

36. Lu, "Zai Jiuloushang" (In the wine shop), in *Panghuang Lu Xun Quanji* (1924; reprint, Taipei: Tangshan, 1989), 4:38.

37. Lu, introduction to *Xiaoshuo erji*, 16.

38. Lu, introduction to *Xiaoshuo erji*, 8.

39. See, for instance, Ivy, *Discourses of the Vanishing*, 106–7.

40. Liang Shanding, *Lüsede Gu* (Green valley) (1942; reprint, Shenyang: Chunfeng Wenyi chubanshe, 1987).

41. Liang Shanding, "Wenxuede guxiang" (The hometown of literature), in *Dongbei xiandai wenxue shiliao* (Historical materials from modern literature of the Northeast), vol. 2 (Shenyang: Liaoning shehui kexueyuan, 1980), 93–99.

42. Okada Hideki"Manshū no kyōdo bungei—Shan Ding 'Lüsede gu' o jiku toshite" (Native-place literature in Manzhouguo, with reference to Shan Ding's *Green Valley*), *Nogusa* 44 (1989): 29.

43. Liang Shanding, *Lüsede Gu*, 235.

44. Feng Weiqun, "'Wenyi zhidao gangyao' chulong yihou" (After the appearance of the "Summary of Guidelines to Art and Literature") in *Weiman wenhua*, ed. Sun Bang et al., Weiman shiliao congshu (Series of Manchukuo historical materials) (Changchun: Jilin renmin chubanshe, 1993), 13–14.

45. Feng, "'Wenyi zhidao gangyao' chulong yihou," 15–16; Jie Xueshi, "Riwei shiqide wenhua tongzhi zhengce" (Cultural control policy in the period of Manchukuo), in *Dongbei lunxian shiqi wenxue* (Literature of the occupation period in the Northeast), ed. Feng Weiqun et al. (Shenyang: Shenyang chubanshe, 1992), 182–98.

46. Quoted in Feng, "'Wenyi zhidao gangyao,'" 14.

47. *SJSB*, December 14, 1943, 447; Lü Qinwen, "Dongbei lunxianqude wailai wenxue yu xiangtu wenxue" (Foreign and native-place literature in the literature of occupied northeast China), in *Zhongri zhanzheng yu wenxue*, ed. Yamada Keizō and Lü Yuanming (Changchun: Dongbei shifandaxue chubanshe, 1992), 153–54.

48. See Kawamura Minato, *Manshū Hōkai*, 7–32. Quoted in Lü Qinwen, "Dongbei lunxianqude wailai wenxue yu xiangtu wenxue," 152.

49. "Zenme xie Manzhou?" (How to write about Manchuria?) [seminar transcription], *Yiwenzhi* (Literary records) 1, no.3 (1944): 27–37.

50. "Zenme xie Manzhou?" 29, 34.

51. Lü Qinwen, "Dongbei lunxianqude wailai wenxue yu xiangtu wenxue," 147. See also Sun, "Lüsede gu yu xiangtu wenxue," (*Green Valley* and native-place literature), in *Dongbei lunxian shiqi wenxue* (Literature of the occupation period in northeast China), ed. Feng Weiqun et al. (Shenyang: Shenyang Chubanshe, 1992), 225; and Pang Zengyu, "Dongbei lunxianqi xiangtu wenxue yu Zhongguo xiandai wenxue shishang xiangtu wenxue zhi bijiao" (Comparison of occupied Northeast native-place literature and native-place literature in modern Chinese literary history), in *Dongbei lunxian shiqi wenxue* (Literature of the occupation period in northeast China), ed. Feng Weiqun et. al (Shenyang: Shenyang Chubanshe, 1992), 65.

52. Hongbaochu, "Summary of Guidelines to Art and Literature," quoted in Sun Zhongtian, "Lüsede gu yu xiangtu wenxue," 225. See also Feng, "'Wenyi zhidao gangyao,'" 14.

53. Liaoning shehui kexueyuan wenxue yanjiusuo (Liaoning Province social science academy literature research institute) et al., ed., *Dongbei xiandai wenxue shiliao* (Historical materials from modern literature of the Northeast), vol. 1 (Shenyang: Liaoning shehui kexueyuan., 1980), 115.

54. See Ōuchi Takayoshi, "Dongbei wenxue ershinian" (Twenty years of Northeast litearature) (1944), selections trans. Wang Wenshi, and "Zuijin Zhongguoren de wenxue" (Recent literature by Chinese people) (1939), trans. Wang Wenshi, in *Dongbei xiandai wenxue shiliao* (Historical materials from modern literature of the Northeast), ed. Liaoning shehui kexueyuan wenxue yanjiusuo et al., vol. 1 (Shenyang: Liaoning shehui kexueyuan, 1980), 87–115.

55. Lü Qinwen, "Dongbei lunxianqude wailai wenxue yu xiangtu wenxue," 152–53.

56. Okada, "Manshū no kyōdo bungei," 30–31. Writers under state surveillance probably also had little choice but to attend the various literary conferences. Several of them, including Shanding, did attend these, although there is also evidence that by 1944 they were merely going through the motions of participation. See Kawamura, *Manshū Hōkai*, 26–27.

57. Huang Wanhua, "Liang Shanding he tade 'Lüse de Gu'" (Liang Shanding and his *Green Valley*), in *Dongbei wenxue yanjiu shiliao* (Northeast literature research materials), vol. 5 (Harbin: Harbin wenxueyuan, 1986), 11.

58. Liang Shanding, *Lüsede Gu*, 235–36. See also Liang Shanding, "Wenxuede guxiang," 94.

59. Pang, "Dongbei lunxianqi xiangtu wenxue," and Lü, "Dongbei lunxianqude wailai wenxue yu xiangtu wenxue."

60. Pang, "Dongbei lunxianqi xiangtu wenxue," 66.

61. See Okada, "Manshū no kyōdo bungei," 11, and Lü, "Dongbei lunxianqude wailai wenxue yu xiangtu wenxue," 137–45.

62. Sun, "Lüsede gu yu xiangtu wenxue," 225.

63. Lü, "Dongbei lunxianqude wailai wenxue yu xiangtu wenxue," 129–30.

64. Lü, "Dongbei lunxianqude wailai wenxue yu xiangtu wenxue," 144.

65. Sun, "Lüsede gu yu xiangtu wenxue," 233.

66. Sun, "Lüsede gu yu xiangtu wenxue," 234.

67. See Lü, "Dongbei lunxianqude wailai wenxue yu xiangtu wenxue," 144–45.

68. Okada Hideki, "Geibunshi ha no bungaku kiseki—Manshū ni okeru Chūgokujin sakka" (Tracks of the Literary Records group: Chinese writers in Manchuria), *Nogusa* 39 (1987): 96–101.

69. Okada, "Geibunshi ha no bungaku kiseki," 87–92, 95.

70. However, Okada, who is often sympathetic to the PRC scholars and Shanding, insists that Japanese writers in Manchuria such as Ōtani actually sought to cultivate a vision of Manchuria independent of Japan, and shared Shanding's desire for a regional literature of the Northeast reflecting its special qualities for both Chinese and Japanese writers. See Okada Hideki, "Geibunshi ha no bungaku kiseki—Manshū ni okeru Chūgokujin sakka" (Tracks of the Literary Records group: Chinese writers in Manchuria), *Nogusa* 38 (1986): 2–3, and "Wei Manzhouguo wenyi zhengcede zhankai—cong 'wenhuahui' dao 'yiwen lianmeng'" (The development of literary policy in the puppet state of Manzhouguo: From "cultural association" to "literary federation"), in *Dongbei lunxian shiqi wenxue* (Literature of the occupation period in northeast China), ed. Feng Weiqun et al. (Shenyang: Shenyang chubanshe, 1992), 159–61. Okada also believes that PRC scholars from the region have not fully acknowledged

this fact. However, see Zhang Yumao, "Zongxu" (General introduction), in *Dongbei xiandai wenxue daxi, 1919–1949* (Modern literature of the Northeast, 1919–1949), 14 vols., ed. Zhang Yumao (Shenyang: shenyang chubanshe, 1996), 1:1–24. Okada is perhaps right in pointing to the nationalistic exaggerations of the PRC scholars, particularly in relation to Japanese writers. But he fails to see that quite apart from what Shanding and the Japanese writers may have desired, their effort to produce an authenticity in the region was easily appropriable by metropolitan interests.

71. Liang Shanding, *Lüsede Gu*, 75.

72. Liang Shanding, *Lüsede Gu*, 187.

73. Liang Shanding, *Lüsede Gu*, 166.

74. My understanding of the relationship between history and fiction is inspired by Paul Ricoeur. See his analysis of event (figuration), historiography (con-figuration) and fiction (re-figuration) in historical process in *Time and Narrative*, vols. 1 and 2 (Chicago: University of Chicago Press, 1984–85), and his shorter piece, "The Function of Fiction in Shaping Reality," in *Reflection and Imagination: A Paul Ricoeur Reader*, ed. Mario J. Valdes (Toronto: University of Toronto Press, 1991), 117–36.

75. H. E. M. James, *The Long White Mountain or Journey into Manchuria* (London: Longmans, Green, 1888), 14, and R. Lee, *Manchurian Frontier*, 110.

76. James, *Long White Mountain*, 252–53.

77. R. Lee, *Manchurian Frontier*, 91–92.

78. James, *Long White Mountain*, 306, 318.

79. Alice Tisdale, *Pioneering Where the World Is Old* (New York: Henry Holt, 1917), 25.

80. McCormack, *Chang Tso-lin*, 17–19, 43.

81. Lattimore, *Manchuria*, 234.

82. Tisdale, *Pioneering Where the World Is Old*, 24.

83. Ma Zhengfu, "Dongximeng Menggu shiji (xu)" (Investigations in Eastern and Western Mongolia [continued]) *Xibei zazhi* (Northwest miscellany), no. 2 (Beijing: Xibei xiejing hui [Northwest coordination association], 1912), 35–41.

84. *SJSB*, March 3–25, 1943, 430, 439, 446, 454, 462.

85. For a detailed account of this resistance, see Lee Chong-sik, *Counterinsurgency in Manchuria: The Japanese Experience, 1931–1940* (Santa Monica, Calif.: Rand Corporation, 1967), 6–10. Lee also discusses the changed relationship between Korean and Chinese resistance forces after the establishment of Manchukuo (18–19). See also Willard Price, "Japan Faces Russia in Manchuria," *National Geographic*, November 1942, 603–14.

86. Pang Zengyu, *Heitudi wenhua yu dongbei zuojia qun* (Black soil culture and a group of Northeastern writers) (Changsha: Hunan jiaoyu chubanshe, 1995), 119–49.

87. Shih Nai-an, *Water Margin*, trans. J. H. Jackson (reprint, New York: Paragon, 1968).

88. Where the sworn brotherhood of the Water Margin occupied the marshes at the foot of the mountains (*shanpo*), Shanding (which translates as "mountain peak") has them occupy the mountaintop.

89. Arseniev, *Dersu the Trapper*, 136, 143, 176, 185, 213–14, 224–25.

90. Lattimore, *Manchuria*, 224; Arseniev, *Dersu the Trapper*, 179–80.

91. See his "Manzhou wenxue bitan" (Chatting about Manzhou literature), quoted in Ōuchi Takayoshi, "Dongbei wenxue ershinian," 99.

92. Williams, *Country and the City*, and Leo Marx, *The Machine in the Garden: Technology and the Pastoral Ideal in America* (Oxford: Oxford University Press, 1964).

93. Timothy S. Oakes, "Shen Congwen's Literary Regionalism and the Gendered Landscape of Chinese Modernity," *Geografiska Annaler* 77, no. 2 (1995): 93–107; see also Shen Congwen, *Imperfect Paradise: Stories by Shen Congwen*, ed. Jeffrey Kinkley, trans. Jeffrey Kinkley et al. (Honolulu: University of Hawaii Press, 1995), especially the section entitled, "The Vitality of the Primitive," 81–118.

94. See Kawamura, *Manshū Hōkai*, 68–76; Kleeman, "Mysticism and Corporeality."

95. Kam Louie, introduction to *Strange Tales from Strange Lands: Stories by Zheng Wanlong*, ed. Kam Louie (Ithaca: Cornell University Press, 1993), 1–22.

96. Zheng Wanlong, *Strange Tales from Strange Lands*, 35–44.

97. Zheng Wanlong, *Strange Tales from Strange Lands*, 45–58.

98. Cited in Mineo Nakajima, *The Kao Kang Affair and Sino-Soviet Relations*, Review: The Study of Communism and Communist Countries in Japan, no. 44 (Tokyo: Japan Institute of International Affairs, 1977), 2. In 1954, a power struggle within the CCP led to the purge of Politburo member Gao Gang and Party Organization Department head Rao Shushi (from East China) on the charge that they were illicitly trying to seize control of the party. Gao Gang, who had been the top party, government, and military leader in the Northeast, was alleged to have a special, even colonial, relationship with Stalin. While the purge represented an inner-party struggle, the incident suggests that Gao Gang may have continued to pursue power on the contested borderlands pattern of the region in his bid for national power. See also Frederick C. Teiwes, *Politics at Mao's Court: Gao Gang and Party Factionalism in the Early 1950s* (Armonk, N.Y.: Sharpe, 1990).

99. This and the information on contemporary Northeastern literature below was related to me by Professor Sun Zhongtian and Dr. Lü Qinwen, Deputy Director, Party Propaganda Department of Jilin Province, previously Deputy Director, Jilin Academy of Social Sciences.

100. Zhang Yumao, "Zongxu" (General introduction), 1:12–13.

~

Conclusion

My concluding remarks fall into three parts. The first seeks to explore the significance of Manchukuo in the changing relationship between imperialism and nationalism in the world and to discern the distinctiveness of Japanese imperialism in the inter-war period. The second marshals the findings of this study to reflect upon the relationship between authenticity and sovereignty in the East Asian modern. Finally, the study of Manchukuo presents an opportunity to probe the relationship between the globally circulatory notion of culture (and civilization), transnational identities, and nationalist ideology in the twentieth century.

Manchukuo and Imperialism

European colonial states in Asia and Africa did not resemble the modern governmental state until well into the inter-war years and later. Meghan Vaughan has explored the differences between the more repressive types of power exercised in colonial regimes and the more "productive" power of governmentality. Of course, the distinction is not absolute, and in my reading of Foucault modern power is also repressive: it is based as much upon surveillance and discipline as upon care for the population. Nonetheless, one can agree with Vaughan that in the European colonies power was overwhelmingly repressive and sought to reproduce the difference between colonizers and colonized on racial grounds. Moreover, while it introduced new forms of enumeration and classification, this power frequently served the needs of the capitalist metropole by reproducing or articulating with older modes of production and practices in the colonies.[1]

While several scholars show that Japanese imperialism was different in certain ways, it also shared a great deal with European colonialism—certainly in violence and repressiveness—until World War I and the March 1919 Korean movement.[2] Komagome Takeshi has argued that Japanese imperialism reflected the extension of the principles underlying national integration. Japanese nationalism was a contradictory affair composed not only of the principle of "blood descent," but also of common language and culture (or civilization). Whereas language and culture created possibilities for integrating the colonized based on assimilation or alliance, historically, the exclusionary principle of blood descent raised its head by inventing new ways—institutional, legal, or attitudinal—to circumvent the incorporation of non-Japanese in the empire as citizens. Colonial laws in Korea and Taiwan before 1920 reflected the European conception that civilized laws were not necessarily suited to the colonized, and the colonial regimes endorsed various historical and bodily forms of coercion. In Korea, for instance, flogging—modeled on the flogging law in Taiwan—remained the central method of punishment until 1920.[3] Nonetheless, Komagome traces a trajectory in Japanese expansionism whereby experiments with the forms of empire led to the increased visibility of models of assimilation and alliance. After the 1919 independence movement in Korea, groups within the colonial regime pointed to the necessity of overhauling the existing colonial government. Responding equally to the new nationalism and to a growing awareness of new models of reform and international development, the regime experimented with liberalizing the multinational state during what is known as the period of Cultural Rule in Korea in the 1920s. But the experiment was not sustained and the ideas and energies were transferred to Manchukuo.[4]

While Manchukuo evolved out of the trajectory of Japanese colonialism, it also represented a beginning, the first step in the realization of the autarkic sphere that included a pan-Asianist alliance, the yen bloc, and new strategies of development and mobilization. Pan-Asianism, which flourished as part of the civilizational discourse of the inter-war period, seemed to predestine Japan's mission on the mainland for many Japanese. Without reference to this discourse, we cannot fully grasp how an Ishiwara Kanji conceived of Manchukuo not simply as a colony, but as the nucleus of an anti-Western alliance of East Asian states (*Tōa remmei*), thus establishing the conceptual basis for a strong, developmental state. The idea of a pan-Asianist alliance produced a different kind of tension in Manchukuo than that which dominated the Japanese relationship with Korea and Taiwan. Manchukuo was undermined by the contradiction between an alliance based on independence—hence the quest for sovereignty—and the imperialist power structure, whereas in Korea and Taiwan the tension developed chiefly between assimilation and exclusion. This would have different implications for identity projects, especially in the 1930s, when the *kominka* movement in the colonies sought to produce the colonized as imperial Japanese subjects. Such projects were officially rejected in Manchukuo.

Indeed, Manchukuo signals fundamental changes in the nature of the Japanese empire. The truly intensive phase of industrialization and development in Korea and Taiwan came after 1931 and emerged as part of the plan for strategic autarky centered on Manchukuo. The rapid growth in industrialization, education, and other aspects of development in Korea and Taiwan began mostly in the early 1930s, and accelerated with the invasion of China in 1937.[5] Even in rural Korea, where landlord-based local control continued through the 1920s, new patterns of state-led corporatist mobilization led to the restraining of landlord power and implementation of reforms by the 1930s.[6] War, as global competition by other means, had led, as in World War I, to the mobilization of resources and identity. This time the Self that was the object of integration was not merely wider than the nation, it had already been or was in the process of becoming shaped by regimes of national authenticity for all parties concerned—Japanese, Chinese, and Korean. Integration on the basis of assimilation and alliance would still confront enormous challenges.

To be sure, the strategy of alliance also reflected other historical circumstances of the time and place. Rana Mitter has persuasively argued that factors ex-centric to the Japanese metropole were central to Japanese rule in Manchukuo.[7] Ronald Robinson's formulation of "ex-centric imperialism" explains this rule as an expression not only of metropolitan impulses, but of the circumstances of local allies who would "bargain" with imperial powers.[8] Indeed, I would argue that Manchukuo represented the endgame for imperialists and their allies in the face of rising nationalism. Confronted by the ascendancy of the KMT and its impending integration of Manchuria, the Guandong Army and the regional power structure forged an alliance with local elites, redemptive societies, and the old power structure. These allies had few choices given the reality of Japanese military power, but it was also clear to the Japanese that some kind of autonomous "national" status would be necessary to maintain the alliance. In this respect, Manchukuo was consistent with global imperialism in the inter-war years, when direct rule by aliens and sheer exploitation gave way to alternatives such as indirect rule, collaborative arrangements with local elites, self-government, quasi independence, and other means to secure imperialist interests.[9]

In its quest for modernity and formal sovereignty, however, Manchukuo represented something more than the sum of these inter-war arrangements. It foreshadowed the imperialism of the postwar period—especially of the Cold War—when, despite the independence declared by many countries, the new "imperial" powers retained considerable economic and military control over their client nation-states. While the Soviet Union controlled many socialist nations tightly, the Anglo-American empire—whether in Iraq until 1958, Congo, or Vietnam, to cite just a few examples—developed new patterns of dominance. In the words of Roger Louis and Ronald Robinson, the new imperialism "needed a good deal of old-fashioned imperial and financial intervention along with [the] economic attraction. Such was the imperialism of decolonization."[10] Manchukuo not only prefigured this kind of client state, the actions of the state in these changed circumstances—increased bargaining power of local groups, rights discourse, new strategies of control, new institutions of governmentality, and most of all, the institutionalization of identity-building projects—made for a new type of society.

Manchukuo and the East Asian Modern

The contradiction between sovereignty claims and an imperialist power structure that shadowed Manchukuo from its birth became increasingly intolerable over the war years, and the entire enterprise started to fall apart after the outbreak of the Pacific War. The troubles with the redemptive societies evident in this period reveal that even the pact with civilizational groups was increasingly overtaken by militarist goals. In this sense, while this book has deepened and fleshed out the historical picture of Manchukuo, the principal narrative of a puppet state increasingly dominated by an imperialistic power structure remains in place.

If we look beyond such a narrative, however, the paradoxes of Manchukuo provoke questions relevant to understanding modern nation formation in East Asia and the wider nation-state system in the post–World War I period as well. First, the indubitable expansion of state power and fascistic governmentality raises questions about the relationship between modern state- and nation-formation. The kind of state building we see in Manchukuo reflects, in many respects, the most sophisticated and powerful technologies of state expansion of the time. Since most of these states—for instance, Japan, Germany, and the Soviet Union—were also constructed as nation-states, the question arises as to whether such forms of state building and governmentality could develop without reference to the identities and loyalties of its citizens. Even in the earlier part of the nineteenth century, before nationalism became the norm for defining the body politic, the European nation-states had, as Giddens points out, "an administrative and territorially ordered unity which they did not possess before." This unity could not remain purely administrative if only because "the very co-ordination of activities involved presumes elements of cultural homogeneity."[11] We can imagine how much more acute this tension was for statebuilders in Manchukuo, which was founded upon and continued to invoke the rhetoric of nation. Indeed, when the Japanese power structure, subservient to a suicidal military expansionism, overwhelmed the national interests of Manchukuo, it led to the destruction of a laboriously constructed machinery of social power in Manchuria, as in Japan.

Specifically, Manchukuo became linked to the identity projects of nationalism through the state's immersion in a historicist discourse, in its self-perception as a subject progressing in historical time. This immersion produced the tension, familiar to modern nationalism, between commitment to modernization (including associated notions of governmentality, mobilization, and rights discourse) and the search for identity and authenticity. Out of this tension emerged a symbolic regime of authenticity, control of which was necessary for the state to achieve its goals of order, mobilization, and sovereignty. Conversely, these needs of the state required the maintenance of the symbolic regime.

Manchukuo state-builders certainly recognized the importance of identity formation, both for purposes of mobilization and control and for its domestic and international sovereignty claims. Their problem was that they could not, to any great extent, build a strong nationalist identity that either excluded the interests of Japan or compromised the ingrained colonial sense of superiority among the Japanese in the region. Hence the identity they sought to cultivate tended to be weakly territorial, expressed in ethnic nationality within the Concordia framework, in Asian civilizational forms, and in the spatial representation of a frontier nation built around the forest. Whereas the regime sanctioned Asian civilizational forms, including Confucianism and the syncretic notions of the redemptive societies, to appeal to the majority Chinese population, the representation of Manchukuo as a natural frontier appeared to limit Chinese claims and endorse the Japanese as caretakers of the autochthonous peoples and primeval nature. While different efforts were made to harmonize these contradictory conceptions of authenticity, the regime seemed simply to juggle them most of the time.

In some ways, the authenticity of a natural space served as a pivot in Manchukuo ideology. As the primeval home of the Tungus, the region became linked, via the Ural-Altaic myth, to the Japanese. The forest also hinged the representation of the frontier with Chinese heartland traditions, as we saw in *Green Valley* and its framings. Shanding bridged the contradiction from his own perspective: he found authenticity in a natural place, but with Chinese characteristics, as it were. In the historical narrative of the state, Manchuria as natural place was the birthplace of nonagri*cultural* empires that engendered a non-Chinese imperial tradition. When this empire extended over China, especially with the Manchus, it had controlled an ethnic alliance and a Confucian universalism that shaped the loyalties of many Chinese. Manchukuo state-builders evidently took a leaf from this imperial history in its model of the multinational state. Each of these representations was imbricated with the other to design loyalty to a state that was not quite nationalist. But this state possessed and deployed the means to produce identity, like any other nation-state.

Precisely because it was such a self-consciously constructed project, Manchukuo reveals the process of identity formation with relative clarity. Globally circulating concepts and practices of governmentality and fascistic mobilization, nationality, civilization and womanhood, indigeneity and nativism, were often transformed by the use of historical imagery, models, and language into immanent traditions. The specification of a realm of authenticity, whether through the identification of classical traditions or shamanism, the figure of the self-sacrificing woman, the native place, or the sacred forest, was designed—for different segments of the population—to secure the custodial sovereignty of the new nation-state. Such designation of the authentic also often served to justify the penetration of state power, as we have seen with the state's reshaping of the redemptive societies and women's groups as repositories of Eastern tradition, the reservation system for the Oroqen, and the state's effort to frame native-place cultural production. There were still other ways in which the regime sought to represent the authenticity of the polity and its rule: for instance, in Confucian state rituals and patronage of Mongol Lamaism. The highly deliberate and urgent search for authenticity belied its anxiety and must have seemed parodic to many—the discourse of an over-imagined nation.

How did Manchukuo exemplify what I have called the East Asian modern? I have tried to probe the ways in which institutional innovations were indigenized, and occasionally even shaped, by historical symbols and ideologies of the region.

Historical resources were evoked to moralize state initiatives and subordinate civil society and family for purposes of state making and governmentality. New Life Confucianism and "moral suasion" permitted mobilization through state-administered mass organizations, and the cultural investment of the periphery was interiorized by extending heartland traditions to these zones. In these ways, the experience of Manchukuo was consistent with that of Japan, Korea, and China.

Further, Bruce Cumings has identified an East Asian model of development, which he traces to the experience of Japanese modernization and its extension to the colonies in Korea and Taiwan. What he calls "the bureaucratic-authoritarian industrializing regime" comprises a bureaucratic state combining Confucian statecraft traditions with European-style civil service, high levels of mass education, state direction of the economy, total surveillance, involvement in the regional political economy, and an ideology of national essence.[12] Several features of this model outside Japan derive, I believe, principally from the period of strategic autarky in which Manchukuo and its pattern of industrial development, corporatist organization, surveillance, and mobilization played a central role. Indeed, postwar state-builders in South Korea were deeply shaped by their experiences in Manchukuo.[13] The particular cultural deployment, during this period, of the East Asian *modern*—enabling exaltation of the state, commitment of the bureaucracy, appeals to discipline and self-sacrifice, and "moral suasion," among other developments—is a significant precondition of the East Asian *model*.

But just as significant, Manchukuo exemplified what was *excised* from the dominant representations of the modern nation-state in Japan and China. With respect to Japan, Manchukuo served as a laboratory for what was not possible to achieve within Japan itself. Militarists, state-planners, economists, scientists, technocrats, modernist architects, city-builders, museum designers, forest conservationists, and germ warfare experimentalists sought to realize their designs, visionary and monstrous, here. That they were able to implement some of these ideas and plans in Japan in the openings provided by the postwar situation is a measure of the continuing role of Manchukuo in the formation of Japanese modernity, as is only now being revealed.[14]

With respect to China, state-builders in Manchukuo fostered in rhetoric and policy, if not always in practice, precisely those elements that had been problematic for modern Chinese nationalism. This nationalism had opposed the redemptive and popular religious societies and tried to rapidly assimilate various ethnic and indigenous groups. By unleashing the activism of redemptive and sectarian societies, first in Manchukuo and subsequently in China proper (*guannei*), the Manchukuo model of governance, which sought to reconcile traditionalism with fascistic mobilization, revealed a gaping hole in Chinese nationalist mobilization. The Chinese state's refusal to accept the conception of transcendence and self-empowerment in these societies has continued to haunt it to this day.

While Chinese policies towards non-Han ethnic groups during the Republic basically reflected the praxis of a homogenizing and assimilationist nation-state, this praxis had to accommodate an understanding of the rights of nationality and minority groups. Consciousness of these rights, of course, circulated globally, but it was brought home with decisive clarity by Manchukuo and other claims on peripheral territories during the war. A historical, Confucian model of voluntary assimilation— much like *jiaohua*—emerged as a response to the challenge posed by this wartime experience.

Sovereignty and the Scales of Identity

The curious phenomenon of Manchukuo as a modern identity project that cultivated sub- and transnational identities presents us with an opportunity to explore the dynamics of identity formation across different scales more widely in the nation-state system of the early twentieth century. "Civilization" in the identity projects of Manchukuo represented modes of self-fashioning that combined modern ideas with historical, religious, and civilizational conceptions of community not always compatible with territorially de-limited national models. We have seen how notions of transcendence and faith embedded in such conceptions could produce highly motivated subjects among the men and women of the redemptive societies. At the same time, civilization, which Redfield defined as a subset of culture, retained and realized the potential to define a community sharply against an Other, as in the war of the East against the West.[15]

We can see in the early twentieth century the growing importance of the principle of culture—the repository of authenticity—as the basis of the sovereign community over much of the world, as in Manchukuo. If the notion of culture was ever once simply "received tradition," by the end of World War I it no longer possessed that innocence. Neither did culture refer to an upper-class formation relatively unrestricted by territory, nor principally to a methodology of meaning production,[16] but to a bounded and holistic set of ideas, institutions, and practices that constituted and distinguished a people. Epistemologically it had become rewired to serve identity. With the ascendancy of several critical intellectual and political forces—the (originally German) counter-evolutionary tradition, the Soviet model of cultural nationality, the Wilsonian ideal of linguistic nationality, and anti-imperialist nationalism itself—this notion of culture/civilization became a globally produced knowledge.

The novelty of the relationship between culture and rights (of which authenticity and sovereignty are specifications), particularly during the inter-war period, does not lie in the equation or congruence of culture with the nation-state. Culture became an identificatory concept, an identified entity, and a potential object of identity, all of which could be either greater or lesser than the nation-state. Cultures could be as small as Boas's autochthonous communities or as vast as Asian or Islamic civilization; but once identified, cultures became vehicles of potential subjecthood and rights. When they became objects of identity, they also seeded a regime of authenticity.

While in the post–World War I period much political energy was expended and violence committed in seeking to match linguistic and cultural nationality with nation-state boundaries in Europe, the dynamics of scalar identity were being tested in the Soviet Union and Asia. Here, nationalizing states that sought to inherit empires—motivated perhaps by the conditions of rights awareness in the regions— experimented with alternative relationships between cultural nationality and state. In 1912, even before the appearance of the multinational Soviet Union, the Republic of China declared itself a Republic of Five Nationalities. Japanese state-builders in Manchukuo were not only informed by their own colonial experiments with nationality, they were influenced by Chinese Republican and Soviet ideas. The problems the model of the multinational state encountered in Manchukuo were distinct because of the minority, Japanese-dominated power structure. But the form of the new nation-state was continuous with that in the Soviet Union and China.

In all of these societies and in many postwar nations, old and new, the idea of nations as homogenous, organic entities gave way to a multinational or multicultural idea that forced the nation-state to acknowledge, and sometimes to foster, minority ethnic or nationality rights. The implicit rationale may be expressed as a contract wherein cultural subjecthood is granted in exchange for loyalty to the nation-state. Such a development should be seen as a response to various factors. The spread of rights consciousness and anti-imperialist ideology were among them, as was the rapid construction of bounded nation-states from heterogeneous social formations, in particular where such nation-states sought to inherit old empires, but also where more recent demographic movements had produced new populations, such as the Chinese in southeast Asia or the Koreans in Manchuria. In many ways, the multinational idea was itself a circulating response to the quickening circulation of people, ideas, and resources that was designed to stabilize the nation as a viable, competitive, and moral power. The problem of authenticity, of course, did not disappear.

Permitting as they do a measure of voluntarism and porousness, nations as cultural formations lack the predeterminism and exclusivism of racial nationalism. The cultural nation has the capacity to develop into the multicultural nation organized around two scales of identity, which we may think of as "territorial-national" versus "sub- and transnational." These two scales, embedded in different narratives and institutions, ought to be compatible, normatively speaking. But whether because of global competitiveness, rights consciousness, or the reaction to this consciousness, the identities are still susceptible to the politics of closure, and the two scales are not infrequently at odds. In the Japanese case, we have seen how the racialized ideal of the Yamato nation consistently subverted the wider goal of assimilation into an alliance with a common culture and civilization that the Japanese state also sought to build. While this common culture and civilization was conceived, in part at least, as necessary for dominance in a competitive world, the regime of authenticity built around the racialized nation tended to trump this goal. The Chinese Republic revealed a pattern where, although scholars and nationalists also worked with the idea of autochthonous and separate nationalities, they consistently emphasized assimilationist institutions, narratives of voluntary assimilation, and the cultural investment of peripheral spaces as part of the national imaginary. The Republic collapsed in the face of a revolutionary uprising, but its institutional and cultural efforts at nationalizing the peripheries served as the foundation for the PRC's consolidation of these regions in its version of the multinational state.[17]

The multinationalism of Manchukuo, inspired by the Soviet model and institutionalized through the Concordia Association, did not often clarify the relationship between (ethnic) nationality and the larger nation-state, or what General Koiso Kuniaki called *Daikoku*. A classified document circulated anonymously in 1940 (cited in chapter 2) engaged a Hegelian discussion of Soviet nationality. It argued that "the spirit of universal citizenship" embodied in the state "moves from the outside to the inside" of nationalities; in this movement, the culture of the individual nationalities becomes the basis for the realization of spirit.[18] Texts like this acknowledge, however philosophically, the reality of the subordination of nationality (it is unclear if this included the Japanese) to the Manchukuo state. At the same time, as Suk-jung Han has argued, the rhetoric of state building (*kenkoku* or *jianguo*) replaced that of the "kingly way" over time, signaling the ascendancy of statism and loyalty to the state over civilizational ideals. As the terrible costs of war bore down on Manchukuo society, the state become increasingly alienated from its own sub- and transnational identity projects. Since, from the beginning, it had a weak sense of territorial nationality, Manchukuo ended as a strong—military fascist—state that represented only itself.[19] We are reminded of the Soviet Union at its end. Rogers Brubaker has suggested that, in contrast to the various nationalities that became the focus of identity formation, the Soviet state never succeeded in generating its own narrative or symbolism of nationhood.[20] The legitimacy of the twentieth-century state, no matter how strong and modern, appears to have been built around narratives of identity.

Nations are continuously produced by global competition and globalizing forces; they are also simultaneously the moral constructs empowered to regulate, contain, and sometimes combat these forces. It is in order to escape the paralyzing effects of this contradiction that their authority tends to be located beyond the system, in the immanence of the symbolic regime. The different scales of identity reflect to some extent this tension between the universal and the particular, and by no means do all identities come to be imbued with authority or controlled by power. At the same time, as the ur-form and model of identity politics, nationalism and its regime of authenticity frequently become reproduced in identities at different levels. It is not yet clear whether the new turn in the current globalization will cause identity politics to wither or further empower it to develop beyond the need even for a state.

In the course of writing this book, I have become aware that the critique of nationalism as a symbolic regime of power is beset by an acute moral quandary. When faced by a monstrous imperialism or terror, nationalism may represent the only available means of self-defense in a world of nation-states. I faced this quandary with the Chinese resistance to a brutal Japanese occupation, where there were few alternatives but for the resistance to mobilize as nationalism. We continue to encounter this dilemma in relation to communities weak or strong, whether it be the nationalization of an indigenist movement, crafted as a survival strategy, or nationalism as the reaction of a global power to an indefensible terrorism. Moreover, for some liberal nationalists in the world, the idea of an authentic culture may also be the precondition of cosmopolitanism. Should we then grasp these differences through the distinction between good and bad nationalisms?

The character of nationalism does not appear to be fixed. Rather, all nationalisms contain the potential to convert an enabling, context-based, and coalitional understanding of the self into a deep history of belonging and/or an exclusivist moral force. This transformation is, of course, most evident in the case of Japanese nationalism. I have also tried to grasp the moment at which militarism converted the universalism of redemptive societies in Manchukuo, and have pointed to ways in which Chinese nationalism transformed a practical defense and alliance into a deep history of inalienability. There must surely be a place in our understanding of nationalism in the real world that is strategic or coalitional in character.

But while recognizing the limits of a historical situation, it is also the responsibility of scholars to grasp when, how, why, and with what consequences nationalism as alliance can be converted into a deep history. The deep nation is secured by a regime of authenticity that, no matter how frail or defensive, has the potential to harden boundaries and shut out the world morally. I write in the hope that isolating the dynamic, context, and moment of the realization of this potential is not a useless venture.

Notes

1. Megan Vaughan, *Curing Their Ills: Colonial Power and African Illness* (Cambridge, England: Polity Press, 1991), 8–12; Michel Foucault, *The History of Sexuality*, vol. 1, *An Introduction* (New York: Pantheon, 1978), 12.

2. For similarities and differences see Myers, "Creating a Modern Enclave Economy," 137–39. See also Mark Peattie, introduction to *The Japanese Colonial Empire, 1895–1945*, ed. Ramon H. Myers and Mark Peattie (Princeton: Princeton University Press, 1984); Bruce Cumings, "Colonial Formations and Deformations," 73–74; and Gi-Wook Shin and Michael Robinson, eds., *Colonial Modernity in Korea* (Cambridge: Harvard University Asia Center, 1999).

3. Komagome, *Shokuminchi Teikoku Nippon no Bunka Tōgō*. 356–70. Chulwoo Lee, "Modernity, Legality, and Power in Korea under Japanese Rule," in *Colonial Modernity in Korea*, ed. Gi-Wook Shin and Michael Robinson (Cambridge: Harvard University Asia Center, 1999), 31–34.

4. Komagome, *Shokuminchi Teikoku Nippon no Bunka Tōgō*. 359–60. See also Michael A. Schneider, "The Limits of Cultural Rule: Internationalism and Identity in Japanese Responses to Korean Rice," in *Colonial Modernity in Korea*, ed. Gi-Wook Shin and Michael Robinson (Cambridge: Harvard University Asia Center, 1999), 98–100.

5. Soon-Won Park, "Colonial Industrial Growth and the Emergence of the Korean Working Class," in *Colonial Modernity in Korea*, ed. Gi-Wook Shin and Michael Robinson

(Cambridge: Harvard University Asia Center, 1999), 143–47. Park shows that the overall elementary school enrollment rate in Korea doubled in the 1930s, from 14.5 percent in 1930 to 33.8 percent in 1940. In Meiji Japan the enrollment rate was 62 percent in 1886 (147); see Myers, "Creating a Modern Enclave Economy," 137–39, and Cumings, "Colonial Formations and Deformations," 76–79. In 1940, Manchukuo authorities claimed that 43 percent of school-age children were receiving some form of education; see Jones, *Manchuria since 1931*, 49.

6. Gi-Wook Shin and Do-Hyun Han, "Colonial Corporatism: The Rural Revitalization Campaign, 1932–1940," in *Colonial Modernity in Korea*, ed. Gi-Wook Shin and Michael Robinson (Cambridge: Harvard University Asia Center, 1999), 70–96.

7. Mitter, *Manchurian Myth*, 16–19.

8. Ronald Robinson, "The Ex-centric Idea of Imperialism, with or without Empire," in *Imperialism and After: Continuities and Discontinuities*, ed. Wolfgang G. Mommsen and Jurgen Osterhammel (London: Allen and Unwin, 1986), 267–89.

9. Barraclough, *Introduction to Contemporary History*, 166–67.

10. Louis and Robinson, "Empire Preserv'd," *Times Literary Supplement*, May 5, 1995, 16; see also Suk-Jung Han, "The Problem of Sovereignty: Manchukuo, 1932–1937" (forthcoming in *Positions*).

11. Giddens, *Nation-State and Violence*, 219.

12. Cumings, "Colonial Formations and Deformations," 88–92.

13. Suk-jung Han, "Those Who Imitated the Colonizers: The Influence of State-Making from Manchukuo to South Korea" (paper prepared for the conference volume, *Japanese Colonialism in Manchuria*), University of California at Los Angeles, January 2001.

14. See Kobayashi Hideo, *"Nihon kabushiki gaisha" o tsukutta otoko: Miyazaki Masayoshi no shōgai* (The man who created "Japan, Inc.": The career of Miyazaki Masayoshi) (Tokyo: Shōgakkan, 1995); Janis Mimura, "From 'Manchukuo' to Japan's 'New Order'" (unpublished paper, n.d.); and Young, *Japan's Total Empire*. On the origins of the postwar Japanese "construction state" in Manchukuo, see Tucker, "Building 'Our Manchukuo.'"

15. Having already written at length about nationalism, I had embarked on the Manchukuo project to explore regional and transnational processes and identities. While this topic did indeed provide such an opportunity, as an early-twentieth-century phenomenon, the problem of nationalism unavoidably returned to primacy. The discourses of civilization, locality, and religion could not be grasped apart from nationalism or national structures, whether in Japan, China, or even Manchukuo.

16. See Raymond Williams, *The Country and the City*, for the former, and Clifford Geertz, *The Interpretation of Cultures* (New York: Basic, 1973), for the latter.

17. Liu Xiaoyuan, "The Chinese Communist Party and the 'Nationality Question,' 1921–1945."

18. *Soren no minzoku seisaku* (Soviet nationality policy), Publication of the Research Institute of the National Foundation University (Shinkyō: Kenkoku Daigaku kenkyūin kan, 1940), 1–2.

19. Suk-jung Han, "The Problem of Sovereignty."

20. Rogers Brubaker, *Nationalism Reframed: Nationhood and the National Question in the New Europe* (Cambridge: Cambridge University Press, 1996), 24–35.

Glossary of Chinese Terms

Note: The Chinese terms are followed by Japanese pronunciation, where relevant.

badao　霸道

baihua　白話

bang　幫

baojia　保甲

baojing anmin yundong
　保境安民運動

baonü yixueyuan　保女義學院

bense　本色

Bianjiang tongxun　邊疆通訊

bianjiang wuli de guofanghua
　邊疆武力的國防化

Bianzheng gonglun　邊政公論

Bohai　渤海

Cai Yuanpei　蔡元培

Chahar sheng　察哈爾省

Changbai (Mountain)　長白（山）

Changchun　長春

Chen Duxiu　陳獨秀

Chen Tianhua　陳天華

Chen Yifu　陳毅夫

chengshi　誠實

chengxian qihou
　承先啓後

chi　恥

choubeichu　籌備處

Chu　楚

Cixi　慈禧

congfu　從夫

Da Yaxiyazhuyi　大亞細亞主義

Dalian　大連　Dairen

datong　大同

Datongbao　大同報

Datong weiyi shijie　大同唯一世界

Dai Jitao　戴季陶

Dan Di　但娣

dao　道

Daodehui　道德會

daotong　道通

Daoyuan　道院

difang　地方　chihō

257

difangxing　地方性

diyu　地域　chiiki

Dongbei Jiuguo Hui　東北救國會

Dongfangzazhi　東方雜誌

Donghu　東胡

Du Yaquan　杜亞泉

Duanmu Hongliang　端木 蕻良

dushen zhuyi sixiang
　獨身主義思想

Elunchun　鄂倫春　Oroqen
　(Orochon/Oronjon)

er taitai　二太太

falu shehui　法律社會

fanbang　番邦

Fei Xiaotong　費孝通

Feng Youlan　馮友蘭

Feng zhuren　馮主人

feng　風

fengjian　封建

fengjian-junxian debate　封建郡縣

fengjin　封禁

fengsu　風俗

fengtu　風土　fudō

foxing　佛性

Fu Sinian　傅斯年

fudao　婦道

Funü fuwutuan　婦女服務團

Funü shenghuo gaijinhui
　婦女生活改進會

funü shimin　婦女市民

Funü Zazhi　婦女雜誌

funü　婦女

fuxing benxing　復興本性

ganhuale　感化了

Gaoli　高麗　Koryo

Ge Suicheng　葛綏成

Gelaohui　哥老會

geming jianguo　革命建國

geming　革命

gexin　革新

Geyao　歌謠

gongxin　公心

Gu Ding　古丁

Gu Hongming　辜鴻銘

Gu Jiegang　顧頡剛

Gu Yanwu　顧炎武

Guandi　關帝

Guandongjun　關東軍　Kantōgun

guanmin yizhi　官民一致

guannei　關內

Guizhou (sheng)　貴州（省）

guohuo　國貨

Guorong　國榮

Guowei　國威

Guxiang　故鄉

guxiang　故鄉　kyōdo

guyazhouren　古亞洲人

guyou renxin　固有人心

Han Dynasty　漢朝

hanjian　漢奸

Hanjun　漢軍

Hanyu Dacidian　漢語大辭典

Harbin　哈爾濱

Hebei sheng　河北省

Heilongjiang sheng　黑龍江省

Hezhezu　赫哲族

Hongbaochu　弘報處

honghuzi　紅鬍子

Hongwanzihui　紅卍字會

Hu Shi　胡適

hua　化

huashi　化世

Huang Wenshan　黃文山

Hunan (sheng)　湖南（省）

hunhe　混合

Hunxie Er　混血兒

huozhe neng sheshen shujie
　活者能捨身淑界

Jiaji diaocha baogao
　家計調查報告
　　Kakei chōsa hōkoku

Jiali tongxiang jiujihui
　家裡同鄉救濟會

Jiali　家裡

jiating yanjiushe　家庭研究社

jiaxiang he diyu　家鄉和地域

Jian Xian'ai　蹇先艾

Jiandao　間島

jianguo jingshen he jiating funü
　建國精神和家庭婦女

Jianguo xuangao　建國宣告

jianguo　建國　kenkoku

jianshang　奸商

jianghu　江湖

jiaohua　教化　kyōka

jie　界

jie　節

Jilin sheng　吉林省

jin caizhu　金財主

jinbu　進步

jinhua　進化

jinxin　盡心

jingpai　京派

jingsui　精髓

jiuji　救己

jiuren　救人

Jiushi Fotuan　救世佛團

Jiushi Xinjiao　救世新教

jiushi　救世　kyūsei

Jurchen (Jin)　女真（金）

kaiming　開明

Kang Youwei　康有爲

ketou　磕頭

Khitan　契丹

Langgou　狼溝

laogen　老根

laozi zhi ling　老子之靈

letu　樂土

Lei Haizong　雷海宗

lengjing　冷靜

Li Dazhao　李大釗

Li Xianglan　李香蘭　Ri Kōran

li　禮

lian　廉

lianheguo tongzhihui
　聯合國同志會

L Liang Qichao　梁啓超
　　Ryō Keichō

Liang Shanding　梁山丁

Liang Shuming　梁漱溟

liangjie　諒解

liangxin　良心

Liao　遼

Liji　禮記

Lijiaoke　禮教科

lishen duanzheng fang ke weiren
　立身端正方可爲人

lishen　立身

lisu shehui　禮俗社會

lixin yundong　離心運動

liye　立業

liyong　利用

lizhi　立志

Lin Yutang　林語堂

lingmiao　靈廟

Lu Xun　魯迅

lülin haohan　綠林好漢

Lüsede gu　綠色的谷

maiban　買辦

maikong maikong　買空賣空

mantou　饅頭

Manzhou shehui shiye lianhehui
　滿州社會事業聯合會

Manzhou Wenxue　滿州文學

Manzhou Wenyixiehui
　滿州文藝協會

Manzhouguo guofang funüren hui
　滿州國國防婦女人會

Manzhouguo　滿州國　Manchukuo

Manzu　滿族　Manshū

Miao　苗

ming　命

mingyun　命運

minjian　民間

Minshengbu　民生部

minsuxue　民俗學　minzokugaku

Minzhengbu　民政部

minzu xiehe
　民族協和　minzoku kyōwa

minzu　民族　minzoku

Minzuxue Yanjiu jikan
　民族學研究季刊

minzuxue　民族學

modeng　摩登

Fengtian (Mukden)　奉天

muyuan　母院

Nanmanzhan (Nanzhan)
　南滿站（南站）

neidi　內地

neisheng　內聖

Niangniang　娘娘

nitude qixi　泥土的氣息

nüshe　女社

nüxingde chujiao　女性的觸角

Pei Wenzhong　裴 文中

Pingfang　平房

Puyi　溥儀

qipao　旗袍

qianhua minzu　前化民族

Qin Dynasty　秦朝

qing　輕

quwei　趣味

Rehe sheng　熱河省

renleixue　人類學

renqing　人情

renzhongxue　人種學

rong　榮

ronghe　融合

rudao　乳道

sancong　三從

san gang　三綱

sanjiaoheyi　三教合一

Shandong sheng　山東省

shanlindui　山林隊

shanren　善人

Shang　商

shangkan　上坎

shangxin　傷心

Shehui yundong zhidao weiyuanhui
　　社會運動指導委員會

shehui　社會

Shexi　社戲

Shen Congwen　沈從文

shen　身

shenkan　神龕

Shengjing Shibao　盛京時報

shengmingxian　生命線

Shengyihui jiangchang
　　省議會講長

shi　士

Shi Jun　石軍

shijian tong kongjian de bianhua
　　時間同空間的變化

shijie datong　世界大同

Shijie Zongjiao Datonghui
　　世界宗教大同會

Shun　舜

Shuntian Shibao　順天時報

Sima Qian　司馬遷

sishu　私塾

Song Meiling　宋美齡

su　俗

tai　胎

taijiao　胎教

tianliu　天留

tianming　天明

tianxing　天性

tie caizhu　鐵財主

tongbao　同胞

tonghua　同化

tongjiao　同教　dōkyō

Tongshanshe　同善社

tongshi　通史

tongwen　同文　dōbun

tongye　同業

tongzhong　同種　dōshu

tui zhi jiating shehui
　　推之家庭社會

waiwang　外王

Wanguo Daodehui　萬國道德會

wanyou genyuan　萬有根源

Wang Fengyi　王鳳儀

Wang Fuzhi　王夫之

Wang Jingwei　汪精衛

Wang Luyan　王魯彥

wang tianxia　亡天下

wangdao　王道　ōdō

wei Manzhouguo　偽滿州國

weikaihua minzu　未開化民族

wen　文

wenhua　文化　bunka

Wenjiaobu　文教部

wenming　文明

wenyi　文藝

wenzhi jiaohua　文治教化

wenzhipai　文治派

Wu　吳

Wushanshe　吳善社

Wushenglaomu　無生老母

wusi　無私

wuwei　無爲

wuwo　無我

wuxing　五性

wuxing　五行

wuxingde wuqi　無形的武器

wuyü　無欲

xi　系

Xia　夏

xiakan　下坎

xianbingdui　憲兵隊

xiandai　現代

xianqi liangmu　賢妻良母

　ryōsaikenbo

xiangtu bense　鄉土本色

Xiangtu Dili Yanjiufa

　鄉土地理研究法

xiangtu wenxue　鄉土文學

xiangtu yanjiu

　鄉土研究　kyōdo kenkyū

Xiangtu Zhongguo　鄉土中國

xiangtu　鄉土　kyōdo

Xiao Hong　蕭紅

Xiao Jun　蕭軍

xiaoshuohuade youji

　小說化的遊記

Xiehehui　協和會　Kyōwakai

Xiezu　血族

xiezu　血族

xisheng　犧牲

Xin Yaxiya　新亞細亞

xin　心

Xinjiang　新疆

Xinjing　新京　Shinkyō

Xinminhui　新民會

xing dao shenshang, na jiao shizi

　行到身上那叫識字

xing　性

Xing'an Mountains　興安嶺

Xingyayuan　興亞院

Xiong Xiling　熊希齡

Xiongnu　匈奴

xiucai　秀才

xiudao　修道

xiushen　修身

Xu Qinwen　許欽文

xunfu　馴服

xungen　尋根

Yao　堯

yi　義

Yiguandao　一貫道

Yili sangfuzhuan　儀禮喪服傳

yiqi　義氣

yisheng　義聖

yiwenzhipai　藝文志派

Yixiang yiwen　異鄉異文

Yixin tiandao longhua shengjiao

　一心天道龍華聖教

Yiyongjun　義勇軍

youhuo　誘惑

youjihuade xiaoshuo

　遊記化的小說

yousede minzu　有色的民族

Yu Chonghan　于沖漢

Yu gong　禹貢

Yuan Jinkai　袁金鎧

Yuan Shikai　袁世凱

yuan 圓

yuanshi lin 原始林

yuanshi tezhi 元始特質

Yue 越

Zai Jiuloushang 在酒樓上

Zaijiali 在家裡

Zailijiao 在理教

Zang sniyi 臟式毅

Zenme xie Manzhou 怎麼寫滿州

Zhang Binglin (Zhang Taiyan)
章炳麟（章太炎）

Zhang Dongsun 張東蓀

Zhang Jinghui 張景惠

Zhang Xueliang 張學良

Zhang Zhidong 張之洞

Zhang Zuolin 張作霖

zhaojian 召見

zhen 貞

zhen 鎮

zhennü yixue 真女義學

zhenzhende qinggan 真真的情感

Zheng Wanlong 鄭万隆

Zheng Xiaoxu 鄭孝胥

zhengfu zuzhifa 政府組織法

zhengshen 正身

zhengyi 正義 seigi

zhi 志

Zhibian Yuekan 殖邊月刊

ziming 知命

zhixing 知性

zhizhi 知止

Zhongguo minzuxuehui
中國民族學會

Zhongguo Tuozhisuo 中國拓殖所

Zhonghua minzu 中華民族

Zhongtongju 中統局

zhongyi 忠義

Zhongyuan rujiao datong wenhua
中原儒教大同文化

zhongzu 種族 shuzoku

Zhou 周

zhou 州

Zhou Zuoren 周作人

Zhufu 祝福

zhuren 主人

zhuxia 諸夏

ziji xiuyang 自己修養

zili 自立

ziran biaoxiang 自然表像

zizhi zhidaobu 自治指導部

zongfa 宗法

zongjiao 宗教 shūkyō

zongwuting 總務廳

zu 族

zuguo 祖國

zuoren 做人

Glossary of Japanese Terms

Note: The Japanese terms are followed by Chinese pronunciation, where relevant.

ajia gakkai　アジア学会

Akamatsu Chijō　赤松智城

Akiba Takashi　秋葉隆

Amaterasu　天照

Ayukawa Yoshisuke　鮎川義介

bunka　文化　wenhua

bunmei kaika　文明開化

bunmeiteki　文明的

bushidō　武士道

chihō　地方　difang

chiiki　地域　diyu

Daikoku　大国

daikokumin　大国民

Dainihon rengō fujinkai
　大日本連合婦人会

Dairen　大連　Dalian

Dai-Tōa Kyōeiken　大東亜共栄圏

Daiyūhōkai　大雄峯会

datsua　脱亜

Deguchi Nao　出口尚

Deguchi Ōmotokyō　出口大本教

dentōteki seikatsu shisō
　伝統的生活思想

dōbun　同文　tongwen

doken kokka　土建国家

dōkyō　同教　tongjiao

dōshu　同種　tongzhong

fudō　風土　fengtu

Fujiyama Kazuo　藤山一雄

Fukuzawa Yukichi　福沢諭吉

furusato　故郷　guxiang

Genyōsha　玄洋社

hakkō-ichiu　八紘一宇

heisha hōmu　兵者ホーム

Hisama Jūgi　久間十儀

Hitonomichi　人の道

hōken　封建　fengjian

honshitsu　本質

Inaba Kunzan　稲葉君山

Ishiwara Kanji　石原莞爾

Isshinkai　一心会

jinja　神社

junsuisei　純粋性

Kada Tetsuji　加田哲二

kagakuka　科学化

kakei chōsa hōkoku　家計調査報告

kakumei　革命　geming

Kantōgun　関東軍　Guandongjun

Kasagi Ryōmei　笠木良明

Katō Hiroyuki　加藤弘之

Kayahara Kazan　茅原華山

kenkoku　建国　jianguo

ketsuzoku　血族

Kitagawa Fuyuhiko　北川冬彦

Koiso Kuniaki, General　小磯国昭

kokubō fujinkai　国防婦人会

Kōmin　公民

kominka　皇民化

kōsei　厚生

kyōdo kenkyū
　郷土研究　xiangtu yanjiu

kyōdo　郷土　xiangtu

kyōdōtai　共同体

kyōdōteki　共同的

kyōka　教化　jiaohua

Kyōwa undō　協和運動

kyōwa　協和

kyōwakai　協和会　xiehehui

kyūsei　救世　jiushi

Mamiya Rinzo　間宮林蔵

Manei　満映

Manmō no minzoku to shūkyō
　満蒙の民族と宗教

Manmō　満蒙

Manshū Hyōron　満州評論

Manshū Seinen Renmei
　満州青年連盟

Manshūkoku kokuritsu chūō
hakubutsukan
　満州国国立中央博物館

Mantetsu Shainkai　満鉄社員会

Meiji　明治

minkan　民間

minzoku kyōwa
　民族協和　minzu xiehe

minzoku　民族　minzu

minzokugaku　民族学　minzuxue

minzokuggaku　民俗学　minsuxue

Murakami Haruki　村上春樹

Nagata Uzumaro　永田珍麿

Naitō Konan　内藤湖南

Nakagami Kenji　中上健二

nichiman yūwa　日満融和

nihonjinron　日本人論

Nippon Sangyō Kaisha
　日本産業会社

Nogawa Takashi　野川隆

nōhonshugi　農本主義

ōdō　王道　wangdao

Okakura Tenshin　岡倉天心

Ōkawa Shūmei　大川周名

Ōmotokyō　大本教

Orochon/Oronjon　オロンジョン
　(Elunchun/Oroqen)

Ōtani Takeo　大谷健夫

Ōuchi Takayoshi　大内隆雄

Ozaki Hotsumi　尾崎秀実

rikugun　陸軍

rōnin　浪人

ryōsai kenbo

　良妻賢母　xianqi liangmu

sambōchō　参謀長

Satō Daishirō　佐藤大四郎

seigi　正義　zhengyi

seken seikatsu　世間生活

Shibunkai　斯文会

Shimoda Utako　下田歌子

shinjitsusei　真実性

Shinmei Masamichi　新名正道

Shiratori Kurakichi　白鳥倉吉

shojochi　処女地

shūkyō　宗教　zongjiao

shuzoku　種族　zhongzu

Sōka Gakkai　創価学会

Suemitsu Takayoshi　末光高義

Suenaga Misao　末永節

Tachibana Shiraki　橘樸

Taishō　大正

Takizawa Toshiro　瀧澤俊亮

Tōa Dōbun shoin　東亜同文書院

Tōa kyōdōtai　東亜共同体

Tōa renmei　東亜連盟

Tokugawa　徳川

Torii Ryūzō　鳥居龍蔵

Tsuboi Shōgorō　坪井正五郎

Uchida Ryōhei　内田良平

Watsuji Tetsurō　和辻哲郎

Yanagita Kunio　柳田國男

zaibatsu　財閥

Zenman fujin dantai rengōkai

　全満婦人団体連合会

Bibliography

Abbreviations

DMDY

    Manzhouguo Daodehui bianjike (Manzhouguo Morality Society editorial department), ed. *Disanjie Manzhouguo Daodehui daode jiangxi yulu* (Oral records of morality seminars of the Third Manzhouguo Morality Society). Xinjing: Manzhouguo Daodehui huijike, 1936.

DTB

    Datongbao (Great Unity Daily). Xinjing.

EJB

    Elunchunzu jianshi bianxiezu (Editorial committee of the Brief History of the Oroqen), ed. *Elunchunzu jianshi* (Brief history of the Oroqen). Huhehote: Neimenggu renmin chubanshe, 1983.

GWXSY

    Committee on Party History, Central Committee, Chinese Nationalist Party (KMT), ed. *Geming Wenxian: Xin Shenghuo yundongshi* (Revolutionary documents: Historical materials on the New Life movement). Vol. 68. Taipei: Zhongyang wenwu gongyingshe, 1976.

HZN

    Xingya zongjiao xiehui (Revive Asian Religions Association), ed. *Huabei zongjiao nianjian* (Yearbook of the religions of north China). Beiping: Xingyayuan Huabei lianluobu, 1941.

JG

    Jilinsheng gongshu xunling (Jilin provincial government order) 480.44. June 12, 1936; 06.95, June 29, 1936. Jilin Provincial Archives, Changchun.

JTB

    Jiaji tiaocha baogao/Kakei chōsa hōkoku (Household statistical survey reports). Compiled by Guowuyuan, Zongwuting tongjichu (General Affairs Board, Statistical Office). Xingjing: Kangde tushu yinshwa suo, 1935.

MDNJ

    Wanguo Daodehui Manzhouguo zonghui bianjike (Editorial department of the head office of the World Morality Society of Manchukuo), ed. *Manzhouguo Daodehui nianjian* (Yearbook of the Manzhouguo Morality Society). Xinjing: Wanguo Daodehui Manzhouguo zonghui bianjike, 1934.

MGFH

Manchukuo Guofang funüren hui (National Defense Women's Association). Dalian: Manchukuo Guofang funürenhui zongbenbu (Manchukuo National Defense Women's Association general headquarters), 1938–39.

MQX

Xinshenghuo zujin zonghui (New Life Promotion general committee), ed. *Minguo Ershisannian quanguo xinshenghuo yundong* (1934 National New Life movement). Nanjing: Xinshenghuo zujin zonghui, 1934.

MSSJ

Manzhouguo shehui shiye lianhehui (Manchukuo Federation of Social Enterprises), ed. *Manzhouguo shehui shiye jikan* (Manchukuo social welfare seasonal report). Vols. 1 (May) and 2 (September). Xinjing, 1934.

SHT

Nagoyashi hakubutsukan, ed. *Shin Hakubutsukan Taisei: Manshūkoku no hakubutsukan ga sengō Nihon ni tsutaeteiru koto* (The shape of the new museum: What the Manchukuo museum had to say to postwar Japan). Nagoya: Nagoyashi hakubutsukan, 1995.

SJHWZ

Shijie Hongwanzihui Zhonghua zonghui dangan (Archives of the central committee of the World Red Swastika Society, Republic of China). Second Historical Archive, Nanjing. Archive 257, cases 73, 86, 143.

SJSB

Shengjing Shibao (Shengjing Times). Changchun.

SSJYB

Shanghaishi shehuiju yewu baogao (Reports of the Shanghai Municipality Social Bureau on Enterprises and Activities). Shanghai, 1930; 1931; January–June 1932; January 1946.

WJYK

Wenjiaobu Yuekan (Monthly of the Ministry of Education and Culture). Xinjing: Wenjiaobu.

WWD

Wang Weizhengfu dangan (Archives of the puppet government of Wang Jingwei). Second Historical Archive, Nanjing. Archive 2018, cases 48, 69, 93, 107, 108, 113, 146; Archive 2013, cases 303, 764, 767, 775.

XSY

Xinshenghuo yundong (The New Life movement). Nanjing: Xinzhengyuan, xinwenju (Information bureau of the administrative yuan), 1947.

XYDB

Xin shenghuo yundong gaijin zonghui (General promotion committee of the New Life movement), ed. *Xinyun daobao* (New Life guidance bulletin). Nanjing, 1937.

ZDLSG

Wang Chengli, ed. *Zhongguo dongbei lunxian shisinianshi gangyao* (Compendium of the fourteen-year history of the occupation of China's Northeast). Beijing: Zhongguo dabaike quanshu chubanshe, 1991.

ZTJ

Zhongtongju baogao (Report of the Bureau of Investigation and Statistics, Central Committee, Chinese Nationalist Party). Second Historical Archive, Nanjing. Archive 11, cases 1442–448, 1480.

Sources

Acton, John, E. E. D. *Essays in the Liberal Interpretation of History: Selected Papers.* 1862. Edited by William H. McNeill. Chicago: University of Chicago Press, 1967.

Adas, Michael. "The Great War and the Decline of the Civilizing Mission." In *Autonomous Histories: Particular Truths*, edited by Laurie Sears, 101–21. Madison: University of Wisconsin Press, 1993.

Adelman, Jeremy, and Stephen Aron. "From Borderlands to Borders: Empires, Nation-States and the Peoples in Between in North American History." *American Historical Review* 104 (June 1999): 814–41.

Agamben, Giorgio. *Homo Sacer: Sovereign Power and Bare Life.* Translated by Daniel Heller-Roazen. Stanford: Stanford University Press, 1998.

Akamatsu Chijō and Akiba Takashi. *Manmō no minzoku to shūkyō* (Peoples and religions of Manchuria and Mongolia). Tokyo: n.p., 1939.

Alitto, Guy S. *The Last Confucian: Liang Shu-ming and the Chinese Dilemma of Modernity.* Berkeley: University of California Press, 1979.

Allen, Chizuko T. "Northeast Asia Centered around Korea: Ch'oe Namson's View of History." *Journal of Asian Studies* 49 (1990): 787–806.

Allen, J. Michael. "In the Beginning: National Origins and National Identity in Korea." Paper prepared for the conference, Korea's Minjung Movement: The Origins and Development of Populist Nationalism, Bloomington, Ind., 1989.

Alonso, Ana Maria. "Gender, Power, and Historical Memory: Discourses of Serrano Resistance." In *Feminists Theorize the Political*, edited by Judith Butler and Joan Scott, 404–25. New York: Routledge, 1992.

Althusser, Louis. "Ideology and Ideological State Apparatuses (Notes towards an Investigation)." In *Lenin and Philosophy, and Other Essays*, translated by Ben Brewster, 127–86. New York: Monthly Review Press, 1971.

Anderson, Benedict. *Imagined Communities: Reflections on the Origins and Spread of Nationalism.* London: Verso, 1991.

Andrew, Barry, Thomas Osborne, and Nikolas Rose, eds. *Foucault and Political Reason: Liberalism, Neo-liberalism and Rationalities of Government.* Chicago: University of Chicago Press, 1996.

Arendt, Hannah. *The Origins of Totalitarianism.* 1948. Reprint, New York: Harcourt Brace, 1973.

Arkush, R. David. *Fei Xiaotong and Sociology in Revolutionary China.* Cambridge, Mass.: Council on East Asian Studies, 1981.

Arrighi, Giovanni. *The Long Twentieth Century: Money, Power, and the Origins of Our Times.* New York: Verso, 1994.

Arseniev, V. K. *Dersu the Trapper.* Translated by Malcolm Burr. 1941. Reprint, New York: McPherson, 1996.

Atwood, Christopher P. *Young Mongols and Vigilantes in Inner Mongolia's Interregnum Decades, 1911–1931.* Leiden: Brill, forthcoming.

Bai Changqing. Preface to *Dongbei xiandai wenxue daxi, 1919–1949* (Northeast Modern Literature Series), edited by Zhang Yumao, 2:1–17. Shenyang: Shenyang chubanshe, 1996.

Bakhtin, M. M. *Speech Genres and Other Late Essays.* Translated by Vern W. McGee. Austin: University of Texas Press, 1986.

Balibar, Etienne. "The Nation Form: History and Ideology." In *Race, Nation, Class: Ambiguous Identities,* edited by Etienne Balibar and Immanuel Wallerstein, 86–106. London: Verso, 1991.

Barclay, Paul. "An Historian among the Anthropologists: Inō Kanori and the Legacy of Japanese Ethnography in Taiwan," *Japanese Studies* 21 (2001): 117–37.

———. "A Tale of Two Meiji Ethnologists: Inō Kanori and Torii Ryūzō in Taiwan." Paper presented to the Association of Asian Studies, San Diego, Calif., 2000.

Barraclough, Geoffrey. *An Introduction to Contemporary History.* Hammondsworth, England: Penguin, 1964.

Bartelson, Jens. *A Genealogy of Sovereignty.* Cambridge: Cambridge University Press, 1995.

Beahan, Charlotte L. "Feminism and Nationalism in the Chinese Women's Press, 1902–1911." *Modern China* 1 (1975): 379–416.

Bechert, Heinz. "Buddhist Revival in East and West." In *The World of Buddhism: Buddhist Nuns and Monks in Society and Culture,* edited by Heinz Bechert and Richard Gombrich, 273–85. London: Thames and Hudson, 1984.

Befu, Harumi. "Nationalism and *Nihonjinron.*" In *Cultural Nationalism in East Asia: Representation and Identity,* edited by Harumi Befu, 107–38. Berkeley: University of California Press, 1993.

Bentley, Jerry H. *Shapes of World History in Twentieth Century Scholarship.* Washington, D.C.: American Historical Association, 1996.

Bhabha, Homi K. *The Location of Culture.* London: Routledge, 1994.

"Bianbao fuwu gongzuo" (Service among our siblings in the border regions). 1944. In *GWXSY,* 298–303.

Boli, John, and George M. Thomas, eds. *Constructing World Culture: International Nongovernmental Organizations since 1875.* Stanford: Stanford University Press, 1999.

Boli-Bennet, John, and John W. Meyer. "The Ideology of Childhood and the State: Rules Distinguishing Children in National Constitutions, 1870–1970." *American Sociological Review* 43 (1978): 797–812.

Bosco, Joseph. "Yiguan Dao: 'Heterodoxy' and Popular Religion in Taiwan." In *The Other Taiwan: 1945 to the Present,* edited by Murray Rubinstein, 423–44. Armonk, N.Y.: Sharpe, 1994.

Brown, Carolyn T. "Woman as Trope: Gender and Power in Lu Xun's 'Soap.' " In *Gender Politics in Modern China,* edited by Tani E. Barlow, 74–89. Durham, N.C.: Duke University Press, 1993.

Brubaker, Rogers. *Nationalism Reframed: Nationhood and the National Question in the New Europe.* Cambridge: Cambridge University Press, 1996.

Buck, David D. "Railway City and National Capital: Two Faces of the Modern in Chang-chun." In *Remaking the Chinese City: Modernity and National Identity, 1900–1950*, edited by Joseph Esherick, 65–89. Honolulu, University of Hawai Press, 2000.

Bunzl, Matti. "Franz Boas and the Humboldtian Tradition: From *Volksgeist* and *National-charakter* to an Anthropological Concept of Culture." In *Volksgeist as Method and Ethic: Essays on Boasian Ethnography and the German Anthropological Tradition*, edited by George W. Stocking Jr., 17–78. Madison: University of Wisconsin Press, 1996.

Byington, Mark E. "Claiming the Koguryo Heritage: Territorial Issues in the Management of Koguryo Archaelogical Sites in Northeast China." Paper presented at the Second World-wide Conference of the Society for East Asian Archaeology, Durham, England, 2000.

Cai Yuanpei. "Minzuxueshang zhi jinhuaguan" (The evolutionary view in ethnology). 1933. In *Cai Yuanpei minzuxue lunzhu* (Cai Yuanpei discourses on ethnology), edited by Zhong-guo Minzu Xuehui, 17–22. Taipei: Zhonghua Shuju, 1962.

———. "Shehuixue yu minzuxue" (Sociology and ethnology). 1930. In *Cai Yuanpei min-zuxue lunzhu* (Cai Yuanpei discourses on ethnology), edited by Zhongguo Minzu Xuehui, 12–16. Taipei: Zhonghua Shuju, 1962.

———. "Shuo minzuxue" (On ethnology). 1926. In *Cai Yuanpei minzuxue lunzhu* (Cai Yuanpei discourses on ethnology), edited by Zhongguo Minzu Xuehui, 1–11. Taipei: Zhonghua Shuju, 1962.

Carlitz, Katherine. "Desire, Danger, and the Body: Stories of Women's Virtue in Late Ming China." In *Engendering China: Women, Culture and the State*, edited by Christina Gilmar-tin et al., 101–24. Cambridge: Harvard University Press, 1994.

Carter, James H. *Creating a Chinese Harbin: Nationalism in an International City, 1916–1932*. Ithaca: Cornell University Press, 2002

Chan, Wing-tsit. *Religious Trends in Modern China*. New York: Columbia University Press, 1953.

Chaoyang xianzhi (Chaoyang County Gazetteer). Compiled by Zhou Tiejing and Sun Qing-wei. 1930.

Chatterjee, Partha. *The Nation and Its Fragments: Colonial and Postcolonial Histories*. Princeton: Princeton University Press, 1993.

Chen Lifu. "Xin shenghuo yu minsheng shiguan" (New Life and the Minsheng conception of history). In *GWXSY*, 128–46.

Chen Shiwei. "Legitimizing the State: Politics and the Founding of Academica Sinica in 1927." *Papers on Chinese History* 6 (1997): 23–41.

Chen Yin. "'Xiaoshuo youjihua' de jieshi" (Explanation of the conversion of fiction into travel writing). *Xinyaxiya* 1, no. 6 (1931): 151–52.

Cheng, Weikun. "Going Public through Education: Female Reformers and Girls' Schools in Late Qing Beijing." *Late Imperial China* 21 (2000): 107–44.

Cheung, Siu-woo. "Subject and Representation: Identity Politics in Southeast Guizhou." Ph.D. diss., University of Washington, Seattle, 1996.

Chianbu keisatsushi (Law and Order Ministry, Police Department), ed. *Kōmin* (Citizen). Shinkyō: Manshūkoku tosho kabushiki gaisha, 1940.

Chiang Kai-shek. *China's Destiny*. Translated by Wang Chung-hui. New York: Macmillan, 1947.

Chiang Kai-shek (Huizhang). "Xinshenghuo yundong qizhounian jinian xunci" (Exhortation speech commemorating the seventh anniversary of the New Life movement). 1940. In *GWXSY*, 75–84.

Chow, Kai-wing. *The Rise of Confucian Ritualism in Late Imperial China: Ethics, Classics, and Lineage Discourse.* Stanford: Stanford University Press, 1994.

Chow, Rey. *Primitive Passions: Visuality, Sexuality, Ethnography, and Contemporary Chinese Cinema.* New York: Columbia University Press, 1995.

Christy, Alan S. "Representing the Rural: Place as Method in the Formation of Japanese Native Ethnology, 1910–1945." Ph.D. diss., University of Chicago, 1997.

Clarke, M. Desmond, and Charles Jones, eds. *The Right of Nations: Nations and Nationalism in a Changing World.* New York: St. Martin's, 1999.

Clausen, Soren, and Stig Thogersen. *The Making of a Chinese City: History and Historiography in Harbin.* New York: Sharpe, 1996.

Committee on Party History, Central Committee, Chinese Communist Party (KMT), ed. *Geming Wenxian: Xin Shenghuo yundongshi* (Revolutionary documents: Historical materials on the New Life movement). Vol. 68. Taipei: Zhongyang wenwu gongyingshe, 1976.

Cooper, Frederick, and Ann Laura Stoler. "Between Metropole and Colony: Rethinking a Research Agenda." In *Tensions of Empire: Colonial Cultures in a Bourgeois World,* edited by Frederick Cooper and Ann Laura Stoler, 1–56. Berkeley: University of California Press, 1997.

Crowley, James B. *Japan's Quest for Autonomy: National Security and Foreign Policy, 1930–1938.* Princeton: Princeton University Press, 1966.

Cumings, Bruce. "Colonial Formations and Deformations: Korea, Taiwan and Vietnam." In *Parallax Visions: Making Sense of American–East Asian Relations at the End of the Century,* 69–94. Durham, N.C.: Duke University Press, 1999.

Dan Di. "Guanyu nuhua sixiang ji weiman zuojia" (Regarding slavish thought and writers in puppet Manchukuo). *Dongbei Wenxue* 1, no. 2 (1946): 6–8.

———. "Xiezu" (Blood lineage). *Dongbei Wenxue* 1, no. 1 (1945): 4–31.

Daruvala, Susan. *Zhou Zuoren and an Alternative Chinese Response to Modernity.* Cambridge: Harvard University Press, 2000.

Deal, David M. "Policy towards Ethnic Minorities in Southwest China, 1927–1965." In *Nationalism and the Crises of Ethnic Minorities in Asia,* edited by Tai S. Kang, 33–40. Westport, Conn.: Greenwood, 1979.

Denis-Shelton, Marie. "Primitive Self: Colonial Impulses in Michel Leiris's 'L'Afrique fantome.'" In *Prehistories of the Future: The Primitivist Project and the Culture of Modernism,* edited by Elazar Barkan and Ronald Bush, 326–38. Stanford: Stanford University Press, 1995.

Derrida, Jacques. "Ousia and Gramme: Note on a Note from *Being and Time.*" In *Margins of Philosophy,* translated by Alan Bass, 29–67. Chicago: University of Chicago Press, 1982.

Deutsch, Karl W. "Social Mobilization and Political Development." *American Political Science Review* 55 (1961): 493–514.

Diamond, Norma. "Women under Kuomintang Rule: Variations on the Feminine Mystique." *Modern China* 1 (1975): 3–45.

Dikötter, Frank. *The Discourse of Race in Modern China.* Stanford: Stanford University Press, 1992.

Dirlik, Arif. "The Ideological Foundations of the New Life Movement: A Study in Counterrevolution." *Journal of Asian Studies* 34 (August 1975): 945–80.

Dongbei fangzhi renwu zhuanji ziliao suoyin: Liaoning juan (Index of biographical materials from Northeast local gazetteers: Liaoning volume). Shenyang: Liaoningsheng chubanshe, 1991.

Dower, John W. *War without Mercy: Race and Power in the Pacific War*. New York: Pantheon, 1986.

Duara, Prasenjit. "The Regime of Authenticity: Timelessness, Gender, and National History in Modern China." *History and Theory* 37 (October 1998): 287–308.

———. *Rescuing History from the Nation: Questioning Narratives of Modern China*. Chicago: University of Chicago Press, 1995.

———. "Transnationalism and the Challenge to National Histories." In *Rethinking American History in a Global Age*, edited by Thomas Bender, 25–46. Berkeley: University of California Press, 2002.

———. "Transnationalism and the Predicament of Sovereignty, China, 1900–1945." *American Historical Review* 102 (October 1997): 1030–51.

Duus, Peter, Ramon H. Myers, and Mark Peattie, eds. *The Japanese Wartime Empire, 1931–1945*. Princeton: Princeton University Press, 1996.

Edmonds, Richard Louis. "Northern Frontiers of Qing China and Tokugawa Japan: A Comparative Study of Frontier Policy." Research Paper, no. 213. Chicago: University of Chicago, Department of Geography, 1985. ,.

Egami Namio. "The Formation of the People and the Origin of the State in Japan." *Memoirs of the Research Department of the Tōyō Bunko*, no. 23 (1964): 34–70.

Elias, Norbert. *The Civilizing Process: The Development of Manners*. Translated by Edmund Jephcott. New York: Urizen, 1978.

Elliott, Mark C. "The Limits of Tartary: Manchuria in Imperial and National Geographies." *Journal of Asian Studies* 59 (August 2000): 603–47.

———. *The Manchu Way: The Eight Banners and Ethnic Identity in Late Imperial China*. Stanford: Stanford University Press, 2001.

Elunchunzu jianshi bianxiezu (Editorial committee of the brief history of the Oroqen), ed. *Elunchunzu jianshi* (Brief history of the Oroqen). Huhehote: Neimenggu renmin chubanshe, 1983.

Elvin, Mark. "Female Virtue and the State in China." *Past and Present* 104 (1984): 111–52.

Fabian, Johannes. *Time and the Other: How Anthropology Makes Its Object*. New York: Columbia University Press, 1983.

Falundafa jianjie (Introduction to Falungong). Online at http://falundafa.org (accessed January 30, 2000).

Fang Qiuwei. *Feichang shiqizhi bianwu* (Frontier affairs during the emergency period). Hong Kong: Zhonghua shuju, 1937–38.

Febvre, Lucien P. V. "Civilisation: Evolution of a Word and a Group of Ideas." In *A New Kind of History and Other Essays*, edited by Peter Burke, 219–57. New York: Harper and Row, 1973.

Fei Xiaotong. "Special Characteristics of Rural Society." In *From the Soil: The Foundations of Chinese Society—A Translation of Fei Xiaotong's Xiangtu Zhongguo*. With an introduction and epilogue by Gary G. Hamilton and Wang Zheng, 37–44. Berkeley: University of California Press, 1992.

———. "Xiangtu bense." In *Xiangtu Zhongguo*. 1–7. Shanghai: Guanchashe, 1947.

Feng Jiasheng. "Wode yanjiu dongbei shidi de jihua" (My research plan of the history and geography of the Northeast) *Yugong* 1, no. 10 (1934) 2–6.

Feng Weiqun. "'Wenyi zhidao gangyao' chulong yihou" (After the appearance of the "Summary of Guidelines to Art and Literature"). In *Weiman wenhua*, edited by Sun Bang et al.,

13–20. Weiman shiliao congshu (Series of Manchukuo historical materials). Changchun: Jilin renmin chubanshe, 1993.

Ferrara, Alessandro. *Modernity and Authenticity: A Study of the Social and Ethical Thought of Jean-Jacques Rousseau.* Albany: State University of New York Press, 1993.

Fitzgerald, John. *Awakening China: Politics, Culture, and Class in the Nationalist Revolution.* Stanford: Stanford University Press, 1996.

Fogel, Joshua. *Politics and Sinology: The Case of Naitō Konan (1866–1934).* Cambridge: Harvard University Press, 1984.

Foucault, Michel. "An Ethics of Pleasure." In *Foucault Live*, edited by S. Lotringer, 257–76. New York: Semiotext(e), 1989.

———. "Governmentality." In *The Foucault Effect: Studies in Governmentality*, edited by Graham Burchell, Colin Gordon, and Peter Miller, 87–104. Chicago: University of Chicago Press, 1991.

———. *The History of Sexuality.* Vol. 1, *An Introduction.* New York: Pantheon, 1978.

———. "The Political Technology of Individuals." In *Technologies of the Self: A Seminar with Michel Foucault*, edited by Luther H. Martin, Huck Gutman, and Patrick H. Hutton, 145–162. Amherst: University of Massachusetts Press, 1988.

———. *The Use of Pleasure.* Vol. 2 of *The History of Sexuality.* Translated by Robert Hurley. New York: Vintage, 1990.

Freeman, Michael. "The Right to National Self-Determination." In *The Right of Nations: Nations and Nationalism in a Changing World*, edited by M. Desmond Clarke and Charles Jones, 45–64. New York: St. Martin's, 1999.

Fu Sinian. *Dongbei Shigang* (Outline of Northeastern History). 1932. In *The Complete Works of Fu Sinian.* Vol. 5. Taipei: Lianjing Press, 1980.

Fu Zhong, ed. *Yiguandao Lishi* (History of the Yiguandao). Taipei: Zhengyi shanshu, 1997.

Fujiansheng xinyunhui (Fujian province New Life committee). "Fujian Lianjiang, Jiangyue xian hunsang lisu tiaocha" (Survey of wedding and funeral customs in Fujian's Lianjiang and Jiangyue counties). In *XYDB*, 5 and 6 (April 1937): 58–59.

Fujitani, Takashi. "Inventing, Forgetting, Remembering: Toward a Historical Ethnography of the Nation-State." In *Cultural Nationalism in East Asia: Representation and Identity*, edited by Harumi Befu, 77–106. Berkeley: University of California Press, 1993.

Fujiwara Kazuo. "Hōten ni okeru shokuba kōjō undō no genjō" (The circumstances of the workplace labor movement in Fengtian [Mukden]). *Kyōwa undo* 5, no. 9 (September 1943): 43–61.

Fujiyama Kazuo. *Manshū no shinrin to bunka.* Shinkyō: Tōhō Kokumin Bunkō, 1937.

Fukui Naohide. "Yanagita Kunio no Ajia ninshiki" (Yanagita Kunio's view of Asia). In *Kindai Nihon no Ajia ninshiki* (Modern Japan's perceptions of Asia), edited by Furuya Tetsuo, 469–508. Kyoto: Kyoto Daigaku Jinbun Kagaku Kenkyūjo, 1994.

Fukunaga Tadashi. *Manshūkoku no minzoku mondai* (The nationality question of Manchukuo). Shinkyō: Manshō Fuzanbō, 1944.

"Funü xinyun gongzuo gaixu" (General statement of the work of women's new life) (1944). In *GWXSY*, 303–10.

Furth, Charlotte. "The Patriarch's Legacy: Household Instructions and the Transmission of Orthodox Values." In *Orthodoxy in Late Imperial China*, edited by Kwang-ching Liu, 187–211. Berkeley: University of California Press, 1990.

———, ed. *The Limits of Change: Essays on Conservative Alternatives in Republican China.* Cambridge: Harvard University Press, 1976.

Furuya Tetsuo, ed. *Kindai Nihon no Ajia Ninshiki* (Modern Japan's perception of Asia). Kyoto: Jinbun kagaku kenkyūjo, 1994.

Gardener, William O. "Colonialism and the Avant-Garde: Kitagawa Fuyuhiko's Manchurian Railway." *Stanford Humanities Review* 7 (1999): 12–21.

Garon, Sheldon. *Molding Japanese Minds: The State in Everyday Life*. Princeton: Princeton University Press, 1997.

———. "Women's Groups and the Japanese State: Contending Approaches to Political Integration, 1890–1945." *Journal of Japanese Studies* 19 (1993): 5–41, 70–71.

Ge Suicheng. *Xiangtu Dili Yanjiufa* (The research methods of community geography). Shanghai: Zhonghua shuju, 1939.

Geertz, Clifford. *The Interpretation of Cultures*. New York: Basic Books, 1973.

Gellner, Ernest. *Nations and Nationalism*. Ithaca: Cornell University Press, 1983.

Gerth, Karl. *Nationalizing Consumer Culture in Modern China*. Cambridge: Harvard University Asia Center, forthcoming.

Geyer, Dietrich. "Modern Imperialism? The Tsarist and the Soviet Examples." In *Imperialism and After: Continuities and Discontinuities*, edited by Wolfgang G. Mommsen and Jurgen Osterhammel, 48–62. London: Allen and Unwin, 1986.

Giddens, Anthony. *The Nation-State and Violence*. Vol. 2 of *A Contemporary Critique of Historical Materialism*. Berkeley: University of California Press, 1987.

Glahn, Richard Von. "The Enchantment of Wealth: The God Wutong in the Social History of Jiangnan." *Harvard Journal of Asiatic Studies* 51 (1991): 651–714.

Gluck, Carol. *Japan's Modern Myths: Ideology in the Late Meiji Period*. Princeton: Princeton University Press, 1985.

Godlewska, Anne. "Napoleon's Geographers (1797–1815): Imperialists and Soldiers of Modernity." In *Geography and Empire*, edited by Anne Godlewska and Neil Smith, 31–53. Oxford: Blackwell, 1994.

Godlewska, Anne, and Neil Smith, eds. *Geography and Empire*. Oxford: Blackwell, 1994.

Gong, Gerrit W. *The Standard of "Civilization" in International Society*. Oxford: Clarendon, 1984.

Goodman, Bryna. *Native Place, City, and Nation: Regional Networks and Identities*. Berkeley: University of California Press, 1995.

Gottschang, Thomas. "Economic Change, Disasters, and Migration: The Historical Case of Manchuria." *Economic Development and Cultural Change* 35 (1987): 461–90.

Grieder, Jerome B. *Intellectuals and the State in Modern China*. New York: Free Press, 1981.

Gu Jiegang. "Qin–Han tongyide youlai he zhanguoren duiyu shijiede xiangxiang" (The origins of Qin–Han unification and the image of the world during the Warring States). 1926. In *Gushibian*, edited by Gu Jiegang, vol. 2, no.1, 1–10. Beijing: Pu she, 1930.

Gu Jinshi, ed. "Kangzhanyilai woguo minzuxue xuanmu." *Minzuxue Yanjiu jikan* 4 (1944): 129–69.

Guangdongsheng xinyunhui (Guangdong province New Life committee). "Guangdongsheng Renhua deng xian lisu tiaocha" (Survey of customs in Guangdong's Renhua and other counties). In *XYDB*, 5 and 6 (April 1937): 60–64.

Guldin, Gregory E. *The Saga of Anthropology in China: From Malinowski to Moscow to Mao*. New York: Sharpe, 1994.

Han Suk-jung. "The Problem of Sovereignty: Manchukuo, 1932–1937." Forthcoming in *Positions*.

———. "Puppet Sovereignty: The State Effect of Manchukuo, from 1932 to 1936." Ph.D. diss., University of Chicago, 1995.

———. "Those Who Imitated the Colonizers: The Influence of State-Making from Manchukuo to South Korea." Paper prepared for the conference, Japanese Colonialism in Manchuria, University of California at Los Angeles, January 2001.

Hanyu Dacidian bianji weiyuanhui (Hanyu Dacidian editorial committee), ed. *Hanyu Dacidian*. Shanghai: Sanlian chuban, 1987.

Harootunian, H. D. "Disciplinizing Native Knowledge and Producing Place: Yanagita Kunio, Origuchi Shinobu, Takata Yasuma." In *Culture and Identity: Japanese Intellectuals during the Interwar Years*, edited by J. Thomas Rimer, 99–132. Princeton: Princeton University Press, 1988.

Hasegawa Yūichi. "Taishō chūki tairiku kokka e no imeiji—'Daikōraikoku' (Dagaoli, Koryo) kōsō to sono shūhen" (The image of a mainland nation in the mid-Taishō era: The conception of the "Great Koryo nation" and the area around it). *Kokusai Seiji* 71 (1982): 93–108.

Hashikawa, Bunso. "Japanese Perspectives on Asia: From Dissociation to Coprosperity." In *The Chinese and the Japanese: Essays in Political and Cultural Interactions*, edited by Akira Iriye, 331–41. Princeton: Princeton University Press, 1980.

Hatada Takashi. *Chūgoku sonraku to kyōdōtai riron* (Chinese villages and the theory of village community). Tokyo: Iwanami shoten, 1976.

He Guanzhou. "You Qian zaji" (Random notes of travels in Guizhou). *Xinyaxiya* 5, no. 5 (1933): 135–49; 5, no. 6 (1933): 133–35.

He Liankai. "Cai Jiemin xiansheng duiyu minzuxuezhi gongxian" (The contributions of Mr. Cai Yuanpei to ethnology) (1959). Introduction to *Cai Yuanpei minzuxue lunzhu* (Cai Yuanpei discourses on ethnology), edited by Zhongguo minzu xuehui, 1–19. Taipei: Zhonghua Shuju, 1962.

———. "Jieshao Zhongguo minzuxuede wenxian yu gongzuo" (Introduction to materials and works in Chinese ethnology). In *Minzuwenhua yanjiu* (Research of nationality cultures), selected by He Liankai. N.p., 1951.

———. "Sishinianlaizhi Zhongguo minzuxue" (Forty years of Ethnology in China). *Zhongguo minzuxuebao* 1 (1955): 1–24.

Hechter, Michael. *Internal Colonialism: The Celtic Fringe in British National Development, 1536–1966*. Berkeley: University of California Press, 1975.

Hegel, Georg W. F. *The Philosophy of History*. Translated by J. Sibree. 1837. Reprint, New York: Dover, 1956.

Hinsley, F. H. *Sovereignty*. Cambridge: Cambridge University Press, 1986.

Hirano, Kenichiro. "The Japanese in Manchuria, 1906–1931: A Study of the Historical Background of Manchukuo." Ph.D. diss., Harvard University, 1983.

Hobsbawm, Eric. *Nations and Nationalism since 1780*. Cambridge: Cambridge University Press, 1990.

Hofstadter, Richard. *Social Darwinism in American Thought*. Boston: Beacon, 1955.

Holston, James. "Alternative Modernities: Statecraft and Religious Imagination in the Valley of the Dawn." *American Ethnologist* 26 (August 1999): 605–31.

Hoshina Kiyoji. *Josei yo Manshū yo* (To women and Manchuria). Dairen: Dairen Fujin Taimuzu sha, 1931–34.

Howland, Douglas. *Borders of Chinese Civilization: Geography and History at Empire's End*. Durham, N.C.: Duke University Press, 1996.

Hua Min. "Guangfu yu wenren" (Recovery and writers). *Dongbei Wenxue* 1, no. 2 (1946): 13–17.

Hua Qiyun. *Manmeng wenti* (The problem of Manchuria and Mongolia). Shanghai: Dadong shuju, 1931.

Huang Wanhua. "Liang Shanding he tade 'Lüse de Gu'" (Liang Shanding and his *Green Valley*). In *Dongbei wenxue yanjiu shiliao* (Northeast literature research materials), vol. 5. Harbin: Harbin wenxueyuan, 1986.

———. Preface to *Dongbei xiandai wenxue daxi, 1919–1949* (Modern literature of the Northeast, 1919–1949), edited by Zhang Yumao, 11:1–19. Shenyang: Shenyang chuban-'she, 1996.

Huang Wenshan. "Minzuxue yu Zhongguo minzu yanjiu" (Ethnology and the study of China's peoples). *Minzuxue Yanjiu jikan* 1 (1936): 1–26.

Humphrey, Caroline. "Shamanic Practices and the State in Northern Asia: Views from the Center and Periphery." In *Shamanism, History and the State*, edited by Nicholas Thomas and Caroline Humphrey, 191–228. Ann Arbor: University of Michigan Press, 1994.

Huntington, Samuel. "The Clash of Civilizations?" *Foreign Affairs* 72 (1993): 22–49.

Inaba Kunzan. *Manshū Hattatsushi* (The history of the development of Manchuria). Tokyo: Osaka yagō shuppanbu, 1918.

Ishikawa Shinobu, ed. *Zenman fujin dantai rengōkai hōkokusho* (Report of the All Manchukuo Women's Federation). Dairen: Zenman fujin dantai rengōkai, 1933.

Ishikawa Yoshihiro. "Bunmei, bunka, soshite Ryō Keichō" (Civilization, culture, and Liang Qichao). Unpublished manuscript, 1995.

———. "Tōzai bunmeiron to Nihon no rondan" (The discourse of East–West civilization and the Sino-Japanese world of letters). In *Kindai Nihon no Ajia ninshiki* (Modern Japan's perceptions of Asia), edited by Furuya Tetsuo, 395–432. Kyoto: Kyōtō Daigaku Jinbun Kagaku Kenkyūjo, 1994.

Ito Takeo. *Life Along the South Manchurian Railway: The Memoirs of Ito Takeo*. Translated by Joshua A. Fogel. Armonk, N.Y.: Sharpe, 1988.

Ivy, Marilyn. *Discourses of the Vanishing: Modernity, Phantasm, Japan*. Chicago: University of Chicago Press, 1995.

James, H. E. M. *The Long White Mountain, or Journey into Manchuria*. London: Longmans, Green, 1888.

Janelli, Roger L. "The Origins of Korean Folklore Scholarship." *Journal of American Folklore* 99 (1986): 24–49.

Jiang Zhongzheng (Chiang Kai-shek). *Zhongguozhi mingyun* (China's destiny). N.p.: Zhengzhong shuju, 1943.

Jie Xueshi. "Riwei shiqide wenhua tongzhi zhengce" (Cultural control policy in the period of Manchukuo). In *Dongbei lunxian shiqi wenxue* (Literature of the occupation period in the Northeast), edited by Feng Weiqun et al., 182–98. Shenyang: Shenyang chubanshe, 1992.

Jin Hua. "Bushi pian" (Not literature). *Dongbei Wenxue* 1, no. 2 (1946): 10–12.

Jin Qisan. "Woguo nanbei zhi dili guandian" (Geographical perspectives on the north and south of our nation). *Fangzhi Yuekan* 8 (1935): 7–8.

Jinan Daoyuan, ed. *Li Daodayuan yishilu* (Record of the virtuous events of the establishment of the Great Dao Yuan). Jinan, 1932.

Jones, F. C. *Manchuria since 1931*. New York: Oxford University Press, 1949.

Judge, Joan. "Talent, Virtue, and the Nation: Chinese Nationalisms and Female Subjectivities in the Early Twentieth Century." *American Historical Review* 106 (June 2001): 765–803.

Kang Baiqing. "Du Wang jun Zhuomin daxue buyi nannü tongxiao lun shangdui" (A response to Mr. Wang Zhuomin's essay on the inappropriateness of coeducation in the universities). *Funü zazhi* 4 (1918): 1–4.

Kang Chao. *The Economic Development of Manchuria: The Rise of a Frontier Economy.* Ann Arbor: Center for Chinese Studies, 1982.

Karmel, Solomon, M. "Ethnic Nationalism in Mainland China." In *Asian Nationalism: China, Taiwan, Japan, India, Pakistan, Indonesia, The Philippines,* edited by Michael Leifer, 38–62. New York: Routledge, 2000.

Kasza, Gregory J. *The Conscription Society: Administered Mass Organization.* New Haven: Yale University Press, 1995.

Kawamura Minato. *"Daitōa minzokugaku" no kyojitsu* (The truths and falsehoods of "Great East Asian folklore"). Tokyo: Kōdansha, 1996.

———. *Manshū Hōkai: "Daitōa bungaku" to sakkatachi* (The collapse of Manchukuo: Writers and "Greater East Asia literature"). Tokyo: Bungei shunjū, 1998.

Kelly, John D. "Diaspora and World War, Blood and Nation in Fiji and Hawai'i." *Public Culture* 7 (1995): 475–98.

Ketelaar, James E. *Of Heretics and Martyrs in Meiji Japan: Buddhism and Its Persecution.* Princeton: Princeton University Press, 1990.

Kirby, William C. *Germany and Republican China.* Stanford: Stanford University Press, 1984.

Kishimoto Mio. "'Fengsu' to Jidaikan—Minmatsu Shinsho no keiseironsha kara mita Sō, Gen, Minsho" (Chinese history in *"fengsu"* perspective: The Song-Yuan-Ming transition and statecraft discourse in the sixteenth century). Paper presented at the Song-Yuan-Ming Transition in Chinese History Conference, Lake Arrowhead, Calif., June 5–11, 1997.

Kleeman, Faye Yuan. "Mysticism and Corporeality: Re-envisioning Manchuria in a Postcolonial Japan." Paper presented at the conference, Contemporary Japanese Popular and Mass Culture, Montreal, Canada, 1999.

Ko, Dorothy. *Teachers of the Inner Chambers: Women and Culture in Seventeenth-Century China.* Stanford: Stanford University Press, 1994.

Kobayashi Hideo. *"Nihon kabushiki gaisha" o tsukutta otoko: Miyazaki Masayoshi no shōgai* (The man who created "Japan, Inc.": The career of Miyazaki Masayoshi). Tokyo: Shōgakkan, 1995.

Koiso Kuniaki. "Zenman fujin dantai rengōkai kai'in shoshi ni tsugeru no sho" (Letter to all our sisters of the All Manchukuo Women's Federation). In *Zenman fujin dantai rengōkai hōkokusho* (Report of the All Manchukuo Women's Federation), edited by Ishikawa Shinobu, 5–7. Dairen: Zenman fujin dantai rengōkai, 1933.

Komagome Takeshi. *Shokuminchi Teikoku Nippon no Bunka Tōgō* (The cultural integration of the Japanese colonial empire). Tokyo: Iwanami Shoten, 1996.

Konoye, Fumimaro. "Manchoukuo, Precursor of Asiatic Renaissance and the Government by *Wang-tao* (Kingly Way) based on Theocracy." *Contemporary Manchuria* 2 (July 1937): 1–17.

Koselleck, Reinhart. *Futures Past: On the Semantics of Historical Time.* Translated by Keith Tribe. Cambridge: MIT Press, 1985.

Krasner, Stephen D. "Organized Hypocrisy in Nineteenth Century East Asia." *International Relations of the Asia-Pacific* 1 (2001).

Landes, Joan. *Women and the Public Sphere in the Age of the French Revolution.* Ithaca: Cornell University Press, 1988.

Laski, Harold J. *The Foundations of Sovereignty and Other Essays.* 1921. Reprint, Freeport, N.Y.: Books for Libraries, 1968.

Lattimore, Owen. *Manchuria: Cradle of Conflict.* New York: Macmillan, 1935.

League of Nations Commission of Enquiry on Manchuria [Lytton Commission]. *The Far Eastern Problem: Official Texts and Summary of the Lytton Report.* Worcester, Mass.: New York Carnegie Endowment for International Peace, Division of Intercourse and Education, 1933.

Lee Chong-sik. *Counterinsurgency in Manchuria: The Japanese Experience, 1931–1940.* Santa Monica, Calif.: Rand Corporation, 1967.

———. *Revolutionary Struggle in Manchuria: Chinese Communism and Soviet Interest, 1922– 1945.* Berkeley: University of California Press, 1983.

Lee, Robert H. G. *The Manchurian Frontier in Ch'ing History.* Cambridge: Harvard University Press, 1970.

Lefebvre, Henri. *The Production of Space.* Translated by Donald Nicholson-Smith. Oxford: Blackwell, 1992.

Levenson, Joseph R. "The Province, the Nation, and the World: The Problem of Chinese Identity." In *Approaches to Modern Chinese History,* edited by Albert Feuerwerker et al., 268–88. Berkeley: University of California Press, 1967.

Levin, M. G. *Ethnic Origins of the Peoples of Northeastern Asia.* Arctic Institute of North America Translations from Russian Sources, no. 3. Toronto: University of Toronto Press, 1972.

Li Changdan. "Dongbei yuanshi minzu he zhongguo benbuminzu zai renzhongshangde guanxi" (Racial relationships between the primitive peoples of the Northeast and the peoples of China proper). *Xinyaxiya* 11, no. 4 (1936): 31–36.

Li, Lincoln. *The China Factor in Modern Japanese Thought: The Case of Tachibana Shiraki, 1891–1945.* Albany: State University of New York Press, 1996.

Li Shiyu. *Xianzai Huabei mimi zongjiao* (Secret religions in north China today). 1948. Reprint, Taipei: Guding shuwu, 1975.

Li Youning and Zhang Yufa, eds. *Jindai Zhongguo nuquan yundong shiliao 1842–1911* (Documents on feminist movements in modern China, 1842–1911). Vols. 1 and 2. Taipei: Zhuanji wenxueshe, 1975.

Liang Shanding. *Lüsede Gu* (Green valley). 1942. Reprint, Shenyang: Chunfeng Wenyi chubanshe, 1987.

———. "Wenxuede guxiang" (The home of literature). In *Dongbei xiandai wenxue shiliao* (Historical materials from modern literature of the Northeast), 2:93–99. Shenyang: Liaoning shehui kexueyuan, 1980.

Lin Anwu. "Yin dao yi li jiao—yi Wang Fengyi 'shierzi xinchuan' wei gaixin zhankai" (Establishing "the Way" as religion: Explorations centered upon Wang Fengyi's "twelve character teachings"). In *Zhonghua minzu zongjiao xueshu huiyi lunwen fabiao* (Publication of the Conference on the Study of Chinese Religion), 11–19. Taipei: n.p., 1989.

Ling Chunsheng. *Songhuajiang xiayoude Hezhezu* (The Hezhe people downstream on the Sunghua River). Nanjing: Guoli zhongyang yanjiuyuan lishi yuyan yanjiusuo, 1934.

Liu, Lydia. "The Female Body and Nationalist Discourse: The Field of Life and Death Revisited." In *Scattered Hegemonies: Postmodernity and Transnational Feminist Practices,* edited by Inderpal Grewal and Caren Kaplan, 37–62. Minneapolis: University of Minnesota Press, 1995.

———. *Translingual Practice: Literature, National Culture, and Translated Modernity, China, 1900–1937*. Stanford: Stanford University Press, 1995.

———, ed. *Tokens of Exchange: The Problem of Translation in Global Circulations*. Durham, N.C.: Duke University Press, 1999.

Liu Xiaoyuan. "The Chinese Communist Party and the 'Nationality Question,' 1921–1945." Unpublished paper, 1999.

———. "The Kuomintang and the 'Mongolian Question' in the Chinese Civil War, 1945–1949." *Inner Asia* 1 (1999): 169–94.

Loya, Thomas A., and John Boli. "Standardization in the World Polity: Technical Rationality over Power." In *Constructing World Culture: International Nongovernmental Organizations since 1875*, edited by John Boli and George M. Thomas, 169–97. Stanford: Stanford University Press, 1999.

Lu Hsün [Lu Xun]. *Dawn Blossoms Plucked at Dusk*. Translated by Yang Hsien-yi and Gladys Yang. Beijing: Foreign Languages Press, 1976.

———. "Soap." In *Selected Stories of Lu Hsün*. Translated by Yang Hsien-yi and Gladys Yang, 164–75. New York: Norton, 1960.

Lu Kuangbin, Han Youfeng, and Du Yongji, eds. *Elunchunzu sishinian, 1953–1993* (Forty years of the Oroqen nationality). Beijing: Zhongyang minzu daxue chubanshe, 1994.

Lü Meiyi and Zheng Yongfu. *Zhongguo Funü Yundong, 1840–1921* (The Chinese women's movement). Zhengzhou: Henan Renmin chubanshe, 1990.

Lü Qinwen. "Dongbei lunxianqude wailai wenxue yu xiangtu wenxue" (Foreign and native-place literature in the literature of occupied northeast China). In *Zhongri zhanzheng yu wenxue*, edited by Yamada Keizō and Lü Yuanming, 127–61. Changchun: Dongbei shifan-daxue chubanshe, 1992.

Lu Xun. "Feizao" (Soap). 1924. In *Panghuang, Lu Xun Quanji* (Hesitation, Lu Xun collected works). Vol. 4, 57–73. Taipei: Tangshan, 1989.

———. "Guxiang" (My old home). 1921. In *Nahan, Lu Xun Quanji* (Call to arms, Lu Xun collected works). Vol. 2, 80–94. Taipei: Tangshan, 1989.

———. Introduction to *Xiaoshuo erji* (Second collection of fiction), edited by Lu Xun, 1–18. Shanghai: Liangyou gongsi, 1935.

———. "Shexi" (Village opera). 1922. In *Nahan, Lu Xun Quanji* (Call to arms, Lu Xun collected works). Vol. 2, 185–98. Taipei: Tangshan, 1989.

———. "Wozhi jielieguan" (My views on chastity). 1918. In *Fen, Lu Xun Quanji* (Grave, Lu Xun collected works). Vol. 1, 101–13. Taipei: Tangshan, 1989.

———. "Zai Jiuloushang" (In the wine shop). 1924. In *Panghuang, Lu Xun Quanji* (Hesitation, Lu Xun collected works). Vol. 4, 31–45. Taipei: Tangshan, 1989.

———. "Zhufu" (New Year's sacrifice). 1924. In *Panghuang, Lu Xun Quanji* (Hesitation, Lu Xun collected works). Vol. 4, 7–30. Taipei: Tangshan, 1989.

Ma Hongtian. "Guanyu 'Dayaxiya' yu 'Xinyaxiya' timingde huiyi" (Remembering the titles of Great Asia and New Asia). *Xinyaxiya* 1, no. 1 (1930): 139–40.

———. "Kaifa xibei shi jiejue Zhongguo shehui minsheng wentide genben fangfa" (Opening up the Northwest is a basic means of solving the problem of livelihood in Chinese society). *Xinyaxiya* 1, no. 1 (1930): 37–40.

———. "Zhongguo tuozhi xuehui yu Zhongguo biandi xuehuizhi taolun yu shoubei" (The planning and discussion of the China Settlement and Colonization Institute and the China Border Regions Institute). *Xinyaxiya* 1, no. 1 (1930): 141–42.

Ma Zhangshou. "Shaoshu minzu wenti" (The problem of minority nationalities). *Minzuxue Yanjiu jikan* 6 (1948): 8–23.

Ma Zhengfu. "Dongximeng Menggu shiji (xu)" (Investigations in Eastern and Western Mongolia [continued]). *Xibei zazhi* (Northwest miscellany), no. 2 (December 1912): 1–41.

Malkki, Liisa H. *Purity and Exile: Violence, Memory, and National Cosmology among Hutu Refugees in Tanzania.* Chicago: University of Chicago Press, 1995.

Manchukuo Guofang funüren hui (National Defense Women's Association). Dalian: Manchukuo Guofang funüren hui zongbenbu (Manchukuo National Defense Women's Association general headquarters), 1938–39.

Mann, Susan. *Precious Records: Women in China's Long Eighteenth Century.* Stanford: Stanford University Press, 1997.

Manzhouguo Daodehui bianjike (Manzhouguo Morality Society editorial department), ed. *Disanjie Manzhouguo Daodehui daode jiangxi yulu* (oral records of morality seminars of the Third Manzhouguo Morality Society). Xinjing: Manzhouguo Daodehui huijike, 1936.

Manzhouguo shehui shiye lianhehui, ed. *Manzhouguo shehui shiye jikan* (Manchukuo social welfare seasonal report). Vols. 1 (May) and 2 (September). Xinjing, 1934.

Mao Dun. "Mud." In *Furrows: Peasants, Intellectuals, and the State: Stories and Histories from Modern China,* edited by Helen F. Siu, 33–39. Stanford: Stanford University Press, 1990.

Marshall, T. H. *Class, Citizenship and Social Development.* Westport, Conn.: Greenwood, 1973.

Martin, Bernd. "The Politics of Expansion of the Japanese Empire: Imperialism or Pan-Asiatic Mission?" In *Imperialism and After: Continuities and Discontinuities,* edited by Wolfgang G. Mommsen and Jurgen Osterhammel, 63–82. London: Allen and Unwin, 1986.

Marx, Leo. *The Machine in the Garden: Technology and the Pastoral Ideal in America.* Oxford: Oxford University Press, 1964.

Matsuoka, Yosuke. *The Manchurian Question: Japan's Case in the Sino-Japanese Dispute as Presented before the League of Nations.* Observations of the Japanese Government on the Report of the Commission of Inquiry, Memorandum of the Japanese Delegation. Geneva: League of Nations, 1933.

Matsusaka, Yoshihisa Tak. *The Making of Japanese Manchuria, 1904–1932.* Cambridge: Harvard University Press, 2001.

Maza, Sarah. "Stories in History: Cultural Narratives in Recent Works in European History." *American Historical Review* 101 (1996): 1493–515.

McClintock, Anne. "'No Longer in Future Heaven': Nationalism, Gender, and Race." In *Becoming National: A Reader,* edited by Geoff Eley and Ron Suny, 260–84. New York: Oxford University Press, 1996.

McCormack, Gavan. *Chang Tso-lin in Northeast China, 1911–1928: China, Japan, and the Manchurian Idea.* Stanford: Stanford University Press, 1977.

———. "Manchukuo: Constructing the Past." *East Asian History* 2 (December 1991): 105–24.

———. "Manchukuo: Vision, Plan, and Reality." Unpublished paper, 1987.

McNeill, William H. *Arnold Toynbee: A Life.* New York: Oxford University Press, 1989.

Meng, Chih. *China Speaks: On the Conflict between China and Japan.* New York: Macmillan, 1932.

Meng Yue. "Female Images and National Myth." In *Gender Politics in Modern China*, edited by Tani E. Barlow, 118–36. Durham, N.C.: Duke University Press, 1993.

Mihailoff, I. A., ed. *North Manchuria and the Chinese Eastern Railway.* Harbin: CER Printing Office, 1924.

Mill, John Stuart. *Considerations on Representative Government.* 1861. Reprint, Buffalo: Prometheus, 1991.

Mimura, Janis. "From 'Manchukuo' to Japan's 'New Order': Bureaucratic Visions of a Totalitarian State." Unpublished paper, 1999.

Mita Masao. "Shukei tokuhihatsu" (Capital police special secret publication), no. 3650. Submitted to the police headquarters. November 29, 1943.

Mitani Takeshi. "Senzenki Nihon no Chūgoku himitsu kessha ni tsuite no chōsa" (Surveys of Chinese secret societies in prewar Japan). In *Senzenki Chūgoku jittai chōsa shiryō no sōgōteki kenkyū* (Composite studies of prewar surveys of actual conditions in China), ed. Honjō Hisako. N.p., 1998.

Mitchell, Timothy. *Colonising Egypt.* Berkeley: University of California Press, 1991.

Mitter, Rana. *The Manchurian Myth: Nationalism, Resistance, and Collaboration in Modern China.* Berkeley: University of California Press, 2000.

Miyake, Yoshiko. "Doubling Expectations: Motherhood and Women's Factory Work under State Management in Japan in the 1930s and 1940s." In *Engendering China: Women, Culture and the State*, edited by Christina Gilmartin et al., 267–95. Cambridge: Harvard University Press, 1991.

Mizuno Naoki. "Senkyūhyaku nijū nendai Nihon, Chōsen, Chūgoku ni okeru Ajia ninshiki no ichidanmen—Ajia minzoku kaigi o meguru sangoku no ronchō" (An aspect of the perception of Asia in the three countries of Japan, Korea, and China during the 1920s: The arguments of the three countries surrounding the conference on Asian peoples). In *Kindai Nihon no Ajia ninshiki* (Modern Japan's perceptions of Asia), edited by Furuya Tetsuo, 509–44. Kyoto: Kyoto Daigaku Jinbun Kagaku Kenkyūjo, 1994.

Mommsen, Wolfgang G., and Jurgen Osterhammel, eds. *Imperialism and After: Continuities and Discontinuities.* London: Allen and Unwin, 1986.

Morefield, Jeannie Marie. " 'Families of Mankind': Liberal Idealism and the Construction of Twentieth-Century Internationalism." Ph.D. diss., Cornell University, 1999.

Morris-Suzuki, Tessa. *Re-inventing Japan: Time, Space, Nation.* London: Sharpe, 1998.

———. "Through Ethnographic Eyes." Unpublished paper, n.d.

Moseley, George V. H., III. *The Consolidation of the South China Frontier.* Berkeley: University of California Press, 1973.

Murphey, David T. "Space, Race, and Geopolitical Necessity: Geopolitical Rhetoric in German Colonial Revanchism, 1919–1933." In *Geography and Empire*, edited by Anne Godlewska and Neil Smith, 173–87. Oxford: Blackwell, 1994.

Myers, Ramon H. "Creating a Modern Enclave Economy: The Economic Integration of Japan, Manchuria, and North China, 1932–1945." In *The Japanese Wartime Empire, 1931–1945*, edited by Peter Duus, Ramon H. Myers, and Mark R. Peattie, 136–70. Princeton: Princeton University Press, 1996.

Myers, Ramon H., and Mark Peattie, eds. *The Japanese Colonial Empire, 1895–1945.* Princeton: Princeton University Press, 1984.

Nagata Uzumaro. *Manshū ni okeru Oronjon no kenkyū* (Studies of the Oroqen in Manchuria). Vol. 1. Shinkyō: Chianbu Sambōshi chōsaka (Investigative Division of the Security Bureau of the General Staff), 1939.

Nagoyashi hakubutsukan, ed. *Shin Hakubutsukan Taisei: Manshūkoku no hakubutsukan ga sengō Nihon ni tsutaeteiru koto* (The shape of the new museum: What the Manchukuo museum had to say to postwar Japan). Nagoya: Nagoyashi hakubustkan, 1995.

Nakajima, Mineo. *The Kao Kang Affair and Sino-Soviet Relations.* Review: The Study of Communism and Communist Countries in Japan, no. 44. Tokyo: Japan Institute of International Affairs, 1977.

Nakami, Tatsuo. "A Protest against the Concept of the 'Middle Kingdom': The Mongols and the 1911 Revolution." In *The 1911 Revolution in China,* edited by Eto Shinkichi and Harold Z. Schiffrin. Tokyo: University of Tokyo Press, 1984, 129–49.

Nakao Katsumi. "Shokuminchi no minzokugaku—Manshū minzokugakkai no katsudō" (Colonial ethnology: The activities of the Ethnological Association of Manchuria). *Herumesu* 52 (December 1994): 135–43.

———. "Shokuminchishugi to Nihon minzokugaku" (Colonialism and Japanese anthropology). *Chūgoku—Shakai to Bunka (China: Society and Culture)* 8 (June 1993): 231–42.

Neocleus, Mark. *Administering Civil Society: Towards a Theory of State Power.* New York: St. Martin's, 1996.

Ninkovich, Frank A. *The Wilsonian Century: U.S. Foreign Policy since 1900.* Chicago: University of Chicago Press, 1999.

Nish, Ian. "Nationalism in Japan." In *Asian Nationalism: China, Taiwan, Japan, India, Pakistan, Indonesia, The Philippines,* edited by Michael Leifer, 182–89. London: Routledge, 2000.

———. "Some Thoughts on Japanese Expansionism." In *Imperialism and After: Continuities and Discontinuities,* edited by Wolfgang G. Mommsen and Jurgen Osterhammel, 82–89. London: Allen and Unwin, 1986.

Nishimura Shigeo. *Chūgoku kindai tōhoku chiikishi kenkyū* (A regional history of Northeast China). Kyoto: Hōritsu bunkasha, 1984.

———. "Research in Japan on the History of North-East China: Present State and Problems." Translated by Gavan McCormack. Unpublished manuscript, 1992.

Nolte, Sharon H., and Sally Ann Hastings. "The Meiji State's Policy Toward Women, 1890–1910." In *Recreating Japanese Women, 1600–1945,* edited by Gail Lee Bernstein, 151–74. Berkeley: University of California Press, 1991.

Oakes, Timothy S. "Shen Congwen's Literary Regionalism and the Gendered Landscape of Chinese Modernity." *Geografiska Annaler* 77 B.2 (1995): 93–107.

Oguma Eiji. "The Green of the Willow, the Flower's Scarlet: Public Debate on the U.S. Exclusion Movement and the Colonization of Korea under the Japanese Empire." Translated by Joseph Murphy. Unpublished paper.

Okada Hideki. "Bungaku hyōka no kijun to sono tekiyō" (The criteria of literary evaluation and its application). *Nogusa* 47 (1991): 57–67.

———. "Geibunshi ha no bungaku kiseki—Manshū ni okeru Chūgokujin sakka" (Tracks of the Literary Records group: Chinese writers in Manchuria). *Nogusa* 38 (1986): 1–22; 39 (1987): 79–102.

———. "Manshū no kyōdo bungei—Shan Ding 'Lüsede gu' o jiku toshite" (Native-place literature in Manzhouguo, with reference to Shan Ding's *Green Valley*). *Nogusa* 44 (1989): 10–33.

———. "Wei Manzhouguo wenyi zhengcede zhankai—cong 'wenhuahui' dao 'yiwen lianmeng'" (The development of literary policy in the puppet state of Manzhouguo: From "cultural association" to "literary federation"). In *Dongbei lunxian shiqi wenxue* (Literature of the occupation period in northeast China), edited by Feng Weiqun et al., 156–81. Shenyang: Shenyang chubanshe, 1992.

Oniki Isamu, comp. *Manshū kyōdo dokuhon* (Textbook of the Manchurian native place). Dairen: Ōsaka Yagō Shotenzō, 1935.

Ono, Kazuko. *Chinese Women in a Century of Revolution, 1850–1950*. Translated and edited by Joshua Fogel. Stanford: Stanford University Press, 1989.

Ōtani Komme. *Shūkyō chōsa shiryō* (Materials from the survey of religions). Vol. 2, *Kitsurin, Kantō, Hinkō, kakushō shūkyō chōsa hōkoku* (Report on religious surveys of the various provinces of Jilin, Jiandao, and Binjiang). Shinkyō: Minseibu, 1937.

Ōtsuka Kazuyoshi. "Shiberia—Nihon ni okeru minzoku kenkyū" (Siberia: Anthropological Research in Japan). In *Nihon minzokugaku no genzai*, edited by Joseph Kriner, 317–26. Tokyo: Shin'yōsha, 1996.

Ōuchi Takayoshi. "Dongbei wenxue ershinian" (Twenty years of Northeast literature). 1944. Selections translated by Wang Wenshi. In *Dongbei xiandai wenxue shiliao* (Historical materials from modern literature of the Northeast), edited by Liaoning shehui kexueyuan wenxue yanjiusuo (Liaoning Province social science academy literature research institute) et al. Vol. 1, 87–115. Shenyang: Liaoning shehui kexueyuan, 1980.

———. "Zuijin Zhongguoren de wenxue" (Recent literature by Chinese people). 1939. Translated by Wang Wenshi. In *Dongbei xiandai wenxue shiliao* (Historical materials from modern literature of the Northeast). Vol. 1, 113–15. Shenyang: Liaoning shehui kexueyuan, 1980.

Ownby, David. "Chinese Millenarian Traditions: The Formative Age." *American Historical Review* 104 (December 1999): 1513–30.

———. "Imperial Fantasies: The Chinese Communists and Peasant Rebellions." *Comparative Studies in Society and History* 43 (2001): 65–91.

Ōyama Hikoichi. *Samankyō to Manshūzoku no kazoku seido*. Xinjing: Jianguo daxue yanjiuyuan, 1942.

Ozaki Fumiaki. "Shū Sakujin (Zhou Zuoren) no shinson teishō to sono hamon" (Zhou Zuoren's advocacy of the New Village movement and its ripples). *Meiji Daigaku Kyōyō Ronshū* 207 (1988): 119–36; 237 (1991): 67–85.

Pai, Hyung-il. "Japanese Anthropology and the Discovery of Prehistoric 'Korea.'" *Journal of East Asian Archaeology* 1 (1999): 354–82.

Pang Zengyu. "Dongbei lunxianqi xiangtu wenxue yu Zhongguo xiandai wenxue shishang xiangtu wenxue zhi bijiao" (Comparison of occupied Northeast native-place literature and native-place literature in modern Chinese literary history). In *Dongbei lunxian shiqi wenxue wenxue* (Literature of the occupation period in northeast China), edited by Feng Weiqun et al., 63–74. Shenyang: Shenyang Chubanshe, 1992.

———. *Heitudi wenhua yu dongbei zuojia qun* (The culture of black soil and the group of dongbei writers). Changsha: Hunan jiaoyu chubanshe, 1995.

Peattie, Mark R. *Ishiwara Kanji and Japan's Confrontation with the West*. Princeton: Princeton University Press, 1975.

Pocock, J. G. A. *The Machiavellian Moment: Florentine Thought and the Atlantic Republican Tradition*. Princeton: Princeton University Press, 1975.

Postone, Moishe. *Time, Labor, and Social Domination: A Reinterpretation of Marx's Critical Theory*. Cambridge: Cambridge University Press, 1993.

Price, Willard. "Japan Faces Russia in Manchuria." *National Geographic*, November 1942, 603–14.

Puett, Michael. *The Ambivalence of Creation: Debates Concerning Innovation and Artifice in Early China.* Stanford: Stanford University Press, 2001.

Redfield, Robert. *Human Nature and the Study of Society: The Papers of Robert Redfield.* Edited by Margaret Park Redfield. Vol. 1. Chicago: University of Chicago Press, 1962–63.

Renan, Ernest. "What Is a Nation?" In *Nation and Narration*, edited by Homi Bhabha, 8–22. New York: Routledge, 1990.

Reynolds, Douglas R. *China, 1898–1912: The Xinzheng Revolution and Japan.* Cambridge, Mass.: Council on East Asian Studies, 1993.

Ricoeur, Paul. *Reflection and Imagination: A Paul Ricoeur Reader.* ed. Mario J. Valdes. Toronto: University of Toronto Press, 1991.

———. *Time and Narrative.* 3 vols. Chicago: University of Chicago Press, 1984–88.

Robinson, Michael. "National Identity and the Thought of Sin Ch'aeho: Sadaejuui and Chuch'e in History and Politics." *Journal of Korean History* 5 (1984): 121–42.

Robinson, Ronald. "The Ex-centric Idea of Imperialism, with or without Empire." In *Imperialism and After: Continuities and Discontinuities*, edited by Wolfgang G. Mommsen and Jurgen Osterhammel, 267–89. London: Allen and Unwin, 1986.

Rose, Nikolas. "Governing 'Advanced' Liberal Democracies." In *Foucault and Political Reason: Liberalism, Neo-liberalism, and Rationalities of Government*, edited by Andrew Barry, Thomas Osborne, and Nikolas Rose, 37–64. Chicago: University of Chicago Press, 1996.

Rouse, Roger. "Questions of Identity: Personhood and Collectivity in Transnational Migration to the United States." *Critique of Anthropology* 15 (1995): 351–80.

Sanetō Keishū. *Nihon bunka no Shina e no eikyō* (The influence of Japanese culture on China). Tokyo: Keisetsu shoin, 1940.

Sasaki Tōru. "Nihon ni okeru Orochon in kansuru minzokugakuteki hōkoku no hikaku kenkyū—'Orochon no jissō' o chūshin to shite" (A comparative study of Japanese ethnological reports regarding the Orochon, with particular reference to "the real facts about the Orochon"). *Hokkaidoritsu Hoppō Minzoku Hakubutsu Kenkyū kiyō* 3 (1994): 93–137.

Schirmer, Jennifer. "The Claiming of Space and the Body Politic within National-Security States: The Plaza de Mayo Madres and the Greenham Common Women." In *Remapping Memory: The Politics of Timespace*, edited by Jonathan Boyarin, 185–220. Minneapolis: University of Minnesota Press, 1994.

Schmid, Andre. "Rediscovering Manchuria: Sin Ch'aeho and the Politics of Territorial History in Korea." *Journal of Asian Studies* 56 (1997): 26–46.

Schneider, Laurence A. *Ku Chieh-kang and China's New History: Nationalism and the Quest for Alternative Traditions.* Berkeley: University of California Press, 1971.

Schwab, Raymond. *Oriental Renaissance: Europe's Rediscovery of India and the East, 1680–1880.* Translated by Gene Patterson-Black and Victor Reinking. New York: Columbia University Press, 1984.

Shao Dan. "Gender in the Construction and Deconstruction of Manchoukuo." Unpublished paper, 2001.

Shao Ge. "Yougan yiti" (The topic of feeling). *Dongbei Wenxue* 1, no. 2 (1946): 8–10.

Shao Yong. *Zhongguo huidaomen* (China's religious societies). Shanghai: Remmin chubanse, 1997.

Shen Congwen. *Imperfect Paradise: Stories by Shen Congwen.* Edited and translated by Jeffrey Kinkley et al. Honolulu: University of Hawaii Press, 1995.

Shen Jie. "Japanese Women and Their War Responsibility: Regarding Fascist Female Organizations in the Spurious Manchuria Country." Paper presented to the International Federation of Women's Historians Conference, University of Melbourne, 1997.

Shi Jun. "Hun Xie'er" (Children of mixed blood). *Qingnian wenhua* 1 (August 1943), 107–15.

Shih Nai-an. *Water Margin*. Translated by J. H. Jackson. Reprint, New York: Paragon, 1968.

Shimizu, Akitoshi. "Colonialism and the Development of Modern Anthropology in Japan." In *Anthropology and Colonialism in Asia and Oceania*, edited by Jan van Bremen and Akitoshi Shimizu, 115–71. Surrey, England: Curzon Press, 1999.

Shin, Gi-wook, and Michael Robinson, eds. *Colonial Modernity in Korea*. Cambridge: Harvard University Asia Center, 1999.

Shinohara, Hatsue. "Forgotten Crusade: The Quest for a New International Law." Ph.D. diss., University of Chicago, 1996.

Shirokogoroff, S. M. "Ethnological and Linguistic Aspects of the Ural-Altaic Hypothesis." *Qinghua Xuebao* (Tsinghua Journal) 6, no. 3 (1931): 199–396.

———. *Social Organization of the Northern Tungus*. 1929. Reprint, Oosterhout, Netherlands: Anthropological Publications, 1966.

Silverberg, Miriam. "The Modern Girl as Militant." In *Recreating Japanese Women, 1600–1945*, edited by Gail Lee Bernstein, 239–66. Berkeley: University of California Press, 1991.

Skinner, G. William. "Marketing and Social Structure in Rural China." *Journal of Asian Studies* 24 (1964–65): 3–43, 195–228.

Smith, Anthony. "Theories of Nationalism: Alternative Models of Nation Formation." In *Asian Nationalism: China, Taiwan, Japan, India, Pakistan, Indonesia, The Philippines*, edited by Michael Leifer, 1–20. London: Routledge, 2000.

Smith, Sara R. *The Manchurian Crisis 1931–1932: A Tragedy in International Relations*. Westport, Conn., Greenwood, 1948.

Smith, Warren H., Jr. *Confucianism in Modern Japan: A Study of Conservatism in Japan's Intellectual History*. Tokyo: Hokuseido, 1959.

Song Meiling (Zhidaozhang). "Xinshenghuo yundong" (New Life movement). 1936. In *GWXSY*, 107–12.

———. "Funü xinshenghuo yingyoude jingshen" (The spirit that women's new life ought to have). 1938. In *GWXSY*, 113–19.

Song Ruohua. *Nü Lunyu* (The analects of women). ca. 780. Shanghai: Shanghai dazhong shuju, 1936.

"Soren no minzoku seisaku" (Soviet nationality policy). Publication of the Research Institute of the National Foundation University. Shinkyō: Kenkoku Daigaku kenkyūin kan, 1940.

Spencer, Philip, and Howard Wollman. "Good and Bad Nationalisms: A Critique of Dualism." *Journal of Political Ideologies* 3 (1998): 255–74.

Spengler, Oswald. *The Decline of the West*. Abridged edition, edited by Helmut Werner. New York: Knopf, 1962.

Stephenson, Shelley. "The Occupied Screen: Star, Fan, and Nation in Shanghai Cinema, 1937–1945." Ph.D. diss., University of Chicago, 2000.

Stocking, George W., Jr. *Victorian Anthropology*. New York: Free Press, 1987.

———, ed. *Volksgeist as Method and Ethic: Essays on Boasian Ethnography and the German Anthropological Tradition*. Madison: University of Wisconsin Press, 1996.

Suemitsu Takayoshi. *Shina no himitsu kessha to jizen kaisha* (China's secret societies and charitable societies). Dairen: Manshū hyōronsha, 1932.

Suleski, Ronald. *Civil Government in Warlord China: Tradition, Modernization, and Manchuria.* New York: Peter Lang, 2002.

Sun, Kungtu C. *The Economic Development of Manchuria in the First Half of the Twentieth Century* (assisted by Ralph W Huenemann). Cambridge, Mass.: East Asian Research Center, Harvard University, 1969.

Sun Yat-sen. "Da Yaxiyazhuyi" (Great Asianism). *Xinyaxiya* 1, no. 1 (1930): 2–7.

Sun Zhongtian. "Lüsede gu yu xiangtu wenxue" (*Green Valley* and native-place literature). In *Dongbei lunxian shiqi wenxue wenxue* (Literature of the occupation period in northeast China), edited by Feng Weiqun et al., 224–35. Shenyang: Shenyang Chubanshe, 1992.

Szpilman, Christopher W. A. "The Dream of One Asia: Ōkawa Shūmei and Japanese Pan-Asianism." In *The Japanese Empire and Its Legacy in East Asia*, edited by Harald Fuess, 49–64. Munich: German Institute of Japanese Studies, 1988.

Tachibana Shiraki. *Dōkyō to Shinwa Densetsu* (Daoism and myths and legends). Tokyo: Kaizōsha, 1947.

———. *Shina Shakai Kenkyū* (Studies of Chinese society). Tokyo: Nihon Hyōronsha, 1934.

Takeuchi, Keiichi. "The Japanese Imperial Tradition, Western Imperialism, and Modern Japanese Geography." In *Geography and Empire*, edited by Anne Godlewska and Neil Smith, 188–209. Oxford: Blackwell, 1994.

Takizawa Toshihiro. *Manshū no gaison shinkō* (Beliefs of Manchuria's towns and villages). Shinkyō: Manshū jijō annaijo, 1940.

———. *Shūkyō chōsa shiryō* (Materials from the survey of religions). Vol. 3, *Minkan shinkō chōsa hōkokushō* (Report on the survey of popular beliefs). Shinkyō: Minseibu, 1937.

Tamanoi, Mariko Asano. "Knowledge, Power, and Racial Classifications: The 'Japanese' in 'Manchuria,'" *Journal of Asian Studies* 59 (May 2000): 248–76.

Tamir, Yael. "The Age of Atonement: The Emergence of a New Political Paradigm." In *The Right of Nations: Nations and Nationalism in a Changing World*, edited by Jones Clarke, 88–99. New York: St. Martin's, 1999.

Tanaka, Stefan. *Japan's Orient: Rendering Pasts into History.* Berkeley: University of California Press, 1993.

Teiwes, Frederick C., *Politics at Mao's Court: Gao Gang and Party Factionalism in the Early 1950s.* Armonk, N.Y.: Sharpe, 1990.

Tian Lin. "Yiwei baojing fengshuang de zuojia—fang nüzuojia Tian Lin" (A weather-beaten writer: An interview with Tian Lin). Interview by Feng Weiqun and Li Chunyan. In *Dongbei lunxian shiqi wenxue xinlun* (New interpretations of the literature of occupied Dongbei), 244–49. Changchun: Jilin daxue chubanshe, 1991.

Tisdale, Alice. *Pioneering Where the World Is Old.* New York: Henry Holt, 1917.

Todorov, Tzvetan. *On Human Diversity: Nationalism, Racism, and Exoticism in French Thought.* Translation by Catherine Porter. Cambridge: Harvard University Press, 1993.

Tomiyama, Ichiro. "Colonialism and the Sciences of the Tropical Zone: The Academic Analysis of Difference in 'the Island Peoples.'" In *Formation of Colonial Modernity in East Asia*, edited by Tani E. Barlow, 199–21. Durham, N.C.: Duke University Press, 1997.

Tongshihui zhiyin (Management committee [of the Wansi Chungshan Lodge]). *Wansi Chungshantang zhuankan.* Pamphlet of the Wansi Chungshan Lodge. Hangzhou, 1935.

Toynbee, Arnold J. "Christianity and Civilization." In *Civilization on Trial.* 225–52. New York: Oxford University Press, 1948.

―――. "World Sovereignty and World Culture." *Pacific Affairs* 4 (September 1931): 753–78.

Tucker, David Vance. "Building 'Our Manchukuo': Japanese City Planning, Architecture, and Nation-Building in Occupied Northeast China." Ph.D. diss., University of Iowa, 1999.

Uchida Ryōhei. *Manmō no dokuritsu to Sekai Kōmanjikai no katsudō* (The independence of Manchuria-Mongolia and the activities of the World Red Swastika Society). Tokyo: Senshinsha, 1932.

Ueda Makoto. "Okakura Tenshin—aru kyōkaijin no Ajia kan" (Okakura Tenshin: A view of Asia from a certain margin). *Kokusai kyōryū* 77 (1996): 56–58.

United Nations. "International Covenant on Economic, Social, and Cultural Rights," and "The Covenant on Civil and Political Rights." Online at www.hrweb.org/legal/undocs. html#CPR (accessed June 19, 2002).

Vaughan, Megan. *Curing their Ills: Colonial Power and African Illness.* Cambridge, England: Polity, 1991.

Wallerstein, Immanuel. "The Construction of Peoplehood: Racism, Nationalism, Ethnicity." In *Race, Nation, Class: Ambiguous Identities,* edited by Etienne Balibar and Immanuel Wallerstein, 71–85. London: Verso, 1991.

Wang, David Der-wei. *Fictional Realism in Twentieth-Century China: Mao Dun, Lao She, Shen Congwen.* New York: Columbia University Press, 1992.

Wang Guohua, ed. *Yisheng Wang Fengyi duxinglu* (Record of the profound actions of the righteous sage, Wang Fengyi). 1934. Reprint, Taipei: Wanguo Daodehui zonghui, 1981.

Wang Horng-luen. "In Want of a Nation: State, Institutions, and Globalization in Taiwan." Ph.D. diss., University of Chicago, 1999.

Wang Jingwei. "Duiyu nüjiede ganxiang" (Reflections on women's world). *Funü zazhi* 10 (1924): 106–8.

Wang Qingyu. *Dongbei wenti* (The Northeastern problem). Shanghai: shangwu chubanshe, 1931.

Wang Zhuomin. "Lun wuguo daxue shang buyi nannü tongxiao" (On the inappropriateness of co-education in our universities). *Funü zazhi* 4, no. 5 (1918) 1–8.

Watsuji Tetsurō. *Climate and Culture: A Philosophical Study.* 1935. Translated by Geoffrey Bownas. New York: Greenwood Press in cooperation with Yushodo Co., 1988.

Wei Huilin. "Zhanhou Zhongguo minzu zhengce yu bianjiang jianshe" (Postwar Chinese nationality policy and frontier construction). *Minzuxue Yanjiu jikan* 4 (1944): 1–6.

Welch, Holmes. *The Buddhist Revival in China.* Cambridge: Harvard University Press, 1968.

Wigen, Karen. "Teaching about Home: Geography at Work in the Prewar Nagano Classroom." *Journal of Asian Studies* 59 (2000): 550–74.

Williams, Raymond. *The Country and the City.* London: Chatto and Windus, 1973.

Willoughby, Westel W. *The Sino-Japanese Controversy and the League of Nations.* Baltimore: Johns Hopkins University Press, 1935.

Wilson, Richard. *Learning to Be Chinese: The Political Socialization of Children in Taiwan.* Cambridge: MIT Press, 1970.

Winnichakul, Thongchai. *Siam Mapped: A History of the Geo-Body of a Nation.* Honolulu: Hawaii University Press, 1994.

Wolfe, Patrick. "The Dreamtime in Anthropology and in Australian Settler Culture." *Comparative Studies in Society and History* 33 (1991): 197–224.

———. "Nation and Miscegenation: Discursive Continuity in the Post-Mabo Era." *Social Analysis* 36 (1994): 93–152.

Wong, Aida Yuen. "In Search of the East: Art History and Sino-Japanese Relations." Ph.D. diss., Columbia University, 1999.

Wu Meiji. *Zhongguo renwen dili* (Human geography in China). Nanjing: Nanjing Zhongshan shuju, 1929.

Wu Shangquan. *Dongbei dili yu minzu shengcunzhi guanxi* (The relationship of the geography of the Northeast and the survival of the nation). Chongqing: Duli chubanshe, 1944.

Wu Ying. "Manzhou nüxing wenxuede ren yu zuopin" (Female writers and their works in Manchuria). 1944. In *Dongbei xiandai wenxue daxi, 1919–1949* (Modern literature of the Northeast, 1919–1949). 14 vols. Edited by Zhang Yumao, 1:342–56. Shenyang: Shenyang chubanshe, 1996.

"Xiezai juanmo." Postscript to *Xinyaxiya* 1, no. 3 (1930): 15–16.

"Xinyaxiyazhi shiming" (The mission of New Asia). Preface to *Xinyaxiya* (New Asia) 1, no. 1 (1930).

Yamada Seizaburō. *Manshūkoku bunka kensetsuron* (The theory of cultural construction in Manchukuo). Shinkyō: Geibun shobō, 1943.

Yamamuro Shinichi. "Ajia ninshiki no kijiku" (The axes of perceiving Asia). In *Kindai Nihon no Ajia ninshiki* (Modern Japan's perceptions of Asia), edited by Furuya Tetsuo, 3–46. Kyoto: Kyōtō Daigaku Jinbun kagaku kenkyūjo, 1994.

———. *Kimera: Manshūkoku no shōzō* (Chimera: A portrait of Manzhouguo). Tokyo: Chūō Kōronsha, 1993.

Yamazaki Mugen. "Kyōiku zasshi ni miru Ajia ninshiki no tenkai" (The development of the perception of Asia as seen in educational journals). In *Kindai Nihon no Ajia ninshiki* (Modern Japan's perceptions of Asia), edited by Furuya Tetsuo, 299–350. Kyoto: Jinbun kagaku kenkyūjo, 1994.

Yamazaki Seika. *Nekka, Kinshū ryōshō shūkyō chōsa hōkokusho* (Report of the survey of religion in the two provinces of Rehe and Jinzhou). Shūkyō Chōsa Shiryō (Materials from the survey of religions), vol 4. Shinkyō: Minseibu, 1937.

Yan Pinzao. "Nanchang mofan laodong fuwutuan fangwenji" (Record of a visit to Nanchang's model labor service team). In *XYDB*, 5 and 6 (April 1937), 106–114.

Yan Shi. "Nannü tongxue yu lian'ai shang de zhidao" (Coeducation and guidance on amorous relationships). *Funü zazhi* 9, no. 10 (1923) 18–19.

Yang, Mayfair Mei-hui. "From Gender Erasure to Gender Difference: State Feminism, Consumer Sexuality, and Women's Public Sphere in China." In *Spaces of Their Own: Women's Public Sphere in Transnational China*, ed. Mayfair Mei-hui Yang, 35–67. Minneapolis: University of Minnesota Press, 1999.

Yao Congwu. *Dongbei shi lun cong* (Collection of historical essays on the Northeast). 2 vols. Taipei: Zhengzhong shuju, 1959.

Yasutomi Ayumu. "Teikiichi to kenjō keizai—1930 nen zengo ni okeru Manshū nōson shijō no tokuchō" (The rural marketing system in Manchuria around 1930: Periodic markets and the economy of the county town). Paper submitted to *Ajia Keizai*, 2002.

Yasutomi Ayumu and Fukui Chie, *Manshū no kenryūtsūken* (Manchuria and county currencies). Paper submitted to *Ajia Keizai*, 2002.

Young, C. Walter. *The International Relations of Manchuria: A Digest and Analysis of Treaties, Agreements and Negotiations Concerning the Three Eastern Provinces of China*. Chicago: University of Chicago Press, 1929.

Young, Louise. *Japan's Total Empire: Manchuria and the Culture of Wartime Imperialism.* Berkeley: University of California Press, 1998.

Zanasi, Margherita. "Chen Gongbo and the Construction of a Modern Nation in China." In *Nation Work: Asian Elites and National Identities*, edited by Timothy Brook and Andre Schmid, 125–57. Ann Arbor: University of Michigan Press, 2000.

"Zenme xie Manzhou?" (How to write about Manchuria?) [seminar transcription]. *Yiwenzhi* (Literary Records) 1, no. 3 (1944): 27–37

Zerubavel, Eviatar. *Hidden Rhythms: Schedules and Calendars in Social Life.* Berkeley: University of California Press, 1981.

Zhang Qiyun. *Zhongguo rendi guanxi gailun* (An introduction to relations between humans and land in China). Shanghai: Dadong shuju, 1947.

Zhang Yumao. "Zongxu." General introduction to *Dongbei xiandai wenxue daxi, 1919–1949* (Modern literature of the Northeast, 1919–1949), edited by Zhang Yumao. 14 vols. 1:124. Shenyang: Shenyang chubanshe, 1996.

Zhao Jinghua. "Shū Sakujin (Zhou Zuoren) to Yanagita Kunio: Koyū shinkō o chūshin to suru minzokugaku" (Zhou Zuoren and Yanagita Kunio: Folklore centered on traditional beliefs). *Nihon Chūgoku gakkaihō* 47 (1995): 195–209.

Zhongguo shehui kexueyuan jindaishi yanjiusuo, ed. *Minguo Renwuzhuan* (Republican biographies). 8 vols. Beijing: Zhonghua shuju, 1978.

Zhou Zuoren. "Difang yu wenyi" (Locality and literature). 1923. In *Zhou Zuoren zaoqi sanwenxuan* (Selections from the early prose of Zhou Zuoren). Shanghai: Shanghai wenyi chubanshe, 1984, 308–11.

———. "Guxiang de yecai" (Wild herbs of the old home). 1924. In *Zhou Zuoren zaoqi sanwenxuan* (Selections from the early prose of Zhou Zuoren). Shanghai: Shanghai wenyi chubanshe, 1984, 199–201.

Index

About the Author

Educated in India and the United States, Prasenjit Duara is currently professor of history and East Asian languages and civilizations at the University of Chicago. He is the author of *Culture, Power, and the State: Rural Society in North China, 1900–1942*, which won the American Historical Association's J. K. Fairbank Prize for 1989 and the Association of Asian Studies' Joseph R. Levenson Prize for 1990. He is also the author of *Rescuing History from the Nation: Questioning Narratives of Modern China* (1995). His work has been widely translated into Chinese and Japanese.

Duara has also contributed to volumes on historiography and historical thought. His most recent essays are "Transnationalism and the Challenge to National Histories," in *Rethinking American History in a Global Age*, edited by Thomas Bender (2002), and "Postcolonial History," in *A Companion to Western Historical Thought*, edited by Sarah Maza and Lloyd Kramer (2002). He is currently editing a reader on decolonization.